Integrated Series in Information Systems

Volume 36

Series Editors

Ramesh Sharda
Oklahoma State University, Stillwater, OK, USA

Stefan Voß
University of Hamburg, Hamburg, Germany

More information about this series at http://www.springer.com/series/6157

Shan Suthaharan

Machine Learning Models and Algorithms for Big Data Classification

Thinking with Examples for Effective Learning

 Springer

Shan Suthaharan
Department of Computer Science
UNC Greensboro
Greensboro, NC, USA

ISSN 1571-0270   ISSN 2197-7968   (electronic)
Integrated Series in Information Systems
ISBN 978-1-4899-7640-6   ISBN 978-1-4899-7641-3   (eBook)
DOI 10.1007/978-1-4899-7641-3

Library of Congress Control Number: 2015950063

Springer New York Heidelberg Dordrecht London

Printed on acid-free paper

Springer International Publishing AG Switzerland is part of Springer Science+Business Media (www.
springer.com)

It is the quality of our work which will please God and not the quantity – Mahatma Gandhi

If you can't explain it simply, you don't understand it well enough – Albert Einstein

Preface

The interest in writing this book began at the IEEE International Conference on Intelligence and Security Informatics held in Washington, DC (June 11–14, 2012), where Mr. Matthew Amboy, the editor of *Business and Economics: OR and MS*, published by Springer Science+Business Media, expressed the need for a book on this topic, mainly focusing on a topic in data science field. The interest went even deeper when I attended the workshop conducted by Professor Bin Yu (Department of Statistics, University of California, Berkeley) and Professor David Madigan (Department of Statistics, Columbia University) at the Institute for Mathematics and its Applications, University of Minnesota on June 16–29, 2013.

Data science is one of the emerging fields in the twenty-first century. This field has been created to address the big data problems encountered in the day-to-day operations of many industries, including financial sectors, academic institutions, information technology divisions, health care companies, and government organizations. One of the important big data problems that needs immediate attention is in big data classifications. The network intrusion detection, public space intruder detection, fraud detection, spam filtering, and forensic linguistics are some of the practical examples of big data classification problems that require immediate attention.

We need significant collaboration between the experts in many disciplines, including mathematics, statistics, computer science, engineering, biology, and chemistry to find solutions to this challenging problem. Educational resources, like books and software, are also needed to train students to be the next generation of research leaders in this emerging research field. One of the current fields that brings the interdisciplinary experts, educational resources, and modern technologies under one roof is machine learning, which is a subfield of artificial intelligence.

Many models and algorithms for standard classification problems are available in the machine learning literature. However, a few of them are suitable for big data classification. Big data classification is dependent not only on the mathematical and software techniques but also on the computer technologies that help store, retrieve, and process the data with efficient scalability, accessibility, and computability features. One such recent technology is the distributed file system. A particular system that has become popular and provides these features is the Hadoop distributed file system, which uses the modern techniques called MapReduce programming model (or a framework) with Mapper and Reducer functions that adopt the concept called the (key, value) pairs. The machine learning techniques such as the decision tree (a hierarchical approach), random forest (an ensemble hierarchical approach), and deep learning (a layered approach) are highly suitable for the system that addresses big data classification problems. Therefore, the goal of this book is to present some of the machine learning models and algorithms, and discuss them with examples.

The general objective of this book is to help readers, especially students and newcomers to the field of big data and machine learning, to gain a quick understanding of the techniques and technologies; therefore, the theory, examples, and programs (Matlab and R) presented in this book have been simplified, hardcoded, repeated, or spaced for improvements. They provide vehicles to test and understand the complicated concepts of various topics in the field. It is expected that the readers adopt these programs to experiment with the examples, and then modify or write their own programs toward advancing their knowledge for solving more complex and challenging problems.

The presentation format of this book focuses on simplicity, readability, and dependability so that both undergraduate and graduate students as well as new researchers, developers, and practitioners in this field can easily trust and grasp the concepts, and learn them effectively. The goal of the writing style is to reduce the mathematical complexity and help the vast majority of readers to understand the topics and get interested in the field. This book consists of four parts, with a total of 14 chapters. Part I mainly focuses on the topics that are needed to help analyze and understand big data. Part II covers the topics that can explain the systems required for processing big data. Part III presents the topics required to understand and select machine learning techniques to classify big data. Finally, Part IV concentrates on the topics that explain the scaling-up machine learning, an important solution for modern big data problems.

Greensboro, NC, USA   Shan Suthaharan

Acknowledgements

The journey of writing this book would not have been possible without the support of many people, including my collaborators, colleagues, students, and family. I would like to thank all of them for their support and contributions toward the successful development of this book. First, I would like to thank Mr. Matthew Amboy (Editor, *Business and Economics: OR and MS*, Springer Science+Business Media) for giving me an opportunity to write this book. I would also like to thank both Ms. Christine Crigler (Assistant Editor) and Mr. Amboy for helping me throughout the publication process.

I am grateful to Professors Ratnasingham Shivaji (Head of the Department of Mathematics and Statistics at the University of North Carolina at Greensboro) and Fadil Santosa (Director of the Institute for Mathematics and its Applications at University of Minnesota) for the opportunities that they gave me to attend a machine learning workshop at the institute. Professors Bin Yu (Department of Statistics, University of California, Berkeley) and David Madigan (Department of Statistics, Columbia University) delivered an excellent short course on applied statistics and machine learning at the institute, and the topics covered in this course motivated me and equipped me with techniques and tools to write various topics in this book. My sincere thanks go to them. I would also like to thank Jinzhu Jia, Adams Bloniaz, and Antony Joseph, the members of Professor Bin Yu's research group at the Department of Statistics, University of California, Berkeley, for their valuable discussions in many machine learning topics.

My appreciation goes out to University of California, Berkeley, and University of North Carolina at Greensboro for their financial support and the research assignment award in 2013 to attend University of California, Berkeley as a Visiting scholar—this visit helped me better understand the deep learning techniques. I would also like to show my appreciation to Mr. Brent Ladd (Director of Education, Center for the Science of Information, Purdue University) and Mr. Robert Brown (Managing Director, Center for the Science of Information, Purdue University) for their support to develop a course on big data analytics and machine learning at University of North Carolina at Greensboro through a sub-award approved by the National Science Foundation. I am also thankful to Professor Richard Smith, Director of the

Statistical and Applied Mathematical Sciences Institute at North Carolina, for the opportunity to attend the workshops on low-dimensional structure in high-dimensional systems and to conduct research at the institute as a visiting research fellow during spring 2014. I greatly appreciate the resources that he provided during this visiting appointment. I also greatly appreciate the support and resources that the University of North Carolina at Greensboro provided during the development of this book.

The research work conducted with Professor Vaithilingam Jeyakumar and Dr. Guoyin Li at the University of New South Wales (Australia) helped me simplify the explanation of support vector machines. The technical report written by Michelle Dunbar under Professor Jeyakumar's supervision also contributed to the enhancement of the chapter on support vector machines. I would also like to express my gratitude to Professors Sat Gupta, Scott Richter, and Edward Hellen for sharing their knowledge of some of the statistical and mathematical techniques. Professor Steve Tate's support and encouragement, as the department head and as a colleague, helped me engage in this challenging book project for the last three semesters. My sincere gratitude also goes out to Professor Jing Deng for his support and engagement in some of my research activities.

My sincere thanks also go to the following students who recently contributed directly or indirectly to my research and knowledge that helped me develop some of the topics presented in this book: Piyush Agarwal, Mokhaled Abd Allah, Michelle Bayait, Swarna Bonam, Chris Cain, Tejo Sindhu Chennupati, Andrei Craddock, Luning Deng, Anudeep Katangoori, Sweta Keshpagu, Kiranmayi Kotipalli, Varnika Mittal, Chitra Reddy Musku, Meghana Narasimhan, Archana Polisetti, Chadwik Rabe, Naga Padmaja Tirumal Reddy, Tyler Wendell, and Sumanth Reddy Yanala.

Finally, I would like to thank my wife, Manimehala Suthaharan, and my lovely children, Lovepriya Suthaharan, Praveen Suthaharan, and Prattheeba Suthaharan, for their understanding, encouragement, and support which helped me accomplish this project. This project would not have been completed successfully without their support.

Greensboro, NC, USA   Shan Suthaharan
June 2015

About the Author

Shan Suthaharan is a Professor of Computer Science at the University of North Carolina at Greensboro (UNCG), North Carolina, USA. He also serves as the Director of Undergraduate Studies at the Department of Computer Science at UNCG. He has more than 25 years of university teaching and administrative experience and has taught both undergraduate and graduate courses. His aspiration is to educate and train students so that they can prosper in the computer field by understanding current real-world and complex problems, and develop efficient techniques and technologies. His current teaching interests include big data analytics and machine learning, cryptography and network security, and computer networking and analysis. He earned his doctorate in Computer Science from Monash University, Australia. Since then, he has been actively working on disseminating his knowledge and experience through teaching, advising, seminars, research, and publications.

Dr. Suthaharan enjoys investigating real-world, complex problems, and developing and implementing algorithms to solve those problems using modern technologies. The main theme of his current research is the signature discovery and event detection for a secure and reliable environment. The ultimate goal of his research is to build a secure and reliable environment using modern and emerging technologies. His current research primarily focuses on the characterization and detection of environmental events, the exploration of machine learning techniques, and the development of advanced statistical and computational techniques to discover key signatures and detect emerging events from structured and unstructured big data.

Dr. Suthaharan has authored or co-authored more than 75 research papers in the areas of computer science, and published them in international journals and refereed conference proceedings. He also invented a key management and encryption technology, which has been patented in Australia, Japan, and Singapore. He also received visiting scholar awards from and served as a visiting researcher at the University of Sydney, Australia; the University of Melbourne, Australia; and the University of California, Berkeley, USA. He was a senior member of the Institute of Electrical and Electronics Engineers, and volunteered as an elected chair of the Central North Carolina Section twice. He is a member of Sigma Xi, the Scientific Research Society and a Fellow of the Institution of Engineering and Technology.

Contents

Chapter 1
Science of Information

Abstract The main objective of this chapter is to provide an overview of the modern field of data science and some of the current progress in this field. The overview focuses on two important paradigms: (1) big data paradigm, which describes a problem space for the big data analytics, and (2) machine learning paradigm, which describes a solution space for the big data analytics. It also includes a preliminary description of the important elements of data science. These important elements are the *data*, the *knowledge* (also called responses), and the *operations*. The terms *knowledge* and *responses* will be used interchangeably in the rest of the book. A preliminary information of the data format, the data types and the classification are also presented in this chapter. This chapter emphasizes the importance of collaboration between the experts from multiple disciplines and provides the information on some of the current institutions that show collaborative activities with useful resources.

1.1 Data Science

Data science is an emerging field in the twenty-first century. The article by Mike Loukides at the O'reilly website [1] provides an overview, and it talks about data source, and data scalability. We can define data science as the management and analysis of data sets, the extraction of useful information, and the understanding of the systems that produce the data. The system can be a single unit (e.g., a computer network or a wireless sensor network) that is formed by many interconnecting subunits (computers or sensors) that can collaborate under a certain set of principles and strategies to carry out tasks, such as the collection of data, facts, or statistics of an environment the system is expected to monitor. Some examples of these systems include network intrusion detection systems [2], climate-change detection systems [3], and public space intruder detection systems [4]. These real-world systems may produce massive amounts of data, called *big data*, from many data sources that are highly complex, unstructured, and hard to manage, process, and

© Springer Science+Business Media New York 2016   1
S. Suthaharan, *Machine Learning Models and Algorithms for Big
Data Classification*, Integrated Series in Information Systems 36,
DOI 10.1007/978-1-4899-7641-3_1

analyze. This is currently a challenging problem for many industries, institutions, and organizations, including businesses, health care sectors, information technology divisions, government agencies, and research organizations. To address this problem, a separate field, big data science, has been created and requires a new direction in research and educational efforts for its speedy and successful advancements [5].

One of the research problems in big data science is the big data classification, as reported in [6, 7], which involves the classification of different types of data and the extraction of useful information from the massive and complex data sets. The big data classification research requires technology that can handle problems caused by the data characteristics (volume, velocity, and variety) of big data [5]. It also requires mathematical models and algorithms to classify the data efficiently using appropriate technology, and these mathematical models and algorithms form the field of machine learning discussed in [8–10].

1.1.1 Technological Dilemma

One of the technological dilemmas in big data science is the nonexistence of a technology that can manage and analyze dynamically growing massive data efficiently and extract useful information. Another dilemma is the lack of intelligent approaches that can select suitable techniques from many design choices (i.e., models and algorithms) to solve big data problems. Additionally, if we invest in expensive and modern technology, assuming that the data in hand is big data, and we later find out that the data is not big data (which could have been solved by simple technology and tools), then the investment is basically lost. In this case, the machine-learning techniques like the supervised learning [11] and the dimensionality reduction [8, 12] techniques are useful. A simple explanation on supervised learning can be found at the MATLAB website [13]. One of the dimensionality reduction approaches is called principal component analysis (PCA), and a simple tutorial on PCA can be found at Brian Russell's website [14]. In addition to these techniques, a framework (or a systematic design) to test and validate the data early is also required and a framework for this purpose is presented in Chap. 3.

1.1.2 Technological Advancement

The current advancements in the technology include the modern distributed file systems and the distributed machine learning. One such technology is called Hadoop [15, 16], which facilitates distributed machine learning using external libraries, like the scikit-learn library [17], to process big data. Among several machine-learning techniques in the libraries, most of them are based on classical models and algorithms, may not be suitable for big data processing. However, some techniques, like the decision tree learning and the deep learning, are suitable for big data classification, and they may help develop better supervised learning techniques in the upcoming years. The classification techniques evolved from these models and algorithms are the main focus, and they will be discussed in detail in the rest of the book.

1.2 Big Data Paradigm

In this book, it is assumed that the big data paradigm consists of a big data system and an environment. The goal of a system is to observe an environment and learn its characteristics to make accurate decisions. For example, the goal of a network intrusion detection system is to learn traffic characteristics and detect intrusions to improve the security of a computer network. Similarly, the goal of a wireless sensor network is to monitor changes in the weather to learn the weather patterns for forecasting. The environment generates events, and the system collects the facts and statistics, transforms them into knowledge with suitable operations, learns the event characteristics, and predicts the environmental characteristics.

1.2.1 Facts and Statistics of a System

To understand a system and develop suitable technology, mathematical/statistical models, and algorithms, we need clear definitions for two important terms, data and knowledge, and for three operations, physical, mathematical, and logical operations. The descriptions of these terms and operations are presented below.

1.2.1.1 Data

Data can be described as the hidden digital facts that the monitoring system collects. Hidden digital facts are the digitized facts that are not obvious to the system without further comprehensive processing. The definition of data should be based on the knowledge that must be gained from it. One of the important requirements for the data is the format. For example, the data could be presented mathematically or in a two-dimensional tabular representation. Another important requirement is the type of data. For example, the data could be labeled or not labeled. In the labeled data, the digital facts are not hidden and can be used for training the machine-learning techniques. In the unlabeled data, the digital facts are hidden and can be used for testing or validation as a part of the machine-learning approach.

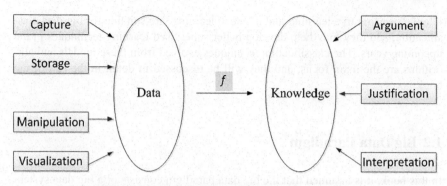

Fig. 1.1 Transformation of data into knowledge

1.2.1.2 Knowledge

Knowledge can be described as the learned information acquired from the data. For example, the knowledge could be the detection of patterns in the data, the classification of the varieties of patterns in the data, the calculation of unknown statistical distributions, or the computation of the correlations of the data. It forms the responses for the system, and it is called the "knowledge set" or "response set" (sometimes called the "labeled set"). The data forms the domain, called "data domain," on which the responses are generated using a model f as illustrated in Fig. 1.1. In addition to these two elements (i.e., the data and the knowledge), a monitoring system needs three operations, called physical operations, mathematical operations, and logical operations in this book. The descriptions of these three important operations are presented in the following subsections.

1.2.1.3 Physical Operation

Physical operations describe the steps involved in the processes of data capture, data storage, data manipulation, and data visualization [18]. These are the important contributors to the development of a suitable data domain for a system so that the machine-learning techniques can be applied efficiently. Big data also means massive data, and the assumption is that it cannot be solved with a single file or a single machine. Hence, the indexing and distribution of the big data over a distributed network becomes necessary. One of the popular tools available in the market for this purpose is the Hadoop distributed file system (http://hadoop.apache.org/), which uses the MapReduce framework (http://hadoop.apache.org/mapreduce/) to accomplish these objectives. These modern tools help enhance the physical operations of a system which, in turn, helps generate sophisticated, supervised learning models and algorithms for big data classifications.

1.2.1.4 Mathematical Operation

Mathematical operations describe the theory and applications of appropriate mathematical and statistical techniques and tools required for the transformation of data into knowledge. This transformation can be written as a knowledge function $f : D \Rightarrow K$ as illustrated in Fig. 1.1, where the set D stands for the data domain and the set K stands for the knowledge or response set. In this knowledge function, if the data (i.e., the data domain) is structured, then the executions of these operations are not difficult. Even if the structured data grows exponentially, these operations are not difficult because they can be carried out using existing resources and tools. Hence, the size of the data does not matter in the case of a structured data in general.

1.2.1.5 Logical Operation

Logical operations describe the logical arguments, justifications, and interpretations of the knowledge, which can be used to derive meaningful facts. For example, the knowledge function $f : D \Rightarrow K$ can divide (classify) the data domain and provide data patterns, and then the logical operations and arguments must be used to justify and interpret the class types from the patterns.

1.2.2 Big Data Versus Regular Data

In addition to the terminologies mentioned earlier, we also need to understand the distinction between the new definition of big data and the definition of regular data. Figure 1.2 demonstrates this distinction. Before we understand the information in this figure, we need to understand three parameters, n, p, and t of a system, because they determine the characteristics of data whether it is a big data set or a regular data set.

1.2.2.1 Scenario

An element of a monitoring system's data can also be called an observation (or an event). This book will use the term "observation" and the term "event" interchangeably. For example, an observation of a network intrusion detection system is the traffic packet captured at a particular instance. Millions of events (n) may be captured within a short period of time (t) using devices like sensors and network routers and analyzed using software tools to measure the environmental characteristics. An observation generally depends on many independent variables called *features*, and they form a space called *feature space*. The number of features (p) determines the dimensionality of the system, and it controls the complexity of processing the data. The features represent the characteristics of the environment that is monitored by

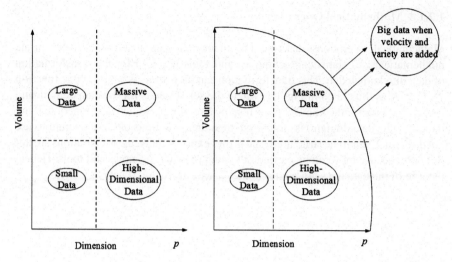

Fig. 1.2 Big data and regions of interest

the system. As an example, the source bytes, destination count, and protocol type information found in a packet can serve as features of the computer network traffic data. The changes in the values of feature variables determine the type (or the class) of an event. To determine the correct class for an event, the event must be transformed into knowledge.

In summary, the parameter n represents the number of observations captured by a system at time t, which determines the size (*volume*) of the data set, and the parameter p represents the number of features that determines the dimension of the data and contributes to the number of classes (*variety*) in the data set. In addition, the ratio between the parameters n and t determines the data rate (*velocity*) term as described in the standard definition of big data [6].

Now referring back to Fig. 1.2, the horizontal axis represents p (i.e., the dimension) and the vertical axis represents n (i.e., the size or the volume). The domain defined by n and p is divided into four subdomains (small, large, high dimension, and massive) based on the magnitudes of n and p. The arc boundary identifies the regular data and massive data regions, and the massive data region becomes big data when velocity and variety are included.

1.2.2.2 Data Representation

A data set may be defined in mathematical or tabular form. The tabular form is visual, and it can be easily understood by nonexperts. Hence this section first presents the data representation tool in a tabular form, and it will be defined mathematically from Chap. 2 onward. The data sets generally contain a large number of events as mentioned earlier. Let us denote these events by $E_1, E_2, \ldots, E_{mn}$. Now assume that these observations can be divided into n separable classes denoted by $C_1, C_2, \ldots, C_n$ (where n is much smaller than mn), where C_1 is a set of events $E_1, E_2, \ldots, E_{m_1}$, C_2 is a set of events $E_1, E_2, \ldots, E_{m_2}$, and so on (where $m_1 + m_2 + \cdots = mn$). These classes of events may be listed in the first column of a table. The last column of the table identifies the corresponding class types. In addition, every set of events depends on p features that are denoted by $F_1, F_2, \ldots, F_p$, and the values associated with these features can be presented in the other columns of the table. For example, the values associated with feature F_1 of the first set $E_1, E_2, \ldots, E_{m_1}$ can be denoted by $x_{11}, x_{12}, \ldots, x_{1m_1}$, indicating the event E_1 takes x_{11}, event E_2 takes x_{12}, and so on. The same pattern can be followed for the other sets of events.

1.3 Machine Learning Paradigm

Machine learning is about the exploration and development of mathematical models and algorithms to learn from data. Its paradigm focuses on classification objectives and consists of modeling an optimal mapping between the data domain and the knowledge set and developing the learning algorithms. The classification is also called *supervised learning*, which requires a training (labeled) data set, a validation data set, and a test data set. The definitions and the roles of these data sets will be discussed in Chap. 2. However, to briefly explain, the training data set helps find the optimal parameters of a model, the validation data set helps avoid overfitting of the model, and the test data set helps determine the accuracy of the model.

1.3.1 Modeling and Algorithms

The term *modeling* refers to both mathematical and statistical modeling of data. The goal of modeling is to develop a parametrized mapping between the data domain and the response set. This mapping could be a parametrized function or a parametrized process that learn the characteristics of a system from the input (labeled) data. The term *algorithm* is a confusing term in the context of machine learning. For a computer scientist, the term algorithm means step-by-step systematic instructions for a computer to solve a problem. In machine learning, the modeling, itself, may have several algorithms to derive a model; however, the term algorithm here refers to a *learning algorithm*. The learning algorithm is used to train, validate, and test the model using a given data set to find an optimal value for the parameters, validate it, and evaluate its performance.

1.3.2 Supervised and Unsupervised

It is best to define supervised learning and unsupervised learning based on the class definition. In supervised learning, the classes are known and class boundaries are

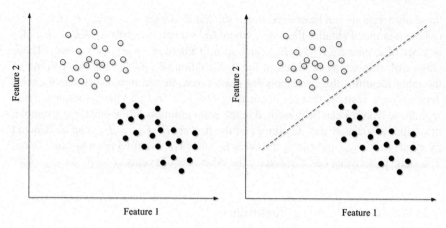

Fig. 1.3 Classification is defined

well defined in the given (training) data set, and the learning is done using these classes (i.e., class labels). Hence, it is called classification. In unsupervised learning, we assume the classes or class boundaries are not known, hence the class labels themselves are also learned, and classes are defined based on this. Hence, the class boundaries are statistical and not sharply defined, and it is called clustering.

1.3.2.1 Classification

In classification problems [11], we assume labeled data (classes) are available to generate rules (i.e., generate classifiers through training) that can help to assign a label to new data (i.e., testing) that does not have labels. In this case, we can derive an exact rule because of the availability of the labels. Figure 1.3 illustrates this example. It shows two classes, labeled with white dots and black dots, and a straight line rule that helps to assign a label to a new data point. As stated before, the labeled data sets are available for the purpose of evaluating and validating machine-learning techniques, hence the classification problem can be defined mathematically.

The classification problem may be addressed mathematically based on the data-to-knowledge transformation mentioned earlier. Suppose a data set is given, and its data domain D is R^l, indicating that the events of the data set depend on l features and form an l-dimensional vector space. If we assume that there are n classes, then we can define the knowledge function (i.e., the model) as follows:

$$f : R^l \Rightarrow \{0, 1, 2, \ldots, n\} \tag{1.1}$$

In this function definition, the range $\{0, 1, 2, \ldots, n\}$ is the knowledge set which assigns the discrete values (labels) $0, 1, 2, \ldots, n$ to different classes. This mathematical function helps us to define suitable classifiers for the classification of the data. Several classification techniques have been proposed in the machine learning

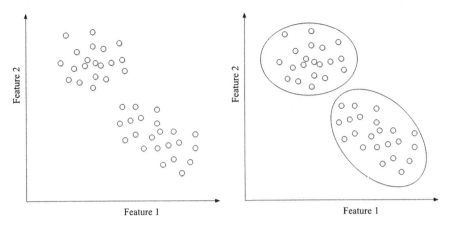

Fig. 1.4 Clustering is defined

literature, and some of the well-known techniques are: support vector machine [19], decision tree [20], random forest [21], and deep learning [22]. These techniques will be discussed in detail in this book with programming and examples.

1.3.2.2 Clustering

In clustering problems [23, 24], we assume data sets are available to generate rules, but they are not labeled. Hence, we can only derive an approximated rule that can help to label new data that do not have labels. Figure 1.4 illustrates this example. It shows a set of points labeled with white dots; however, a geometric pattern that determines two clusters can be found. These clusters form a rule that helps to assign a label to the given data points and thus to a new data point. As a result, the data may only be clustered, not classified. Hence, the clustering problem can also be defined as follows with an approximated rule. The clustering problem may also be addressed mathematically based on the data-to-knowledge transformation mentioned earlier. Once again, let us assume a data set is given, and its domain D is R^l, indicating that the events of the data set depend on l features and form an l-dimensional vector space. If we extract structures (e.g., statistical or geometrical) and estimate there are $\hat{n}$ classes, then we can define the knowledge function as follows:

$$\hat{f} : R^l \Rightarrow \{0, 1, 2 \dots, \hat{n}\} \tag{1.2}$$

The range $\{0, 1, 2, \dots, \hat{n}\}$ is the knowledge set which assigns the discrete labels $0, 1, 2, \dots, \hat{n}$ to different classes. This function helps us to assign suitable labels to new data. Several clustering algorithms have been proposed in machine learning: k-Means clustering, Gaussian mixture clustering, and hierarchical clustering [23].

1.4 Collaborative Activities

Big data means big research. Without strong collaborative efforts between the experts from many disciplines (e.g., mathematics, statistics, computer science, medical science, biology, and chemistry) and the dissemination of educational resources in a timely fashion, the goal of advancing the field of data science may not be practical. These issues have been realized not only by researchers and academics but also by government agencies and industries. This momentum can be noticed in the last several years. Some of the recent collaborative efforts and the resources that can provide long-term impacts in the field of big data science are:

- Simons Institute UC Berkeley—http://simons.berkeley.edu/
- Statistical Applied Mathematical Science Institute—http://www.samsi.info/
- New York University Center for Data science—http://datascience.nyu.edu/
- Institute for Advanced Analytics—http://analytics.ncsu.edu/
- Center for Science of Information, Purdue University—http://soihub.org/
- Berkeley Institute for Data Science—http://bids.berkeley.edu/
- Stanford and Coursera—https://www.coursera.org/
- Institute for Data Science—http://www.rochester.edu/data-science/
- Institute for Mathematics and its Applications—http://www.ima.umn.edu/
- Data Science Institute—http://datascience.columbia.edu/
- Data Science Institute—https://dsi.virginia.edu/
- Michigan Institute for Data Science—http://minds.umich.edu/

An important note to the readers: The websites (or web links) cited in the entire book may change rapidly, please be aware of it. My plan is to maintain the information in this book current by updating the information at the following website: http://www.uncg.edu/cmp/downloads/

1.5 A Snapshot

The snapshot of the entire book always helps readers by informing the topics covered in the book ahead of time. This allows them to conceptualize, summarize, and understand the theory and applications. This section provides a snapshot of this book under three categories: the purpose and interests, the goals and objectives, and the problems and challenges.

1.5.1 The Purpose and Interests

The purpose of this book is to provide information on big data classification and the related topics with simple examples and programming. Several interesting topics contribute to big data classification, including the characteristics of data, the relationships between data and knowledge, the models and algorithms that can help learn the characteristics (or patterns) in the data, and the emerging technologies that help manage, process, and analyze data.

1.5.2 The Goal and Objectives

The goal of this book is to teach the details of the development of models and algorithms to address big data classification. To achieve these goals, the chapter objectives are developed: (1) the analysis and the understanding of big data, (2) the configuration and the understanding of big data systems, (3) the exploration and the understanding of supervised learning models and algorithms, (4) the development of the models and algorithms with the focus of reducing the classification errors and computational complexity, and (5) the understanding of the scalability problems.

1.5.3 The Problems and Challenges

Problems are the controlling of the following three errors: (1) approximation errors, (2) estimation errors, and (3) optimization errors. The challenges are how to control the above errors under the following three data conditions (or characteristics): (1) class characteristics, (2) error characteristics, and (3) domain characteristics.

Problems

1.1. A Physical System
Suggest a physical system capable of handling big data management, processing, and analysis. Think about an application you are interested in and familiar with, and use the knowledge gained in Sect. 1.2 to develop a solution for this question.

1.2. Network Traffic Data
A data set has been created at a network router by capturing network traffic over a period of 15 min. Do you think it is regular data, large data, high-dimensional data, massive data, or big data? Justify your opinion with examples.

1.3. Is a Data Set a Big Data Set?
(a) Empirically show a data set is evolving into a big data set. You may select a data set, identify its features, and increase observations of each feature assuming they follow a statistical distribution (e.g., Gaussian or uniform).
(b) Develop a theory that proves or shows a data set is a big data set if the data set is actually big data, otherwise it is not a big data set.

Acknowledgements Thanks to the Department of Statistics, University of California, Berkeley; the Center for Science of Information, Purdue University; the Statistical Applied Mathematical Science Institute; and the Institute for Mathematics and its Applications, University of Minnesota for their support which contributed to the development of this book.

References

1. M. Loukides. "What is data science?" http://radar.oreilly.com/2010/06/what-is-data-science.html, 2010.
2. A. Lazarevic, V. Kumar, and J. Srivastava, "Intrusion detection: A survey," Managing Cyber Threats, vol.5, Part I, pp. 19–78, June 2005.
3. S. Suthaharan, M. Alzahrani, S. Rajasegarar, C. Leckie and M. Palaniswami. "Labelled data collection for anomaly detection in wireless sensor networks," in Proceedings of the 6th International Conference on Intelligent Sensors, Sensor Networks and Information Processing, pp. 269–274, 2010.
4. S. Bandari and S. Suthaharan. "Intruder detection in public space using suspicious behavior phenomena and wireless sensor networks," in Proceedings of the 1st ACM International Workshop on Sensor-Enhanced Safety and Security in Public Spaces at ACM MOBIHOC, pp. 3–8, 2012.
5. P. Zikopoulos, C. Eaton, et al. "Understanding big data: Analytics for enterprise class hadoop and streaming data." McGraw-Hill Osborne Media, 2011.
6. S. Suthaharan. "Big data classification: Problems and challenges in network intrusion prediction with machine learning," ACM SIGMETRICS Performance Evaluation Review, vol. 41, no. 4, pp. 70–73, 2014.
7. H. Tong. "Big data classification," Data Classification: Algorithms and Applications. Chapter 10. (Eds.) C.C. Aggarwal. Taylor and Francis Group, LLC. pp. 275–286. 2015.
8. C.M. Bishop. "Pattern recognition and machine learning," Springer Science+Business Media, LLC, 2006.
9. T. Hastie, R. Tibshirani, and J. Friedman. The Elements of Statistical Learning. New York: Springer, 2009.
10. T. G. Dietterich, "Machine-learning research: Four current directions," AI Magazine, vol. 18, no. 4, pp. 97–136, 1997.
11. S. B. Kotsiantis. "Supervised machine learning: A review of classification techniques," Informatica 31, pp. 249–268, 2007.
12. S. Yan, D. Xu, B. Zhang, H.J. Zhang, Q. Yang, and S. Lin, "Graph embedding and extensions: A general framework for dimensionality reduction," IEEE Transactions on Pattern Analysis and Machine Intelligence, vol. 29, no. 1, pp. 40–51, 2007.
13. http://www.mathworks.com/help/stats/supervised-learning-machine-learning-workflow-and-algorithms.html
14. http://www.cggveritas.com/technicalDocuments/cggv_0000014063.pdf
15. K. Shvachko, H. Kuang, S. Radia, and R. Chansler. "The hadoop distributed file system," In Proceedings of the IEEE 26th Symposium on Mass Storage Systems and Technologies, pp. 1–10, 2010.
16. T. White. Hadoop: the definitive guide. O'Reilly, 2012.
17. http://scikit-learn.org/stable/
18. P. C. Wong, H.-W. Shen, C. R. Johnson, C. Chen, and R. B. Ross. "The top 10 challenges in extreme-scale visual analytics." Computer Graphics and Applications, IEEE, 32(4):63–67, 2012.
19. M. A. Hearst, S. T. Dumais, E. Osman, J. Platt, and B. Scholkopf. "Support vector machines." Intelligent Systems and their Applications, IEEE, 13(4), pp. 18–28, 1998.

20. S.K. Murthy. "Automatic construction of decision trees from data: A multi-disciplinary survey," Data Mining and Knowledge Discovery, Kluwer Academic Publishers, vol. 2, no. 4, pp. 345–389, 1998.
21. L. Breiman, "Random forests." Machine learning 45, pp. 5–32, 2001.
22. L. Wan, M. Zeiler, S. Zhang, Y. LeCun, and R. Fergus. "Regularization of neural networks using dropconnect." In Proceedings of the 30th International Conference on Machine Learning (ICML-13), pp. 1058–1066, 2013.
23. http://www.mathworks.com/discovery/cluster-analysis.html
24. A. K. Jain. "Data clustering: 50 years beyond K-means." Pattern recognition letters, vol. 31, no. 8, pp. 651–666, 2010.

Part I
Understanding Big Data

Chapter 2
Big Data Essentials

Abstract The main objective of this chapter is to organize the big data essentials that contribute to the analytics of big data systematically. It includes their presentations in a simple form that can help readers conceptualize and summarize the classification objectives easily. The topics are organized into three sections: big data analytics, big data classification, and big data scalability. In the big data analytics section, the big data controllers that play major roles in data representation and knowledge extraction will be presented and discussed in detail. These controllers, the problems and challenges that they bring to big data analytics, and the solutions to address these problems and challenges will also be discussed. In the big data classification section, the machine learning processes, the classification modeling that is characterized by the big data controllers, and the classification algorithms that can manage the effect of big data controllers will be discussed. In the big data scalability section, the importance of the low-dimensional structures that can be extracted from a high-dimensional system for addressing scalability issues will be discussed as well.

2.1 Big Data Analytics

In [1], Philip Russom defined the term "Big data analytics" by dividing it into two keywords "big data" and "analytics," and he described them individually based on their combined influence on business intelligence. Business intelligence is one of the applications that can benefit from the big data techniques and technologies. Big data analytics also has a scientific significance in real-world applications; therefore, it is appropriate to define it based on class characteristics, feature characteristics, and observation characteristics—the three important controllers of big data. This chapter discusses these big data controllers in detail. The understanding of big data controllers, the analysis of the problems that the controllers create in a big data environment, the confrontation of the challenges for solving these problems efficiently,

© Springer Science+Business Media New York 2016

S. Suthaharan, *Machine Learning Models and Algorithms for Big Data Classification*, Integrated Series in Information Systems 36, DOI 10.1007/978-1-4899-7641-3_2

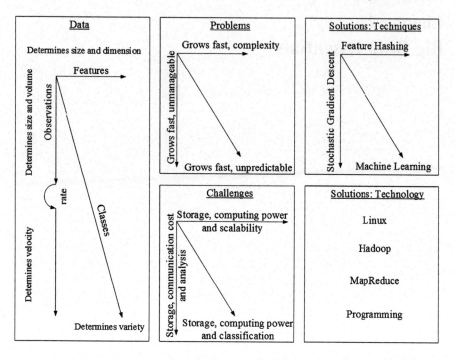

Fig. 2.1 The contributors to the analytics of big data: the controllers, problems, challenges, and solutions (techniques and technologies)

and the development of techniques and technologies to address big data classification are the important contributors in big data analytics. The definition of big data analytics based on the contributors would help the classification of the structured and unstructured data significantly. Whether a data set is structured or unstructured may be determined by proper understanding of the controllers.

2.1.1 Big Data Controllers

The main goal of this book is to address big data classification problems, challenges, and solutions. In [2], these topics are presented focusing on network intrusion detection, which is considered a big data application. A complete understanding of the class characteristics, feature characteristics, and observation characteristics can help address these issues. These three controllers are illustrated in Fig. 2.1. Let us first understand the information presented in the first column of this figure. It presents a 3D representation of a set of data. The observations (the vertical axis) represent the events that are recorded or observed by a system, and they describe the big data's term volume. The number of observations, n, states that the size of the data set is n.

They may also describe the big data's term velocity which may be defined by the availability of data on demand. Hence, the observation controls the classification issues that resulted from the volume and velocity of the big data. The features (the horizontal axis) represent the independent variables that generate the events (or responses), and hence they determine the volume and the dimensionality of the data. The number of features, p, means the data set has p-dimensions. They control the scalability of the data, and the parameters, n and p, together define the characteristics of dimensionality. For example, if $n < p$, then the data set is said to be high dimensional. The third big data controller, the classes (the diagonal axis), represents the types of the events and determines the variety term of big data. It helps to group the data and creates the need for dividing the data domain robustly.

2.1.2 Big Data Problems

The individualization of the controllers and their uncoordinated efforts can create problems in the big data realm. Each controller defines its own contribution to big data, and it affects the individualization of the other controllers orthogonally, and hence we define the controllers' problems using a three-dimensional space as shown in the second column of Fig. 2.1. As it is defined, the controller class contributes to the unpredictability of big data. It means that the detection (or classification) of classes with the growth in big data is very difficult and unpredictable. The growth in the class types is system dependent, and it is independent to the users' knowledge and the experience. Hence, the big data classification becomes unpredictable, and the application of machine-learning models and algorithms becomes difficult.

Similarly, the controller feature contributes to the complexity of big data. It makes the classification of patterns difficult by increasing the dimensionality of data. It is one of the major contributors to the scalability problems in a big data paradigm. The third controller observation contributes to the difficulties of managing, processing, and analyzing the data. Its growth increases the volume of data and makes the processing difficult with the current technologies. Therefore, if we understand the individuality of these controllers and their uncoordinated efforts clearly, then we should be able to confront the challenges that they bring to big data classification.

2.1.3 Big Data Challenges

The individualization and orthogonality problems reported in the previous section create several challenges to the current techniques and technologies. The bottom figure in the second column of Fig. 2.1 illustrates the challenges. The challenges associated with the techniques may be categorized as classification, scalability, and analysis. The challenges associated with the technologies may be categorized as computation, communication, and storage. In addition, the problems can bring security challenges as reported in the papers [2, 3] as well. Let us now connect these challenges with the corresponding big data controllers.

The problems caused by the controller class can impact the performance degradation of the classification techniques, while imposing challenges on the choice of computing power and storage requirements. The problems caused by the controller feature challenge the reduction of dimensionality and the storage and computing power. Similarly the controller observation brings challenges in the data processing, storage requirements, and communication issues when the data are distributed as demonstrated in [2] to solve intrusion detection problems.

2.1.4 Big Data Solutions

The big data solutions are illustrated in the third column of Fig. 2.1. The big data solutions are divided into techniques and technologies as illustrated in these figures. The techniques involve solving problems by addressing the challenges associated with the big data controllers with respect to their speed, complexity, unpredictability, (un)manageability, and scalability. The techniques may be divided into modeling and algorithms whereas the technologies may be divided into systems and framework. The modeling and algorithms may be described more specifically with supervised machine learning (related to classes) [4], feature hashing (related to features) [5, 6], and stochastic gradient descent (related to observations) [7, 8]. Similarly the systems and framework may be described more specifically with the modern distributed file systems like the Hadoop distributed file system [9, 10] and modern programming frameworks like the MapReduce programming model [11, 12].

2.2 Big Data Classification

The main focus of this book is on big data classification [2, 13], which is one of the important and difficult problems in big data analytics. In simple terms, big data classification is a process of classifying big data under the problems and challenges introduced by the controllers of big data. The steps involved in the big data classification objectives are presented in the top figure of Fig. 2.2, which shows the processes involved with the management of big data, the configuration of big data technology, and the development of machine-learning techniques.

In the top figure of Fig. 2.2, the steps involved in the classification process are clearly presented: collecting the input data, understanding the data, shaping up the data (e.g., data cleaning and representation learning), and understanding the big data environment based on the hardware requirements and constraints of controllers. Finally, the understanding of the modeling and algorithms is also required for the success of big data classifications. The first bottom figure of Fig. 2.2 shows the specific parameters that influence the management of the big data controllers and lead

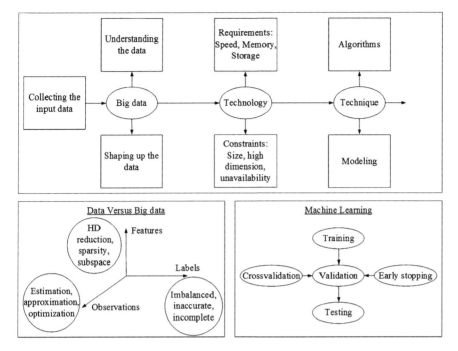

Fig. 2.2 *Top*: the classification processes of big data are illustrated. *Bottom left*: the classification modeling of big data is illustrated. *Bottom right*: the classification algorithms of big data are illustrated

to challenges in the development of learning models. In the second bottom figure of Fig. 2.2, the steps involved in learning algorithms are presented. It shows the flow from training phase to validation phase and then to testing phase. In the validation phase, cross-validation techniques can be applied and an early stopping decision may be made to avoid a so-called overfitting problem.

2.2.1 Representation Learning

The representation learning techniques [14, 15] are useful for understanding and shaping the data. These techniques require statistical measures and processes. Statistical measures like the mean, standard deviation, and covariance can help detect the patterns numerically. Similarly, the graphical tools like pie charts, histograms, and scatter plots can help in understanding the patterns. Statistical processes like normalization and standardization can manipulate data to extract and understand patterns. Representation learning mainly focuses on the big data controller feature, and its goal is the feature selection. Hence it contributes to the dimensionality

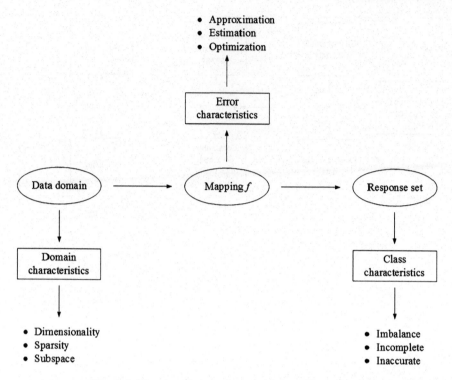

Fig. 2.3 Characteristics problems with the modeling

reduction objectives in machine learning. In big data analytics, the data sets grow dynamically; therefore, the representation learning techniques take the dynamically changing data characteristics into consideration. In general, representation learning techniques have been applied to understand the data, but it does not incorporate the domain division (class-separate) objectives. The recent cross-domain representation learning framework proposed by Tu and Sun [16] may be useful to understand the data for big data analytics.

2.2.2 Distributed File Systems

Distributed file systems are suitable for big data management, processing, and analysis [17]. They may be customized to satisfy the hardware requirements and remove computing environmental constraints. They must be configured to handle a large volume of data (big data storage), real-time data (big data on demand), and large varieties of computations associated with the data types (computer memory). The modern Hadoop distributed file system can be configured to meet these requirements, thus eliminating the constraints that arise from the size, dimensionality, and data unavailability for on demand applications.

2.2.3 Classification Modeling

Classification modeling was illustrated in Fig. 1.1 and discussed in Chap. 1. As we recall, it defines a map f between a data domain and a knowledge (or response) set. This definition may be extended to the analysis of class labels in order to describe the class characteristics defined by imbalanced [18], incomplete [19], and inaccurate data [20]; to the analysis of the observations in order to describe the error characteristics defined by the approximation, the estimation, and the optimization [21, 22] errors; and to the analysis of the features in order to describe the domain characteristics defined by the degree of dimensionality, the sparsity, and the subspace. This extended definition is illustrated in Fig. 2.3. It also shows the relationships between the three characteristics. It states that the approximation, estimation, and optimization issues must be taken into consideration, when the mapping f is defined, the dimensionality, sparsity, and subspace must be taken into consideration when the data domain is divided, and the imbalance, incomplete, and inaccurate class characteristics must be considered when the subdomains are mapped to the responses.

2.2.3.1 Class Characteristics

Imbalanced, incomplete, and inaccurate class characteristics can be defined in the response set portion of the modeling objective (see Fig. 2.3). These characteristics are influenced by the big data controllers: classes, features, and observations. We can describe these characteristics using simple examples.

Let us take two classes: $\{(1,5),(1.5,5.2),(2,4.6)\}$ and $\{(5,1),(6,0.5),(6.5,1.4)\}$. This is balanced data, the observations are represented by (x_1,x_2) with two features and the number of observations in each class is 3. If we assume these are the true observations, but a system generates $\{(1,5),(1.5,5.2),(2,4.6)\}$ and $\{(6,0.5),(6.5,1.4)\}$, then we can call this imbalanced data [18]. You will see a detailed explanation in Chap. 3. That is, if we have more observations in one class than in the other class, then we can say the data is imbalanced, and the smaller class is the minority class, and the other class is the majority class.

If the system generates $\{(1,5),(1.5,5.2),(2,4.6)\}$ and $\{(5,1),(6,0.5),(6.5,-)\}$ then we can call this incomplete data, because a class has missing information and is not complete. Similarly, if the system generates $\{(1,5),(1.5,5.2),(6.5,1.4)\}$ and $\{(5,1),(6,0.5),(2,4.6)\}$, then we can call it inaccurate data because class observations are labeled incorrectly.

This scenario is illustrated visually in Fig. 2.4. The top row shows two classes "class 1" and "class 2" with the balanced, complete, and accurate data. In the first image of the second row, an imbalanced data example is shown; in the second image of this row, an incomplete data example (data are missing) is illustrated; and in the third image, an example of inaccurate data (labels are switched) is shown. In [19], Little and Rubin provide different examples for explaining the patterns that are expected when the data is incomplete. These three class characteristics are the major players for the deformation of patterns.

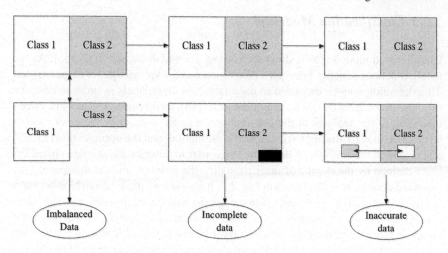

Fig. 2.4 Examples of imbalanced data, incomplete data, and inaccurate data based on the class labels and information abnormalities

2.2.3.2 Error Characteristics

The error characteristics can be defined in the mapping portion of the modeling process. This is shown in Fig. 2.3. Bottou and Bousquet [21] discuss the decomposition of classification errors using estimation, approximation, and optimization errors, and then Dalessandro [22] simplifies it in his paper. Based on these references, the estimation error may be defined as the differences in the models derived from the data sets of different sizes (e.g., finite and infinite sizes); the approximation error may be defined as the differences in the models derived from the parametrized models assumed (e.g., linear and nonlinear models); and the optimization error may be defined as the differences in the algorithms used to derive the models (e.g., efficient and inefficient algorithms). It is described in Fig. 2.5.

Suppose there is a true model, and we don't know that model; hence, we assume a model and develop a classification technique. Then the error between the true model and the model that we assumed will impact the accuracy of the classification model that we developed. This error is called the approximation error. Similarly, suppose there is a best algorithm, but we don't know that, and we develop an algorithm and use it for our classification. This error will impact the classification accuracy as well. This is called the optimization error. In the third error, suppose we use the true model and the best algorithm, in that case, we would get the actual results, but if we use our assumed model and the algorithm, we produce a different result. This error is called the estimation error. The task of big data classification is to minimize these three errors in the modeling and the algorithms. These three error characteristics are the major players for the classification errors.

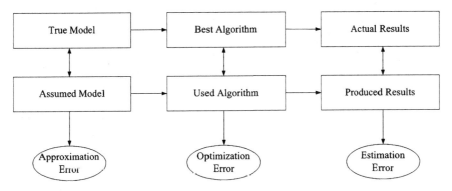

Fig. 2.5 Differences in modeling, algorithm and results can define approximation, optimization and estimation errors respectively

2.2.3.3 Domain Characteristics

Dimensionality, sparsity, and subspace can be defined based on the information of the features (one of the big data controllers). The number of features determines the dimensionality of the data. However, some of the features may not be relevant features, and they may not contribute to the patterns in the data. This can lead to dimensionality reduction, and the new space with fewer features is called the subspace. For example, take three observations with three features: (2,6,1.1), (4,8,2.2), and (3,7,0.5); they are drawn from two classes, "even" and "odd." They form a three-dimensional data domain. We can easily classify them with only the first two features, so it means new data points are (2,6), (4,8), and (3,7), and they now form a two-dimensional subspace. The first two points represent the "even" class and the last one represents "odd" class. Therefore, the subspaces can have low-dimensional structures that are useful for classification. Let us now define sparsity using a modified example. In this example, let us take the following three observations with three features: (2,0,0), (0,8,0), and (0,0,3). Here the features are sparse and they create the sparsity problem of big data classification.

2.2.4 Classification Algorithms

The classification algorithms mainly involve machine-learning processes, which are training, validation, and testing [4]. However, cross-validation and early stopping processes must be incorporated in the validation step.

2.2.4.1 Training

The training phase provides an algorithm to train the model. In other words, we can say that the parameters of a machine-learning model are estimated, approximated, and optimized using a labeled data set, the domain characteristics (dimensionality, sparsity, and subspace), and the class characteristics (imbalanced, incomplete, and inaccurate). The data set used in this phase is called the training set, and when a data set is called a training set then we can assume that it is a labeled data set. That is when the class labels are known.

2.2.4.2 Validation

The validation phase provides an algorithm to validate the effectiveness of the model using another data set, which was not used in the training phase. In this case, the data set is called the validation set, and it is also labeled. The validation phase helps to show that the parameters derived in the training phase work based on a quantitative measure. Hence, the quantitative measure plays a major role in this validation process. Some of these measures are entropy and root mean-squared error.

If the results are not satisfactory, then the model must be trained again to obtain better parameter values. This is the phase where the effects of the problems (the selection of an incorrect model, or the use of an inefficient algorithm) reported in Fig. 2.5 can be seen and corrected. The validation phase can also help to correct the over-training problem, which leads to the overfitting problem. The main technique used for this purpose is called the cross-validation [23].

2.2.4.3 Testing

This is a simple phase, and provides an algorithm to test if the trained and cross-validated model works using another data set, which was not used in the training or validation phases. In this algorithm, the labeled data set is used only to compare the results produced by the final model in terms of classification accuracy and computational time. Several measures are available for this purpose, and they are called qualitative measure as they are used to measure the performance of the model. Some of these measures are listed in [24], and they are: accuracy, sensitivity, specificity, and precision. These measures are used later in this book for performance analysis.

2.3 Big Data Scalability

Scalability is an unavoidable problem in big data applications [25]. Uncontrollable and continuous growth in the features create the scalability problem. In simple terms, the classification results obtained with a set of features expires instantaneously because of the new additions in the features. Scalability occurs in high-dimensional systems, and it may be addressed using efficient representation learning and feature hashing algorithms.

2.3.1 High-Dimensional Systems

A large number of feature does not mean the data is high dimensional. A data set is high dimensional only if the number of features (p) of the data set are larger than the number of observations (n) in the data set. In big data analytics, the problem, challenges, and solution related to scalability have been treated separately, as it forms a separate problem space and gives significant challenges to different applications like text processing (spam filter) and forensic linguistics. The features are the main controller that contribute to this scalability problem and associated challenges. Hence, the scalable machine learning topic emerged into the big data paradigm. In this problem space, the features dynamically grow, and the system becomes high dimensional and difficult to manage. Therefore, one solution is to understand the patterns in low dimensions to develop efficient big data classification models and algorithms. Removal of irrelevant features can bring the number of features to less than the number of observations and, hence, help define low-dimensional structures.

2.3.2 Low-Dimensional Structures

In this section, two approaches are discussed: representation learning and feature hashing. Representation learning [14] provides models and algorithms to represent data at the preprocessing stage and help learn data characteristics through understanding of the roles of controllers and extracting geometrical and statistical structures. In [15], a simple representation learning technique, called a single-domain, representation-learning model, has been proposed, and its objective is to separate two classes over two-dimensional subspaces. It adopts the concept of unit-circle algorithm proposed in [26]. The main big data controller that may be manipulated to extract low-dimensional structures by generating subspaces in the representation-learning algorithms is the features.

Therefore, the techniques called *hashing techniques* have been proposed in the field to create low-dimensional subspaces. The feature hashing techniques provide dimensionality reduction to the data through the mapping of entire feature space to subspaces that are formed by subsets of features. Hence, it is sensitive to the inferiority of the algorithm used to generate such mappings.

Problems

2.1. Select several data sets from the University of California, Irvine, Machine Learning repository and explore: What is the purpose of the data sets? How many observations are there? How many features are there? How many classes are there? Is it useful to analyze the data sets? Will they evolve into big data sets?

2.2. Data Analytics

(a) Identify two data sets based on the answers that you found for the question in the first problem.
(b) Apply statistical analysis tools (such as scatter plots, histograms, pie charts, statistical distributions, etc.) and determine if the data sets are imbalanced, incomplete, or inaccurate.
(c) Make the data sets balanced, complete, and correct through randomization. Assume Gaussian properties for each feature, or conduct a distribution test to find a suitable distribution. Have you succeeded?

Acknowledgements I would like to thank Bin Yu and Richard Smith for the opportunities they gave me to attend several big data related workshops at their respective institutions. The knowledge gained from these workshops helped me write some of the topics presented in this book.

References

1. P. Russom, "Big data analytics," TDWI Best Practices Report, Fourth Quarter, Cosponsored by IBM, pp. 1–38, 2011.
2. S. Suthaharan. 2014. "Big Data Classification: Problems and challenges in network intrusion prediction with machine learning," ACM SIGMETRICS Performance Evaluation Review, vol. 41, no. 4, pp. 70–73.
3. J. Whitworth and S. Suthaharan. 2014. "Security problems and challenges in a machine learning-based hybrid big data processing network systems," ACM SIGMETRICS Performance Evaluation Review, vol. 41, no. 4, pp. 82–85.
4. S. B. Kotsiantis. "Supervised machine learning: A review of classification techniques," Informatica 31, pp. 249–268, 2007.
5. K. Weinberger, A. Dasgupta, J. Langford, A. Smola, and J. Attenberg. "Feature hashing for large scale multitask learning." In Proceedings of the 26th Annual International Conference on Machine Learning, pp. 1113–1120. ACM, 2009.
6. Q. Shi, J. Petterson, G. Dror, J. Langford, A. Smola, and V. Vishwanathan. "Hash kernels for structured data." The Journal of Machine Learning Research 10, pp. 2615–2637, 2009.
7. Y. LeCun, L. Bottou, Y. Bengio, and P. Haffner. "Gradient-based learning applied to document recognition." Proceedings of the IEEE, vol. 86, no. 11, pp. 2278–2324, 1998.
8. T. Zhang. "Solving large scale linear prediction problems using stochastic gradient descent algorithms." In Proceedings of the International Conference on Machine learning, pp. 919–926, 2004.
9. P. Zikopoulos, C. Eaton, et al. Understanding big data: Analytics for enterprise class hadoop and streaming data. McGraw-Hill Osborne Media, 2011.
10. T. White. Hadoop: the definitive guide. O'Reilly, 2012.

11. J. Dean, and S. Ghemawat, S. "MapReduce: simplified data processing on large clusters." Communications of the ACM, vol. 51, no. 1, pp. 107–113, 2008.

12. J. Dean, and S. Ghemawat. "MapReduce: a flexible data processing tool." Communications of the ACM, vol. 53, no. 1, pp. 72–77, 2010.

13. H. Tong. "Big data classification," Data Classification: Algorithms and Applications. Chapter 10. (Eds.) C.C. Aggarwal. Taylor and Francis Group, LLC. pp. 275–286. 2015.

14. Y. Bengio, A. Courville, and P. Vincent. "Representation learning: A review and new perspectives," IEEE Transactions on Pattern Analysis and Machine Intelligence, vol. 35, no. 8, pp. 1798–1828, 2013.

15. S. Suthaharan. "A single-domain, representation-learning model for big data classification of network intrusion," Machine Learning and Data Mining in Pattern Recognition, Lecture Notes in Computer Science Volume 7988, pp. 296–310, 2013.

16. W. Tu, and S. Sun, "Cross-domain representation-learning framework with combination of class-separate and domain-merge objectives," In: Proc. of the CDKD 2012 Conference, pp. 18–25, 2012.

17. K. Shvachko, H. Kuang, S. Radia, and R. Chansler. "The hadoop distributed file system," In Proc. of the IEEE 26th Symposium on Mass Storage Systems and Technologies, pp. 1–10, 2010.

18. K. Kotipalli and S. Suthaharan. 2014. "Modeling of class imbalance using an empirical approach with spambase data set and random forest classification," in Proceedings of the 3rd Annual Conference on Research in Information Technology, ACM, pp. 75–80.

19. R.J.A. Little and D.B. Rubin. "Statistical analysis with missing data," Wiley Series in Probability and Statistics, John Wiley and Sons, Inc. second edition, 2002.

20. B. Frenay and M. Verleysen, "Classification in the presence of label noise: a survey," IEEE Transactions on Neural Networks and Learning Systems, vol. 25, no. 5, pp. 845–869, 2014.

21. L. Bottou, and O. Bousquet. "The tradeoffs of large scale learning." In Proceedings of NIPS, vol 4., p. 8, 2007.

22. B. Dalessandro. "Bring the noise: Embracing randomness is the key to scaling-up machine learning algorithms." Big Data vol. 1, no. 2, pp. 110–112, 2013.

23. S. Arlot, and A. Celisse. "A survey of cross-validation procedures for model selection," Statistics surveys, vol. 4, pp. 40–79, 2010.

24. Machine Learning Corner (Design models that learn from data), "Evaluation of Classifier's Performance," https://mlcorner.wordpress.com/tag/specificity/, Posted on April 30, 2013.

25. P. Domingos, and G. Hulten. "A general method for scaling-up machine learning algorithms and its application to clustering." In Proceedings of the International Conference on Machine Learning, pp. 106–113. 2001.

26. S. Suthaharan. 2012. "A unit-circle classification algorithm to characterize back attack and normal traffic for network intrusion detection systems," in Proceedings of the IEEE International Conference on Intelligence and Security Informatics, pp. 150–152.

Chapter 3
Big Data Analytics

Abstract An in-depth analysis of data can reveal many interesting properties of the data, which can help us predict the future characteristics of the data. The objective of this chapter is to illustrate some of the meaningful changes that may occur in a set of data when it is transformed into big data through evolution. To make this objective practical and interesting, a split-merge-split framework is developed, presented, and applied in this chapter. A set of file-split, file-merge, and feature-split tasks is used in this framework. It helps explore the evolution of patterns from the cause of transformation from a set of data to a set of big data. Four digital images are used to create data sets, and statistical and geometrical techniques are applied with the split-merge-split framework to understand the evolution of patterns under different class characteristics, domain characteristics, and error characteristics scenarios.

3.1 Analytics Fundamentals

The statistical and geometrical properties are the main analytics fundamentals that can help us understand the evolution of patterns. One of the focuses of big data classification is the development of an efficient domain division technique; therefore, the analytics fundamentals must be understood clearly. Some of the statistical measures that contribute to accomplishing this objective are the counting, the mean, the variance (or standard deviation), the covariance, and the correlation [1, 2]. The connection between these statistical measures and the geometrical properties of the data must be clearly defined. In addition to these numerical measures, several graphical tools that support visual analytics are also available, and three of them considered in this chapter are: graphs, histograms, and scatter plots [3]. These numerical and visual measures, alone, are not enough to understand the evolution of patterns in a big data environment. The statistical processes that contribute to this objective are also required, and the important processes incorporated in the analytics discussed in this chapter are: standardization, normalization, linear transformation,

© Springer Science+Business Media New York 2016
S. Suthaharan, *Machine Learning Models and Algorithms for Big Data Classification*, Integrated Series in Information Systems 36,
DOI 10.1007/978-1-4899-7641-3_3

and orthogonalization. Some of these statistical measures and the statistical processes are discussed in detail in the book by Layth C. Alwan [4], and I encourage readers to consult this book for additional information.

3.1.1 Research Questions

The above-mentioned statistical and geometrical measures are useful to answer several questions, and these answers can play a major role in understanding and developing machine-learning models and algorithms for big data classification. Some of the questions related to big data sets are listed and briefly described below:

- Is the data set a regular data set or a big data set? This means the data in hand may be analyzed and processed by current techniques and technologies. Therefore, it is important to understand some of the basic properties of data so that advanced technologies may be deployed if the data is big data or expected to grow to big data.
- Does the data set have separable classes or non-separable classes? The answer can help determine the processes, modeling, and algorithms required to learn the classification characteristics and develop efficient classifiers. Non-separable classes will have to face higher false positives than the separable classes and, hence, linear algorithms may not work as expected.
- Is the data set an imbalanced, inaccurate, or incomplete? Data sets have their own structures that may lead to complicated structures when a set of data is transformed into big data. These properties may be described using imbalance, inaccurate, and incomplete data characteristics. They will be discussed in detail with examples later in the chapter.
- Does the data set have a scalability problem? As we discussed in the previous chapter, scalability is the problem that results from the growing number of features and the complicated data structures. This problem is elevated, in general, when the data has grown to big data, and this problem must be identified correctly.
- Is the data set high dimensional? If the number of observations in a data set is significantly lower than the number of features, then we can define the data set as high dimensional, and significant care must be taken to extract useful information.
- Does the data set have low-dimensional structures? High-dimensional data may carry very useful information in low dimensions; and these low-dimensional structures must be extracted to process data, and these structures may be used to process and analyze big data.

The questions were grouped according to the structures of the data, characteristics of the data, scalability of the data, dimensionality of the data, and the existence of meaningful low-dimensional structures. In general, the machine learning (more specifically, the supervised learning) attempts to answer the question: Which class does the observation belong to? To answer this question, we develop a classifier (a supervised learning model), and train and validate it using a labeled data set. However, in a big data system, we need to answer: Which class does the group of observations belong to? Say, for example, we want to decide if a photo (face image) transmitted over a computer network belongs to person A or person B. In this example, each image has many sub-image blocks ($8 \times 8 = 64$ pixels) that are transmitted using a network protocol. These blocks are available together for deciding whether a group of blocks belongs to the picture of A or B. Thus, batch learning of a single class is highly feasible in a big data system. This chapter mainly focuses on the techniques that are suitable for a similar batch learning environment. Hence, the data sets and the way they are manipulated and interpreted are important for big data analytics.

3.1.2 Choices of Data Sets

Two simple data sets are selected for the first set of simulations, and they are called *Hardwood Floor* and *Carpet Floor*. The images are presented in Figs. 3.1 and 3.2. These are simple examples, and they satisfy Gaussian models with minimum inseparability problems, and thus, they are chosen for the simulations first. Note that two more complex data sets, Biltmore Estate and MyPrismaColors, are also considered, and they will be used later for different examples since they provide good examples of a mixture of Gaussian models.

The choices of data sets and the way they are handled to explain the big data classification are very important. It is also important to address these problems computationally and provide explanation scientifically. Therefore, it is necessary to write programs to read the data and carry out the machine-learning tasks systematically. It is also vital to make the data balanced (if it is imbalanced), accurate (if it is inaccurate), and complete (if it is incomplete) through a randomization process. As per a recent study by Dalessandro [5], randomization is a good solution to address most of the big data problems. Therefore, randomization is used to create larger data sets from these data sets. The split-merge-split framework requires these expanded data sets, and it will be discussed later in the chapter.

You can download these images and their corresponding .csv files from the website [6] at the Department of Computer Science, University of North Carolina at Greensboro. The images are of the size 256×256 pixels. Considering these images, it is possible to obtain many images of these objects (or places), or many subblocks of these images. This book considers 1024 subblocks of size 8×8 pixels. Each block is of size 8×8 pixels, and it is considered an observation of the data set. Each pixel is considered a feature, hence there are 1024 observations and 64 features.

The data patterns may be extracted from the numerical measures and visual aids. Some of the simple statistical pattern detectors are the mean, median, mode, variance, pie chart, and histogram. In this section, a few of these pattern detectors are applied to the data sets, and results are presented with discussions.

3.2 Pattern Detectors

The statistical and geometrical pattern detectors significantly contribute to the successful understanding of data characteristics to optimize the classification accuracies of the machine-learning models. In this section, some of the statistical and visual measures are presented and discussed with examples.

3.2.1 Statistical Measures

Statistical measures can help understand the measurements of various patterns hidden within the data. They can help us characterize the data based on their size, number of distinct patterns, the spread of the patterns, and so on. The counting, mean, and standard deviations are discussed below. I strongly suggest that readers refer to a statistics book like [4] to learn the analysis of statistical processes.

3.2.1.1 Counting

Counting is a simple measure, but it is very powerful and helpful in many aspects of big data analytics, including pattern detection, resource allocation, and data management. Some of the questions that can be answered using the counting measure are: How many observations are there? How many features are there? and How many classes are there? This measure is the major player in addressing imbalanced data problems (minority class versus majority class) in big data classification.

Thinking with Example 3.1:

Consider the hardwood floor and carpet floor data sets. Each observation in these data sets comes from one of these two classes of images; therefore, we have a two-class classification problem. These images were divided into 1024 nonoverlapping blocks of size 8×8 ($= 64$) pixels, hence we have 1024 observations from each class, and 64 features (where each pixel is a feature). Simply, we have two classes, 64 features, and 2048 observations; therefore, the volume of data is 2048, the dimensionality of data is 64, and there are two balanced classes.

3.2.1.2 Mean and Variance

The statistical mean and the variance can also be used to measure the effect of the big data controllers. Some questions that can be answered using these measures are: What are the differences in the feature characteristics? How do the between-class observations differ? Are there any subgroups of features (subspace)? Are there any similarities between the subgroups?

Fig. 3.1 Hardwood floor

Fig. 3.2 Carpet floor

Thinking with Example 3.2:

Figure 3.3 presents an example that illustrates the meanings of mean and variance. It shows the two-dimensional data domain formed by two features named Feature 1 and Feature 2, and four points that are connected by straight lines to show the deformation of patterns. The original four points are connected to form a square (in blue), and its mean and variance are calculated and plotted on the data domain.

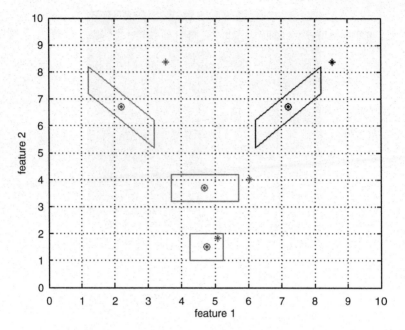

Fig. 3.3 A toy example—mean and variance are illustrated

The means of the features (1 and 2) are 4.75 and 1.5, and their variances are 0.3333. The horizontal sides show the variability in Feature 1, and the vertical sides show the variability in Feature 2. However, when Feature 1 varies, there is no variability in Feature 2. Similarly when Feature 2 varies, there is no variability in Feature 1. It indicates zero covariance and correlation. If we now disperse the data (square) horizontally and move it upward over Feature 2 as shown in the rectangle (in red), then the new means and variances are: 4.70, 3.7, 1.3333, and 0.3333. Feature 1 is dispersed, but Feature 2 is not, hence the variance of Feature 1 has changed significantly. Similarly, the mean of Feature 2 has changed because of the vertical shift. Once again, Feature 2 does not change with respect to Feature 1 or Feature 1 does not change with respect to Feature 2; hence, we have zero covariance and correlation.

Thinking with Example 3.3:

As mentioned before, the images considered have 64 features (because each block of 64 pixels is considered an observation). Suppose we are interested in understanding the features' properties. We can calculate their mean and standard deviations. These values are presented in Figs. 3.5 and 3.6. We can clearly see the hardwood floor

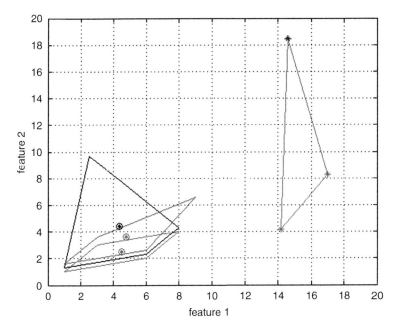

Fig. 3.4 A toy example—covariance and correlation are illustrated

has lower intensity values than the carpet floor. It also has lower local variations than that of the carpet floor. These properties can help to classify these images and predict if a new block of data belongs to a hardwood floor or carpet floor.

3.2.1.3 Covariance and Correlation

The covariance and correlation measures are also illustrated in Fig. 3.3. Suppose we change the values of the four points to form the parallelogram shown in the right-hand side of the data domain (in black), then we can see the changes in Feature 2 values with respect to Feature 1 and vice versa. In this case, we have co-variability (means the covariance). The calculation of the statistical measures (means, variances, covariance, and correlation) for this example are: 7.20, 6.70, 1.3333, 1.6667, 1.00, and 0.6708, respectively. We can see the Feature 2 values increase with respect to Feature 1, which indicates the positive covariance and correlation. Similarly, if we change the values of the four points to form the parallelogram shown in the left-hand side of the data domain (in magenta), then the values of the statistical measures can be calculated as: 2.2000, 6.7000, 1.3333, 1.6667, −1.0000, and −0.6708. It shows the negative covariance and correlation because the Feature 2 values decrease with respect to Feature 1.

Another example is shown in Fig. 3.4 which illustrates the effect on the covariance and correlation with respect to geometrical pattern deformation. In this example, the blue parallelogram is the original shape formed by the original data points on the data domain. The covariance and correlation are 2.2500 and 0.5606 respectively. If we disperse the top right-hand corner point to form the polygon shape shown in red, then the new covariance and correlation are: 4.7500 and 0.6282, respectively. It clearly shows the increase in the magnitude of these measures. Similarly, if we disperse the top left-hand point to form the polygon shown in black, then the covariance and correlation values are: -0.8125 and -0.0678. It clearly shows the negative correlation. Therefore, the southwest $\Leftrightarrow$ northeast dispersion will give a positive increase, and the northwest $\Leftrightarrow$ southeast dispersion will give a negative increase in the covariance and correlation.

3.2.2 Graphical Measures

In the statistical field, there are several visual tools available that can be used for visual analytics. The paper by Wong et al. [7] reports several challenges in visual analytics problems; however, simple statistical tools like pie charts, histograms, and scatter plots, and their applications to big data analytics must be first understood.

3.2.2.1 Histogram

An important visual tool that can help detect the statistical distribution of data and validate the numerical statistical hypothesis testing is the histogram [4]. It can be used to answer the following questions as a part of data analytics: Does the data follow a single distribution? Are there any multiple distributions to determine multi-class property? Does the data follow a Gaussian distribution? The histograms of the hardwood floor and carpet floor data sets presented in Figs. 3.7 and 3.8 show the Gaussian properties (approximately) of the images.

3.2.2.2 Skewness

Skewness is one of the visual tools that can help classification objectives. It may be used as a numerical measure as well when computed. If the distribution of one class is skewed on one side (say left-positively skewed), and the distribution of another class is skewed on the other side (i.e., right-negatively skewed), then these classes can be easily classified based on the skewness [4]. If a data set contained within-class multiple distributions, then the different skewness of within-class distributions can also help to explain the data characteristics. Therefore, skewness is a helpful measure to achieve classification objectives.

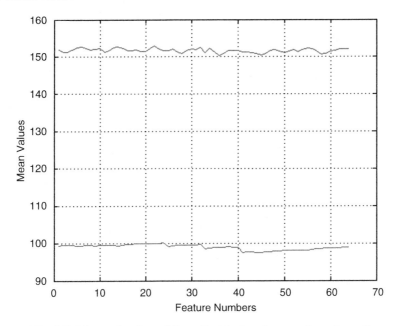

Fig. 3.5 Mean—hardwood floor (in *blue*) and carpet floor (in *red*)

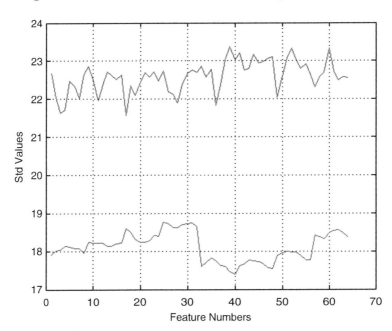

Fig. 3.6 STD—hardwood floor (in *blue*) and carpet floor (in *red*)

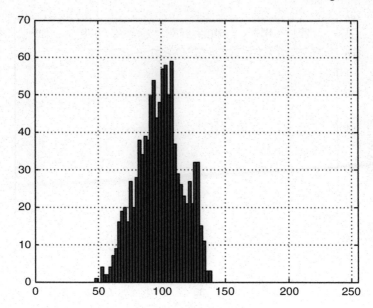

Fig. 3.7 Histogram: hardwood floor

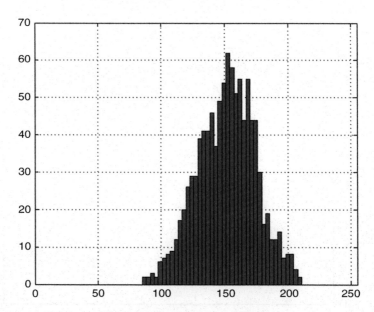

Fig. 3.8 Histogram: carpet floor

3.2.2.3 Scatter Plot

A scatter plot is also a very useful visual tool, and it can show local distribution of a class [4]. It can show the visual aspects of central tendency, dispersion, and association very clearly. It can also show the relationships between the original domain and a transformed domain if the data is transformed into another domain based on the features. It can also help to see the effect of dimensionality reduction and identify meaningful low-dimensional structures. Figures 3.9 and 3.10 show scatter plots of hardwood floor and carpet floor, and they clearly show the separable (approximate) properties of these classes in three and two dimensions, respectively.

3.2.3 Coding Example

Use the coding example provided in this subsection to reproduce the figures presented in Figs. 3.1 and 3.2, and Figs. 3.5, 3.6, 3.7, 3.8, 3.9, and 3.10, and understand the properties of the data sets given. This program may be modified to input your own data sets and produce results for understanding their data characteristics.

Listing 3.1 A Matlab example—plotting some of the pattern detectors

```
1   clear all;
2   close all;
3
4   I1=double(imread('hardwood.jpeg'));
5   aa1=imresize(I1(:,:,1),[256 256]);
6   figure;imshow(aa1,[]);
7
8   kk=1;nn=8;
9   for ii=1:8:256
10      for jj=1:8:256
11          bb1=aa1(ii:ii+7,jj:jj+7);
12          cc1(kk,:)=reshape(bb1,1,64);
13          kk=kk+1;
14      end
15  end
16  csvwrite('hardwood.csv',cc1);
17  bt=csvread('hardwood.csv');
18
19  I2=double(imread('carpet.jpeg'));
20  aa2=imresize(I2(:,:,1),[256 256]);
21  figure;imshow(aa2,[]);
22
23  kk=1;
24  for ii=1:8:256
25      for jj=1:8:256
26          bb2=aa2(ii:ii+7,jj:jj+7);
27          cc2(kk,:)=reshape(bb2,1,64);
28          kk=kk+1;
29      end
```

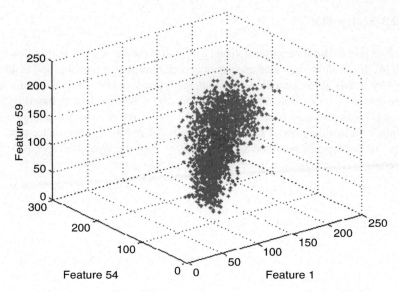

Fig. 3.9 A 3D scatter plot of hardwood (*blue*) and carpet (*red*) floors

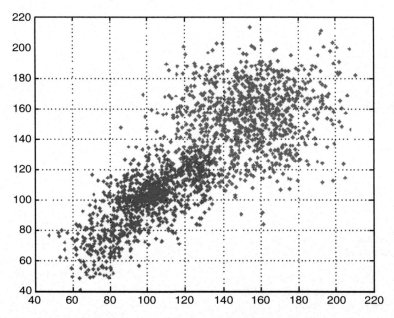

Fig. 3.10 A 2D scatter plot of hardwood (*blue*) and carpet (*red*) floors

```
30  end
31  csvwrite('carpet.csv',cc2);
32  ct=csvread('carpet.csv');
33
34  mcc1=mean(bt);
35  scc1=std(bt);
36
37  mcc2=mean(ct);
38  scc2=std(ct);
39
40  figure;plot(mcc1);hold on;plot(mcc2,'color','red');grid on;
41  xlabel('Feature_Numbers');ylabel('Mean_Values');
42  figure;plot(scc1);hold on;plot(scc2,'color','red');grid on;
43  xlabel('Feature_Numbers');ylabel('Std_Values');
44
45  f1=1;f54=54;f59=59;
46
47  figure;hist(bt(:,f1),40);grid on;
48  axis([0 255 0 70]);
49  figure;hist(ct(:,f1),40);grid on;
50  axis([0 255 0 70]);
51
52  figure;plot3(bt(:,f1),bt(:,f54),bt(:,f59),'.');
53  hold on;plot3(ct(:,f1),ct(:,f54),ct(:,f59),'r.');grid on;
54  xlabel('Feature_1');ylabel('Feature_54');zlabel('Feature_59');
55
56  figure;plot(bt(:,f1),bt(:,f54),'.');
57  hold on;plot(ct(:,f1),ct(:,f54),'r.');grid on;
58  xlabel('Feature_1');ylabel('Feature_54');
```

The block of code from lines 4 to 17 reads the original 256×256 pixel hardwood floor image, displays it (Fig. 3.1), reshapes it to 1024, 8×8 pixel blocks, saves them to a .csv file as 1024 observations, and then reads them from the file for processing. The .csv files can be found at http://www.uncg.edu/cmp/downloads. Similar tasks are carried out on the original 256×256 pixel carpet floor image, and this block of codes is given in lines 19–32. Figure 3.2 shows the image that was produced by this block of code. There are 64 pixels in each block, and they represent 64 features for the observation, represented from left to right and then top to bottom.

The statistical means and standard deviations are calculated for both images in lines 34–38, then these measures are plotted in Figs. 3.5 and 3.6 using the codes in lines 40–43. Line 45 shows the selection of features 1, 54, and 59 from the 64 features. The block of code in lines 47–50 produces the histograms presented in Figs. 3.7 and 3.8. The lines from 52 to 54 show the block of codes that plot the three feature values as the 3D plot presented in Fig. 3.9. Similarly, lines 56–58 plot the features 1 and 54 as a 2D plot illustrated in Fig. 3.10.

3.3 Patterns of Big Data

Evolution of patterns is a natural phenomenon in a big data environment. We know that the changes happen in an environment over time; therefore, the conclusion made based on the information at a given time may not be valid later in the time sequence. However, some similarity may be available at both instances that may be used to devise conclusions. In real big data systems, the patterns may propagate, may deform or new patterns may evolve. The evolution of patterns increases the complexity of the data, and, therefore, the development of supervised learning models and algorithms for big data classification is difficult.

Let us now look at a more complex example. For this purpose, the Biltmore Estate and MyPrismaColors images presented in Figs. 3.11 and 3.12 are considered. Only a part (256×256 pixels) of the gray scale version [24] of the Biltmore Estate image in Fig. 3.11 is used to construct the data set. If we create a scatter plot of features 1, 22, and 59 of these image data sets, then we can obtain the plots in Fig. 3.13 for the two classes (blue for Biltmore Estate and red for MyPrismacolors). Recall we divided the images into 1024 blocks, where each block has 8×8 pixels. In this scatter plot, we can clearly see complex structures (e.g., a mixture Gaussian model), and thus the classification of the images is not an easy task. However, some interesting patterns are hidden in the plot, and we should be able to bring them out using *standardization, normalization, linear transformation* (e.g., with Gaussian weights), and *orthogonalization* over the feature variables.

Thinking with Example 3.4:

In the Biltmore Estate and MyPrismaColor examples, we have 64 features, 1024 observations, and 2 classes. For example, if we want to standardize the 800th observation, then each feature value, $x_{800j}; j = 1 \ldots 64$, of that observation is updated as follows: $\hat{x}_{800j} = (x_{800j} - \bar{x}_{800})/s_{800}$, where $\bar{x}_{800}$ and s_{800} represent the mean and standard deviation of the observation 800 over the 64 features. Let us now plot the 800th observation before (blue) and after (red) the standardization process. The graphs are shown in Fig. 3.14. We can see the standardization process bring up the local variations. Now if we plot the features 1, 22, and 59 of the standardized image data sets then we can obtain the scatter plot shown in Fig. 3.15. If we compare the corresponding plots in Figs. 3.13 and 3.15, we can see the image class MyPrismaColors is separated from the plot of class Biltmore Estate, and it makes the classification task much easier. However, we notice still some points belong to Biltmore Estate class (blue) are present in the subdomain where the MyPrismaColors class (red) points are. This subdomain is zoomed in Fig. 3.16. We can see fewer blue points than red, indicating that the MyPrismaColors class dominates in that subdomain.

Fig. 3.11 Biltmore Estate

Fig. 3.12 MyPrismaColors

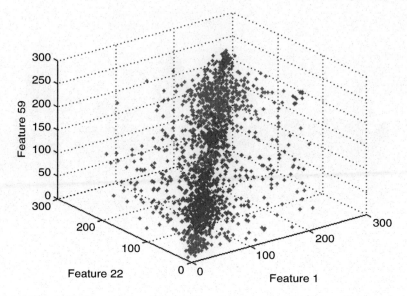

Fig. 3.13 Scatter plot of both Biltmore Estate and MyPrismaColors

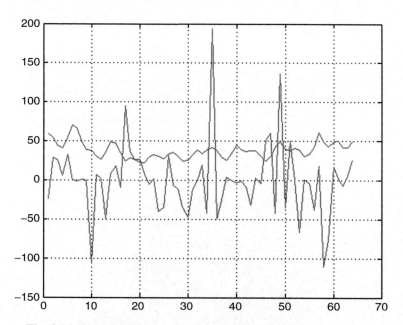

Fig. 3.14 Comparison between the original and standardized data

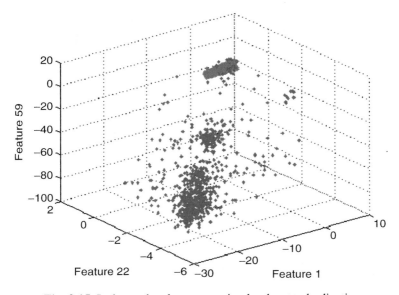

Fig. 3.15 It shows the class separation by the standardization

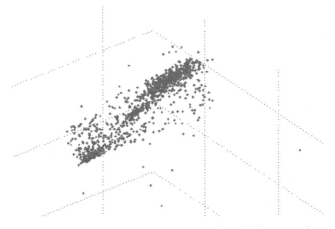

Fig. 3.16 It shows that the subdomain (*red*) is zoomed

3.3.1 Standardization: A Coding Example

You can use the coding example provided in this subsection to reproduce the figures presented in Figs. 3.11, 3.12, 3.13, 3.14, 3.15, and 3.16 and understand the properties of these complex data sets given. You can also modify this program, use your own data sets to produce similar results, and understand the data characteristics.

Listing 3.2 A Matlab example—standardization example

```
1   clear all;
2   close all;
3
4   I1=double(imread('biltmore31.jpg'));
5   figure;imshow(I1,[]);
6
7   I2=double(imread('MyPrismacolors1.jpg'));
8   figure;imshow(I2,[]);
9
10  [num1,txt1,raw1]=xlsread('biltmore31.csv');
11  [num2,txt2,raw2]=xlsread('MyPrismacolors1.csv');
12
13  nn=64;
14  i1=1;i2=22;i3=59;
15
16  figure;plot3(num1(:,i1),num1(:,i2),num1(:,i3),'.');grid on;
17  hold on;plot3(num2(:,i1),num2(:,i2),num2(:,i3),'r.');grid on;
18  xlabel('Feature_1');ylabel('Feature_22');zlabel('Feature_59');
19
20  [a1,b1,c1]=xlsread('randnums1.xls');
21  [a2,b2,c2]=xlsread('randnums2.xls');
22
23  a1=(a1-mean(a1))/std(a1);
24  a2=(a2-mean(a2))/std(a2);
25
26  a1=a1/max(abs(a1));
27  a2=a2/max(abs(a2));
28
29  mn1=mean(num1');
30  sd1=std(num1');
31  mn2=mean(num2');
32  sd2=std(num2');
33
34  for jj=1:nn
35      new1(:,jj)=a2(jj)*(num1(:,jj)-mn1(:,jj))./(1+sd1(:,jj));
36  end
37
38  for jj=1:nn
39      neww1(:,jj)=a2(jj)*(num2(:,jj)-mn2(:,jj))./(1+sd2(:,jj));
40  end
41
42  figure;plot(num1(800,:));hold on;plot(new1(800,:),'color','red');
        grid on;
43
44  figure;plot3(new1(:,i1),new1(:,i2),new1(:,i3),'b.');grid on;
45  xlabel('Feature_1');ylabel('Feature_22');zlabel('Feature_59');
46  hold on;plot3(neww1(:,i1),neww1(:,i2),neww1(:,i3),'r.');grid on;
47  xlabel('Feature_1');ylabel('Feature_22');zlabel('Feature_59');
```

The block of code from lines 4 to 8 reads the image files (Biltmore Estate and MyPrismaColors) and displays them on the screen. These images are presented in Figs. 3.11 and 3.12, respectively. Lines 10 and 11 read their corresponding .csv files and assign the data to the variables *num*1 and *num*2. The number of features and the selected features are initialized in lines 13 and 14. The 3D scatter plot of the data stored in the variables *num*1 and *num*2 is plotted in lines 16–18, and the result is presented in Fig. 3.13. Two files with Gaussian random numbers are read and stored in two variables *a*1 and *a*2 in lines 20–21. These values are standardized and then normalized in the block of codes in 23 to 24 and 26 to 27, respectively.

In lines 29–32, the mean and standard deviation of each observation over the features are calculated for both data sets. You can interpret this as the calculation of mean and the standard deviation of each block. Lines 34–36 transform the original Biltmore Estate data stored in *num*1 to *new*1 using a weighted standardization process. Note: Integer 1 is added to the standard deviation to avoid the *NAN* error in Matlab coding. Similarly, the MyPrismaColors data is transformed and stored in a new variable *neww*1 in lines 38–40. Also, note that the same Gaussian weight *a*2 is used in both transformations. In line 42, the 800th observation is of the original data, and the transformed data are plotted to see the effect of the Gaussian weighted standardization process. Figure 3.14 shows the results of this code. The block of codes in lines 44–47 plots the features 1, 22, and 59 of the data sets and the resulted scatter plot is presented in Fig. 3.15. In this scatter plot, the blue points show the Biltmore Estate data and the red points show the MyPrismaColors data. The subdomain around the MyPrismaColors data is zoomed and presented in Fig. 3.16 to highlight the patterns of the MyPrismaColors data.

3.3.2 Evolution of Patterns

To understand the evolution of patterns better, it is important to create big data simulations and study the patterns under different class characteristics, domain characteristics, and error characteristics. To support this goal, a split-merge-split framework is introduced. This framework is illustrated in Fig. 3.17 and presents a two-class and three-feature classification example. It shows an input table (i.e., the data domain and response set) which has three features f_1, f_2, and f_3, and two classes: C_1 and C_2. It also shows the split, merge, and split processes.

In the first split process, the input table is divided into two tables such that each table has the data domain for a single class. Then it shows the integration of a data expansion technique that adds more observations to each table (i.e., each feature's values are expanded). These tables are then merged to get much larger table (big data) than the original input table. In the next split process, this big data is divided by pairing only two features at a time and creating two-dimensional data domains. This framework allows us to change the data expansion technique, obtain results, and analyze the data in low dimensions to understand the future data characteristics.

The framework presented in Fig. 3.17 is used in this simulation. The main unit in this framework is the data expansion unit, and we can adopt different techniques in this unit and see their effects in the analytics unit. The localization and globalization of the data patterns may help to create big data based on a set of data available. Mainly, localization contributes to the evolution of local patterns by maintaining

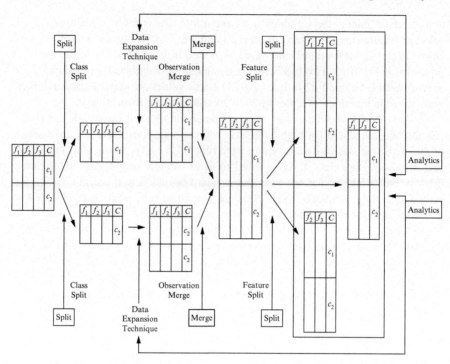

Fig. 3.17 A big data analytics framework that helps integrate expansion techniques and study the effect for future data characteristics over a big data environment

the similarity and propagating the patterns. It also contributes to the evolution of new patterns. In contrast, globalization contributes to the removal of the original data characteristics and induces complexity of big data classification. The example considered in this section is the development of big data for analytics based on the globalization principles. The creation of new data is performed based on the assumption of a single Gaussian model. If the localization principle was considered, we could have adopted a mixture Gaussian model [8].

The data expansion is divided into four methods based on three objectives. The three objectives are: (a) we want to shift the classes based on their respective statistical means, (b) we want to add weights to shift the features, and (c) we want to assume certain distribution to the observations. The four methods are:

- No mean-shift, Max Weights, Gaussian Increase,

- Mean-shift, Max Weights, Gaussian Increase,

- No mean-shift, Gaussian weights, Gaussian Increase,

- Mean-shift, Gaussian weights, Gaussian Increase.

These four approaches are explained in the subsequent sections using the highly complex data sets, Biltmore Estate and MyPrismaColors, in Figs. 3.11 and 3.12. The scatter plot of these images in Fig. 3.13 clearly shows the complexity of these data sets and the difficulties of classification. The evolution of patterns will be studied and compared using the scatter plots so that the big data classification problems can be clearly understood. For this purpose a simple parametrized data expansion model must first be developed and this is the objective of the next subsection.

3.3.3 Data Expansion Modeling

The data expansion model is the major player in the split-merge-split framework for big data analytics simulation. Data expansion can provide evolution and the deformation of patterns to study the data characteristics. We can model it using statistical and mathematical approaches. The generalized model for the data expansion is based on the standardization using the standard score formula [2]. It also uses normalization, linear transformation, and orthogonalization. The standard score is also called z-score and it is defined by Berry and Lindgren [2]:

$$z = (x - \mu)/\sigma. \tag{3.1}$$

The variable z is assumed to follow normal distribution when the population parameters μ and σ are known. As mentioned in [4], the sample mean ($\bar{x}$) and the sample standard deviation (s_x) can be used to replace the population parameters μ and σ in the standardization process. Therefore, it can be rewritten as follows:

$$t = (x - \bar{x})/s_x. \tag{3.2}$$

In this case, the variable t follows a t-distribution [4]. This standard score or the standardization can be interpreted differently, and it can help formulate big data applications. Suppose we have n observations $x_{1j}, x_{2j}, \ldots, x_{nj}$ of the feature x_j, where $j = 1 \ldots p$. Let us also assume its population mean μ and the standard deviation σ are not known then with $(1 - \alpha)\%$ confidence; we can define the following interval:

$$\bar{x}_j - t s_{x_j} \leq \mu_j \leq \bar{x}_j + t s_{x_j}. \tag{3.3}$$

In other words, we can interpret this as: the values of the feature x_j are dense toward the mean μ_j and dispersed by $t s_{x_j}$, and therefore, we can assume all the observations of the feature x_j fall inside this range. With this confidence interval, we have a range of values from $\bar{x}_j - t s_{x_j}$ to $\bar{x}_j + t s_{x_j}$, and they may be divided into n values: $\bar{x}_j + t_{1j} s_{x_j}, \bar{x}_j + t_{2j} s_{x_j}, \ldots, \bar{x}_j + t_{nj} s_{x_j}$. Let us now use the divided values to score the n observations:

$$x_{ij} = \bar{x}_j + t_{ij} s_{x_j}, \tag{3.4}$$

where $i = 1 \ldots n$ and $j = 1 \ldots p$. If we rearrange this equation, we will get:

$$s_{x_j} t_{ij} = x_{ij} - \bar{x}_j. \tag{3.5}$$

If $s_{x_j} \neq 0$, then we can divide both sides of the equation, but in an environment like big data, we cannot make such an assumption for all the feature variables. Therefore, let us divide both sides by $1+s_{x_j}$, and it will give us the following equation:

$$\frac{s_{x_j}}{1+s_{x_j}} t_i = \frac{x_{ij} - \bar{x}_j}{1+s_{x_j}},\qquad(3.6)$$

where $i = 1\ldots n$ and $j = 1\ldots p$. Hence, we can take the weighted score on the left-hand side as an approximated standardized score w_{ij} for big data applications:

$$w_{ij} = \frac{x_{ij} - \bar{x}_j}{1+s_{x_j}},\qquad(3.7)$$

where $i = 1\ldots n$. This process will also take care of the coding problem (like the undefined term *NAN* in Matlab) in the implementation of the standardization process. Using this weighted standard score, we can build the following parametrized data expansion model (where the approximated standard score is scaled using a parameter β and mean-shift using the parameter α):

$$x' = \alpha\bar{x} + \beta(x - \bar{x})/(1 + s_x).\qquad(3.8)$$

The parameters α and β are normalized. A proper selection of the values for these parameters can induce orthogonality properties between classes. It is illustrated in the next section.

3.3.3.1 Orthogonalization: A Coding Example

Notice that an orthogonalization of classes may be achieved with a certain set of β values corresponding to the data sets (images) considered. The coding example is given in Listing 3.3 and the results of images in Figs. 3.18 and 3.19. It can be clearly seen that the classes displayed in Fig. 3.18 are orthogonal, and this property is validated using the vector dot-product values displayed in Fig. 3.19. You can see the dot-product values of two vectors are closer to zero.

Listing 3.3 A Matlab example—orthogonalization example

```
1   clear all;
2   close all;
3
4   [num1,txt1,raw1]=xlsread('biltmore31.csv');
5   [num2,txt2,raw2]=xlsread('MyPrismacolors1.csv');
6
7   nn=64; alpha=0.00001;
8   i1=1;i2=22;i3=59;
9
10  figure;plot3(num1(:,i1),num1(:,i2),num1(:,i3),'.');grid on;
11  hold on;plot3(num2(:,i1),num2(:,i2),num2(:,i3),'r.');grid on;
```

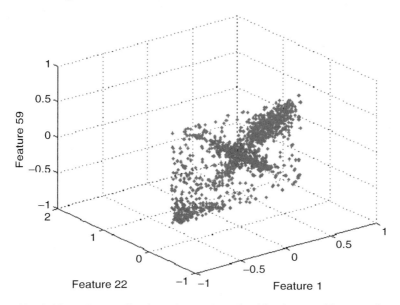

Fig. 3.18 Orthogonalization of two-class classification—a 3D example

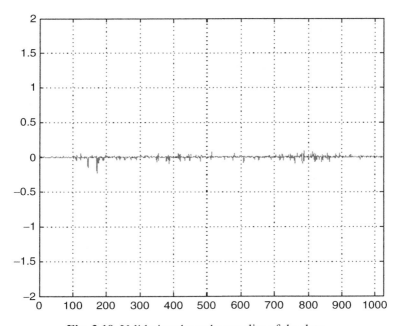

Fig. 3.19 Validating the orthogonality of the data

```
12  xlabel('Feature_1');ylabel('Feature_22');zlabel('Feature_59');
13
14  [a1,b1,c1]=xlsread('randnums1.xls');
15  [a2,b2,c2]=xlsread('randnums2.xls');
16
17  a1=(a1-mean(a1))/std(a1);
18  a2=(a2-mean(a2))/std(a2);
19
20  a1=a1/max(abs(a1));
21  a2=a2/max(abs(a2));
22
23  mn1=mean(num1);
24  sd1=std(num1);
25  mn2=mean(num2);
26  sd2=std(num2);
27
28  for jj=1:nn
29        new1(:,jj)=alpha*mn1(jj)+a1(jj)*(num1(:,jj)-mn1(jj))./(1+
               sd1(jj));
30  end
31
32  for jj=1:nn
33        neww1(:,jj)=alpha*mn2(jj)+a2(jj)*(num2(:,jj)-mn2(jj))./(1+
               sd2(jj));
34  end
35
36  figure;plot3(new1(:,i1),new1(:,i2),new1(:,i3),'.');grid on;
37  xlabel('Feature_1');ylabel('Feature_22');zlabel('Feature_59');
38  hold on;plot3(neww1(:,i1),neww1(:,i2),neww1(:,i3),'r.');grid on
39  xlabel('Feature_1');ylabel('Feature_22');zlabel('Feature_59');
40
41  %A simple orgthogonality test: dot product must be close to zero
42  v1=[new1(:,i1) new1(:,i2) new1(:,i3)];
43  v2=[neww1(:,i1) neww1(:,i2) neww1(:,i3)];
44
45  %calculation of vectors on the planes
46  v11=v1(1:end-1,:)-v1(2:end,:);
47  v12=v2(1:end-1,:)-v2(2:end,:);
48
49  %calculation of dot product
50  vv=v11.*v12;
51
52  %check the dot product is close to zero
53  uu=sum(vv');
54  mean(uu) %close to zero -0.0012
55
56  figure;plot(uu);grid on;
57  axis([0 1024 -2 2]);
```

The codes in lines 4 and 5 read the .csv files corresponding to Biltmore Estate and MyPrismaColors and assign the data to the variables *num*1 and *num*2. In lines 7 and 8, the number of features and the selected features are initialized. In addition, the value of the mean-shift is selected closer to 0 by assigning 0.0001 to the parameter *alpha*. The block of code from line 10 to line 26 is the same as the block of code in line 16 to line 32. The original Biltmore Estate data is transformed in lines

28–30 and stored in the variable *new*1 using a weighted standardization process as before. However, this time the Gaussian weights stored in variable *a*1 is used. Once again, the integer 1 is added to the standard deviation to avoid the *NAN* error in Matlab coding. Similarly, the MyPrismaColors data is transformed and stored in a new variable *neww*1 in lines 32–34 using the Gaussian weight *a*2.

The differences in the Gaussian weights *a*1 and *a*2 provide the orthogonality, and it is important to note that not all the combinations of *a*1 and *a*2 will give the orthogonality. It must be learned. Figure 3.18 is obtained using the block of code in lines 36–39, and it shows the orthogonality between classes in the data domain formed by the features 1, 22, and 59. Once again, in this scatter plot, the blue points show the Biltmore Estate data, and the red points show the MyPrismaColors data. The rest of the code from lines 41 to 54 performs the orthogonality test using dot-products with vectors. Lines 56 and 57 produce the graph in Fig. 3.19, which shows the dot-products of several vectors (in lines 46 and 47) closer to zero (i.e., −0.0012). Hence, we can confirm they are orthogonal.

3.3.3.2 No Mean-Shift, Max Weights, Gaussian Increase

For the purpose of no mean-shift and max weights, the parameter α is chosen closer to 0 and the parameter β equal to 1. The generalized equation in Eq. (3.8) becomes:

$$x' \approx (x - \bar{x})/(1 + s_x). \tag{3.9}$$

For the purpose of making Gaussian increase, the new data are generated using the mean $\bar{x}'$ and s_x' of the new random variable x', and the following equation results:

$$z = \bar{x}' + s_{x'}.* randn(M, 1); \tag{3.10}$$

In this equation MATLAB function *randn* helps generate M new observations with the random variable z that follows the Gaussian distribution with mean $\bar{x}'$ and standard deviation $s_{x'}$. Figure 3.20 shows the effect of the data increase based on this computational process. The classes are heavily mixed and not easy to classify.

3.3.3.3 Mean-Shift, Max Weights, Gaussian Increase

To integrate the mean-shift effect that can help us understand the data characteristics better, the classes are shifted by the scaled mean $\alpha\bar{x}$ of the features. Therefore, the original data expansion model has changed to the following:

$$x' = \alpha\bar{x} + (x - \bar{x})/(1 + s_x). \tag{3.11}$$

Figure 3.21 shows a mean-shifted version of the plot in Fig. 3.20. In this case, the value of the parameter α is 0.1.

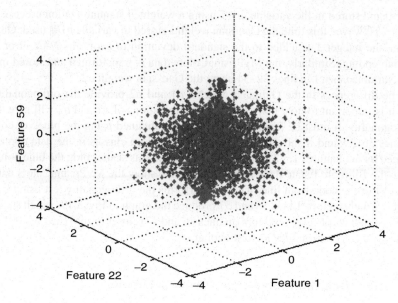

Fig. 3.20 An example of increased data using Biltmore Estate image

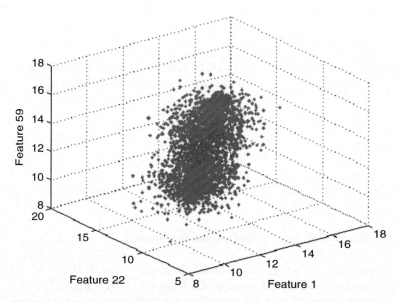

Fig. 3.21 An illustration of a mean-shift using the example in Fig. 3.20

3.3.3.4 No Mean-Shift, Gaussian Weights, Gaussian Increase

The parameter α is selected to be closer to 0. For the purpose of Gaussian weights, the MATLAB's randn() function is used. Hence, we can define the model as:

$$x' \approx \beta(x - \bar{x})/(1 + s_x), \tag{3.12}$$

where the distribution of the parameter β is the standard normal distribution.

3.3.3.5 Mean-Shift, Gaussian Weights, Gaussian Increase

The parameter α is selected to be closer to 1. For the purpose of Gaussian weights, the MATLAB's randn() function is used. Hence, we can define the model as:

$$x' = \alpha\bar{x} + \beta(x - \bar{x})/(1 + s_x), \tag{3.13}$$

where the distribution of the parameter β is also the standard normal distribution $N(0, 1)$ as same as before. We can generate different sets of values for the parameter β related to the features (we considered the features 1, 22, and 59 out of 64 features); however, the values selected give an interesting visual characteristic as shown in Figs. 3.22 and 3.23.

3.3.3.6 Coding Example

The code in Listing 3.4 is provided to illustrate the data expansion processes and the results. You can use this Matlab program to reproduce the figures presented in Figs. 3.20, 3.21, 3.22, and 3.23 and understand the properties of the data expansion techniques. You can also input your own data sets and produce expanded data sets for understanding your own data sets, and conduct big data processing later.

Listing 3.4 A Matlab example—data expansion examples

```
1   clear all;
2   close all;
3
4   [num1,txt1,raw1]=xlsread('biltmore31.csv');
5   [num2,txt2,raw2]=xlsread('MyPrismacolors1.csv');
6
7   nn=64;
8   i1=1;i2=22;i3=59;
9
10  figure;plot3(num1(:,i1),num1(:,i2),num1(:,i3),'.');grid on;
11  hold on;plot3(num2(:,i1),num2(:,i2),num2(:,i3),'r.');grid on;
12  xlabel('Feature 1');ylabel('Feature 22');zlabel('Feature 59');
13
14  mn1=mean(num1);
15  sd1=std(num1);
```

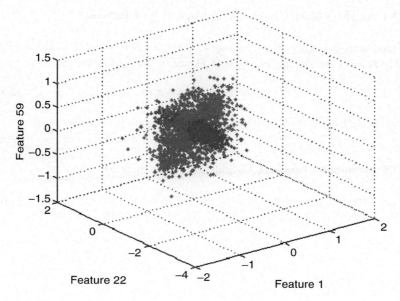

Fig. 3.22 An orthogonalized version of the Biltmore Estate data in Fig. 3.20

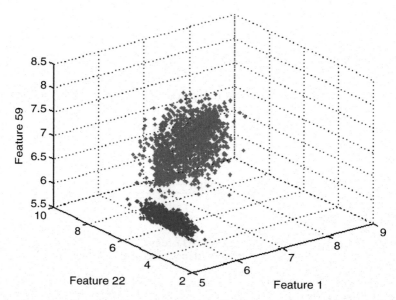

Fig. 3.23 An illustration of a mean-shift using the example in Fig. 3.22

```
16   mn2=mean(num2);
17   sd2=std(num2);
18
19   [a1,b1,c1]=xlsread('randnums1.xls');
20   [a2,b2,c2]=xlsread('randnums2.xls');
21
22   a1=(a1-mean(a1))/std(a1);
23   a2=(a2-mean(a2))/std(a2);
24
25   a1=a1/max(abs(a1));
26   a2=a2/max(abs(a2));
27
28   %%%%%%%%%%% No mean shift and maximum weights
29   alpha=0.00001;
30   for jj=1:nn
31       new1(:,jj)=alpha*mn1(jj)+(num1(:,jj)-mn1(jj))./(1+sd1(jj));
32   end
33
34   mcc1=mean(new1);
35   scc1=std(new1);
36   mm1=length(new1);
37
38   randn('seed',111);
39   for jj=1:nn
40       rr1(:,jj) = mcc1(jj) + scc1(jj).*randn(mm1,1);
41   end
42
43   rrr1=[new1;rr1];
44
45   figure;plot3(rrr1(:,i1),rrr1(:,i2),rrr1(:,i3),'.');grid on
46   xlabel('Feature_1');ylabel('Feature_22');zlabel('Feature_59');
47
48   for jj=1:nn
49       neww1(:,jj)=alpha*mn2(jj)+(num2(:,jj)-mn2(jj))./(1+sd2(jj))
                 ;
50   end
51
52   mccn1=mean(neww1);
53   sccn1=std(neww1);
54   mmm1=length(neww1);
55
56   randn('seed',129);
57   for jj=1:nn
58       rrn1(:,jj) = mccn1(jj) + sccn1(jj).*randn(mmm1,1);
59   end
60
61   rrr11=[neww1;rrn1];
62
63   hold on;plot3(rrr11(:,i1),rrr11(:,i2),rrr11(:,i3),'r.');grid on;
64   xlabel('Feature_1');ylabel('Feature_22');zlabel('Feature_59');
65
66
67   %%%%%%%%%%% Mean shift and maximum weights
68   nn=64;
```

```
69   i1=1;i2=22;i3=59;
70
71   alpha=0.1;
72   for jj=1:nn
73         new1(:,jj)=alpha*mn1(jj)+(num1(:,jj)-mn1(jj))./(1+sd1(jj));
74   end
75
76   mcc1=mean(new1);
77   scc1=std(new1);
78   mm1=length(new1);
79
80   randn('seed',111);
81   for jj=1:nn
82         rr1(:,jj) = mcc1(jj) + scc1(jj).*randn(mm1,1);
83   end
84
85   rrr1=[new1;rr1];
86
87   figure;plot3(rrr1(:,i1),rrr1(:,i2),rrr1(:,i3),'.');grid on
88   xlabel('Feature_1');ylabel('Feature_22');zlabel('Feature_59');
89
90   for jj=1:nn
91         neww1(:,jj)=alpha*mn2(jj)+(num2(:,jj)-mn2(jj))./(1+sd2(jj))
                 ;
92   end
93
94   mccn1=mean(neww1);
95   sccn1=std(neww1);
96   mmm1=length(neww1);
97
98   randn('seed',129);
99   for jj=1:nn
100        rrn1(:,jj) = mccn1(jj) + sccn1(jj).*randn(mmm1,1);
101  end
102
103  rrr11=[neww1;rrn1];
104
105  hold on;plot3(rrr11(:,i1),rrr11(:,i2),rrr11(:,i3),'r.');grid on;
106  xlabel('Feature_1');ylabel('Feature_22');zlabel('Feature_59');
107
108
109  %%%%%%%%%%%% No mean shift and Gaussian weights for orthogonality
110  nn=64;
111  i1=1;i2=22;i3=59;
112
113  alpha=0.00001;
114  for jj=1:nn
115        new1(:,jj)=alpha*mn1(jj)+a1(jj)*(num1(:,jj)-mn1(jj))./(1+
                 sd1(jj));
116  end
117
118  mcc1=mean(new1);
119  scc1=std(new1);
120  mm1=length(new1);
```

```
121
122   randn('seed',111);
123   for jj=1:nn
124           rr1(:,jj) = mcc1(jj) + scc1(jj).*randn(mm1,1);
125   end
126
127   rrr1=[new1;rr1];
128
129   figure;plot3(rrr1(:,i1),rrr1(:,i2),rrr1(:,i3),'.');grid on
130   xlabel('Feature_1');ylabel('Feature_22');zlabel('Feature_59');
131
132   for jj=1:nn
133           neww1(:,jj)=alpha*mn2(jj)+a2(jj)*(num2(:,jj)-mn2(jj))./(1+
                  sd2(jj));
134   end
135
136   mccn1=mean(neww1);
137   sccn1=std(neww1);
138   mmm1=length(neww1);
139
140   randn('seed',129);
141   for jj=1:nn
142           rrn1(:,jj) = mccn1(jj) + sccn1(jj).*randn(mmm1,1);
143   end
144
145   rrr11=[neww1;rrn1];
146
147   hold on;plot3(rrr11(:,i1),rrr11(:,i2),rrr11(:,i3),'r.');grid on;
148   xlabel('Feature_1');ylabel('Feature_22');zlabel('Feature_59');
149
150   %%%%%%%%%%% Mean shift and Gaussian weights for orthogonality
151   nn=64;
152   i1=1;i2=22;i3=59;
153
154   alpha=0.1;
155   for jj=1:nn
156           new1(:,jj)=alpha*mn1(jj)+a1(jj)*(num1(:,jj)-mn1(jj))./(1+
                  sd1(jj));
157   end
158
159   mcc1=mean(new1);
160   scc1=std(new1);
161   mm1=length(new1);
162
163   randn('seed',111);
164   for jj=1:nn
165           rr1(:,jj) = mcc1(jj) + scc1(jj).*randn(mm1,1);
166   end
167
168   rrr1=[new1;rr1];
169
170   figure;plot3(rrr1(:,i1),rrr1(:,i2),rrr1(:,i3),'.');grid on
171   xlabel('Feature_1');ylabel('Feature_22');zlabel('Feature_59');
172
```

```
173   for jj=1:nn
174           neww1(:,jj)=alpha*mn2(jj)+a2(jj)*(num2(:,jj)-mn2(jj))./(1+
              sd2(jj));
175   end
176
177   mccn1=mean(neww1);
178   sccn1=std(neww1);
179   mmm1=length(neww1);
180
181   randn('seed',129);
182   for jj=1:nn
183           rrn1(:,jj) = mccn1(jj) + sccn1(jj).*randn(mmm1,1);
184   end
185
186   rrr11=[neww1;rrn1];
187
188   hold on;plot3(rrr11(:,i1),rrr11(:,i2),rrr11(:,i3),'r.');grid on;
189   xlabel('Feature_1');ylabel('Feature_22');zlabel('Feature_59');
```

You are already familiar with the block of code from line 4 to line 26, therefore no explanation is given again in this section. From line 29 to line 64, the block of code for the method no-mean-shift-and-maximum-weights is given. For the purpose of no-mean-shift, the alpha value is selected as 0.00001. This block of code produced the scatter plot in Fig. 3.20, and we can see a significant overlap in the two classes. The block of code from line 68 to line 106, mean-shift-and-maximum-weight method is illustrated, and in this case alpha = 0.1 is selected for mean-shift. The effect of this selection can be seen in Fig. 3.21, which was produced by this block of code.

The block of code in line 110 to line 148 illustrates the method no-mean-shift-and Gaussian-weights. This method shows the no-mean-shift effect, therefore the alpha = 0.00001 is selected with the Gaussian weights. Figure 3.22 was produced by this block of code. You can see the orthogonality property that was revealed by the use of $a1$ and $a2$ Gaussian weights. Finally, the block of code from line 151 to line 189 illustrates the mean-shift-and-Gaussian-weights method. In this case, the alpha = 0.1 is used, and the effect of mean-shift that was produced by this block of code can be seen in Fig. 3.23.

3.3.4 Deformation of Patterns

The deformation of patterns by big data can be described by three class characteristics: imbalanced data, incomplete data, and inaccurate data. These class characteristics were discussed in Chap. 2 briefly. The class characteristics are the effects of the big data controllers: classes, features, and observations. It can be interpreted as illustrated in Fig. 3.24. It shows the data domain (formed by the features) is divided into two classes (just called class characteristics) by a divisor to make them imbalanced. It also shows some of the features in the top may be characterized as incomplete data. It also shows that the observations may be switched between the classes, and

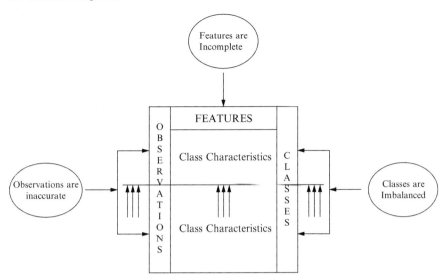

Fig. 3.24 Interpreting the class characteristics with respect to the effect resulted from the big data controllers—classes, features, and observations

hence, it can be characterized as inaccurate observations. Let us now discuss them in detail with the hardwood floor and carpet floor data sets.

3.3.4.1 Imbalanced Data

Imbalanced data means the classes are not balanced (i.e., not informatively equal) [9–12]. In simple terms, using a simple two-class example, we can say that the number of observations in one class is significantly smaller than the other class. It is an example of between-class imbalanced data. In this case, we call the smaller class a minority class and the other class a majority class [10]. In some data sets, to be significantly smaller, the minority class must have only 1 % observations whereas the majority class has 99 % [12] so that they are not informatively equal. The scatter plot at the top left-hand corner of Fig. 3.25 illustrates an example of imbalanced-class characteristics. The hardwood floor and carpet floor data sets are used, where the hardwood floor is undersampled to make it as a minority class.

3.3.4.2 Inaccurate Data

Inaccurate data means the observations are not correct [13–15]. In classification problems, it means some of the observations are not correctly labeled. This problem is called the label noise problem, and the classification objectives have been addressed under this specific problem recently [15]. The scatter plot at the top right-

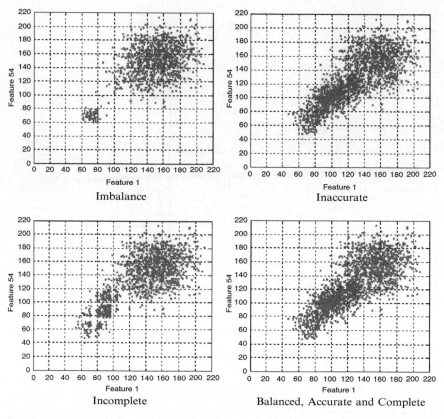

Fig. 3.25 Visually comparing the effect of imbalanced, inaccurate, and incomplete data with the balanced, accurate, and complete data

hand corner of Fig. 3.25 illustrates an example of inaccurate-class characteristics. Once again, the hardwood floor and carpet floor data sets are used here, where some of the labels are switched.

3.3.4.3 Incomplete data

Incomplete data simply means the incomplete features (missing values in some of the features). There are several possible incomplete (i.e., missing data) patterns as reported in [16–20]. One of them is called the "univariate nonresponse," and its effect is illustrated in the bottom left-hand corner of Fig. 3.25. The hardwood floor and carpet floor data sets are used again; the features 1 and 54 are selected and some of the values are removed. The balanced data is presented in the last figure of Fig. 3.25. The four artifacts presented in Fig. 3.25 are created using the Matlab code in Listing 3.5.

3.3.4.4 Coding Example

The scatter plots in Fig. 3.25 are produced using the code in the Listing 3.5. The purpose of this coding example is to show how the imbalanced, inaccurate, and incomplete class characteristics affect the patterns of the data. The data sets *hardwood floor* and *carpet floor* are used to show the effects; however, you can simply modify the code and integrate your data sets to produce similar results.

Listing 3.5 A Matlab example—effect of class characteristics example

```
 1  clear all;
 2  close all;
 3
 4  ht=csvread('hardwood.csv');
 5  ct=csvread('carpet.csv');
 6
 7  i1=1;i2=54;i3=59;
 8
 9  figure;plot(ht(:,i1),ht(:,i2),'.');
10  hold on;plot(ct(:,i1),ct(:,i2),'r.');grid on;
11  xlabel('Feature_1');ylabel('Feature_54');
12  axis([0 220 0 220]);
13
14  % Understand the effect of Imbalanced data
15  rand('seed',131);
16  ind=round(1024*rand(1,10))+1;
17  imb1=ht(abs(ht(:,i1)-70)<10 & abs(ht(:,i2)-70)<10,:);
18  imb2=ht(ind,:);
19  imb=[imb1;imb2];
20
21  figure;plot(imb(:,i1),imb(:,i2),'.');
22  hold on;plot(ct(:,i1),ct(:,i2),'r.');grid on;
23  xlabel('Feature_1');ylabel('Feature_54');
24  axis([0 220 0 220]);
25
26  % Understand the effect of Inaccurate data
27  ind=find(ht(:,i1)<90 & ht(:,i1)>70 & ht(:,i2)<90 & ht(:,i2)>70
           ...
28              | ht(:,i1)<120 & ht(:,i1)>110 & ht(:,i2)<120 & ht(:,i2)
                   >110);
29
30  tmpht=ht;
31  tmpct=ct;
32
33  tmp=tmpht(ind,:);
34  tmpht(ind,:)=tmpct(ind,:);
35  tmpct(ind,:)=tmp;
36
37  figure;plot(tmpht(:,i1),tmpht(:,i2),'.');
38  hold on;plot(tmpct(:,i1),tmpct(:,i2),'r.');grid on;
39  xlabel('Feature_1');ylabel('Feature_54');
40  axis([0 220 0 220]);
41
```

```
42  % Understand the effect of Incomplete data
43  tmpht=ht;
44  tmpct=ct;
45
46  ind=find((abs(ht(:,i1)-75)<3 | abs(ht(:,i2)-75)<3) | abs(ht(:,i1)
        -100)<3 ...
47               | abs(ht(:,i2)-100)<3 | abs(ht(:,i1)-120)<15);
48  tmpht(ind,i1)=0;
49
50  h1=tmpht(tmpht(:,i1)~=0,:);
51
52  figure;plot(h1(:,i1),h1(:,i2),'.');
53  hold on;plot(ct(:,i1),ct(:,i2),'r.');grid on;
54  xlabel('Feature_1');ylabel('Feature_54');
55  axis([0 220 0 220]);
```

There are many ways to produce these effects on the data sets; however, in this example, the magnitude of the data (i.e., the intensity of the pixels in this case) is used to characterize and induce these effects. The block of code from line 14 to line 24 implements the imbalanced data effect; the block of code from line 26 to line 40 implements the inaccurate data effect; and the lines from 42 to 55 implement the incomplete data effects.

The block of code from line 15 to line 19 creates a minority data set from the hardwood floor data set by selecting 10 random observations and the observations with the values of the features 1 and 54 closer to the intensity value 70 (i.e., between 60 and 80). Lines 21 to 24 generated the imbalance scatter plot in Fig. 3.25. Similarly, the block of code in lines 27 to 35 selects some observations based on intensity values and swaps their class labels to introduce label noise, which leads to inaccurate data. Lines 37 to 40 produced the inaccurate scatter plot shown in Fig. 3.25. In lines 43 to 50, some observations are selected, and some of their feature's values are assigned with 0 value to integrate incompleteness. Lines 52 to 55 plotted the incomplete scatter plot in Fig. 3.25.

3.3.5 Classification Errors

The classification error is defined with three error characteristics called approximation error, estimation error, and optimization error, and discussed in detail in [21] and briefly in [5]. These errors are described with simple examples below.

3.3.5.1 Approximation

Approximation is defined as the error in the parametrized model used. For example, suppose the actual unknown model is $y = 0.001x^2 + 1.2x + 3.0$, but the model assumed in training, validation, and testing is $y = 1.2x + 3.0$, then we can say the model is approximated. In this particular case, the trained model will not give the expected classification accuracy no matter how accurately the model was trained and validated.

3.3.5.2 Estimation

Estimation is defined as the error in the parameters used. Suppose the true model is $y = ax + b$ with the values $a = 2.1$ and $b = 4.8$. This is the model that we were trying to find, but we developed the model $y = 2x + 5$, then we can call the parameters a and b in the model $y = ax + b$ are estimated with estimation errors of $\varepsilon_a = |2.1 - 2| = 0.1$ and $\varepsilon_b = |4.8 - 5| = 0.2$.

3.3.5.3 Optimization

Optimization is defined as the error in the learning algorithms used. Suppose there is an efficient algorithm, and it is unknown. Thus we have used an inefficient algorithm, and the best values for a and b cannot be obtained. This is called optimization error, and it cannot be directly obtained. The way to approach this issue is, as an example, if the efficient algorithm is used, we would get $y = 2x + 5$, but if we use a different algorithm we get $y = 2.1x + 4.8$; therefore, the optimization error can be obtained by comparing the estimation errors derived using different algorithms.

3.4 Low-Dimensional Structures

This section mainly focuses on the revelation of meaningful low-dimensional structures [22, 23]. It demonstrates the usefulness of data reduction to low dimensions and data interpretation. Low-dimensional structures can display meaningful patterns. A toy example is given first to transform data from three dimensions to two dimensions, and then the same transformation is applied to real data sets.

3.4.1 A Toy Example

Let us start with a simple example to understand low-dimensional structures. How many points can you observe in the 3D scatter plot shown in Fig. 3.26? We can see only two points that are denoted by stars; however, this plot was generated using three points $(3, 5, -1), (1, 3, -2)$, and $(1, 1, 3)$, and they are shown in Fig. 3.27. Let us now transform the 3D data domain in Fig. 3.26 to a 2D data domain.

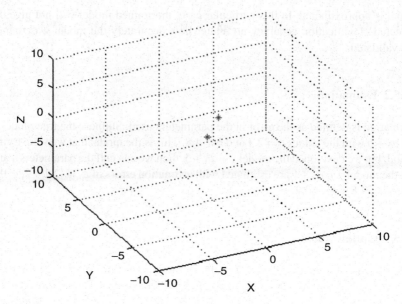

Fig. 3.26 Toy example—you can see two points, but there are three points

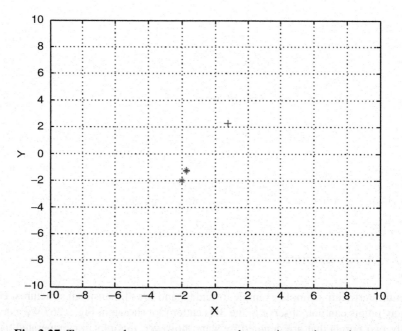

Fig. 3.27 Toy example—now you can see three points and two classes

$$M = \begin{bmatrix} 0.75 & -0.75 & 0.25 \\ 0.25 & -0.25 & 0.75 \end{bmatrix}. \tag{3.14}$$

This transformation provides us the plot in Fig. 3.27. The matrix M transforms $(3,5,-1), (1,3,-2)$, and $(1,1,3)$ to $(-1.75,-1.25), (-2,-2)$, and $(0.75, 2.25)$ respectively. The following matrix multiplication shows one transformation which is the transformation from $(3,5,-1)$ to $(-1.75,-1.25)$:

$$\begin{bmatrix} -1.75 \\ -1.25 \end{bmatrix} = \begin{bmatrix} 0.75 & -0.75 & 0.25 \\ 0.25 & -0.25 & 0.75 \end{bmatrix} * \begin{bmatrix} 3 \\ 5 \\ -1 \end{bmatrix}. \tag{3.15}$$

You can now do the same for the other two points. In this example, we were able to extract some useful information from a low dimension using the following 3D to 2D generalized transformation:

$$\begin{bmatrix} U \\ V \end{bmatrix} = \begin{bmatrix} 0.75 & -0.75 & 0.25 \\ 0.25 & -0.25 & 0.75 \end{bmatrix} * \begin{bmatrix} X \\ Y \\ Z \end{bmatrix}. \tag{3.16}$$

It is important to understand at this point that the matrix used above is not necessarily an optimal matrix. We may parametrize this matrix model and train it to find an optimal value. In real machine-learning applications, optimization algorithms are used to obtain the best matrix. One example is the principal component analysis that performs dimensionality reduction using eigenvectors [8].

3.4.2 A Real Example

You clearly understood the transformation process explained in the above section; therefore, we can now apply the same process to a real example. We can select the complex Biltmore Estate and MyPrismaColors data sets used earlier in this chapter. However, we realize its complex structures can be reduced significantly using a standardization process over the feature variables.

3.4.2.1 Relative Scoring

In Eq. (3.7), we have seen an approximated standardized scoring for the observations of a variable based on its mean and the standard deviation. What will happen if we assign scoring to the observations of a variable based on the mean and standard deviation of another variable? Let us modify Eq. (3.7) as follows:

$$w'_{ij} = \frac{x_{ij} - \bar{y}_i}{1 + s_{y_i}}, \tag{3.17}$$

where x_{ij} is the value that is being scored with respect to the variable y_i which has its mean $\bar{y}_i$ and standard deviation s_{y_i} and $i, j = 1, \ldots, p$. This mean and the standard deviation correspond to values $y_i = \{y_{i1}, y_{i2}, \ldots, y_{ip}\}$. The error caused by the substitution of $\bar{y}_i$ for $\bar{x}_j$, and s_{y_i} for s_{x_j}, where $i, j = 1, \ldots, p$ results in the isolation (and some orthogonality effect) of classes as can be seen in Fig. 3.28. This process, as can be seen, can also help to extract low-dimensional structures.

2D Transformation

The scatter plot in Fig. 3.28 reveals the structures that can help the classification objectives. Now let us transform this 3D scatter plot to a 2D scatter plot using the matrix M in the following equation:

$$\begin{bmatrix} U \\ V \end{bmatrix} = \begin{bmatrix} 0.9526 & 0.8208 & -0.5895 \\ -0.6764 & -1.1584 & -0.0804 \end{bmatrix} * \begin{bmatrix} X \\ Y \\ Z \end{bmatrix}. \tag{3.18}$$

These transformed results are shown in Fig. 3.29. It was easy to select the transformation matrix M for the toy example because of its simplicity. However, the matrix in Eq. (3.18) was selected randomly just to show the structure of these data sets in another low dimension. Once again, they are not necessarily optimal.

3.4.2.2 Coding Example

This coding example provides Matlab code for performing matrix transformation that allows three-dimensional data to a two-dimensional representation. Figures 3.28 and 3.29 are produced by this code. The input to this program is the data shown in Fig. 3.13. You can input your own data sets and transform them to 3D and 2D representations and study their data characteristics.

Listing 3.6 A Matlab example—matrix transformation example

```
1   clear all;
2   close all;
3
4   [num1,txt1,raw1]=xlsread('biltmore31.csv');
5   [num2,txt2,raw2]=xlsread('MyPrismacolors1.csv');
6
7   nn=64;
8   i1=1;i2=22;i3=59;
9
10  figure;plot3(num1(:,i1),num1(:,i2),num1(:,i3),'.');grid on;
11  hold on;plot3(num2(:,i1),num2(:,i2),num2(:,i3),'r.');grid on;
12  xlabel('Feature_1');ylabel('Feature_22');zlabel('Feature_59');
13
14  mn1=mean(num1');
15  sd1=std(num1');
```

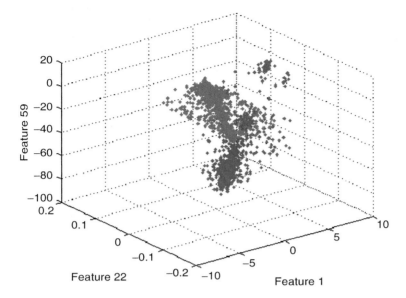

Fig. 3.28 Transformed with first matrix

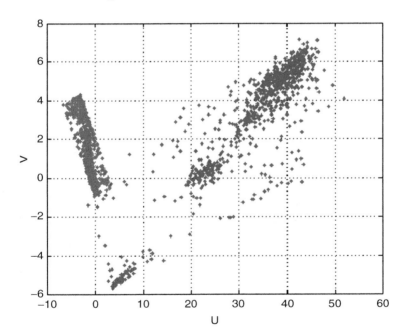

Fig. 3.29 Transformed with the second matrix

```
16   mn2=mean(num2');
17   sd2=std(num2');
18
19   rand('seed',11111);
20   nd=randperm(1024);
21   mmn1=mn1(nd(1:64));
22   mmn2=mn2(nd(1:64));
23   ssd1=sd1(nd(1:64));
24   ssd2=sd2(nd(1:64));
25
26   [a1,b1,c1]=xlsread('randnums1.xls');
27   [a2,b2,c2]=xlsread('randnums2.xls');
28
29   a1=(a1-mean(a1))/std(a1);
30   a2=(a2-mean(a2))/std(a2);
31
32   a1=a1/max(abs(a1));
33   a2=a2/max(abs(a2));
34
35   for jj=1:nn
36         new1(:,jj)=a2(jj)*(num1(:,jj)-mmn1(:,jj))./(1+ssd1(:,jj));
37   end
38
39   for jj=1:nn
40         neww1(:,jj)=a2(jj)*(num2(:,jj)-mmn2(:,jj))./(1+ssd2(:,jj));
41   end
42
43   figure;plot3(new1(:,i1),new1(:,i2),new1(:,i3),'.');grid on;
44   xlabel('Feature_1');ylabel('Feature_22');zlabel('Feature_59');
45   hold on;plot3(neww1(:,i1),neww1(:,i2),neww1(:,i3),'r.');grid on;
46   xlabel('Feature_1');ylabel('Feature_22');zlabel('Feature_59');
47
48   randn('seed',111);
49   M=randn(2,3);
50
51   Zb=M*[new1(:,i1) new1(:,i2) new1(:,i3)]';
52   Zr=M*[neww1(:,i1) neww1(:,i2) neww1(:,i3)]';
53
54   figure;plot(Zb(1,:),Zb(2,:),'b.');
55   hold on;plot(Zr(1,:),Zr(2,:),'r.');grid on;
56   xlabel('U');ylabel('V');
```

You are already familiar with the block of code presented in line 4 to line 12, so the rest of the program is explained here. The block of code in lines from 14 to 17 shows the calculation of the mean and the standard deviation, but this time they are calculated for the observations rather than for the features. The block of code from line 19 to line 24 selects means and standard deviations of 64 observations that are pseudorandomly selected. These statistical measures can be used to assign standard scores for the features. As we can see, the block of code from lines 35 to 41 uses these measures and transforms the feature values *num*1 and *num*2 to *new*1 and *neww*1, respectively. You are already familiar with the standardization and normalization processes showed in lines 29–33, thus no further explanation is not provided for this block of code.

Lines 43–46 plot the transformed features 1, 22, and 59 to show the effect of using the standard score with the statistical measures of the observations instead of those of the corresponding features. In lines 48 and 49, a transformation matrix is created pseudorandomly, and the matrix that was produced is presented in Eq. (3.14). The actual transformation is done in lines 51 and 52, and the resulted scatter plot presented in Fig. 3.29 was produced by the code in lines 54 to 56.

Problems

3.1. Split-Merge-Split

To illustrate big data analytics through simulation, you need data sets that satisfy big data characteristics and a system such as the Hadoop distributed file system that is capable of managing big data problems and challenges. In this problem, you will adopt the big data analytics framework presented in Fig. 3.17 and study how different data expansion techniques will affect the evolution and deformation of patterns. You may use two different distributions, Gaussian and uniform, to implement the data expansion model. Select or create your own data sets. Suppose you have a data set with n number of observations, d number of features, and m number of classes, then complete the following tasks (If your raw data set does not have such a format, you need to transform it to this tabular format).

- Your first task is to read this file, split it according to class labels, and save the output files separately using their class labels as corresponding file names. For example, if you are using the NSL-KDD data set (https://archive.ics.uci. edu/ml/datasets/KDD+Cup+1999+Data), then you have 22 network traffic types, such as normal traffic, back attack traffic, and neptune attack traffic. Hence, you may name the files like normal.txt (or normal.csv if it is a csv file), back.txt, and neptune.txt, respectively.

- Your second task is to—assuming these data follow normal distribution and are identically independently distributed—increase the size of each data set (each file) by randomly adding new observations. Make the files very large to conduct a big data experiment later. Create another expanded data set, assuming that the data follow uniform distribution. The goal of the data expansion is to study the effect of big data, so the size of the expanded data set is subjective, and you must decide its value appropriately based on the data characteristics.

- Your third task is to select any two files randomly and merge them. Observe the effects and performance on both Hadoop and non-Hadoop environments. Now you have a large data set with two classes. You may create multiple pairs (two classes at a time).

- Your fourth task is to split this new large data set into multiple files according to the features and store them separately with their names—you may call the files feature1.txt, feature2.txt, and so on. These files will have data with a particular feature and two classes only.

- Your fifth task is to produce two-dimensional and three-dimensional plots using several combinations of two features and three features, respectively. Once again, do this on both Hadoop and non-Hadoop environments.

Finally, select a few combinations of features based on your visual interpretations, and keep them so that you can classify them using the classification algorithms (e.g., support vector machine, random forest, decision tree, and deep learning techniques such as no-drop and drop-out) that you will learn in detail later in this book.

3.2. Localization

(a) Create big data from the hardwood floor, carpet floor, Biltmore Estate, and MyPrismaColors data sets using localization and globalization properties. Use the programs presented in this chapter to implement this task.
(b) Analyze data sets using the statistical techniques, such as standardization, normalization, orthogonalization, mean and variance, and covariance and correlation presented in this chapter.

Acknowledgements I would like to thank my daughter Prattheeba Suthaharan for generating the "MyPrismaColors" data set (image) presented in Fig. 3.12. I would also like to thank my graduate student Tyler Wendell, who took my Big Data Analytics and Machine Learning course (CSC495/693) in fall 2014 at the Department of Computer Science, the University of North Carolina at Greensboro, and then extended the application of Split-Merge-Split technique to his music data to classify country music and classical music from other genres (e.g., blues, jazz, etc.) using Hadoop distributed file system and Java platform. I greatly appreciate Mr. Brent Ladd and Mr. Robert Brown for their support in developing the Big Data Analytics and Machine Learning course through a subaward approved by the National Science Foundation.

References

1. S.M. Ross. *A Course in Simulation*, Macmillan Publishing Company, 1990.
2. D.A. Berry and B.W. Lindgren. *Statistics: Theory and Methods*, Second Edition, International Thomson Publishing Company, 1996.
3. J. Maindonald, and J. Braun. *Data analysis and graphics using R: an example-based approach*, Second Edition, Cambridge University Press, 2007.
4. L.C. Alwan. *Statistical Process Analysis*, Irwin/McGraw-Hill Publication, 2000.
5. B. Dalessandro. "Bring the noise: Embracing randomness is the key to scaling-up machine learning algorithms." Big Data vol. 1, no. 2, pp. 110–112, 2013.
6. (Electronic Version): LWSNDR, Labelled Wireless Sensor Network Data Repository, The University of North Carolina at Greensboro, 2010. WEB: http://www.uncg.edu/cmp/downloads.
7. P. C. Wong, H. W. Shen, C. R. Johnson, C. Chen, and R. B. Ross. "The top 10 challenges in extreme-scale visual analytics," IEEE Computer Graphics and Applications, pp. 63–67, 2012.
8. C.M. Bishop. "Pattern recognition and machine learning," Springer Science+Business Media, LLC, 2006.
9. R. Akbani, S. Kwek, and N. Japkowicz. "Applying support vector machines to imbalanced datasets." Machine Learning: ECML 2004. Springer Berlin Heidelberg, pp. 39–50, 2004.

10. K. Kotipalli and S. Suthaharan. 2014. "Modeling of class imbalance using an empirical approach with spambase data set and random forest classification," in Proceedings of the 3rd Annual Conference on Research in Information Technology, ACM, pp. 75–80.

11. N. V. Chawla, K. W. Bowyer, L. O. Hall, and W. P. Kegelmeyer. "SMOTE: synthetic minority oversampling technique." Journal of Artificial Intelligence Research, vol. 16, pp. 321–357, 2002.

12. H. He, and E.A. Garcia, "Learning from imbalanced data," IEEE Transactions on Knowledge and Data Engineering, vol. 21, no. 9, pp. 1263–1284, 2009.

13. B. Biggio, B. Nelson, and P. Laskov, "Support vector machines under adversarial label noise," Asian Conference on Machine Learning, JMLR: Workshop and Conference Proceedings, vol. 20, pp. 97–112, 2011.

14. S. Fefilatyev, M. Shreve, K. Kramer, L. Hall, D. Goldgof, R. Kasturi, K. Daly, A. Remsen, and H. Bunke. "Label-noise reduction with support vector machines," 21st International Conference on Pattern Recognition, pp. 3504–3508, 2012.

15. B. Frenay and M. Verleysen, "Classification in the presence of label noise: a survey," IEEE Transactions on Neural Networks and Learning Systems, vol. 25, no. 5, pp. 845–869, 2014.

16. R.J.A. Little and D.B. Rubin. "Statistical analysis with missing data," Wiley Series in Probability and Statistics, John Wiley and Sons, Inc. second edition, 2002.

17. E.A. Gustavo, P.A. Batista, and M.C. Monard. "An analysis of four missing data treatment methods for supervised learning," Applied Artificial Intelligence, Taylor & Francis, vol. 17, pp. 519–533, 2003.

18. M. Ramoni and P. Sebastiani. "Robust learning with missing data," Machine Learning, Kluwer Academic Publishers, vol. 45, pp. 147–170, 2001.

19. S. B. Kotsiantis. "Supervised machine learning: A review of classification techniques," Informatica 31, pp. 249–268, 2007.

20. K. Lakshminarayan, S.A. Harp, R. Goldman, and T. Samad. "Imputation of missing data using machine learning techniques," KDD-96 Proceedings, AAAI, pp. 140–145, 1996. Available at: http://www.aaai.org/Papers/KDD/1996/KDD96-023.pdf

21. L. Bottou, and O. Bousquet. "The tradeoffs of large scale learning." In Proc. of NIPS, vol 4., p. 8, 2007.

22. S. H. Sengamedu. "Scalable analytics – algorithms and systems." Big Data Analytics, Springer Berlin Heidelberg, BDA 2012, LNCS 7678, pp. 1–7, 2012.

23. C. Caragea, A. Silvescu, and P. Mitra. "Combining hashing and abstraction in sparse high dimensional feature spaces." AAAI, p. 7, 2012.

24. S. Suthaharan (2008), "Chaos-based image encryption scheme using Galois field for fast and secure transmission". Real-Time Image Processing 2008, Proceedings of SPIE, vol. 6811, pp. 1–9, 2008, 681105.

Part II
Understanding Big Data Systems

Part II
Understanding File Data Systems

Chapter 4
Distributed File System

Abstract The main objective of this chapter is to provide information and guidance for building a Hadoop distributed file system to address the big data classification problem. This system can help one to implement, test, and evaluate various machine-learning techniques presented in this book for learning purposes. The objectives include a detailed explanation of the Hadoop framework and the Hadoop system, the presentation of the Internet resources that can help you build a virtual machine-based Hadoop distributed file system with the R programming platform, and the establishment of an easy-to-follow, step-by-step instruction to build the Revolution-nAnalytics' RHadoop system for your big data computing environment. The objective also includes the presentation of simple examples to test the system to ensure the Hadoop system works. A brief discussion on setting up a multi node Hadoop system is also presented.

4.1 Hadoop Framework

A Hadoop framework typically has two parts: the Hadoop distributed file system and the MapReduce programming model [1]. The Hadoop distributed file system is a computer network environment that was developed by Doug Cutting and Mike Cafarella to manage big data applications [2] efficiently. It provides modern techniques and technologies to build a distributed network environment with resources, such as multiple processors, storage devices, and software packages for the MapReduce programming model to communicate and process big data, and execute commands dynamically [3, 4]. The MapReduce programming model provides libraries and a graphical user interface to communicate with the Hadoop distributed file system efficiently [5, 6]. The basic components, such as the master and worker computers, data and name nodes, and job-tracker and task-tracker of the Hadoop framework and their communication concepts, with a layering structure for learning are shown in Fig. 4.1. They are clearly explained in the following subsections.

© Springer Science+Business Media New York 2016   79
S. Suthaharan, *Machine Learning Models and Algorithms for Big
Data Classification*, Integrated Series in Information Systems 36,
DOI 10.1007/978-1-4899-7641-3_4

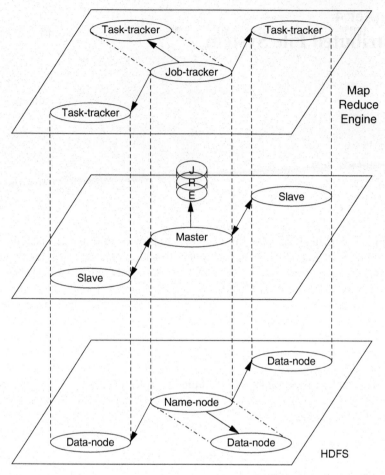

Fig. 4.1 Hadoop computing environment is illustrated with its two basic components: Hadoop distributed file system and MapReduce programming framework

4.1.1 Hadoop Distributed File System

The Hadoop distributed file system can be conceptualized using a master computer and a set of worker (slave) computers with several name-nodes and data-nodes as illustrated in Fig. 4.1. For additional information, refer to the book by Tom White [1]. This system may be conceptualized using three layers as illustrated in the figure. The middle layer shows an example of connections (communications) between the master and two worker computers. One can interpret these as physical connections between the devices. The bottom layer shows name-node and data-nodes associated with the master and the workers and the connections between them. These connections can be conceptualized as logical communications. When jobs are assigned to the workers, they are carried out by the name-nodes and data-nodes.

The main job of the name-node is to maintain the complete directory structure of the distributed file system, while the main job of the data-node is to store the active data associated with the directory structure [1]. If an error message appears related to name-node (for example, missing name node), we know there is a problem in the HDFS layer, and the directory structure of the distributed system must be fixed. We may fix this problem by formatting (or recovering) the directory structure of Hadoop. Hence, the layered structure presented in Fig. 4.1 should help us visualize the internal modules and communication between them, and apply that information when problems, such as a missing name-node message, occur during the installation and configuration of a Hadoop distributed network environment.

4.1.2 MapReduce Programming Model

The MapReduce programming model may be conceptualized using the top two layers illustrated in Fig. 4.1. The master computer and the set of worker-computers in the middle layer are connected to several job-tracker units and several task-tracker units, respectively. For additional information, refer to the MapReduce introduction paper by Dean and Ghemawat [5]. The MapReduce programming model will be discussed in the next chapter in detail, focusing on its programming objectives. The main job of job-tracker is to find the task-trackers that are close to the data-node where the data in process reside. To access these data, as you can see in Fig. 4.1, the job-tracker connects to the name-node via the master and the connection tube, and request the data nodes where the data are. The users of MapReduce programming model can perform these tasks using the three functions: the mapreduce(), the mapper(), and the reducer(). These functions will also be discussed in the next chapter.

4.2 Hadoop System

The Hadoop system can be a physical system or a virtual system. The physical system mainly consists of several networked computers with the Hadoop framework installed on each computer. They are capable of dealing with many big data problems with the addition of extra nodes to the system based on the need for additional resources. The virtual system may be described by the diagram presented in Fig. 4.2. The virtual system has limited capacity, is slow in general, and can only be used under certain restrictions, but it may be cost effective for some applications. The virtual Hadoop computing environment is the best option for testing and learning the big data concepts. A Hadoop system may be divided into the operating system, the distributed system, and the programming platform.

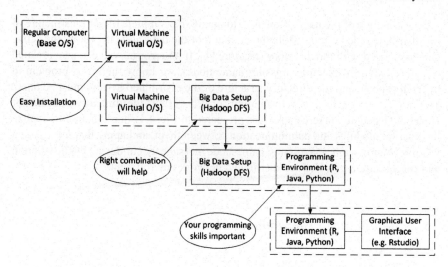

Fig. 4.2 A setting up process of a Hadoop computing environment

4.2.1 Operating System

The operating systems that you may consider when you build a Hadoop framework may be grouped into the base operating system or the virtual operating system. A brief description of these operating systems is presented below:

- *Base Operating System*: The base operating system is the original operating system that you have installed on your computer. It has a direct connection to the hardware and other software resources. In many cases, Microsoft Windows is the base operating system; however, if you have a Unix-based operating system as the base operating system, then you may not need a virtual operating system.

- *Virtual Operating System*: It is also known as the guest operating system. It may be installed on top of the base operating system, and thus it is called the guest operating system. You may install multiple virtual operating systems on top of the base operating system; therefore, you can have multiple virtual machine. In general, the goal is to have a Linux operating system as a virtual operating system on top of the Microsoft Windows operating system.

We really need tools that facilitate the integration of multiple guest operating systems on top of the base operating system. One of the tools available for this purpose is the Oracle VM VirtualBox [7], and its use will be discussed later.

4.2.2 Distributed System

The main goal of the Hadoop framework is parallel processing, which is enabled by the distributed file system with multiple computers (called nodes) and the

MapReduce programming model. This distributed computing environment has at least the following two components:

- *Big Data Platform*: The goal is to create a big data platform to manage massive, unstructured, and scalable data sets. The Cloudera Hadoop [8] is used in this book for the purpose of building a big data platform.

- *Application Packages*: The big data processing jobs must be implemented using models and algorithms, and for this purpose, we need a programming environment with libraries for enabling a distributed system for parallel processing. We may choose R, Java, or Python programming environment for big data processing, but in this book the R programming language has been selected.

The Cloudera Hadoop distributed system [8] with R programming environment is capable of processing big data applications, and it can provide a suitable environment for testing and learning machine-learning models and algorithms.

4.2.3 Programming Platform

The programming languages are the essential tools for the user to communicate with the computers or with a network of computers. They may be grouped into the implementation facilitators and the graphical user interface. They are discussed briefly below:

- *Implementation Facilitator*: The implementation facilitator is a set of built-in functions that help users communicate with the systems. For example, the implementation facilitator in the Hadoop system facilitates the MapReduce developers to run Mapper and Reducer jobs on the Hadoop (for example, RHadoop [9]) system.

- *Graphical User Interface*: The graphical user interface provides a comfortable programming environment to execute commands for big data processing instead of implementing jobs on command lines. Such a graphical user interface for the R programming language is the RStudio [10].

The programming languages used in this book are Matlab [11] and R [12], however, the R programming language and the RStudio graphical user interface have been selected for the big data computing framework because they will enhance your learning experiences in the topics.

4.3 Hadoop Environment

The Hadoop environment should have a suitable operating system, distributed system, and programming platform to build a system that can process big data applications efficiently. To accomplish these objectives, we need a set of essential tools and suitable instructions to install and configure the system successfully. The following two subsections focus on these two important aspects.

4.3.1 Essential Tools

We may need five essential tools to build a Hadoop environment for the big data processing, storage, and analysis. The recommended tools based on my current ins- tallation experience are the Windows 7 operating system (WN) for the base operat- ing system, the Oracle VM VirtualBox (VB) for the virtual machine, the Ubuntu for the guest operating system (UB), the Cloudera Hadoop system (CH) for the Hadoop computing environment, and R programming language with RStudio graphical user interface (RR) for the programming platform.

4.3.1.1 Windows 7 (WN)

The specifications for the use of Microsoft Windows 7 as the base operating sys- tem for the development of the network environment are: (a) Windows 7 Enter- prise, (b) x64, ISP Build model, (c) Intel Core i7-4600U processor with CPU @ 2.10 GHz 2.70 GHz, (d) RAM capacity of 8.00 GB, (e) 64-bit Operating System, and (f) 240 GB storage capacity. The base operating system with these specifications was compatible with the other components installed and did not give any problems in the installation. It also worked very well with the experiments conducted to study the machine-learning models and algorithms with big data classification problems.

4.3.1.2 VirtualBox (VB)

The virtual machine allows another operating system (commonly called the guest operating system) to be installed on top of the base operating system and provides an emulator that creates an environment like the real computers. At the same time, it can allocate computer resources like the memory, the processor tasks, and the necessary storage dynamically. In the system that was built as part of this book project, the Oracle VM VirtualBox [7] was used. The executable file VirtualBox- 4.3.16-95972-Win.exe was downloaded from [7] and used to install the VirtualBox and build Oracle VM VirtualBox for the experiments conducted in this book. As an alternative, you can use VMware player [13]. You can download the necessary files from [13] and build a VMware virtual machine.

4.3.1.3 Ubuntu Linux (UB)

The guest operating system, or the virtual operating system, considered here is the Ubuntu Desktop 14.04 LTS with 64-bit option [14]. The downloaded ISO file from [14] was the "ubuntu-14.04.1-desktop.amd64.iso." You may have the choice of setting up a 32-bit machine or a 64-bit machine; however, my recommendation is to build the entire Hadoop environment as a 64-bit Hadoop system. To ensure you will have a successful system, you must first check if your computer also has 64-bit processors. This may be checked by a right-mouse-click on the "My Com- puter" icon on your desktop, and reading the properties option.

4.3.1.4 Cloudera Hadoop (CH)

This book recommends the Cloudera Hadoop [8] for the Hadoop system if you want to have the R programming environment, and Apache Hadoop [15] if you want to have Java or Python. However, you may have, Cloudera and Java/Python combination which is not discussed, as I have not installed that combination and tested it. The Cloudera Hadoop version that I tested here is ''cdh4-repository_1.0_al l.deb,'' and it provides the following two software packages for processing big data:

- **rmr2-package**: It is an r-map-reduce package [16] that helps MapReduce applications to run on R and Hadoop. This package may be downloaded from [16]. Its library must be included in the r-script. The rmr2 package that I used for my Hadoop environment and tested successfully was ''rmr2_2.3.0.tar.gz.''

- **rhdfs-package**: It is an R-Hadoop-distributed-file-system package [17] that also helps R to be deployed on Hadoop. This package may be downloaded from [17]. Its library must also be included in the r-script followed by rmr2 package. The rhdfs package that I used for my Hadoop environment (and rmr2) and tested successfully was ''rhdfs_1.0.5.tar.gz.''

The directory structure formed as a result of the installation of a Hadoop distributed file system will be presented based on this version of the Cloudera Hadoop. If you install a newer version, check the location of the Cloudera files according to the instructions in the corresponding download pages.

4.3.1.5 R and RStudio (RR)

We now need a programming environment that allows the users to communicate with the Hadoop system. The R programming language can serve that purpose and work with the Cloudera Hadoop system. The instructions available at the following website can help you find the software to build that programming environment:

- http://cran.r-project.org/bin/linux/ubuntu/README.

It provides a command line environment; therefore, RStudio, a graphical user interface, may be downloaded and installed on your system. This software can be found at the following website:

- www.rstudio.com/products/rstudio/download

It is easy to set up this programming environment; follow the instructions provided in the above website to install and configure this programming platform.

4.3.2 Installation Guidance

The process of building a Hadoop environment may be described by the diagram presented in Fig. 4.3. This diagram is provided to help you understand the sequential

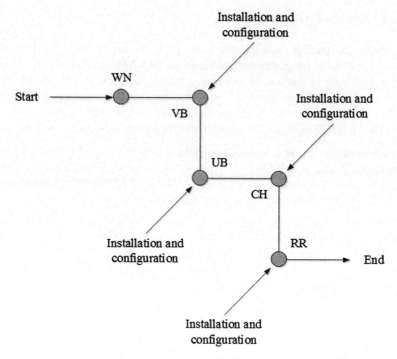

Fig. 4.3 The steps to install a single-node virtual Hadoop system

process of the installation of the entire Hadoop system and record the completed steps for the purpose of the systematic installation and configuration guidance. This installation guidance is divided into six subsection presented below.

4.3.2.1 Internet Resources

The Internet sources listed below provide excellent information and guidelines to install and configure a virtual Hadoop system with the R programming platform:

1. https://www.virtualbox.org/wiki/Downloads. Read the contents of this website to understand and download the Oracle VM VirtualBox software.

2. https://www.youtube.com/watch?v=hK-oggHEetc. Consult this website and watch the entire video before installing the Ubuntu operating system.

3. http://cran.r-project.org/bin/linux/ubuntu/README. This readme file must be consulted to install ubuntu packages that support the R programming platform.

4. https://github.com/RevolutionAnalytics/RHadoop/wiki/Downloads. This Revolution Analytics website provides software packages for the RHadoop system.

5. http://www.cloudera.com/content/cloudera/en/downloads/cdh/cdh-4-1-1.html. Download the Cloudera Hadoop from this website.

6. http://bighadoop.wordpress.com/2013/02/25/r-and-hadoop-data-analysis-rhadoop/. This website provides guidelines to install the R and RHadoop packages.

7. http://www.meetup.com/Learning-Machine-Learning-by- Example/pages/Installing_R_and_RHadoop/. Follow the steps to install the R and RHadoop system.

The information in these Internet sources has been used to build the system adopted in the experiments conducted in this book. Other Internet resources that helped the installation and configuration of the Hadoop system are:

1. http://www.michael-noll.com/tutorials/. It provides additional information to understand the hadoop environment.

2. http://www.rdatamining.com/tutorials/r-hadoop-setup-guide. The information in this website can help install the RHadoop system.

3. http://blog.revolutionanalytics.com/2011/09/mapreduce-hadoop-r.html. It also provides information on the R and RHadoop installation and configuration.

The information in all of these websites tremendously helped me install the RHadoop virtual distributed file system successfully for this book project.

4.3.2.2 Setting Up a Virtual Machine

There may be several options to build a virtual machine, and two of them are the installation and configuration of "Virtualbox" [7] and "VMware Player" [13]. However, the system developed for this book is based on the Oracle VM VirtualBox. Download and install the Oracle VM Virtualbox from the website at [7]. This website provides detailed instructions for the installation. Simply follow the instructions to install it in a few minutes. You may also watch the YouTube video at [18] and follow the instructions to configure the Virtualbox on Ubuntu.

4.3.2.3 Setting Up a Ubuntu O/S

The next step is to install a virtual operating system in the virtual machine that you built using virtualbox package. Once again, the tutorial is available at [18], and this helped me install the Ubuntu Desktop 12.04 LTS inside the Oracle VM VirtualBox. Now download the Ubuntu O/S software from [14]. You most likely will want the desktop version of this software. Note that the website instructions change frequently, hence you need to make an effort to find the binary distribution of the desktop version at the Ubuntu website.

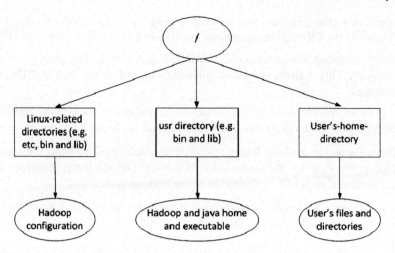

Fig. 4.4 This is an example of the general directory structure that the Linux and Hadoop installations generate. It shows the locations of the HADOOP-HOME, the HADOOP-CMD, the HADOOP-STREAMING, and the JAVA-HOME directories

The instructions to download and install are clear on the website, so simply follow the steps. You have installed a Unix-based operating system on your virtual machine, and type *hadoop* at the command prompt. The system will display the message *command not found'* or a similar message. I also recommend that you draw the directory structure of your Linux environment at this time, similar to the one given in Fig. 4.4; it will help you find where the things are, such as the Linux command, your home directory, and java-home, etc. It will also help to monitor the changes that occur when the new software installed and configured.

4.3.2.4 Setting Up a Hadoop Distributed File System

The instructions on the website at [19] are very helpful to install the Cloudera Hadoop. There are different versions of CDH at the Cloudera website, and you may select the version that you need. Make sure you perform the installation steps while logged in the Unix environment. The following steps may be followed [19]:

1. Download the version cdh4.1.1 by clicking at http://www.cloudera.com/content/cloudera/en/downloads/cdh/cdh-4-1-1.html. If you cannot find this version of the software, install it from another version.

2. Change the directory using the command *cd /home/username/Downloads* and check if you have downloaded the file cdh4-repository_1.1_all.deb for CHD version 4.1.1.

3. Execute the command sudo dpkg -i cdh4-repository_1.1_all.deb as per [19]. It creates a secure ring and imports the public key from Cloudera.

4. Now you have installed new software, which is the Cloudera Hadoop; therefore, you must inform this new addition to the Linux system. To do this, execute the following command:

```
sudo apt-get update
```

Now check your Linux directory structure and find where the Cloudera Hadoop-related files and directories are created. You may develop the directory structure like the one in Fig. 4.5, and it will help you find the files and executables as needed later. When an error occurs, you will find this tree like directory structure especially useful. If you had installed the Apache hadoop [15], then you would have generated the directory structure like the one in Fig. 4.6.

5. In the above steps, you have installed the Hadoop distributed file system, but not the MapReduce framework. To do this, execute the following command: sudo apt-get install followed by the mapreduce-jobtracker file. This file can be found in the directory /usr/lib/hadoop-0.20-mapreduce of the directory hierarchy shown in Fig. 4.5. Therefore, to install the MapReduce framework, you can execute the following command [19]:

```
sudo apt-get install hadoop-0.20-mapreduce-jobtracker
```

6. Type the command *hadoop* on the Linux command prompt, and the system should recognize it now and confirm that the Hadoop system with MapReduce frame has been installed. You should see the Hadoop-related directories have been added to the Linux directory structure, and you should update the directory structure presented in Fig. 4.5 accordingly.

4.3.2.5 Setting Up an R Environment

Install the R programming platform on your system. You can follow the instructions in the README file available at [12]. Note that the instructions on this website help you install the R programming environment, but do not connect it to the Cloudera Hadoop installed in the previous subsection. There are different locations, different versions, and different methods of installation of R programming platform that you can download. Therefore, it is advisable to follow the instructions in the above README file carefully and add the following statement to your /etc/apt/sources.list files as stated in the README file [12].

```
deb http://cran.stat.ucla.edu/bin/linux/ubuntutrusty/
```

Note: Please include a space between unbuntu and trusty in the above link.

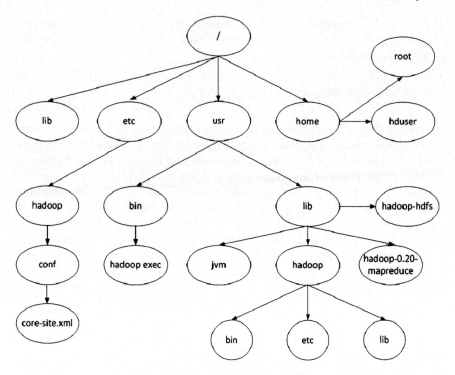

Fig. 4.5 An example of Cloudera Hadoop directory structure with Ubuntu Linux environment

Because of this modification to the Linux environment, you must update the system. To do this, execute the following command as before:

```
sudo apt-get update
```

You might get a GPG error for a public key request—you may ignore it or follow the instructions in the README file to set one up. Either way, your software has already been installed and the system has been updated. You can test to see if the R environment works by executing the following command inside the R environment:

```
sudo R
```

Then quit R using $q()$. Now you can connect the R environment to the Hadoop system. The R environment requires several r-packages to be installed to connect to the Hadoop system, and the ones required at this point are: r-base, r-base-dev, and r-cran-java. These packages may be installed using the following command [19]:

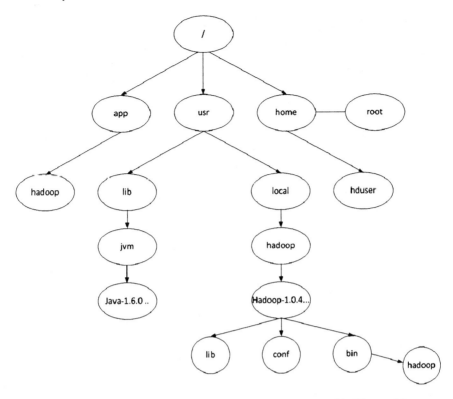

Fig. 4.6 An example of Apache Hadoop directory structure with Ubuntu Linux environment

sudo apt-get install r-base r-base-dev r-cran-rjava

Another package that is required by R is RCurl, and this may be installed using the Ubuntu command line instruction and the following command:

sudo apt-get install libcurl4-openssl-dev

It also requires the package called "plyr," which may be installed within R environment, so invoke the command *sudo R* to bring up the R environment, then use install.package('plyr'). Note that this will ask you to select CRAN repository, and you may select USA(CA1), which is the UC-Berkeley repository.

Another set of packages required by R environment is RJSONIO, itertools, digest, Rcpp, httr, functional, devtools, and as suggested by [19, 20]. They can

be installed from http://cran.revolutionanalytics.com using the install.packages()
command inside the R environment. Make sure you use *sudo R* to bring up the R
environment before executing this command as before. The packages installed for
R programming environment can be found in the /usr/local/R/site-library directory.

4.3.2.6 RStudio

RStudio provides a programming environment for you to comfortably work with
the R programming language. It provides features for you to create, edit, and run
R code for your applications. It also helps to create programs to connect your R
environment to Hadoop in order to run big data applications. The installation of
RStudio can be done by downloading the necessary software from:

- www.rstudio.com/products/rstudio/download

It is important to select the correct version of the software depending on if the
RStudio will be housed on a 32-bit or 64-bit machine. It is also important to make
sure the operating system (in this case, Ubuntu) and the Hadoop distributed file systems are also compatible with either a 32-bit or a 64-bit machine, depending on your
selection. It means that if your Ubuntu and Hadoop are compatible with a 64-bit machine, then you should select RStudio also for the 64-bit machine, otherwise select
the 32-bit version of RStudio. If the software has been downloaded successfully,
you should be able to see rstudio-0.98.1056-amd64.deb in your /usr/home/Down-
loads directory of Ubuntu. The RStudio environment also requires libjpeg62 for the
purpose of graphical displays; therefore, it is important to install it before installing
RStudio. It can be easily installed via the Ubuntu software center. Now change the
directory to *cd your home/Downloads* and execute the following command:

```
sudo dpkg -i rstudio-0.98.1056-amd64.deb
```

The next step is the installation of two other software packages: caTools and re-
shape2. These packages can also be downloaded through the Ubuntu software center to the Rstudio environment. However, it is easier to install them via the RStudio
graphical user interface, and it is highly recommended based on my RStudio installation experience. The applications of R and the RStudio environment require two
RevolutionAnalytics software packages called *rmr2* and *rhdfs* to connect them to a
Hadoop environment and run big data applications. These packages can be downloaded from the following GitHub website:

- https://github.com/RevolutionAnalytics/RHadoop/wiki/Downloads

Now you should be able to see the hadoop-streaming-2.0.0-mr1-cdh4.7.0.jar file
in the download directory /home/username/Downloads, which must be exported
into the RStudio environment as suggested in [19] and [20] using the environment variables HADOOP_HOME, HADOOP_CMD, and HADOOP_STREAMING
as follows:

```
Sys.setenv(HADOOP_HOME='/usr/lib/hadoop-0.20-mapreduce')
Sys.setenv(HADOOP_CMD='/usr/bin/hadoop')
Sys.setenv(HADOOP_STREAMING='/usr/lib/hadoop-0.20-mapreduce/contrib/str
eaming/hadoop-streaming-2.0.0-mr1-cdh4.7.0.jar')
```

These environment variables will be set, as suggested in [19] and [20], in every R program presented in the rest of the book. The next step is to download rhdfs and install it in RStudio. This can be done through Rstudio as suggested on [19].

4.3.3 RStudio Server

This is a separate option so that you can remotely work with R on Hadoop and also allow other users to work remotely. It is a good option if you are an instructor who teaches a course and expects students to work remotely and submit their work on the server. It can also help monitor students' progress.

4.3.3.1 Server Setup

You can download RStudio server software from www.rstudio.com/products/rstudi o/download-server/ and follow the instructions to install it on the machine that you want to set up as a server. You may need to execute the following three commands:

```
sudo apt-get install psmisc
sudo apt-get update
sudo apt-get upgrade
```

You may also have to wait for a long time before the upgrade is complete. Do not forget to create a user in the system so that you can log in as the user from the client after the client is set up.

4.3.3.2 Client Setup

Identify another computer which may be connected to the server over the Internet. Then download the RStudio desktop version from www.rstudio.com/products/rstud io/desktop/ and follow the instructions to install it on the computer. Now go to the server computer and execute the following command:

```
sudo rstudio-server start
```

The server is now running, so you should be able to access the server from the client machine. To do that, bring up a browser and then type:

```
http://ipaddress-of-the-server:8787
```

Replace the phrase *ip-address-of-the-server* with the actual IP address of the server. You should use the user name and password to log in.

4.4 Testing the Hadoop Environment

Once the Hadoop environment is built, you can either use the standard examples available in the Hadoop system, or you can write your own programs and run on the command line to test to see if the system works. The standard examples are packed in the ".jar" file which can be found in the following location in the Ubuntu directory:

```
/usr/lib/hadoop-0.20-mapreduce/hadoop-examples-2.0.0-mr1-cdh4.7.0.jar
```

The standard examples include wordcount, aggregatewordcount, aggregateword-hist, pi, and randomtextwriter. They use the mapreduce(), mapper(), and reduce() functions.

4.4.1 Standard Example

To illustrate the steps involved in running these MapReduce programs using the above ".jar" file and the Hadoop command, the word count example is selected and demonstrated. The following command may be executed:

```
hadoop jar /usr/lib/hadoop-0.20-mapreduce/hadoop-examples-2.0.0-mr1-cdh4.7.0.j
ar wordcount input.txt output-dir
```

This command reads the content of the file input.txt, creates a directory named output-dir, and then writes the word counts as a file with a name like part-00000 inside the directory. You can go (cd) to that directory and issue the "cat" command to look at the content.

4.4.2 Alternative Example

The goal of this example is to use "cat" and "uniq" commands together with Hadoop streaming, mapper, and reducer features to read two files and create a sorted file by removing the duplicate entries. In order to implement this, first create the following two text files using an editor (e.g., vi 1.txt and vi 2.txt):

```
3 Australia Victoria          4 Australia Melbourne
1 America Greensboro          1 Australia Vic
2 India Madras                8 America Arizona
1 Australia Melbourne         6 Greensboro America
                              1 Australia Melbourne
```

Then create a shell script: for example, file-merge.sh, as follows:

```
hadoopjar/usr/lib/hadoop-0.20-mapreduce/contrib/streaming/hadoop-streaming-2.
0.0-mr1-cdh4.7.0.jar-input1.txt2.txt-outputalt-mappercat-reduceruniq

hadoop fs -cat alt/part-00000

hadoop fs -rm -r alt
```

The first command uses the Hadoop's mapreduce streaming capabilities to input the two files and output the results to a directory with a file name part-00000 [21]. The second command reads this file and displays it on the screen. The third command deletes the directory. The output of the first command is:

```
1 America Greensboro
1 Australia Melbourne
1 Australia Vic
2 India Madras
3 Australia Victoria
4 Australia Melbourne
6 Greensboro America
8 America Arizona
```

As you can see, the duplicate entry of "1 Australia Melbourne" is removed.

4.5 Multinode Hadoop

In order to build a multinode Hadoop system, a virtual network must first be established. The Oracle VM virtualbox allows multiple virtual machines to be integrated in the environment. The nodes VB and UB in Fig. 4.7 show the integration of four

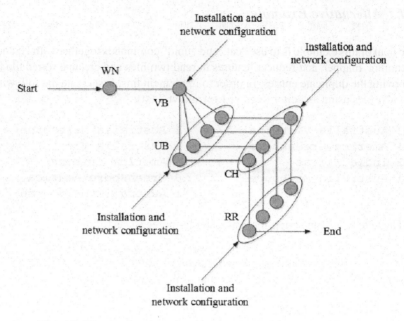

Fig. 4.7 The steps to install a multinode virtual Hadoop system

hosts in the virtual network. The rest of the structure in the figure shows all the installation and network configuration steps to build a complete big data system.

4.5.1 Virtual Network

A virtual network can be created through the Oracle VM VirtualBox Manager by adding several virtual machines and connecting them through network settings. Then, we must install the Ubuntu operating system on every virtual machine as explained in Sect. 4.3.2.3. Using the "ping" command, we can then test to see the virtual machines respond to each other.

4.5.2 Hadoop Setup

As the next step, the Cloudera Hadoop and R programming platforms may be installed on each machine as it has been explained in Sects. 4.3.2.4 and 4.3.2.5, respectively.

Problems

4.1. Virtual Network

Construct a virtual network with four virtual machines (hosts) in the Oracle VM Virtualbox. You must set up IP addresses and the other necessary network parameters. Install the Ubuntu operating system in all virtual machines. Open the shell environment for each operating system and execute ping commands to confirm that these machines can communicate with each other.

4.2. Virtual Hadoop

You have built a virtual network in the previous problem. Now install Cloudera Hadoop in all machines. Confirm all the Hadoop nodes are running.

Acknowledgements I would like to thank my graduate student Sumanth Reddy Yanala for helping to produce the drawing in Fig. 4.1. The information and discussions on "wrapletters" available at http://www.latex-community.org/forum/viewtopic.php?f=44&t=3798 helped the formatting of several long continuous text, like Uniform Resource Locator (URL), in this book.

References

1. T. White. "Hadoop: the definitive guide." O'Reilly Inc, 2009.
2. http://en.wikipedia.org/wiki/Apache_Hadoop
3. D. Borthakur. "The hadoop distributed file system: Architecture and design." Hadoop Project Website 11: 21, 2007.
4. K. Shvachko, H. Kuang, S. Radia, and R. Chansler. "The hadoop distributed file system." In Proceedings of the IEEE Symposium on Mass Storage Systems and Technologies, pp. 1–10, 2010.
5. J. Dean, and S. Ghemawat, "MapReduce: simplified data processing on large clusters." Communications of the ACM, vol. 51, no. 1, pp. 107–113, 2008.
6. J. Dean, and S. Ghemawat. "MapReduce: a flexible data processing tool." Communications of the ACM, vol. 53, no. 1, pp. 72–77, 2010.
7. https://www.virtualbox.org/wiki/Downloads
8. http://www.cloudera.com
9. https://github.com/RevolutionAnalytics/RHadoop/wiki/Downloads
10. http://www.rstudio.com/products/rstudio/download
11. http://www.mathworks.com/products/matlab/index-b.html
12. http://cran.r-project.org/bin/linux/ubuntu/README
13. http://www.vmware.com/products/player
14. http://www.ubuntu.com/download/desktop
15. http://wiki.apache.org/hadoop/Hadoop2OnWindows
16. https://github.com/RevolutionAnalytics/rmr2/tree/master/build
17. https://github.com/RevolutionAnalytics/rhdfs/tree/master/build
18. https://www.youtube.com/watch?v=hK-oggHEetc
19. http://www.meetup.com/Learning-Machine-Learning-by-Example/pages/Installing_R_and_RHadoop/
20. http://bighadoop.wordpress.com/2013/02/25/r-and-hadoop-data-analysis-rhadoop/
21. http://hortonworks.com/blog/using-r-and-other-non-java-languages-in-mapreduce-and-hive/

Chapter 5
MapReduce Programming Platform

Abstract The main objective of this chapter is to explain the MapReduce framework based on RevolutionAnalytics' RHadoop environment. The MapReduce framework relies on its underlying structures, the parametrization, and the parallelization. These structures have been explained clearly in this chapter. The implementation of these structures requires a MapReduce programming platform. An explanation of this programming platform is also presented together with a discussion on the three important functions, mapper(), reducer(), and mapreduce(). These functions help the implementation of the parametrization and parallelization structures to address scalability problems in big data classification. The chapter also presents a set of coding principles, which provide good programming practices to the users of the MapReduce programming platform in the context of big data processing and analysis. Several programming examples are also presented to help the reader to practice coding principles and better understand the MapReduce framework.

5.1 MapReduce Framework

The Mapreduce framework [1] provides techniques and technologies to address big data problems, and they are predominantly useful for solving big data classification problems. The techniques and technologies from RevolutionAnalytics [2] have been selected to apply and explain the MapReduce programming platform. The software packages provided by RevolutionAnalytics can be used to build a Hadoop distributed file system called the RHadoop with a MapReduce programming platform [3]. The MapReduce framework can be easily explained with these packages, and thus the RHadoop system has been selected in this chapter. Let us first explore the underlying structure of the MapReduce framework The underlying structure of the MapReduce framework is a combination of two main concepts called parametrization and the parallelization [4]. They help solve the main scalability problems in big data environment. These two concepts are discussed in the following subsections.

© Springer Science+Business Media New York 2016

S. Suthaharan, *Machine Learning Models and Algorithms for Big Data Classification*, Integrated Series in Information Systems 36, DOI 10.1007/978-1-4899-7641-3_5

Table 5.1 A p dimensional data table

f_1	f_2	f_3	..	f_p
f_{11}	f_{21}	f_{31}	..	f_{p1}
f_{12}	f_{22}	f_{32}	..	f_{p2}
:	:	:	..	:
f_{1n}	f_{2n}	n_{3n}	..	f_{pn}

5.1.1 Parametrization

The parametrization of the MapReduce framework enables users to specify two parameters, called the *key* and the *value*, within a data set so that the data can be efficiently processed using a distributed file system. In MapReduce models, these parameters are called the *key-value pair*, and it is represented by a tuple $(key, value)$. What does the parametrization in the MapReduce framework mean exactly?

Suppose we have a data set represented by p columns and n rows as shown in Table 5.1, and it shows the vertical operation, top to bottom. For simplicity, assume the user selects the data in the first column as the parameter key and the third column as the parameter value, then the key-value pair is (f_1, f_3). The user has many choices, some of them are (f_1, f_{10}), $(f_1, \ldots, f_8, f_p)$, and $(f_3, f_i, \ldots, f_j)$. It shows several choices for users to select the (key, value) pair; hence, the tuple (key, value) becomes the parameter for this model. In addition, this process generates a key domain and a value range, and gives a one-to-one mapping between the key domain and the value range from the data based on the user's choice.

Thinking with Example 5.1:

For this example, let us consider the grades (0–100), the rating (good, fair, bad), and the status (U or G) of 13 university students, where U represents undergraduate student and G represents graduate student. In connecting this with Table 5.1, we have $p = 3$ (i.e., 3 columns) and $n = 13$ (i.e., 13 rows). Assume the entries in this table as: $f_1 = \{96, 92, 68, 95, 96, 11, 50, 32, 75, 50, 93, 98, 12\}$, $f_2 = \{$good, good, fair, good, good, bad, fair, fair, good, fair, good, good, bad$\}$, and $f_3 = \{$U, G, G, G, U, G, U, G, U, U, U, U, G$\}$.

Suppose the user, in this case the instructor, selects the rating as the key and the grades as the value for the (key, value) pair, then we have the mapping between $f_2 = \{$good, good, fair, good, good, bad, fair, fair, good, fair, good, good, bad$\}$ and $f_1 = \{96, 92, 68, 95, 96, 11, 50, 32, 75, 50, 93, 98, 12\}$. Therefore, this selection maps: good $\rightarrow$ 96, good $\rightarrow$ 92, fair $\rightarrow$ 68, $\ldots$, bad $\rightarrow$ 12. This process serves the purpose of the mapper concept in the MapReduce framework.

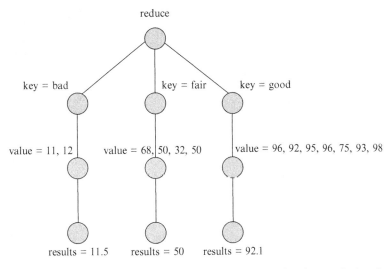

Fig. 5.1 MapReduce programming model that describes the (key, value) pair concept together with user request component and Mapper and Reducer functions

5.1.2 Parallelization

The parallelization of the MapReduce framework converts the one-to-one mapping generated in the Parametrization process to a one-to-many mapping based on the grouping of the same key values. For example, if the key domain has values $\{a, a, b, a, b, b, a\}$ that map to value range $\{v_1, v_2, v_3, v_4, v_5, v_6, v_7\}$, then the grouping may be done using the same key values $\{a, b\}$ map to many like $\{\{v_1, v_2, v_4, v_7\}, \{v_3, v_5, v_6\}\}$. This process helps the MapReduce framework to compress the key domain and maps the compressed keys to their corresponding values as a one-to-many map. This transformation enables each mapping of the compressed keys be processed in parallel by a distributed file system, hence it is called the parallelization. While it helps the parallel processing, it also reduces the data, and thus it serves the purpose of the reducer concept of the MapReduce framework.

Thinking with Example 5.2:

Let us take the same example considered in Thinking with Example 5.1 to understand the parallelization or the reducer better. In that example, we derived a one-to-one mapping as follows: good $\rightarrow$ 96, good $\rightarrow$ 92, fair $\rightarrow$ 68, ..., bad $\rightarrow$ 12. Therefore, we can reduce this data by the following one-to-many mapping to distribute over multiple computers: good $\rightarrow \{96, 92, 95, 96, 75, 93, 98\}$, fair $\rightarrow \{68, 50, 32, 50\}$, and bad $\rightarrow \{11, 12\}$. However, the MapReduce framework sorts the key [5] before transferring the results to this parallelization process, and therefore the correct sequence is the key-sorted list as follows: bad → {11, 12}, fair → {68, 50, 32, 50}, and good → {96, 92, 95, 96, 75, 93, 98}. This example and the processes may be illustrated by the diagram shown in Fig. 5.1. This figure shows three hierarchical branches that facilitate parallelism in the tree like structure where the tasks associated with each branch can be processed by separate processors in parallel. The first level of the tree shows the keys, and the second level shows the value list (or the iterator). The third row is a computation, in this case the averaging, result using the iterator list.

5.2 MapReduce Essentials

The essential tasks of the MapReduce framework, as we have seen in the previous section, are the parametrization and parallelization as well as the sorting performed between these two tasks by the MapReduce framework [5]. We can assign mapper() function for the parametrization process and the reducer() function for the parallelization process, and a main mapreduce() function to execute the mapper() function, sort the output of this function, and transfer the results to the reducer() function. This MapReduce model can be illustrated as shown in Fig. 5.2.

It shows the three process involved in the MapReduce model: the first one is the use of the mapper() function to parametrize the key domain and value range; the second one is the sorting applied by the mapreduce() during the transfer of the results from the mapper() function to the reducer() function; the third process is the use of reducer() function to parallelize the final results. These underlying structures of the MapReduce framework are explained in the following subsections, and these are the extracts of the R code used in the examples presented later in this chapter.

5.2.1 Mapper Function

The mapper() function may be visualized as a vertical operation (or a columnar operation) on the data. Suppose we have p columns (e.g., variables or files) of data with n observations as a table form, then the goal of the mapper() function is to divide the data table vertically as a key domain and value range:

```
grades.map.fn = function(k, v) {
   k=v[,2]
   kk1=keyval(k,v[,1])
   rmr.str(kk1)
}
```

This mapper() function follows the format of the function included in RHadoop software [2, 3] and used in several other applications [6, 7]. In this example, the

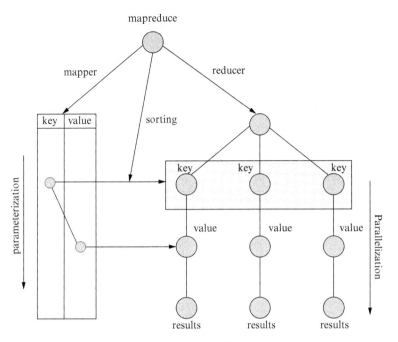

Fig. 5.2 MapReduce programming model is illustrated using the transmission of (key, value) pairs through Mapper function and Reducer function

second column of the data is assigned to a key space, then the key space and the values in the first column are mapped. The *rmr.str* function, in general, helps to debug a *rmr2* program [8], and it has been used here to display the content of the variable *kk*1. The variable *kk*1 is a temporary variable; hence, a proper naming convention is not followed. However, the letter *k* is used to indicate it is a key-related variable.

5.2.2 Reducer Function

The reducer() function may be visualized as a horizontal operation (or a row operation) on the data resulted from the mapper() function. Suppose the key domain has k key labels (i.e., variety of keys) $key_1, key_2, \ldots, key_k$, then the function selects the key's values in their value ranges and performs the operations.

```
grades.reduce.fn = function(k, v) {
   rmr.str(k)
   rmr.str(v)
   kk2=keyval(k,mean(v))
   rmr.str(kk2)
}
```

In this example, the first two *rmr.str* functions display the (key, value) pairs received by the reducer() from the mapper(). In the next statement, the keyval() function performs the horizontal operation, in this case "mean" operation on the value ranges. The resulting reductions based on the key labels are stored in the variable *kk2*, and the subsequent statement displays the stored results. As before, proper naming convention is not followed in the naming of the temporary variable *kk2* which is used to display the results.

5.2.3 MapReduce Function

We now need an engine that reads these functions, executes them correctly, and produces results. The mapreduce() function serves this purpose. It provides a formal parameter list, which copies the input data, the mapper() function, and the reducer() function, and executes them appropriately, according to parametrization, sorting, and parallelization processes. This function may look like this:

```
grades.output.mr = mapreduce(input = grades.input.df,
           map = grades.map.fn, reduce = grades.reduce.fn)
```

It shows three parameters in the formal parameters list: input, map, and reduce. The parameters enable a programmer to transmit the data, mapper(), and reducer() into the mapreduce engine which handles communication with the Hadoop distributed file system. It fetches the results from the Hadoop system and stores them in a variable which may be accessed from outside the Hadoop environment.

5.2.4 A Coding Example

In this coding example, the input file created for Thinking with Example 5.1 is used. It is stored in the file very-first.txt used as an input to the program given in this section. The data in the file are presented below and are listed in three sections for the purpose of display only:

```
96 good U        11 bad  G        93 good U
92 good G        50 fair U        98 good U
68 fair G        32 fair G        12 bad  G
95 good G        75 good U
96 good U        50 fair U
```

The first column of data shows the grades, the second column the rating, and the last column shows the student status. Assuming the data in the second column as key and the first column as value, study the program Listed in 5.1.

Listing 5.1 The parallelization of MapReduce framework

```
1   Sys.setenv(HADOOP_HOME='/usr/lib/hadoop-0.20-mapreduce')
2   Sys.setenv(HADOOP_CMD='/usr/bin/hadoop')
3   Sys.setenv(HADOOP_STREAMING='/usr/lib/hadoop-0.20-mapreduce/
        contrib/streaming/hadoop-streaming-2.0.0-mr1-cdh4.7.0.jar')

5   grades.input.fi <- read.table("very-first.txt", sep="")

7   library(rmr2)
8   library(rhdfs)

10  hdfs.init()

12  grades.input.df = to.dfs(grades.input.fi)

14  grades.map.fn = function(k, v) {
15     k=v[,2]
16     kk1=keyval(k,v[,1])
17     rmr.str(kk1)
18  }

20  grades.reduce.fn = function(k, v) {
21     rmr.str(k)
22     rmr.str(v)
23     kk2=keyval(k,mean(v))
24     rmr.str(kk2)
25  }

27  grades.output.mr = mapreduce(input = grades.input.df, map =
        grades.map.fn, reduce = grades.reduce.fn)

29  grades.output.df = from.dfs(grades.output.mr)
30  grades.output.df
```

In this program, lines 1–3 list the standard settings of the environment variables as performed in [3, 6, 7]; however, the path and the versions of the files are based on the Hadoop system built as a part of this book project. The code in line 5 reads the data file "very-first.txt," which contains the data listed above. Lines 7 and 8 include the libraries rmr2 and rhdfs to execute commands on the RHadoop system. The code in line 10 initializes the hdfs and the code in line 12 inputs the data read in line 5. The block of code in lines 14–18 defines the mapper() function whereas the block of code in lines 20–25 defines the reducer() function.

Within the mapper() function, the second column of the value v is assigned as the key in line 15, and then the key value pair is generated and stored in $kk1$ in line 16. In line 17, the key value pair is displayed. To see the effect of the transformation of the data from mapper to reducer, the key k and value v are displayed in lines 21 and 22. In line 23, the data is reduced and mean values are calculated. The results are printed in line 24. The output of this program, during and after the program execution, in the RStudio platform on the Hadoop system built as a part of this book project is discussed below in segments. The first segment is the output from the mapper() function code in lines 14–18:

```
kk1
List of 2
 $ key: Factor w/ 3 levels "bad","fair","good": 3 3 2
          3 3 1 2 2 3 2 ...
 $ val: int [1:13] 96 92 68 95 96 11 50 32 75 50 ...
```

It shows the key domain and value range generated by the mapper() function using the user's key selection. It lists the key labels, bad, fair, and good, detected in the key domain by the mapper() function. It assigns key labels:1 for bad, 2 for fair, and 3 for good; and stores the values in the value range val:int[1:13]. There are three segments listed below based on the key labels 1, 2, and 3, and the results from the reducer() function in lines 20–25.

```
k
  Factor w/ 3 levels "bad","fair","good": 1

v
  int [1:2] 11 12

kk2
List of 2
 $ key: Factor w/ 3 levels "bad","fair","good": 1
 $ val: num 11.5
```

In the above segment, the data related to the key label 1 (i.e., bad) are processed. As we can see, key 1 is selected, the values 11 and 12 mapped to the key are processed, and then the operation *mean* is performed in the values and calculated as 11.5. In parallel, the next segment is processed:

```
k
  Factor w/ 3 levels "bad","fair","good": 2

v
  int [1:4] 68 50 32 50

kk2
List of 2
 $ key: Factor w/ 3 levels "bad","fair","good": 2
 $ val: num 50
```

In this segment, the sorted key label 2 is selected; its values are processed and operation is performed, and then the result is displayed. Finally, the same sequence of executions take place on the key label 3.

```
k
  Factor w/ 3 levels "bad","fair","good": 3

v
  int [1:7] 96 92 95 96 75 93 98

kk2
List of 2
  $ key: Factor w/ 3 levels "bad","fair","good": 3
  $ val: num 92.1
```

Note that the keys are sorted using the key labels and this task was carried out by the mapreduce() function in line 27 during transfer between the mapper() and reducer() functions. It is also important to note that the reducer() function completes the tasks for the key labels 1, 2, and 3 in parallel as the branches shown in Fig. 5.2. The above information is the display of the program during program execution. The following is the final output of the program:

```
$key
[1] bad  fair good
Levels: bad fair good

$val
[1] 11.50000 50.00000 92.14286
```

In order to implement the mapreduce(), mapper(), and reducer() functions on a big data environment (e.g., Hadoop), it is advisable to strictly adopt a good programming practice. In the following section, a coding principle is presented and recommended, and it will be adopted in the R programs created for the book.

5.3 MapReduce Programming

To be a good programmer, coding discipline is very important, and MapReduce programming has not been exempted from it. The MapReduce coding discipline can be divided into naming convention and coding principles. In this section, a naming convention and a set of coding principles are presented to help readers practice them. They are developed based on the programming styles practiced in [3, 6, 7, 9]; however, this section organizes them for readers structure their programs.

5.3.1 Naming Convention

In MapReduce programming, like object-oriented programming, there are two main attributes: data and functions. However, the data could be input data or output data,

Table 5.2 Coding principles and descriptions

Coding principles	Descriptions
Initialize resources	It makes the program generic to access executables and libraries.
Fork jobs	It allocates the Hadoop-related resources for data processing.
Add input to (h)dfs	It transfers the data from a regular system to Hadoop system.
Define mapper()	It creates (key, value) pairs and an iterator list to match duplicates.
Define reducer()	It receives the (key, value) pair and reduces the data from the list.
Call mapreduce()	It bridges mapper and reducer to sort and transfer iterator list.
Get output from (h)dfs	It transfers results from the Hadoop system to the regular system.

and the functions could be mapper() function, reducer() function, or mapreduce() function. Furthermore, the input data could be the input to the overall program environment or the input to the distributed file systems (dfs), the output could be the output from the mapreduce() function or the output from dfs, and the functions could be the MapReduce-based functions or the user-defined functions.

Therefore, to distinguish these different options for each object, we need to follow naming conventions in our programming practice. The confusion between these different cases can be avoided by naming style that uses the *dot* notation as follows: object_name.attributes_name.descriptor. This is the main contributor to the coding principle presented in this section.

5.3.2 Coding Principles

You can develop your own coding principles and adopt them in your programs. This section suggests a coding principle and adopts the R-codes presented in the rest of the book. The coding principles for MapReduce programming follow the basic programming principles of input-processing-output. Hence, as shown in Table 5.2, they focus on initializing the resources, forking jobs, adding data to hdfs, defining mapper() and reducer() functions, calling the built-in mapreduce() function, and getting the results from hdfs.

5.3.2.1 Input: Initialization

The initialization process mainly focuses on the language-specific tasks such as exporting the paths for the executables and libraries, reading the input files, and initializing variables. As suggested in [6, 7], and mentioned in the previous chapter, the environment variables HADOOP_HOME, HADOOP_CMD, and HADOOP_STREAMING must be set to access certain commands and libraries. These are included in every R program that deals with the MapReduce framework presented in this book, based on the system installed for this book [3, 6, 7]:

```
Sys.setenv(HADOOP_HOME='/usr/lib/hadoop-0.20-mapreduce')
Sys.setenv(HADOOP_CMD='/usr/bin/hadoop')
Sys.setenv(HADOOP_STREAMING='/usr/lib/hadoop-0.20-mapreduce/
contrib/streaming/hadoop-streaming-2.0.0-mr1-cdh4.7.0.jar')
```

Once these variables are set and the paths are available to access the relevant command and libraries, the following libraries must be included [3, 6, 7]:

```
library(rmr2)
library(rhdfs)
```

The "rmr2" and "rhdfs" are the two main libraries to carry out big data processing on RHadoop, and therefore, they are also included in every R program that deals with the MapReduce framework presented in this book.

```
object.input.fi=data
object.input.ki=data
object.input.hi=data
```

The variable name that may be used to store the data is *object.input.id*, where *object* represents the name selected for the object, *input* indicates it is an input, and *fi* describes it is an input data from a file, *ki* describes the data from the keyboard, and *hi* describes the data as hard coded.

5.3.2.2 Input: Fork MapReduce job

This is where you run the commands that invoke Hadoop-related resources, which include Hadoop distributed files system and MapReduce framework [3, 6, 7].

```
hdfs.init()
```

5.3.2.3 Input: Add Input to dfs

In this step, the data to be processed should be stored.

```
object.input.df=to.dfs(data)
```

5.3.2.4 Processing: Mapper

This function assigns initial and intermediate (key, value) pairs [3, 6, 7].

object.map.fn=function(key, value)

5.3.2.5 Processing: Reducer

This function accepts the iterator list of values from the mapper() function and mapreduce() function, and then reduces (e.g., counts) the values [3, 6, 7].

object.reduce.fn=function(key, value)

5.3.2.6 Processing: MapReduce

This function helps sort the output of the mapper() function and create the iterator list of values, which are passed into the reducer() function [3, 6, 7].

object.output.mr=mapreduce(input=object1, map=object2, reduce=object3)

5.3.2.7 Output: Get Output from dfs

The results are in the protected space of Hadoop dfs and regular O/S-based commands cannot be used to get the results. Hence, the Hadoop-related output command must be issued [3, 6, 7].

object.output.df=from.dfs(object4)

5.3.3 Application of Coding Principles

In this section, two simple coding examples (Gaussian and Pythagorean) are presented to show the proper use of the coding principles presented in this section. The blocks of codes presented in the first example have also been extracted and summarized in this section.

5.3.3.1 A Coding Example

The example presented below is based on the following justification: The generation of pseudorandom numbers based on a statistical distribution is needed to study the various machine-learning techniques later in this book. Therefore, this example is provided to generate five pseudo Gaussian random numbers (x) with mean 2.1 and variance 1.1, and transform them using $y = 3x^2 + 2x + 1$, and you may extend this to generate a very large such random set.

Listing 5.2 The use of coding principles with Gaussian samples

```
1   Sys.setenv(HADOOP_HOME='/usr/lib/hadoop-0.20-mapreduce')
2   Sys.setenv(HADOOP_CMD='/usr/bin/hadoop')
3   Sys.setenv(HADOOP_STREAMING='/usr/lib/hadoop-0.20-mapreduce/
        contrib/streaming/hadoop-streaming-2.0.0-mr1-cdh4.7.0.jar')

4
5   set.seed(5)
6   gauss.input.hi = rnorm(5,2.1,1.1)

7
8   library(rmr2)
9   library(rhdfs)
10
11  hdfs.init()
12
13  gauss.input.df = to.dfs(gauss.input.hi)
14
15  gauss.map.fn = function(k, v) {
16      keyval(v,v)
17  }
18
19  gauss.reduce.fn = function(k, v) {
20      keyval(k, 3*v^2+2*v+1)
21  }
22
23  gauss.output.mr = mapreduce(input = gauss.input.df , map = gauss.
        map.fn, reduce = gauss.reduce.fn)
24
25  gauss.output.df = from.dfs(gauss.output.mr)
26  gauss.output.df
```

It is a simple program, and it generates five pseudorandom numbers, which follow the Gaussian distribution properties as shown in lines 5 and 6. These numbers are transferred to the Hadoop system and the mapper() and reducer() functions are executed. In line 16, the values are selected as keys in mapper() and then the reducer() calculates the values based on the quadratic function listed in line 20. The output of this program is: 7.492409, 47.619527, 3.988624, 19.574352, and 56.548119. It confirms the validity of the program. The main advantage of the latest program is the modularity which helps the readability of the program as well as the maintainability.

5.3.3.2 Pythagorean Numbers

We know the integers 4, 5, and 3 form the Pythagorean number, and therefore let us write a simple MapReduce program that reads in these integers in this order, checks for correctness, and then outputs the message "Pythagorean." This program is presented in the Listing 5.3.

Listing 5.3 The use of coding principles with Pythagorean Numbers

```
1   Sys.setenv(HADOOP_HOME='/usr/lib/hadoop-0.20-mapreduce')
2   Sys.setenv(HADOOP_CMD='/usr/bin/hadoop')
3   Sys.setenv(HADOOP_STREAMING='/usr/lib/hadoop-0.20-mapreduce/
        contrib/streaming/hadoop-streaming-2.0.0-mr1-cdh4.7.0.jar')

5   pythag.input.hi = c(4,5,3)

7   library(rmr2)
8   library(rhdfs)

10  hdfs.init()

12  pythag.input.df = to.dfs(pythag.input.hi)

14  pythag.map.fn = function(k, v) {
15    k=1
16    ss=sort(v)
17    val <- ifelse(ss[3]^2==ss[1]^2+ss[2]^2, "Pythagorean", "Not␣
          Pythagorean")
18    keyval(k,val)
19  }

21  pythag.reduce.fn = function(k, v) {
22    keyval(k, v)
23  }

25  pythag.output.mr = mapreduce(input = pythag.input.df, map =
        pythag.map.fn, reduce = pythag.reduce.fn)

27  pythag.output.df = from.dfs(pythag.output.mr)
28  pythag.output.df
```

In this program, the three integers 4, 5, and 3 are assigned to a variable in line 5 and transferred to the Hadoop system in line 12. The mapper() function is then defined in which an "ifelse" statement is used to validate whether the integers satisfy the properties of Pythagorean numbers, then the results are labeled accordingly in line 17. It is important to note that the values are sorted in line 16 to push the largest value to the end of the list. The output of this program is: "Pythagorean."

Table 5.3 Description of coding principles

Coding principles	Coding example
Initialize resources	gauss.input.hi = rnorm(5,2.1,1.1), library(rmr2), library(rhdfs)
Fork job	hdfs.init()
Add input to (h)dfs	gauss.input.df = to.dfs(gauss.input.hi)
Define mapper()	gauss.map.fn = function(k, v) {keyval(v,v)}
Define reducer()	gauss.reduce.fn = function(k, v) {keyval(k, $3 \times v^2 + 2 \times v + 1$)}
Define mapreduce()	gauss.output.mr = mapreduce(input − gauss.input.df, map = gauss.map.fn, reduce = gauss.reduce.fn))
Get output from (h)dfs	gauss.output.df = from.dfs(gauss.output.mr)

5.3.3.3 Summarization

We have seen several examples for the MapReduce model implementation using R programming language and RHadoop environment. Let us now put them together in a tabular form to understand the correct use of the coding principles. This tabular explanation is presented in Table 5.3 using the example code in Listing 5.2. Each block of related codes is mapped to the coding principles discussed based on Table 5.2.

5.4 File Handling in MapReduce

As mentioned earlier, big data processing through efficient file handling with a distributed environment is the main objective of modern distributed file systems like the Hadoop system with MapReduce programming platform. Some of the important tasks that take place during the big data processing management in the Hadoop-like environment are the file input, the file split, and the file merge. Therefore, exploration of the file handling examples will help readers better understand the big data processing environment and develop efficient machine-learning techniques. In this section, three examples are presented where the first example illustrates the file-read mechanism using the Pythagorean numbers, and the next example demonstrates the file split mechanism. The third example elucidates an improved version of the file split example. The file merge example is reserved as an exercise and included in the "problem" section of the chapter for you to develop solutions and write a program using the coding principles learned.

5.4.1 Pythagorean Numbers

Suppose we have a data set with several integers, and we want to find the triples that satisfy the properties of the Pythagorean numbers. Let us also assume the data set is organized with three columns and a number of rows where each row has the three integers to be tested for Pythagorean properties. The data set used in this program is given below (listed in three segments for the purpose of display):

```
1  2  3            13  5   12          19  22  85
4  5  3            32  255 257         5   3   4
2  5  4            29  421 420
```

The ultimate goal is to mark the rows that have Pythagorean integers with the phrase "Pythagorean" and mark others with the phrase "Not Pythagorean."

Listing 5.4 The use of coding principles with Pythagorean numbers

```
1   Sys.setenv(HADOOP_HOME='/usr/lib/hadoop-0.20-mapreduce')
2   Sys.setenv(HADOOP_CMD='/usr/bin/hadoop')
3   Sys.setenv(HADOOP_STREAMING='/usr/lib/hadoop-0.20-mapreduce/
        contrib/streaming/hadoop-streaming-2.0.0-mr1-cdh4.7.0.jar')
4
5   pythag.input.fi <- read.table("pythag.txt", sep="")
6
7   library(rmr2)
8   library(rhdfs)
9
10  hdfs.init()
11
12  pythag.input.df = to.dfs(pythag.input.fi)
13
14  pythag.map.fn = function(k, v) {
15    k=which(v[,1]==v[,1])
16    ss=t(apply(v,1,sort))
17    val <- ifelse(ss[,3]^2==ss[,1]^2+ss[,2]^2, "Pythagorean", "Not
        Pythagorean")
18    keyval(k,val)
19  }
20
21  pythag.reduce.fn = function(k, v) {
22    keyval(k, v)
23  }
24
25  pythag.output.mr = mapreduce(input = pythag.input.df, map =
        pythag.map.fn, reduce = pythag.reduce.fn)
26
27  pythag.output.df = from.dfs(pythag.output.mr)
28  pythag.output.df
```

This program is also similar to other programs; however, the block of code in the mapper() function is presented in lines from 14 to 19. The code in line 15 helps to assign the current index to the key and the code in line 16 helps sort the integers at each index. Then in line 17, the Pythagorean mathematical relationship is validated and labeled with the phrases "Pythagorean" or "Not Pythagorean." The rest of the program has similar code to previous programs, an, thus are not explained. The output of the program follows:

```
$key
[1] 1 2 3 4 5 6 7 8

$val
                        1                    2                    3
                        4
"Not Pythagorean"         "Pythagorean" "Not Pythagorean"
    "Pythagorean"
                        5                    6                    7
                        8
    "Pythagorean"         "Pythagorean" "Not Pythagorean"
    "Pythagorean"
```

We can confirm the result of the key assignment in line 15 with the first output $key and the results of line 17 and the reducer function with the output $val, which has the key as the index and the phrases as the validated results.

5.4.2 File Split Example

Consider an example that illustrates the file split concept using an "ifelse" statement to generate (key, value) pairs. It inputs a file, extracts the unique keys, and writes their corresponding values to the files with filenames associated with those keys. The data in the input file file1.txt are:

```
96 good          50 fair          98 good
92 good          32 fair          10 bad
68 fair          75 good          12 bad
89 good          42 fair
85 good          98 good
```

Once again, the program in Listing 5.5 has many similar blocks of code like the ones that we already reviewed. Therefore, only the main blocks of code in this listing are explained. In this example, both the mapper() function and the reducer() function have significant changes. The key is selected using the "ifelse" statement in line 8, and they will be used as the output file names in the reducer() function at line 23.

Listing 5.5 Identifying the Pythagorean numbers from a set of numbers

```
1   Sys.setenv(HADOOP_HOME='/usr/lib/hadoop-0.20-mapreduce')
2   Sys.setenv(HADOOP_CMD='/usr/bin/hadoop')
3   Sys.setenv(HADOOP_STREAMING='/usr/lib/hadoop-0.20-mapreduce/
        contrib/streaming/hadoop-streaming-2.0.0-mr1-cdh4.7.0.jar')
4
5   grade.input.fi <- read.table("file1.txt", sep="")
6
7   library(rmr2)
8   library(rhdfs)
9
10  hdfs.init()
11
12  grade.input.df <- to.dfs(grade.input.fi )
13
14  grade.map.fn <- function(k,v) {
15    key <- ifelse(v[2] == "good", "good", ifelse(v[2] == "fair", "
        fair", "bad"))
16    keyval(key,v[,1])
17  }
18
19  grade.reduce.fn <- function(k,v) {
20    write(v, paste(k,".txt"))
21    keyval(k, length(v))
22  }
23
24  grade.output.mr <- mapreduce(input=grade.input.df,
25                               map = grade.map.fn,
26                               reduce = grade.reduce.fn)
27
28  grade.output.df = from.dfs(grade.output.mr)
29  grade.output.df
```

The output of this program is similar to the one obtained in the next example, hence the explanation is deferred to the improved version presented in the next example. However, I encourage you to study this program, run the program, obtain results, and interpret them.

5.4.3 File Split Improved

Consider another example that illustrates the file split example without using the "ifelse" statement to generate (key, value) pairs. In big data classification problems, a large number of class types are expected; therefore, the use of an "ifelse" statement is inefficient. The data presented below are the input to the program, and they are stored in the text file named "file2.txt," and the output to the program is the files with the file names based on the class labels and their corresponding data.

90 96 good	60 50 fair	79 98 good
89 92 good	70 32 fair	15 10 bad
69 68 fair	80 75 good	12 12 bad
92 89 good	55 42 fair	
86 85 good	78 98 good	

The use of "ifelse" is inefficient for large files with many numbers of classes (which may serve the purpose of key assignment). Therefore, an alternative approach is required, and this is achieved in the program presented in Listing 5.6.

Listing 5.6 An improved version of the file split example

```
1  Sys.setenv(HADOOP_HOME='/usr/lib/hadoop-0.20-mapreduce')
2  Sys.setenv(HADOOP_CMD='/usr/bin/hadoop')
3  Sys.setenv(HADOOP_STREAMING='/usr/lib/hadoop-0.20-mapreduce/
       contrib/streaming/hadoop-streaming-2.0.0-mr1-cdh4.7.0.jar')
4
5  grades.input.fi <- read.table("file2.txt", sep="")
6
7  library(rmr2)
8  library(rhdfs)
9
10 hdfs.init()
11
12 grades.input.df <- to.dfs(grades.input.fi)
13
14 grades.map.fn <- function(k,v) {
15   key <- v[,3]
16   val <- c(v[,1],v[,2])
17   keyval(key,val)
18 }
19
20 grades.reduce.fn <- function(k,v) {
21   write.table(matrix(v, ncol=2, byrow=FALSE), paste(k,".txt"))
22   keyval(k, length(v))
23 }
24
25 grades.output.mr <- mapreduce(input=grades.input.df,
26                     map = grades.map.fn,
27                     reduce = grades.reduce.fn)
28
29 grades.output.df = from.dfs(grades.output.mr)
30 grades.output.df
```

The main differences are the codes in lines 15, 16, and 21. The key assignment is performed in line 15 using the third column data, and the values are the remaining two columns. The (key, value) pair is generated in line 17 and carried over to the reduce() function via the mapreduce() function in line 25. The reduce function in lines 20–23 generates the matrix using v, assigns keys as the names of the output files, and writes the matrix to the files. The output of this program looks like this:

bad.txt	fair.txt	good.txt
"V1" "V2"	"V1" "V2"	"V1" "V2"
"1" 15 10	"1" 69 68	"1" 90 96
"2" 12 12	"2" 60 50	"2" 89 92
	"3" 70 32	"3" 92 89
	"4" 55 42	"4" 86 85
		"5" 80 75
		"6" 78 98
		"7" 79 98

We can see the three files saved with the names bad.txt, fair.txt, and good.txt as coded in the program. Comparing the output with the content of the input file, we can easily confirm the program correctly split the data files. Note that the file names are manually inserted above only for the purpose of display; they are not the output of the program listed in the Listing 5.6.

Problems

5.1. Small File Merge

(a) Increase the number of observations in the data sets bad.txt, fair.txt, and good.txt created in one of the file split examples presented before. Make sure you write the program to do this task and save the results inside the Hadoop system.

(b) Write a MapReduce program to read these files, merge them, and create a single file. Save it in the Hadoop system.

5.2. Large File Merge

(a) Use the above file merge program to merge the files *hardwood floor* and *carpet floor*, or use your own large files.

(b) Extend this to merge three or more large files, observe the computational time, and interpret the effect of the file size.

5.3. Split-Merge-Split

Read the split-merge-split problem presented in Problem 3.1 of Chap. 3, and repeat the tasks with the RHadoop system and MapReduce programming discussed in Chaps. 4 and 5. Compare the results and computing time.

References

1. J. Dean, and S. Ghemawat. "MapReduce: a flexible data processing tool." Communications of the ACM, vol. 53, no. 1, pp. 72–77, 2010.
2. http://www.revolutionanalytics.com/. Accessed April 23rd, 2015.

3. http://projects.revolutionanalytics.com/rhadoop/. Accessed April 23rd, 2015.
4. J. Dean, and S. Ghemawat, "MapReduce: simplified data processing on large clusters." Communications of the ACM, vol. 51, no. 1, pp. 107–113, 2008.
5. T. White. Hadoop: the definitive guide. O'Reilly, 2012.
6. http://bighadoop.wordpress.com/2013/02/25/r-and-hadoop-data-analysis-rhadoop/. Accessed May 30th, 2015.
7. http://www.meetup.com/Learning-Machine-Learning-by-Example/pages/Installing_R_and_RHadoop/. Accessed May 30th, 2015.
8. https://github.com/RevolutionAnalytics/RHadoop/wiki/user-rmr-Debugging-rmr-programs. Accessed May 31st, 2015.
9. http://www.rdatamining.com/big-data/rhadoop. Accessed May 31st, 2015.

Part III
Understanding Machine Learning

Chapter 6
Modeling and Algorithms

Abstract The main objective of this chapter is to explain the machine learning concepts, mainly modeling and algorithms; batch learning and online learning; and supervised learning (regression and classification) and unsupervised learning (clustering) using examples. Modeling and algorithms will be explained based on the domain division characteristics, batch learning and online learning will be explained based on the availability of the data domain, and supervised learning and unsupervised learning will be explained based on the labeling of the data domain. This objective will be extended to the comparison of the mathematical models, hierarchical models, and layered models, using programming structures, such as control structures, modularization, and sequential statements.

6.1 Machine Learning

The field of Machine Learning provides a ground for scientists to explore learning models and learning algorithms that can help machines (e.g., computers) learn the system from data [1]. In other words, one of the objectives of machine learning is to build an intelligent system. The two main components that can help machine learning approaches achieve this goal are learning models and learning algorithms. Learning models and learning algorithms are, in one way or the other, pattern recognition tools. For example, what will you do if a data set is given to you for analysis? Naturally, you will search for patterns to understand the characteristics of the data for extracting knowledge, predict the trend of the data, or identify the number of groups (or classes) in the data. In a general definition, the machine-learning problem may be described as follows. Suppose a data set and its corresponding response set of a system are given. Then the machine-earning problem may be defined as how to fit a model between them and how to train and validate the model to learn the system's characteristics from data.

© Springer Science+Business Media New York 2016

S. Suthaharan, *Machine Learning Models and Algorithms for Big Data Classification*, Integrated Series in Information Systems 36, DOI 10.1007/978-1-4899-7641-3_6

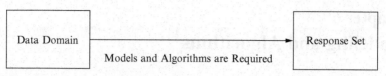

Fig. 6.1 This figure illustrates the relationships between a data domain, a response set, and the learning models and algorithms

6.1.1 A Simple Example

A system produces responses y using $y = 2x + 3$ over the domain $D = [0,2]$ without errors. Then it is easy to find the responses for any data points in the data domain. For example, if we select two points $x = 1.1$ and $x = 1.2$ in D, then we have their responses $y = 5.2$ and $y = 5.4$, respectively. Similarly, we can calculate responses for all the points in the domain, and this will result in the response set $C = [3,7]$. The data domain and the response set of this system are illustrated in Fig. 6.1. It shows the need for mapping between these two sets to establish models and algorithms for classification.

We can represent this relationship with a mathematical function $y = f_{2,3}(x)$ showing its slope and y-intercept as index. Therefore, if the relationship is defined as $y = f_{-2,3.4}(x)$ with the same domain D, then the corresponding equation is $y = -2x + 3.4$ with the response set $C = [-0.6, 3.4]$. Following this mathematical process, we can define a set of straight lines by using slope and y-intercept parameters a and b with the equation as $y = f_{a,b}(x)$. Hence, its corresponding parametrized straight line equation is $y = ax + b$. This linear equation becomes the parametrized model for this particular example.

In the first example, the domain $D = [0,2]$ and the parametrized mapping $y = f_{a,b}(x)$ with $a = 2$ and $b = 3$ were given, and thus we were able to determine the system's response set $C = [3,7]$. However, if the domain $D = [0,2]$ and the response set $C = [3,7]$ are given, then deriving a model is not a straightforward task. We need two tasks to solve this problem: the first task is to derive the parametrized model $y = f_{a,b}(x)$, and the second task is to develop an algorithm for searching for optimal values for $a(= 2)$ and $b(= 3)$ from a large pool of parameter values. For simplicity, suppose that we have derived a model $y = ax + b$ and developed a learning algorithm that provides $a = 1.99$ and $b = 3.01$ then, they are a reasonably well-defined model and an algorithm, because they give the tuples $(1.1, 5.199)$ and $(1.2, 5.398)$, which are close to $(1.1, 5.2)$ and $(1.2, 5.4)$.

The process of deriving a parametrized model and developing a learning algorithm to find an optimal value for the parameters is considered a machine-learning task, and a simple interpretation of this definition is presented in Fig. 6.2. It first shows an input model $y = f_{a,b}(x)$ to the modeling unit, which establishes the parametrized models $f_{a_1,b_1}(x), f_{a_2,b_2}(x), \ldots, f_{a_n,b_n}(x)$ for classification. Then the next learning-algorithm unit takes them as inputs and provides measures that can help optimization. In the subsequent step, these measures (in this case, a simple

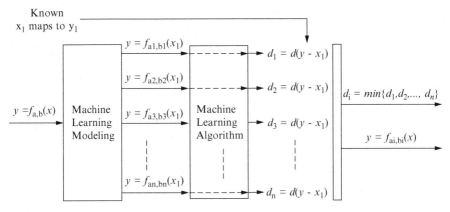

Fig. 6.2 The processes of developing parametrized models, implementing the learning algorithm, and finding optimal parameters are illustrated

distance measure is shown) are compared, and the parameters which give the minimum are selected as optimal values. It also shows the propagation and utilization of the actual labels in this comparison as well as the trained model as the final output $f_{a_i,b_i}(x)$, which gives the minimum distance, assuming a_i and b_i are optimal.

6.1.2 Domain Division Perspective

In machine learning, we come across important terminologies like regression [2], classification [3], clustering [4], supervised learning [5], and unsupervised learning. The description of these terminologies using data domain division can better help us understand their differences. In the machine learning literature, they have been compared and explained in many ways. However, it is easier if they are compared based on the domain division properties so that clear distinctions can be established.

According to domain division properties, regression, classification, and clustering may define the modeling aspect of machine learning, and supervised learning and unsupervised learning may define the learning algorithm aspect of machine learning [5, 6]. Suppose the domain cannot be (or shouldn't be) divided, then we can only study the trend pattern of the data. In this case, the machine-learning approach that we develop is called regression. In other words, we can say that regression is a modeling of the entire data domain. For example, if we use the straight line example considered previously, we can model it using the multiplication and addition operators, and the entire domain as illustrated in Fig. 6.3. It illustrates a linear modeling that the data points x in the data domain are multiplied by the slope parameter a and then incremented by the intercept parameter b to construct a response set. On the other hand, if the domain can be divided (or domain division is allowed), then the modeling can be derived to extract different groups (classes or types) and subgroups

Models and Algorithms

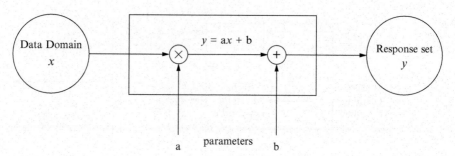

Fig. 6.3 A linear (*straight line*) modeling between a data domain and a response set—it forms a regression scenario

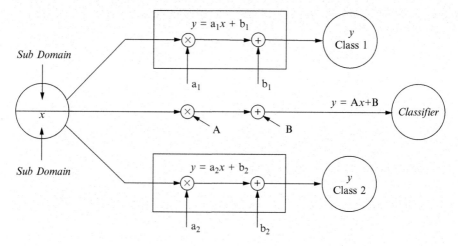

Fig. 6.4 A simple insight of processes that occur during the division of a data domain. The top and the bottom processes may be interpreted as the regression scenarios, and the middle process as the classification scenarios in the subdomains

in the data. Figure 6.4 illustrates this example. In this case, it would have been easier if the two distinct patterns were highlighted as shown in the figure. If that is the case, we can be sure that the classes are labeled with which one is which, so we can divide them. This modeling strategy is called *classification*. In other words, classification is the modeling of subdomains where the parameters A and B play important roles. If these classes are not labeled (i.e., subdomains are not finely defined), and we guess and divide them into two classes, then it is called *clustering* [4].

Domain division can also play an important role in defining learning algorithms. Suppose the domain may be divided and class labels are given, then we can derive a classification model and supervise to obtain optimal parameters. Hence, it is called supervised learning (and classification is assigned under the supervised learning

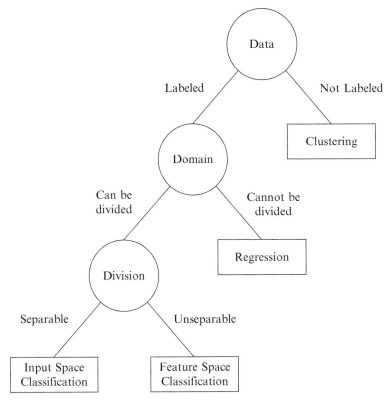

Fig. 6.5 A hierarchical structure that shows the distinction between regression, classification, and clustering based on data-domain-division

paradigm). When a domain is divisible and no class labels are given, then it is called unsupervised learning (it is assigned under the unsupervised learning paradigm).

Suppose the domain may not be divided, then there is no question of where to divide the domain. In this case, the classification or the clustering objective is not possible. Hence, this is a regression learning, and it is always supervised, and it is assigned under the supervised learning category. Therefore, we can create a hierarchical representation of different machine-learning approaches under the categories shown in Fig. 6.5 based on *data → domain → division*. From the top to bottom of the hierarchy, it first shows two categories of data: if the data set is not labeled, then the application is clustering, and if the data is labeled, then the characteristics of the data domain must be understood. In this case, if the data domain cannot be divided or should not be divided, then the application is regression, and if it can be divided, then the ease of the domain division must be analyzed. If the data points associated with the classes are separable, then the original data domain may be divided and the classification may be applied. However, if the classes are nonseparable, then the

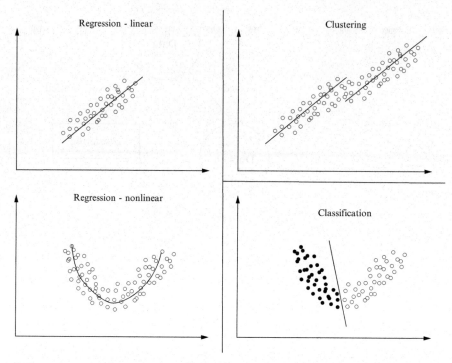

Fig. 6.6 A set of visual examples that can help conceptualize the supervised learning and unsupervised learning techniques based on the domain division

original domain must be transformed to a transformed domain, generally called feature space. Among the three applications highlighted, this book mainly focuses on the classification approaches and their applications. If we focus on big data, then the data node in this hierarchy is "big data," hence the "domain" is highly unstructured, and thus the "division" is complex and difficult. As a result, the classification models and algorithms will encounter significant challenges.

6.1.3 Data Domain

The best way to make an efficient machine-learning algorithm is to develop a robust parametrized learning model. We can now generalize the example discussed above so that the standard definition of a machine-learning model can be established. The example has used a two-dimensional Euclidean space to explain the machine-learning problem, but in a generalized model, a higher-dimensional vector space must be used. Suppose the domain D is a p-dimensional data set with $\mathbf{x} = (\mathbf{x}_1, \mathbf{x}_2, \ldots, \mathbf{x}_n)'$ points in the domain, and there are k responses $y = (y_1, y_2, \ldots, y_k)$, where each response represents a class label. Then each vector $\mathbf{x}_i, (i = 1 \ldots n)$ maps to one of the responses with high probability. Hence, we may develop a model:

$$\mathbf{y}_{k \times 1} = A_{k \times p} \mathbf{x}_{p \times 1} + B_{k \times 1}, \tag{6.1}$$

where A and B are the parameters of the hyperplane formed by the vector $\mathbf{x}$ and y, and these two parameters create the parameter set β as in the generalized parametric model $y = f_\beta(\mathbf{x})$. Each row of matrix A helps assign a point of domain D to a particular response y, and each row of B helps regularize them. As a result, the domain D is divided into k subspaces. Now, the problem is to find a set of optimal values for the matrices A and B for a given set of $\mathbf{x}$ (domain) and y (corresponding responses) so that this model can be used to predict a response y' for a new data vector $\mathbf{x}'$. We can simplify this problem even further so that this process can be clearly explained and understood.

Suppose you have a simple linear model $y = ax + b$, where a and b are the parameters that control the slope and the intercept of this straight line. Then the parametrization means the selection of a suitable value or values for the parameters a and b from a set of values $\{a_1, a_2, \ldots, a_n\}$ and $\{b_1, b_2, \ldots, b_n\}$, respectively. Now suppose we select the parameter combinations (a_i, b_i) and (a_j, b_j) for further analysis to determine which one of these is the best parameter tuple that will maximize the classification accuracy. The process that we adopt to find the best parameter values is called the *optimization*.

6.1.4 Domain Division

The main goal of a learning algorithm is to train a model using a labeled data set in hand (generally, it is large) and obtain optimal values for the parameters. Hence, the best way to define learning algorithms is by integrating the concept of training, validation, and testing procedures. The learning algorithms may be divided into supervised learning algorithms [5] or unsupervised learning algorithms [6]. However, there are other forms of learning algorithms including semi-supervised learning algorithms [7] and reinforcement learning algorithms [8]. The main focus of this book is on the supervised learning algorithms. Let us look at the scatter plots presented in Fig. 6.6. It shows some examples of patterns that highlight the applications of regression (linear and nonlinear), clustering (unsupervised learning), and classification (supervised learning) techniques.

The problem explained in the first figure is a one class problem, and the goal was to fit a model to extract the relationship between $\mathbf{x}$ and $\mathbf{y}$. An example is the data set which consists of the heights ($\mathbf{x}$) and weights ($\mathbf{y}$) of boys (class 1) only or girls (class 2) only. Suppose there are 100 boy participants, and we select a boy with the height x, ask for his weight, and his response is y. Because we have these 100 boys in the participants set, we can use their height and weight information to fit a linear model $\mathbf{y} = A\mathbf{x} + B$ and find the relationship between the heights and weights of the boys. This becomes a predictive model, and it can be used to predict the weight of a new boy based on his height. This type of problem is called regression, and the algorithm that we use to train the model using the data set is called supervised learning because we know where the data $\mathbf{x}$ come from—in this case the boys—so the response $\mathbf{y}$ provides similar answers to the training responses.

In the previous examples, the data vectors $\mathbf{x}$ and $\mathbf{y}$ were given, we came with the model $\mathbf{y} = A\mathbf{x} + B$ and we said we wanted to learn the optimal values that fit the data. Now add one more piece of information. We assume there are two class types in vector $\mathbf{y}$. Suppose we have both girl and boy participants. Then we can divide the problem space into three categories. The first category is the relationship between the height and weight of girls, the second category is the relationship between the height and weight of boys, and the third category is a comparison between girls and boys. The first two cases are regression problems, and the third case is the classification problem.

Now we can define this problem in an interesting way. We may derive two different linear models $\mathbf{y} = A_g\mathbf{x} + B_g$ and $\mathbf{y} = A_b\mathbf{x} + B_b$ for girls and boys, respectively. When a new girl participant arrives, we can measure her height and predict her weight using the first equation, and if a new boy participant comes, we can use the second equation. However, the challenge is to have a single equation (that is, one set of parameters A and B) that helps to determine whether a participant is a girl or a boy using the participant's height and the weight (response) information.

Therefore, in summary, the learning models are: regression, classification, and clustering. The learning algorithms are supervised learning and unsupervised learning. Among the three models stated, the regression and classification require supervised learning; hence, they are called supervised learning models. The clustering model requires unsupervised learning; hence, it is called unsupervised learning model. The interest of this book is the supervised learning models and algorithms; hence, the rest of the book discusses these learning models.

6.2 Learning Models

The term *supervised learning* comes from the analogy that a baby is initially supervised by her mother or father. For example, a baby has learned to identify a pencil or a pen and is able to distinguish them by the labeling done by her parents. Hence, the supervised learning requires label data sets, and we can call this environment a known data domain and known response (labels) set. Therefore, a supervised learning model and an algorithm deal with an environment where the given data is known, and their corresponding responses are also known "see Fig. 6.7". This definition must be extended to a big data environment as well. However, in big data, the data domain is controlled by the three common parameters: volume, variety, and velocity, and the modeling definition is presented in Fig. 6.8. Recently, a new

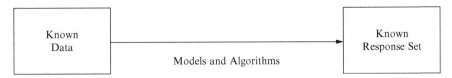

Fig. 6.7 Supervised learning (models and algorithms) is illustrated using the definition of mapping between a known data domain and a known response set

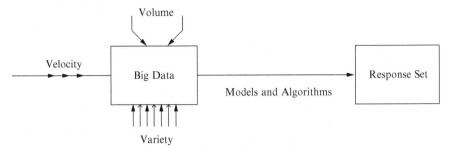

Fig. 6.8 The standard definition of big data classification based on a data domain. It shows the volume, the variety, and the velocity parameters of big data

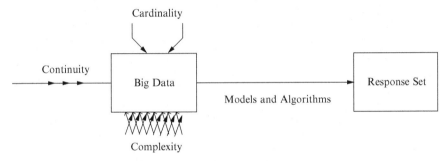

Fig. 6.9 A new definition of big data classification based on data domain. It can help scientific applications to big data environment. It shows cardinality, continuity, and complexity as new parameters for big data

definition has been proposed for big data based on cardinality, continuity, and complexity (C^3) definitions that can help the scientific interpretation of big data [3] for big data classification. This model is illustrated in Fig. 6.9.

As we see in these illustrations, the learning models rely on the characteristics of the data domain. Hence, the learning models must be explained using the characteristics of the data domain. Consider a simple scenario: given the classes (red and blue) shown in Fig. 6.10a and scissors, you are required to have a straight line cut and separate these classes into two pieces. What will you do? You will probably perform a mathematical calculation: (1) you will pick a set of points along the boundary of the class objects as shown in Fig. 6.10b—we may call them support

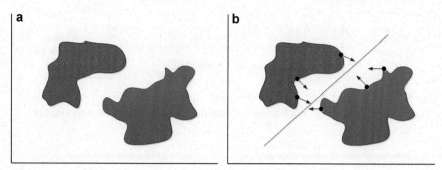

Fig. 6.10 It illustrates a conceptualization of classification as a tool for domain division objectives: (**a**) It shows two classes (*red and blue*), and (**b**) It shows how a linear classifier may be chosen to divide data domain

points, (2) then you will visualize them by moving them along the boundary to find the best straight line (optimal) between the objects (i.e., you include a direction to the points)—hence, we can call them support vectors, and (3) then draw a slope and intercept for the line. Therefore, we can say that you have modeled (or selected) a straight line using some support vectors, and then you applied an optimization algorithm (machine) to select the best straight line. As such, we can call it a support vector algorithm—this became the support vector machine (SVM) [9] in the field of machine learning. As such, we may interpret this classification goal in four ways (or four choices) as shown in Fig. 6.11a–d. The first choice is a linear (straight line) cut, and the linear SVM performs as the cut shown in Fig. 6.11a. In this case, the question is what should be the slope and the intercept of the straight line—they become parameters for the model.

The second choice is to have a few vertical and horizontal cuts as shown in Fig. 6.11b, and this process is performed by a decision tree (DT) technique [10]. In this case, the question is where to cut vertically and horizontally, and they are the parameters for this model. The third choice is to have several vertical and horizontal cuts as shown in Fig. 6.11c. This process is performed by random forest (RF) using many decision trees [11]. In this case, the parameters include the decision trees and their locations of the vertical and horizontal cuts. The fourth choice is to have a smooth cut as demonstrated in Fig. 6.11d. This process is done by deep learning (DL) techniques [12]. These four cases may be grouped as follows: (1) the first case is a mathematical model—SVM, (2) the second and third cases are hierarchical models—DT and RF, and (3) the fourth case is a layered model—DL. There is always one question remaining: which one is the best algorithm? (i.e., which one is the optimal technique?) This can be determined by the machine-learning algorithms.

6.2.1 Mathematical Models

The first approach is mathematical modeling, which classifies by dividing the data domain into two pieces (for example). The first important thing you should know

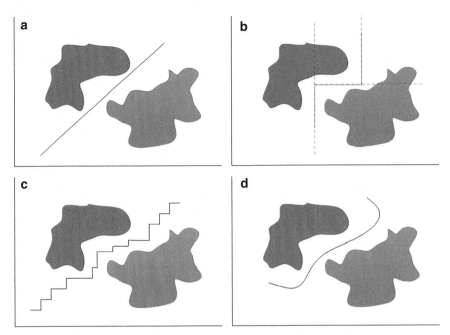

Fig. 6.11 Visualization examples for the classification characteristics of well-known supervised learning algorithms: SVM, DT, RF, and DL. You can now see how these algorithms classify the data by dividing the data domain. (**a**) Linear model: SVM; (**b**) hierarchical model: decision tree; (**c**) hierarchical model: random forest; (**d**) nonlinear model: deep learning

about mathematical modeling is that *they use all the data points in the data domain together to find classifiers*. Therefore, they require that the data domain is defined a priori and available for developing the learning models and algorithms. Several mathematical models have been proposed in the machine learning literature for this purpose. Among them, the support vector machine-based approaches have been well accepted, but they are mathematically intensive. Some of the approaches are: the linear (or standard) support vector machine [9], the nonlinear support vector machine [13], the Lagrangian support vector machine [14], the pq-SVM [15], and the RK-pq-SVM [16]. They can also be grouped into two-class [17] and multi-class [18] support vector machines. Recently scalable support machine algorithms have also been proposed [19], and they are highly suitable for big data applications.

We can conceptualize the working mechanisms of these techniques as follows: We place a straight line (or a hyperplane for higher dimensions) on the data domain and rotate and shift it with the goal of maximizing the classification accuracy using the class label information available on the data domain. Take the example shown in Fig. 6.10 which illustrates the placement of a straight line, adjusting its placement and the orientation so that the straight line can separate the classes optimally. This conceptualized modeling is incorporated in the mathematical derivation of the

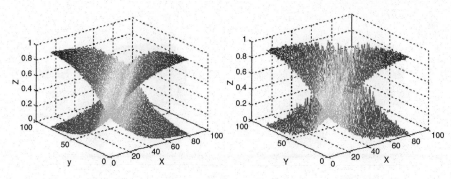

Fig. 6.12 A softmax function and a degraded version

support vector machines. Instead of placing one straight line and transforming it to an optimal one, we can perform it another way and interpret it as follows: For example, you place many straight lines between the classes so that they can separate the classes, and then you calculate their distances from all the points of the classes. Then, maximize the average distances and select the one that is farthest from both classes as the best straight line to classify. In essence, both scenarios parametrize the model and optimize the parameters to reach the maximum classification accuracy.

6.2.2 Hierarchical Models

The second set of approaches is the hierarchical approaches, and they divide the data domain into a few pieces using a small number of vertical and horizontal cuts. While dividing the data domain, it also cuts the classes into pieces and merges them later to form the actual classes. Like the mathematical models, the hierarchical models also *use all the data points in the data domain together to find classifiers*. The well-known hierarchical approaches are the decision tree [10] and random forest [11]. However, several hierarchical models have been proposed based on the DT and RF concepts. Note that the RF approach is a decision tree-based approach, but it uses bootstrap sampling and bagging approaches [20] to create forests of trees randomly and combine them by voting to select the best trees. We can now conceptualize the working mechanisms of the hierarchical techniques as follows: Draw a vertical or horizontal line (or a hyperplane for higher dimensions) to divide the data domain. Suppose we pick the vertical line to split, then shift it horizontally to get the optimal line by using the class label information of all the data points. Now we have two subdomains, and we repeat the same process to both of these domains to divide into more subdomains. We repeat it until no more division is required—the decision may be applied when only the data points of a single class are present in a subdomain.

6.2.3 Layered Models

The layered models are significantly different from the standard mathematical and hierarchical models. They do not use all the data points in the data domain together; instead, they process one data point at a time through a sequence of layers, where each layer carries out a set of related tasks. Thus, they are called layered models. They can divide the data domain like an expert tailor cuts cloth using scissors to form a smooth, curved cut. The concept of layered models is borrowed from the neural network techniques used in artificial intelligence. One of the modern sub-fields of machine learning is called deep learning [12], and its use is significant for big data classification because of its online learning capability. There are several approaches, and they are called deep learning, deep nets, etc. Some of the recent ones are no-drop, drop-out, and dropconnect models [21]. The layered models generally require that the probabilities are defined; therefore, it can benefit from some mathematical functions like softmax function. A two-dimensional softmax function may be defined as follows, based on the generalized function shown in [2]:

$$p_x = \frac{e^{\beta_1 x}}{\left(e^{\beta_1 x} + e^{\beta_2 y}\right)} \tag{6.2}$$

$$p_y = \frac{e^{\beta_2 y}}{\left(e^{\beta_1 x} + e^{\beta_2 y}\right)}, \tag{6.3}$$

where $p_x + p_y = 1$. The first figure in Fig. 6.12 shows a plot of this function, and we can clearly see two properties: (1) the values are mapped between 0 and 1, and (2) both of these functions, p_x and p_y, are complement to each other. These two properties make the softmax function useful to assign probabilities to each data point and classify it. The second figure is a modified version of the softmax function using an additive Gaussian noise.

6.2.4 Comparison of the Models

The three learning models were explained individually based on their ability to divide the data domain and the subdomains that they create. However, it is important to compare them focusing on applications. The following two subsections are dedicated to comparing them with respect to the availability of the data domain and the programming structures.

6.2.4.1 Data Domain Perspective

It is obvious that the domain division is practical only if the data domain is available. In this case, the mathematical and hierarchical models are applicable. As we have seen, the main goal of these models is to divide the data domain using all the data

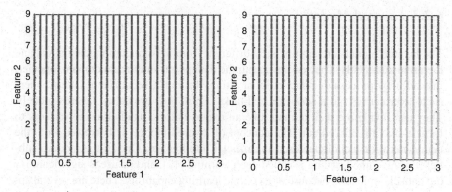

Fig. 6.13 The domain division examples of the mathematical and hierarchical models produced by the code in Listing 6.1

points (observations) in the domain. Each observation can be compared with other observations, and then the data domain can be divided. Thus, these models facilitate batch learning. When the data domain is not available, we only have one observation at a time, and it is not possible to use the information from the other observations. Thus, the models for this scenario can only perform online learning. However, we may create probabilities for the observations to assign a class label. In order to carry this out, we need to establish randomness over each observation and assign certain sets of operations which form layers of tasks, and they are called the layered models.

6.2.4.2 Programming Perspective

In the programming point of view, we can think of mathematical models as the models that adopt the *if-then-else* coding structure. The hierarchical models can be conceptualized as the nested *if-then-else* statements. In contrast, the layered models can be described as a sequence of function calls, where each function performs separate tasks using the results received from the previous function (or the layer). Now the question is how to write such programming structures efficiently, and this objective is the learning algorithm that optimizes the parameters used in the conditions of *if-then-else* statements or in the functions argument list. The coding examples in Listings 6.1 and 6.2 demonstrate the differences in the three types of learning models.

Listing 6.1 A Matlab example—mathematical and hierarchical models

```
1   clear all;
2   close all;
3
4   %%%% Mathematical Modeling
5   figure;
6   for x1=0:0.1:3
7       %mathematical model
```

```
8      x2=2*x1+3;
9      for yy=0:0.1:9
10         %if-then-else
11         if yy>x2
12             aa='.';
13         else
14             aa='r.';
15         end
16         plot(x1,yy,aa);hold on;
17     end
18 end
19
20 %%%% Hierarchical Modeling
21 figure;
22 for x1=0:0.1:3
23     for x2=0:0.1:9
24         %hierarchical model
25         %nested if-then-else
26         if x1<1
27             if x2<3
28                 aa='.';
29             else
30                 aa='r.';
31             end
32         else
33             if x2<6
34                 aa='g.';
35             else
36                 aa='m.';
37             end
38         end
39         plot(x1,x2,aa);hold on;
40     end
41 end
```

The main purpose of the coding in Listing 6.1 is to provide you with a simple insight on mathematical and hierarchical modeling. The block of code in lines 5–18 illustrates a programming structure that can describe the properties of mathematical modeling. In line 8, a simple linear model is presented and lines 11–15 mark the data points above the line with a *blue dot* symbol and the points below the line with a *red dot* symbol. The code in line 16 takes this information and plots it as shown in the first figure in Fig. 6.13. Similarly, the block of code in lines 21–41 illustrates a programming structure which can describe the properties of hierarchical modeling. In hierarchical modeling, the parametrization and domain division are done simultaneously, as shown in the code from line 26 to line 38. When feature 1 is less than 1, if feature 2 is less than 3, then mark the data point with the *blue dot* symbol; otherwise, mark it with the *red dot* symbol. This process is presented in lines 26–31. Similarly, when feature 1 is greater than or equal to 1, if feature 2 is less than 6, then mark the data point with the *green dot* symbol; otherwise, mark it

with the *magenta dot* symbol. The *plot* function in line 39 takes this information as
input and plots it as the second figure shown in Fig. 6.13.

Listing 6.2 A Matlab example—layered models

```
1   clear all;
2   close all;
3
4   randn('seed',138);
5   cc=randn(3,2);
6   randn('seed',534);
7   uu=randn(2,3);
8
9   figure;
10  for x1=0:0.01:1
11      for x2=0:0.01:1
12          %layer 1 tasks
13          y=rlines(cc,[x1;x2]);
14
15          %layer 2 tasks
16          z=renhance(uu,y);
17
18          %layer 3 tasks
19          [p1 p2] = sftmxcal(z);
20
21          if(p1>p2)
22             aa='.';
23          else
24              aa='r.';
25          end
26          plot(x1,x2,aa);hold on;
27      end
28  end
29  xlabel('Feature_1');ylabel('Feature_2');
```

The Listing 6.2 provides a coding example that can help you understand the
meaning of layering the layered model. The layered models also perform the
parametrization and the domain division simultaneously. The block of code in lines
4–7 generates two matrices *cc* and *uu* using Gaussian random numbers. These matrices (i.e., the random numbers) are used to generate some straight lines using the
user-defined function *rlines* in line 13. These straight lines are enhanced using another user-defined function *renhance* in line 16. The purpose of using these user-
defined functions is to show a layering effect. To incorporate the third layer, another
user-defined function *sftmaxcal*, which uses the softmax function to create probabilities for the data points, is added in line 19. These probabilities are used to mark
the data points with a blue dot and a red dot as shown in lines 21–25. Then the data
points are plotted using this color coding, and the resulted image is presented in
Fig. 6.14. The three functions, *rline*, *renhance*, and *sftmaxcal* used in this program
are presented in Listing 6.3.

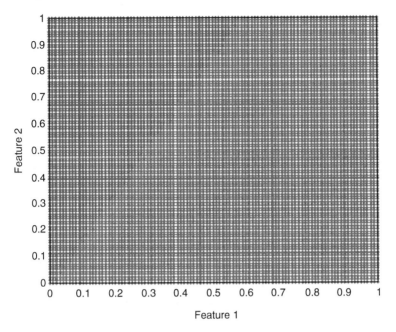

Fig. 6.14 An example layered model's domain division produced by the code in Listing 6.2

Listing 6.3 It presents the functions used in the previous program

```
1  function [y] = rlines(cc,xx)
2
3      y = cc*xx;
4
5  end
6
7  function [z] = renhance(uu,y)
8
9      z=uu*y+0.03*rand(2,1);
10
11 end
12
13 function [p1 p2] = sftmxcal(z)
14
15     p1=exp(z(1))/(exp(z(1))+exp(z(2)));
16     p2=exp(z(2))/(exp(z(1))+exp(z(2)));
17
18 end
```

6.3 Learning Algorithms

Supervised learning algorithms make use of the known data and known responses (as labels—see Fig. 6.7) and use that information to train and validate the model. They can fine-tune the parameters using the labels to derive an optimal model based on the data available. A larger training data set is better because it may have enough labels to train the model to face all possible circumstances; however, it may also lead to a problem called overfitting. Hence, the validation process is required to stop the training early and help alleviate the problem.

6.3.1 Supervised Learning

Supervised learning algorithms for trivial data varies from application to application; however, they fall under three categories: training phase, validation phase, and testing phase [5]. The actual algorithms developed for a particular problem under these categories rest on the designer and the developer of the algorithm. Supervised learning algorithms for big data is more complex. They must take the physical operation into consideration. The volume of the data is unmanageable, the number of class types are large, and the speed required to process the data is high. Hence, it needs distributed file sharing, parallel processing technology, lifelong learning techniques, and cross-domain representation learning techniques [22].

> Supervised learning means building a parametrized model that can divide the data domain, and then optimizing the parameters using training, validation, and testing algorithms. Classification means dividing the data domain.

The training scenario was presented in Fig. 6.7 with an explanation of a mapping concept between the known data and known response set. In this case, the development of models and the application of training algorithms to learn the model parameters are the mapping between the data domain and the response set. The validation scenario is illustrated in Fig. 6.15, and it shows the application of the trained model using a known validation set and its responses. If the validation fails, retraining is required, or it may need an early stopping to avoid an overfitting problem. The testing scenario is explained in Fig. 6.16, and it shows the trained and validated model applied to a new data, and the responses are predicted. In this phase, the labels are not provided to the model or the algorithm, but they can be used to calculate the classification accuracies.

Fig. 6.15 Validation: It illustrates the validation phase of a supervised learning algorithm. The response that we get from the model is the cross-validated response for the input data

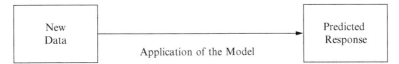

Fig. 6.16 Testing: It illustrates the testing phase of a supervised learning algorithm. The response that we get from the model is the predicted response for the input data

6.3.2 Types of Learning

Supervised learning may be grouped into batch learning and online learning. In batch learning, all the labeled data points in the data domain are used together for learning and optimizing the model parameters. As mentioned before, the mathematical models like the support vector machine and the hierarchical models like the decision tree and the random forest require the entire data set to learn the model parameters. In batch learning, the global information is available for processing because of the availability of the entire data set during training.

The layered models process one data point at a time to learn the model parameters, and thus facilitate online learning. In this approach, the learned parameters are updated at every step using the new observation. Therefore, in the layered models, when an observation is processed, it does not have the information of future data points. In other words, it does not have global information, just the local information. The advantage of the layered models is the online learning, which is highly suitable for big data classification. Additionally, it provides nonlinear classifiers, in contrast to the mathematical and hierarchical models.

In summary, the data domain plays a major role in the machine-learning models and algorithms, especially in the supervised learning paradigm. Therefore, the recommendation is to focus on the data domain and how efficiently it can be divided to maximize the classification accuracy. The classification techniques in the subsequent chapters are explained, focusing on the domain division objectives. If the data domain represents the big data, then the appropriate care must be taken in the development and application of supervised learning models and algorithms. In this case, the big data technologies like the Hadoop distributed file system can also help; however, it is important to understand the properties of the data domain such that the scalable machine learning techniques can be developed.

Problems

6.1. Understanding Parametrization

Write a program to create a data set with the classes similar to the ones shown in Fig. 6.10a and display it on a computer screen with the same color coding. Your program must create a .csv file as well. Then extend your program to generate a straight line as shown in Fig. 6.10b—select your own parameter values for this straight line. Calculate the average of the distances of the points from the lines. Now change the parameter values and select the ones that maximize this distance.

6.2. Steps Toward Understanding Optimization

(a) Write a program to determine whether the point $(2,10)$ is closer to the straight line $y = -x + 5$ or $y = 2x + 3$.
(b) Write a program to create a line that is parallel to $y = 2x + 3$, but closer to the point $(2,10)$ than $y = 2x + 3$. Interpret your results with a detailed discussion.

References

1. T. G. Dietterich, "Machine-learning research: Four current directions," AI Magazine, vol. 18, no. 4, pp. 97–136,1997.
2. T. Hastie, R. Tibshirani, and J. Friedman. The Elements of Statistical Learning. New York: Springer, 2009.
3. S. Suthaharan. "Big data classification: Problems and challenges in network intrusion prediction with machine learning," ACM SIGMETRICS Performance Evaluation Review, vol. 41, no. 4, pp. 70–73, 2014.
4. A. K. Jain. "Data clustering: 50 years beyond K-means." Pattern recognition letters, vol. 31, no. 8, pp. 651–666, 2010.
5. S. B. Kotsiantis. "Supervised machine learning: A review of classification techniques," Informatica 31, pp. 249–268, 2007.
6. O. Okun, and G. Valentini (Eds.), "Supervised and unsupervised ensemble methods and their applications," Studies in Computational Intelligence series, vol. 126, 2008.
7. M. Ji, T. Yang, B. Lin, R. Jin, and J. Han. "A simple algorithm for semi-supervised learning with improved generalization error bound," in Proceedings of the 29th International Conference on Machine Learning, pp. 1223–1230, 2012.
8. M.G. Lagoudakis and R. Parr. "Reinforcement learning as classification: Leveraging modern classifiers," in Proceedings of the 20th International Conference on Machine Learning, vol. 3, pp. 424–431, 2003.
9. M. A. Hearst, S. T. Dumais, E. Osman, J. Platt, and B. Scholkopf. "Support vector machines." Intelligent Systems and their Applications, IEEE, vol. 13, no. 4, pp. 18–28, 1998.
10. L. Rokach, and O. Maimon. "Top-down induction of decision trees classifiers-a survey." IEEE Transactions on Systems, Man, and Cybernetics, Part C: Applications and Reviews, vol. 35, no. 4, pp. 476–487, 2005.
11. L. Breiman, "Random forests." Machine learning 45, pp. 5–32, 2001.
12. G. E. Hinton, N. Srivastava, A. Krizhevsky, I. Sutskever, and R. R. Salakhutdinov. "Improving neural networks by preventing co-adaptation of feature detectors," arXiv preprint arXiv:1207.0580, 2012.
13. D. Meyer, F. Leisch, and K. Hornik. "The support vector machine under test." Neurocomputing 55, pp. 169–186, 2003.

14. O. L. Mangasarian and D. R. Musicant. 2000. "LSVM Software: Active set support vector machine classification software." Available online at http://research.cs.wisc.edu/dmi/lsvm/.

15. M. Dunbar, J. M. Murray, L. A. Cysique, B. J. Brew, and V. Jeyakumar. "Simultaneous classification and feature selection via convex quadratic programming with application to HIV-associated neurocognitive disorder assessment." European Journal of Operational Research 206(2): pp. 470–478, 2010.

16. V. Jeyakumar, G. Li, and S. Suthaharan. "Support vector machine classifiers with uncertain knowledge sets via robust optimization." Optimization, pp. 1–18, 2012.

17. G. Huang, H. Chen, Z. Zhou, F. Yin and K. Guo. "Two-class support vector data description." Pattern Recognition, 44, pp. 320–329, 2011.

18. V. Franc, and V. Hlavac. "Multi-class support vector machine." In Proceedings of the IEEE 16th International Conference on Pattern Recognition, vol. 2, pp. 236–239, 2002.

19. D. Wang, J. Zheng, Y. Zhou, and J. Li. "A scalable support vector machine for distributed classification in ad hoc sensor networks." Neurocomputing, vol. 74, no. 1, pp. 394–400, 2010.

20. L. Breiman. "Bagging predictors." Machine learning 24, pp. 123–140, 1996.

21. L. Wan, M. Zeiler, S. Zhang, Y. LeCun, and R. Fergus. "Regularization of neural networks using dropconnect." In Proceedings of the 30th International Conference on Machine Learning (ICML-13), pp. 1058–1066, 2013.

22. W. Tu, and S. Sun, "Cross-domain representation-learning framework with combination of class-separate and domain-merge objectives," In: Proceedings of the CDKD 2012 Conference, pp. 18–25, 2012.

Chapter 7
Supervised Learning Models

Abstract The main objective of this chapter is to discuss various supervised learning models in detail. The supervised learning models provide parametrized mapping that projects a data domain into a response set, and thus helps extract knowledge (known) from data (unknown). These learning models, in simple form, can be grouped into predictive models and classification models. Firstly, the predictive models, such as the standard regression, ridge regression, lasso regression, and elastic-net regression are discussed in detail with their mathematical and visual interpretations using simple examples. Secondly, the classification models are discussed and grouped into three models: mathematical models, hierarchical models, and layered models. Also discussed are the mathematical models, such as the logistic regression and support vector machine; the hierarchical models, like the decision tree and the random forest; and the layered models, like the deep learning. They are discussed only from the modeling point of view, and they will be discussed in detail together as the modeling and algorithms in separate chapters later in the book.

7.1 Supervised Learning Objectives

Supervised learning [1] has two main objectives: parametrization objectives and optimization objectives. These objectives may be defined and differentiated using the continuous and discrete nature of the response variables [2]. The parametrization objective is defined as regression-related action if the response set is continuous, and it is defined as classification-related action if the response set is discrete. The main idea for defining these objectives is to develop supervised learning models first, then efficient supervised learning algorithms. The regression-related objectives in general have two parts: the prediction and the optimization [3]. It also has a regularization component, but it can be part of the prediction requirement. Similarly, the classification-related objectives have two parts: the classification and the optimization. As an example, look at Fig. 1.3b. It shows two sets (classes) of data points.

© Springer Science+Business Media New York 2016

S. Suthaharan, *Machine Learning Models and Algorithms for Big
Data Classification*, Integrated Series in Information Systems 36,
DOI 10.1007/978-1-4899-7641-3_7

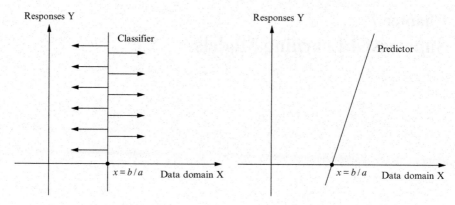

Fig. 7.1 Domain division by a classifier and a predictor

We may divide them by the straight line as shown in the figure—this is a classifier. However, if we ask different people to divide the two classes, they may come up with different straight lines (i.e., the classifiers). Then the question becomes which one is the best classifier; to answer this question, we need an optimizer. This is the reason the support vector machine-based techniques use the so-called support vectors (i.e., some of the most suitable data points) to determine the optimal classifier [4, 5].

7.1.1 Parametrization Objectives

Let us start with a simple example by designating the mathematical expression $ax - b$, where $x \in X$, and X is the data domain. If we assume $ax - b = 0$, then we have a vertical line at $x = b/a$ as shown in Fig. 7.1a. If we assume y is a response variable in the response set Y associated with the changes in the parameters a and b, and define $ax - b = y$, then we have a straight line with a slope a and an intercept $-b$ as shown in Fig. 7.1b. If we consider these two straight lines, we can see both of them divide the data domain into two subdomains, but the first one allows the same labeling to all the points (x) in a subdomain as illustrated in Fig. 7.2a, and the second one does not allow as shown in Fig. 7.2b. Therefore, the first line is suitable for classifications, and the second line is suitable for regression. This is a simple way of distinguishing the classification and regression definitions.

7.1.1.1 Prediction Point of View

The above considered example divided the one-dimensional data domain $(x \in X)$ with a response variable $y \in Y$, and parametrized the domain division. It is illustrated in Fig. 7.3a. Now assume that the data domain is two-dimensional, and they are represented by X_1 and X_2 as shown in Fig. 7.3b. In this particular case, we may

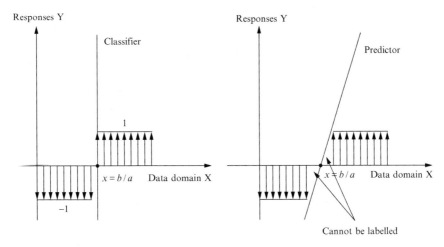

Fig. 7.2 An important difference between a classifier and a predictor

consider the mathematical expression $a_1x_1 + a_2x_2 - b$ as a learning model. If we now incorporate the response variable y, and assume $a_1x_1 + a_2x_2 - b = y$, then we have a regression-related problem. It can be written in the following matrix form: $[a_1, a_2][x_1, x_2]' - b = y$. It expresses the fitting of a regression plane to the data points in a two-dimensional data domain. Following the same parametrization steps, we can define a hyperplane regression for the data points in higher dimensions, and as such we can generalize this regression model and parametrize it in a matrix form:

$$y = A\mathbf{x}' - b \tag{7.1}$$

In this equation, A and b represent the slope and intercept parameters of the regression plane that is defined by this linear equation. Also note that the symbol $\mathbf{x}'$ is the transpose of the matrix $\mathbf{x}$. This section helped you understand the generalization of a regression model from a simple example; now we can take similar steps to define the classification problem.

7.1.1.2 Classification Point of View

For the purpose of classification, we must define $a_1x_1 + a_2x_2 - b = 0$ so that we can create a plane that can divide the data domain X_1X_2 into two subdomains D_1 and D_2, such that all the points in a subdomain can be labeled the same:

$$D_1 = \{(x_1, x_2) : [a_1, a_2][x_1, x_2]' - b \leq 0\} \tag{7.2}$$

$$D_2 = \{(x_1, x_2) : [a_1, a_2][x_1, x_2]' - b > 0\} \tag{7.3}$$

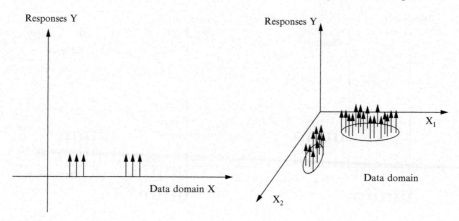

Fig. 7.3 An important difference between classification (classifier) and regression (predictor)

Therefore, our classifiers may be defined: $[a_1,a_2][x_1,x_2]' - b = -1$ for the data points in domain D_1 and $[a_1,a_2][x_1,x_2]' - b = 1$ for the data points in domain D_2. Following the same parametrization steps, we can define the high-dimensional classifiers for the data points in a three-dimensional data domain, four-dimensional data domain, and so on. We can generalize this classification model and parametrize it in the following matrix form:

$$Ax' - b = -1; x \in D_1 \tag{7.4}$$

$$Ax' - b = 1; x \in D_2 \tag{7.5}$$

and the subdomains are:

$$D_1 = \{x : Ax' - B \leq 0\} \tag{7.6}$$

$$D_2 = \{x : Ax' - B > 0\} \tag{7.7}$$

Equation (7.1) and the set of equations in Eqs. (7.4)–(7.7) provide parameter models; however, there are many possible values for the parameters. The selection of such possible values satisfies the parametrization objectives. Once we defined them, then the objective is to select the optimal values for the parameters. It is called the optimization objectives, and it is discussed below.

7.1.2 Optimization Objectives

The simplest way to explain the optimization objective is to select several models, and then select the best model using a distance measure and the labeled data sets provided. The optimization cannot be done unless the labeled data set is given. Therefore, the optimization process must be defined mathematically or structurally, assuming the availability of a labeled data set.

Table 7.1 Regression—results using equation $x_2 = 0.5x_1 + 3.0$

x_1	Predicted x_2	Actual x_2	Difference	Squared	MSE	RMSE
2.0	$0.5 \times 2.0 + 3 = 4.00$	2.0	-2.00	4.00	9.26	3.04
3.0	$0.5 \times 3.0 + 3 = 4.50$	3.0	-1.50	2.25	9.26	3.04
1.0	$0.5 \times 1.0 + 3 = 3.50$	6.0	2.50	6.25	9.26	3.04
2.5	$0.5 \times 2.5 + 3 = 4.25$	9.5	5.25	27.56	9.26	3.04
2.0	$0.5 \times 2.0 + 3 = 4.00$	6.5	2.50	6.25	9.26	3.04

Table 7.2 Classification—results using equation $x_2 = 0.5x_1 + 3.0$

x_1	x_2	Distance Calculation	Distance	Assigned label	Class label	Match label	Avg
2.0	2.0	$(0.5 \times 2.0 - 1 \times 2.0 + 3)/1.12$	1.79	$+1$	$+1$	1	2.46
3.0	3.0	$(0.5 \times 3.0 - 1 \times 3.0 + 3)/1.12$	1.34	$+1$	$+1$	1	2.46
1.0	6.0	$(0.5 \times 1.0 - 1 \times 6.0 + 3)/1.12$	-2.24	-1	-1	1	2.46
2.5	9.5	$(0.5 \times 2.5 - 1 \times 9.5 + 3)/1.12$	-4.69	-1	-1	1	2.46
2.0	6.5	$(0.5 \times 2.0 - 1 \times 6.5 + 3)/1.12$	-2.24	-1	-1	1	2.46

7.1.2.1 Prediction Point of View

It is convenient if we first understand the optimization objectives through a simple example before exploring the actual mathematical implementation. Suppose we have five data points: (2,2), (3,3), (1,6), (2.5,9.5), and (2,6.5), where the first numbers in the tuples are the data points (x), and the second numbers are the responses (y), and we want to fit regression models. Suppose we have selected four models: (1) $y = 0.5x + 3.0$, (2) $y = 1.5x + 0.5$, (3) $y = 2.0x + 2.0$, and (4) $y = 3.5x + 3.0$, then we can select the best model that leads to a minimum mean squared error (MSE) or root mean squared error (RMSE) [3]. The RMSE values of these models are: 3.04, 3.43, 3.21, and 6.19, respectively. From these values, we can determine $y = 0.5x + 3.0$ is the best model, and it is highlighted in red in Fig. 7.4a with other models.

Table 7.1. shows the steps used to calculate the RMSE for the first straight line and, using the same steps, the RMSE values for the other straight lines are calculated. Hence, the best regression line for this data set is the first straight line $y = 0.5x + 3.0$, and it is highlighted in red in Fig. 7.4a. Now suppose we want to find the classifier that defines the classes 1 and -1 shown in Fig. 7.4b. In this case, we should calculate the perpendicular distances from the points to a straight line (a model) and minimize the average distance. The following subsection ellaborates this classification example.

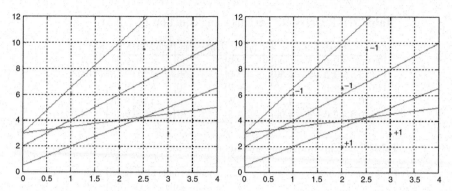

Fig. 7.4 It illustrates four possible classifiers for a set of five points—the horizontal axis represents the variable x_1 and the vertical axis represents the variable x_2

7.1.2.2 Classification Point of View

Suppose we now label the five data points: $(2,2,1)$, $(3,3,1)$, $(1,6,-1)$, $(2.5,9.5,-1)$, and $(2,6.5,-1)$, where the first two points $(2,2)$ and $(3,3)$ are labeled as class 1 (i.e., the response y is equal to 1), and the next three points are labeled as class -1. Hence, in this case we have a two-dimensional data domain with responses 1 and -1 in the third dimension. Now suppose we select the same straight lines for the classification (i.e., to divide the data domain), then the four models are: (1) $x_2 = 0.5x_1 + 3.0$, (2) $x_2 = 1.5x_1 + 0.5$, (3) $x_2 = 2.0x_1 + 2.0$, and (4) $x_2 = 3.5x_1 + 3.0$. In this particular case, we should consider the perpendicular distances of the points from the lines.

Table 7.2 shows the steps to calculate those distances using the first model $y = 0.5x + 3.0$. The variable y is considered as another feature (or independent variable) in this case. Similarly the averages of the perpendicular distances for the other straight lines have been calculated. The averages of the perpendicular distance values, with respect to these lines are: 2.46, 1.75, 1.25, and 1.36, thus the best line is the third straight line, which is highlighted in red in Fig. 7.4b. We can also see that this is one of the straight lines that classifies the classes with zero false positives [6], which is one of the measures that can be used for classification.

7.2 Regression Models

Regression models are predictors and they are suitable for the systems that produce continuous responses. There are several regression models, which include standard regression, ridge regression, lasso regression, and elastic-net regression [7, 8].

7.2.1 *Continuous Response*

The continuous response variable Y of a system may be modeled using a linear relationship between X and the domain variable x. Consider a simple two- dimensional parametrized model for these variables as follows:

$$Y = aX \tag{7.8}$$

If the actual responses are y, and the domain values are x, then we can define a nonlinear error factor as follows:

$$E = (y - ax)^2 \tag{7.9}$$

A minimization of this error and distinct regularization are contributors to the regression models, like regular regression, ridge regression, lasso regression, and elastic-net regression [3, 7]. The continuous property of the variables x and y allows the application of derivatives for minimization. This principle of derivatives is also true when the model is high dimensional with vector model representation as follows:

$$E = (y - A\mathbf{x})^2 \tag{7.10}$$

When a data domain and its corresponding response values are available, we should be able to estimate the parameter (matrix) A from this error minimization, and thus we can have the model defined in Eq. (7.8) as a predictive model.

7.2.2 *Theory of Regression Models*

In the regression models, the parameter a plays a major role in minimizing the error as a slope parameter and a regularization parameter. There are different ways of calculating this parameter, and thus we have different approaches [3, 7]. These approaches are discussed in this section.

7.2.2.1 Standard Regression

In the regular regression, the classification objective is achieved by defining a parametrized model using the simple model $y = ax$. Then the optimization objective is achieved through the minimization of the following error factor with respect to the parameter a:

$$E = (y - ax)^2 \tag{7.11}$$

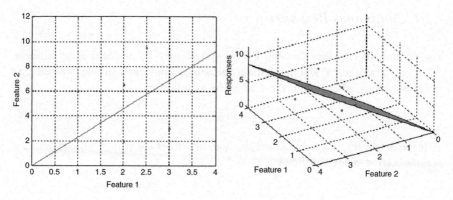

Fig. 7.5 Results of the standard regression model

To minimize the error function with respect to the parameter a, we can operate a partial derivative. This will give us the following:

$$\frac{\partial E}{\partial a} = 2(y - ax)(-x) = 0 \tag{7.12}$$

This equality gives us the following estimate for a that minimizes the error factor:

$$a = \frac{yx}{x^2} \tag{7.13}$$

In another form we can write this estimate as follows:

$$a = yx(x^2)^{-1} \tag{7.14}$$

If we now generalize this estimate for the vector (matrix) model $E = (y - A\mathbf{x})^2$, then we will have the following [3, 7]:

$$A = y\mathbf{x}'(\mathbf{x}\mathbf{x}')^{-1} \tag{7.15}$$

with the model $y = A\mathbf{x}$.

Thinking with Example 7.1:

The coding example listed in Listing 7.1 uses the models in Eqs. (7.14) and (7.15), and fits the one-dimensional regression model (i.e., a straight line) and the two-dimensional regression model (i.e., a plane) to a given set of data. Figures 7.5 and 7.6 show these results, respectively. In this coding example, lines 5 and 6 declare an independent variable x (i.e., one-dimensional data domain) and its response variable y, respectively. These variables are used to calculate the parameter A in line 8 using the equation in Eq. (7.15). The standard regression model defined as a part of Eq. (7.15) is implemented in lines 10 and 11, and the results are then plotted in lines 13 and 14. These blocks of codes produced the scatter plot presented in the first figure of Fig. 7.5. As we can see, the standard regression model fits very well with the data points used and plotted in the figure.

Listing 7.1 A Matlab example—standard regression

```
1   clear all;
2   close all;
3
4   %%% 1D Data Domain
5   x=[2 3 1 2 2.5];
6   y=[2 3 6 6.5 9.5];
7
8   A=y*x'*inv(x*x');
9
10  xt=[0 4];
11  yt=A*xt;
12
13  figure;plot(x,y,'.');axis([0 4 0 12]);grid on;
14  hold on;line(xt,yt);xlabel('Feature_1');ylabel('Feature_2');
15
16  %%% 2D Data Domain
17  x1=[2 3 1 2 2.5];
18  x2=[2 3 2.1 2 2.5];
19  yy=[2 3 6 6.5 9.5];
20
21  xx=[x1; x2];
22  AA=yy*xx'*inv(xx*xx');
23
24  xx1=[0 0 4 4];
25  xx2=[0 4 0 4];
26  xxx=[xx1; xx2];
27
28  yy1=AA*xxx;
29  yy2=reshape(yy1,2,2);
30  [mg1,mg2]=meshgrid(0:4:4);
31
32  figure;plot3(x1,x2,yy,'r.');grid on;axis([0 4 0 4 0 12]);
33  hold on;surf(mg1,mg2,yy2);view([259 44]);
34  xlabel('Feature_1');ylabel('Feature_2');zlabel('Responses');
```

Similarly, a two-dimensional dependent variable (x) (i.e., a two-dimensional data domain) is defined in lines 17 and 18 along with its response variable y in line 19. The block of code in lines 21 and 22 calculate the parameter A presented in Eq. (7.15), and the standard regression model is defined in line 28. The rest of the program generates the three-dimensional plot in Fig. 7.5.

7.2.2.2 Ridge Regression

For this model the regularization parameter λa^2 is added to the error factor stated in the regular regression model [3, 7]:

$$E = (y - ax)^2 + \lambda a^2 \qquad (7.16)$$

To minimize the error function with respect to the parameter a, we can operate a partial derivative. This will give us the following:

$$\frac{\partial E}{\partial a} = 2(y - ax)(-x) + 2\lambda a = 0 \qquad (7.17)$$

This equality gives us the following estimate for a that minimizes the error factor:

$$a = \frac{yx}{x^2 + \lambda} \qquad (7.18)$$

In another form, we can write this estimate as follows:

$$a = yx(x^2 + \lambda)^{-1} \qquad (7.19)$$

If we now generalize this estimate for the vector (matrix) model $E = (y - A\mathbf{x})^2 + \lambda ||A||^2$, then we will have the following [3, 7]:

$$A = y\mathbf{x}'(\mathbf{x}\mathbf{x}' + \lambda I)^{-1} \qquad (7.20)$$

with the model $y = A\mathbf{x}$.

Thinking with Example 7.2:

The coding example provided in Listing 7.2 uses the ridge regression models in Eqs. (7.19) and (7.20). The one-dimensional and two-dimensional ridge regression models are applied to the data sets used in the previous Thinking with Example. The three-dimensional ridge regression result is presented in the first figure of Fig. 7.6.

Listing 7.2 A Matlab example—ridge regression

```
1  clear all;
2  close all;
3
4  %%% 1D Data Domain
5  x=[2 3 1 2 2.5];
6  y=[2 3 6 6.5 9.5];
7  lamda=0.1;
8
```

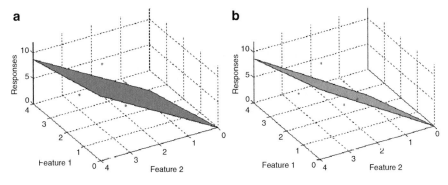

Fig. 7.6 (**a**) Results of the ridge regression. (**b**) Results of the Lasso regression

```
9   A=y*x'*inv(x*x'+lamda);
10
11  xt=[0 4];
12  yt=A*xt;
13
14  figure;plot(x,y,'.');axis([0 4 0 12]);grid on;
15  hold on;line(xt,yt);xlabel('Feature_1');ylabel('Feature_2');
16
17  %%% 2D Data Domain
18  x1=[2 3 1 2 2.5];
19  x2=[2 3 2.1 2 2.5];
20  yy=[2 3 6 6.5 9.5];
21
22  xx=[x1; x2];
23  nn=length(xx*xx');
24  AA=yy*xx'*inv(xx*xx'+lamda*eye(nn));
25
26  xx1=[0 0 4 4];
27  xx2=[0 4 0 4];
28  xxx=[xx1; xx2];
29
30  yy1=AA*xxx;
31  yy2=reshape(yy1,2,2);
32  [mg1,mg2]=meshgrid(0:4:4);
33
34  figure;plot3(x1,x2,yy,'r.');grid on;axis([0 4 0 4 0 12]);
35  hold on;surf(mg1,mg2,yy2);view([-120 47]);
36  xlabel('Feature_1');ylabel('Feature_2');zlabel('Responses');
```

This program is similar to the one in Listing 7.1, but the calculation of the model parameter *A* presented in the corresponding blocks of codes is different, which is based on the ridge regression model.

7.2.2.3 Lasso Regression

The word *lasso* stands for Least Absolute Shrinkage and Selection Operator. The definition of Lasso has been presented in generalized forms in many books and research papers, including [3, 7], and [8]; however, it is easier if we simplify its definition by adding the regularization parameter $\lambda|a|$ to the error factor as shown:

$$E = (y - ax)^2 + \lambda|a| \tag{7.21}$$

To minimize the error factor with respect to the parameter a, we can apply a partial derivative operator. This application will give us the following:

$$\frac{\partial E}{\partial a} = 2(y - ax)(-x) + \lambda\frac{\partial|a|}{\partial a} = 0 \tag{7.22}$$

We can write $|a| = \sqrt{a^2}$, therefore

$$\frac{\partial|a|}{\partial a} = \frac{1}{2}(a^2)^{-\frac{1}{2}}2a = \frac{a}{|a|} \tag{7.23}$$

If we substitute this partial derivative in Eq. (7.22), then we can get the following estimate for the parameter a that minimizes the error factor in Eq. (7.21):

$$a = \frac{yx - \frac{\lambda}{2}\frac{a}{|a|}}{x^2} \tag{7.24}$$

If we assume a is a positive number, then we have the fraction $\frac{a}{|a|} = 1$, and if we assume a is a negative number, then we have $\frac{a}{|a|} = -1$. Therefore, the fraction $\frac{a}{|a|}$ describes the sign of the parameter a. Hence, we can rewrite Eq. (7.24) as follows:

$$a = \left(yx - \frac{\lambda}{2}s\right)(x^2)^{-1} \tag{7.25}$$

where $s = 1$ if a is positive and $s = -1$ if a is negative.

If we now generalize this estimate for the vector (matrix) model $E = (y - A\mathbf{x})^2 + \lambda||A||$, then we will have the following [3, 7]:

$$A = \left(y\mathbf{x}' - \frac{\lambda}{2}s\right)(\mathbf{x}\mathbf{x}')^{-1} \tag{7.26}$$

with the model $y = A\mathbf{x}$.

Thinking with Example 7.3:

The program in Listing 7.3 illustrates the Lasso regression model. The lasso regression model in Eq. (7.26) is implemented as one-dimensional and two-dimensional data domain examples.

Listing 7.3 A Matlab example—lasso regression

```
1   clear all;
2   close all;
3
4   %%% 1D Data Domain
5   x=[2 3 1 2 2.5];
6   y=[2 3 6 6.5 9.5];
7   lamda=0.1;
8
9   A1=y*x'*inv(x*x');
10  S=sign(A1);
11
12  A=(y*x'-S*lamda/2)*inv(x*x');
13
14  xt=[0 4];
15  yt=A*xt;
16
17  figure;plot(x,y,'.');axis([0 4 0 12]);grid on;
18  hold on;line(xt,yt);xlabel('Feature_1');ylabel('Feature_2');
19
20  %%% 2D Data Domain
21  x1=[2 3 1 2 2.5];
22  x2=[2 3 2.1 2 2.5];
23  yy=[2 3 6 6.5 9.5];
24
25  xx=[x1; x2];
26  nn=length(xx*xx');
27
28  AA1=yy*xx'*inv(xx*xx');
29  SS=sign(AA1);
30
31  AA=(yy*xx'-SS*(lamda/2))*inv(xx*xx');
32
33  xx1=[0 0 4 4];
34  xx2=[0 4 0 4];
35  xxx=[xx1; xx2];
36
37  yy1=AA*xxx;
38  yy2=reshape(yy1,2,2);
39  [mg1,mg2]=meshgrid(0:4:4);
40
41  figure;plot3(x1,x2,yy,'r.');grid on;axis([0 4 0 4 0 12]);
42  hold on;surf(mg1,mg2,yy2);view([-120 47]);
43  xlabel('Feature_1');ylabel('Feature_2');zlabel('Responses');
```

The three-dimensional results of this program (i.e., the lasso regression example) are presented in the second figure of Fig. 7.6. Comparing the results of standard regression, ridge regression, and lasso regression results in Figs. 7.5 and 7.6, we can only see a slight difference between the models. Note that the data is small, thus significant differences are not expected. You must apply these techniques to large data sets to observe the differences.

7.2.2.4 Elastic-Net Regression

For this model, both regularization parameters $\lambda_1 a^2$ and $\lambda_2 a$ are added to the error factor stated in the regular regression model [3, 7, 8].

$$E = (y - ax)^2 + \lambda_1 a^2 + \lambda_2 |a| \tag{7.27}$$

To minimize the error function with respect to the parameter a we can operate a partial derivative. This will give us the following:

$$\frac{\partial E}{\partial a} = 2(y - ax)(-x) + 2\lambda_1 a + \lambda_2 \frac{a}{|a|} = 0 \tag{7.28}$$

This equality gives us the following estimate for a that minimizes the error factor:

$$a = \frac{yx - \frac{\lambda_2}{2} s}{x^2 + \lambda_1} \tag{7.29}$$

In another form, we can write this estimate as follows:

$$a = \left(yx - \frac{\lambda_2}{2} s \right) (x^2 + \lambda_1)^{-1} \tag{7.30}$$

If we now generalize this estimate for the vector (matrix) model $E = (y - A\mathbf{x})^2 + \lambda ||A||^2$, then we will have the following [3, 7]:

$$A = \left(y\mathbf{x}' - \frac{\lambda_2}{2} s \right) (\mathbf{x}\mathbf{x}' + \lambda_1 I)^{-1} \tag{7.31}$$

with the model $y = A\mathbf{x}$.

Thinking with Example 7.4:

The coding example for the illustration of the elastic-net regression is presented in Listing 7.4. The results of this program are given in Fig. 7.7. The results from two different viewpoints are presented to show the disappearance of some points; however, it fits the model for the points considered.

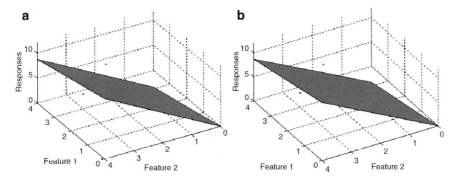

Fig. 7.7 (**a**) Results of the elastic-net regression model at a viewpoint 1. (**b**) Results of the elastic-net regression model at a viewpoint 2

Listing 7.4 A Matlab example—elastic-net regression

```
1   clear all;
2   close all;
3
4   %%% 1D Data Domain
5   x=[2 3 1 2 2.5];
6   y=[2 3 6 6.5 9.5];
7   lamda1=0.1;
8   lamda2=0.2;
9
10  A1=y*x'*inv(x*x');
11  S=sign(A1);
12
13  A=(y*x'-(lamda2/2)*S)*inv(x*x'+lamda1);
14
15  xt=[0 4];
16  yt=A*xt;
17
18  figure;plot(x,y,'.');axis([0 4 0 12]);grid on;
19  hold on;line(xt,yt);xlabel('Feature_1');ylabel('Feature_2');
20
21  %%% 2D Data Domain
22  x1=[2 3 1 2 2.5];
23  x2=[2 3 2.1 2 2.5];
24  yy=[2 3 6 6.5 9.5];
25
26  xx=[x1; x2];
27
28  AA1=yy*xx'*inv(xx*xx');
29  SS=sign(AA1);
30
31  nn=length(xx*xx');
32  AA=(yy*xx'-(lamda2/2)*SS)*inv(xx*xx'+lamda1*eye(nn));
33
```

```
34   xx1=[0  0  4  4];
35   xx2=[0  4  0  4];
36   xxx=[xx1;  xx2];
37
38   yy1=AA*xxx;
39   yy2=reshape(yy1,2,2);
40   [mg1,mg2]=meshgrid(0:4:4);
41
42   figure;plot3(x1,x2,yy,'r.');grid on;axis([0 4 0 4 0 12]);
43   hold on;surf(mg1,mg2,yy2);view([-120 47]);
44   xlabel('Feature_1');ylabel('Feature_2');zlabel('Responses');
45
46   figure;plot3(x1,x2,yy,'r.');grid on;axis([0 4 0 4 0 12]);
47   hold on;surf(mg1,mg2,yy2);view([-120 50]);
48   xlabel('Feature_1');ylabel('Feature_2');zlabel('Responses');
```

Once again, significant differences cannot be observed between the results of the four regression models. These examples are given to help readers understand the theory and implementation of the models.

7.3 Classification Models

Classification models are suitable for the system that produces discrete responses. There are several classification models that may be grouped under mathematically intensive models, hierarchical models, and layered models. Some of these models discussed in this book are the support vector machine [9], decision tree [10], random forest [11], and deep learning [12]. We have discussed their differences in terms of domain division perspectives and programming perspectives. However, they can be distinguished more meaningfully with respect to the data domain and the subspace management and manipulation. The mathematical and hierarchical models manage and manipulate the data domain, and the shallow and deep learning models manage and manipulate feature space. Figure 7.8 illustrates these differences.

7.3.1 Discrete Response

The nature of the discrete responses of a system has been illustrated in Fig. 7.9 using two color labels (red and blue). The first figure in Fig. 7.9 shows a data domain (X) with two classes, but the second figure shows a third dimension that represents the responses (Y), red and blue, from the classes. These discrete responses, red and blue, may be represented by 1 and 0, respectively. Let us first represent the mathematical relationship between the data domain X and the response set Y using the same model we assumed for the continuous case:

$$Y = aX \tag{7.32}$$

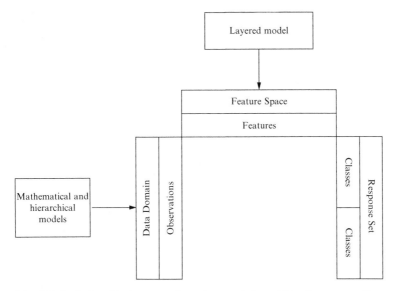

Fig. 7.8 Relationship between learning models and big data controllers

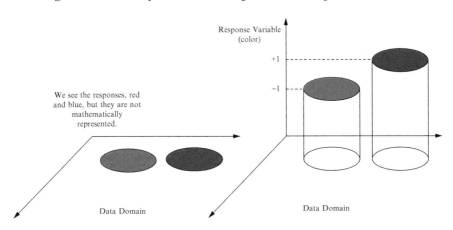

Fig. 7.9 The effect of discrete responses

However, in this equation, X is continuous, and Y is discrete. In a visual sense, this mathematical relationship forms a staircase effect so it is difficult to fit a linear or nonlinear mathematical model for the data. Therefore, we must define an intermediate response set, which is continuous to fit a model and then apply some thresholding techniques to map them to discrete values. This is the reason the logistic regression defines the following intermediate mathematical equation [3]:

$$\log\left(\frac{p}{1-p}\right) = aX \tag{7.33}$$

where the new intermediate variable represents a probability p, and it gives us:

$$p = \frac{e^{ax}}{1 + e^{ax}} \tag{7.34}$$

This definition helps the logistic regression to define an error factor using an entropy with respect to probabilities and find the optimal parameter a. A similar concept of introducing intermediate variables has been used in the SVM models.

7.3.2 Mathematical Models

The two mathematical learning models considered in this section are logistic regression and SVM techniques. The logistic regression model has been built upon the probability nature of the classes, and the SVM model has been built upon the separability nature of the classes. In the following subsections, these two mathematical models are discussed using fewer variables and simple examples. The explanation includes the optimization of an error factor and derivation of the models.

7.3.2.1 Logistic Regression

A discussion on generalized logistic regression can be found in detail in the book by Hastie et al. [3]. The logistic regression provides a classification model, and this model is presented in this section with fewer variables and a simple two-class classification example. The logistic regression focuses on minimizing the entropy E, and it can be defined for a two-class problem as follows:

$$E = y\log(p) + (1 - y)\log(1 - p) \tag{7.35}$$

In this equation, y is the class label either 0 or 1, and p is the probability of the class label y is detected. It can be simplified as follows:

$$E = \log(1 - p) + y\log\frac{p}{(1 - p)} \tag{7.36}$$

If we now assume the probability p satisfies a logistic function with a parameter a, then we can define the probabilities p and $1 - p$ as follows:

$$p = \frac{e^{ax}}{1 + e^{ax}} \tag{7.37}$$

$$1 - p = \frac{1}{1 + e^{ax}} \tag{7.38}$$

By substituting these mathematical expressions for both p and $1 - p$ in Eq. (7.36), we can rewrite it with the following equation:

$$E = \log \frac{1}{1 + e^{ax}} + y \log e^{ax} \tag{7.39}$$

This equation can be simplified as follows:

$$E = -\log(1 + e^{ax}) + yax \tag{7.40}$$

If we now apply a partial derivative operator with respect to the parameter a, then we get the following equation:

$$\frac{\partial E}{\partial a} = yx - \frac{e^{ax}}{1 + e^{ax}} x = 0 \tag{7.41}$$

We have defined a mathematical expression for the probability p in Eq. (7.37), and if we substitute it in the above equation, we can get the following:

$$\frac{\partial E}{\partial a} = (y - p)x = 0 \tag{7.42}$$

The next step is to derive an expression for the second derivative from Eq. (7.41). As discussed by Hastie et al. [3], a second derivative is important to update the parameter a. The results of the application of the second partial derivative are:

$$\frac{\partial^2 E}{\partial a^2} = -\frac{(1 + e^{ax})xe^{ax}x - e^{ax}xe^{ax}x}{(1 + e^{ax})^2} = 0 \tag{7.43}$$

$$\frac{\partial^2 E}{\partial a^2} = -\frac{xe^{ax}x}{(1 + e^{ax})^2} = 0 \tag{7.44}$$

$$\frac{\partial^2 E}{\partial a^2} = -x \frac{e^{ax}}{(1 + e^{ax})} \frac{1}{(1 + e^{ax})} x = 0 \tag{7.45}$$

By substituting the mathematical expression in Eq. (7.37) for p, we can simplify the above equation and obtain the following:

$$\frac{\partial^2 E}{\partial a^2} = -xp(1 - p)x = 0 \tag{7.46}$$

By representing $p(1 - p)$ with w, we can rewrite this equation as follows:

$$\frac{\partial^2 E}{\partial a^2} = -xwx = 0 \tag{7.47}$$

We can now use the Newton–Raphson approach as Hastie et al. used in their book [3] to update the logistic regression parameter a:

$$a_{\text{curr}} = a_{\text{prev}} - \left(\frac{\partial^2 E}{\partial a^2}\right)^{-1} \frac{\partial E}{\partial a} \tag{7.48}$$

Using Eqs. (7.42) and (7.47), we can change the above equation to:

$$a_{\text{curr}} = a_{\text{prev}} - (xwx)^{-1}(y-p)x \tag{7.49}$$

If we now generalize this equation for the parameter updates, then we will have the following: [3, 7]:

$$a_{\text{curr}} = a_{\text{prev}} - \left(\mathbf{x}'W\mathbf{x}\right)^{-1}(y-p)\mathbf{x} \tag{7.50}$$

where W is a matrix with the diagonal elements w.

7.3.2.2 SVM Family

Let us start with a straight line equation used previously to divide the data domain presented in Fig. 7.4:

$$x_2 = ax_1 - b \tag{7.51}$$

Suppose we define the parameter a as a ratio between two new parameters w_1 and w_2 such that $a = -w_1/w_2$, then we can have the following linear equation:

$$x_2 = -\left(\frac{w_1}{w_2}\right)x_1 - b \tag{7.52}$$

We can write it as $w_1x_1 + w_2x_2 + \gamma = 0$, where $\gamma = w_2b$. We can also write this equation in a matrix form as follows: $[w_1, w_2][x_1, x_2]^T + \gamma = 0$. Hence, the generalized straight line equation will be [13]:

$$\mathbf{w}\mathbf{x}^T + \gamma = 0 \tag{7.53}$$

Let us now consider the example illustrated in Fig. 7.10: It shows a straight line represented by $w_1x_1 + w_2x_2 + \gamma = 0$ and a point (a, b) above the line with a perpendicular to the straight line from the point. Then the length of this perpendicular line describes the distance (with the direction) as follows [14]:

$$d_1 = \frac{w_1 a + w_2 b + \gamma}{\sqrt{w_1^2 + w_2^2}} \tag{7.54}$$

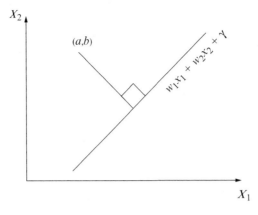

Fig. 7.10 A point and a straight line to illustrate classification

Now if we consider the line $x_2 = 2.0x_1 + 2.0$ (which was the best line chosen in the example illustrated in the second figure of Fig. 7.4), and the point $(2, 6.5)$ exists above that line, then the distance to that point from the line is:

$$d_1 = \frac{2.0 \times 2 - 1 \times 6.5 + 2}{\sqrt{2^2 + 1^2}} = \frac{-0.5}{\sqrt{5}} < 0 \qquad (7.55)$$

The negative distances are true for all the points above the line. Now use the point $(2, 2)$ which exists below the straight line and calculate its distance from the straight line. This will give us:

$$d_2 = \frac{2.0 \times 2 - 1 \times 2 + 2}{\sqrt{2^2 + 1^2}} = \frac{4}{\sqrt{5}} > 0 \qquad (7.56)$$

The positive distances are true for all the points below the line. Note that the points on the line satisfy the equation of the line (i.e., equal to zero). Therefore, we can define the absolute distance measure as follows:

$$d = s \times \frac{w_1 a + w_2 b + \gamma}{\sqrt{w_1^2 + w_2^2}} > 0 \qquad (7.57)$$

where $s = -1$ when the point (a, b) lies above the line and $s = 1$ when the point lies below the line. To optimize the classification accuracy, it is appropriate to select w_1 and w_2 such that they maximize the distances d for the points on both sides of the line. Therefore, the combined distance that should be maximized is:

$$D = 2s \times \frac{w_1 a + w_2 b + \gamma}{\sqrt{w_1^2 + w_2^2}} \qquad (7.58)$$

This will give us:

$$D = s \times \frac{w_1 a + w_2 b + \gamma}{\sqrt{w_1^2 + w_2^2/2}} \tag{7.59}$$

We know that the class response (y) is the dependent variable with the equation $w_1 x_1 + w_2 x_2 + \gamma = y$, so we have the combined distance as follows:

$$D = \frac{s \times y}{\sqrt{w_1^2 + w_2^2/2}} \tag{7.60}$$

It is obvious that we must keep the numerator $s \times y$ greater than or equal to 1 and then minimize the denominator $\sqrt{w_1^2 + w_2^2/2}$ by selecting suitable values for w_1 and w_2 to maximize the distance D. Therefore, we write this as an optimization problem as follows:

$$\begin{aligned} &\underset{w_1, w_2}{\text{Minimize:}} \quad \sqrt{w_1^2 + w_2^2/2} \\ &\text{subject to:} \quad s \times (w_1 x_1 + w_2 x_2 + \gamma) \geq 1 \end{aligned} \tag{7.61}$$

We can now generalize this optimization problem to [13]:

$$\begin{aligned} &\underset{\mathbf{w}}{\text{Minimize:}} \quad ||\mathbf{w}||^2/2 \\ &\text{subject to:} \quad S \times (\mathbf{w}\mathbf{x}^T + \gamma I) \geq I \end{aligned} \tag{7.62}$$

This optimization problem is the basis for the development of the linear SVM models. It can also be used to make an optimal straight line cut (in any direction) that divides the data domain into two for classifying two classes. For additional information, consult the paper [13] by Dunbar et al., which provides the mathematical background of the support vector machine in a simple form, and the reader can easily grasp the concept and the mathematical derivation of SVM. Figure 1 in [13] can help the conceptualization of the technique.

Since the introduction of SVM, several versions (e.g., Lagrangian SVM [15] and pq-SVM) have been proposed, and some of them, including the original SVM, will be discussed later in the book. The SVM can be divided into two categories: the SVM for multiclass classification and the SVM for two-class classification (or binary classification). In general, the multiclass SVMs have been created using combinations of several two-class SVMs; therefore, this book focuses only on the two-class SVM in detail. The readers who are interested in deriving multi-lass SVM from two-class SVM are encouraged to consult the paper [16] by Franc and Hlavac.

7.4 Hierarchical Models

Hierarchical models help classify even isolated groups of points by connecting them with their parent classes using tree like structures. These models are highly suitable for modern requirements, which include big data and distributed machine learning. It adopts both regression and classification strategies with a tree that may be built through a sequence of decisions. Hence, it is also called a decision tree.

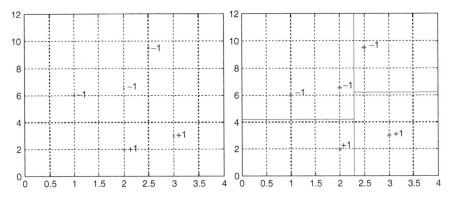

Fig. 7.11 An example that illustrates a domain division by a decision tree

7.4.1 Decision Tree

In machine learning, there are two types of decision trees: regression trees and classification trees [17]. An article that discusses these two types of trees can be found in the blog at [18]. A decision tree uses a rule-based approach to divide the domain into multiple linear spaces and predict responses. If the predicted responses are continuous (i.e., the responses can be a real number), then the decision tree is a regression tree, and if the predicted responses are discrete (i.e., a response can belong to a class), then the tree is a classification tree.

In simple terms, the decision trees make several vertical and horizontal cuts on the data domain, and thus they are highly suitable for multiclass classification as well. The data domain can be mapped to several classes (responses), and the decision tree can classify them by developing multiple subdomains. Consider the same example used in the explanation of SVM: The first figure of Fig. 7.11 shows the five data points $(2,2,1)$, $(3,3,1)$, $(1,6,-1)$, $(2.5,9.5,-1)$, and $(2,6.5,-1)$ that come from two classes 1 and -1. There is a horizontal cut that can separate the classes, but let us assume a vertical cut (horizontal decision—horizontal axis is used for decision) was chosen by the decision tree algorithm. The second figure of Fig. 7.11 shows the vertical cut at 2.2. Note that we need an algorithm to choose a suitable position to cut and this will be explained later in the book. Hence, two subdomains are generated, and they form a left and a right tree. Now a horizontal cut is chosen to cut the left subdomain (left tree) at 4.2. This process separates the classes 1 and -1 on the left side. Similarly, the right subdomain is divided with a horizontal cut at 6.2. We can represent the results as a decision tree shown in Fig. 7.12.

7.4.2 Random Forest

In random forest, the decision tree modeling plays a major role. It is applied to several bootstrap samples of the original data [11]. The bootstrap samples are taken by sampling the original data with replacement, and the number of observation in

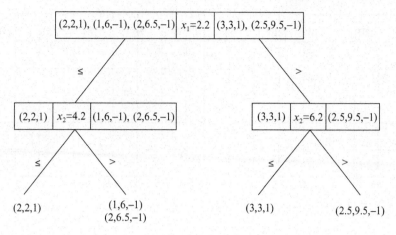

Fig. 7.12 The decision tree that corresponds to the example in Fig. 7.11

each sample is the same as that of the original data. Consider the same example we used for SVM classification: $(2,2,1), (3,3,1), (1,6,-1), (2,6.5,-1)$, and $(2.5,9.5,-1)$. However, add indexes to these points as follows: $(1,2,2,1), (2,3,3,1), (3,1,6,-1)$, $(4,2,6.5,-1)$, and $(5,2.5,9.5,-1)$. The indexes help generate bootstrap samples, and thus let us generate four bootstrap samples, with each sample having five observations. They are presented in Table 7.3. The first, fourth, seventh, and tenth columns show the indexes selected in each bootstrap samples. Other columns show their corresponding points and the labels as we can clearly see.

Table 7.3 Bootstrap samples

Index	Point	Label	Index	Point	Label	Index	Point	Label	Index	Point	Label
1	(2.0,2.0)	+1	5	(2.5,9.5)	−1	1	(2.0,2.0)	+1	3	(1.0,6.0)	−1
2	(3.0,3.0)	+1	1	(2.0,2.0)	+1	4	(2.0,6.5)	−1	3	(1.0,6.0)	−1
5	(2.5,9.5)	−1	2	(3.0,3.0)	+1	5	(2.5,9.5)	−1	3	(1.0,6.0)	−1
3	(1.0,6.0)	−1	2	(3.0,3.0)	+1	1	(2.0,2.0)	+1	1	(2.0,2.0)	+1
5	(2.5,9.5)	−1	3	(1.0,6.0)	−1	4	(2.0,6.5)	−1	1	(2.0,2.0)	+1

These samples are plotted in Fig. 7.13 in their respective order, and we can see the effect of the sampling with replacement (i.e., bootstrap sampling). To show a possible domain division by decision tree, these four examples of vertical split and horizontal split are selected. This set of four decision trees forms a random forest. The features x_1 (horizontal) and x_2 (vertical) are selected to explain the concept of random forest. The example in the first figure of Fig. 7.13 assumes the feature x_2 was selected and an algorithm was used to do a horizontal split (cut) at 4.5. It separates

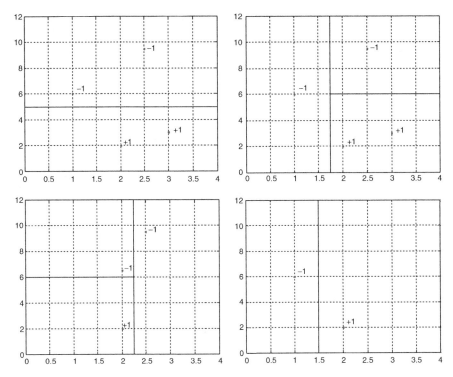

Fig. 7.13 Examples of four bootstrap samples are illustrated

the classes perfectly, and the left side (i.e., top subdomain) of its corresponding tree has the points of class 1, and the right side (i.e., bottom subdomain) has the points of class -1.

7.4.2.1 A Coding Example

The Matlab code in Listing 7.5 was used to produce the samples and figures that are presented in this section. Now suppose a new observation $(1.4, 5.8, ?)$ arrives, and it doesn't have a label. Hence, we must determine the class label of this observation using the random forest classifiers developed and presented in Fig. 7.9. We have run this observation down the trees of the random forest. For example, the first tree (top left) suggests $(1.4, 5.8, -1)$, meaning that the observation belongs to class -1. The second tree (top right) suggests $(1.4, 5.8, -1)$, the third tree suggests $(1.4, 5.8, +1)$, and the fourth tree suggests $(1.4, 5.8, -1)$. Therefore, with a voting mechanism known as bagging [11], we can decide the observation $(1.4, 5.8)$ belongs to class -1. This is the actual process carried out in random forest, and Chap. 11 is dedicated to a full explanation of random forest with its associated algorithms.

Listing 7.5 A Matlab example—bootstrap sampling

```
1   clear all;
2   close all;
3
4   x=[2 3 1 2 2.5];
5   y=[2 3 6 6.5 9.5];
6   L=[1 1 -1 -1 -1];
7
8   rand('seed',131);
9   for ii=1:4
10      ind{ii}=floor(5*rand(5,1))+1;
11  end
12
13  for ii=1:4
14      xx{ii}=x(ind{ii});
15      yy{ii}=y(ind{ii});
16      ll{ii}=L(ind{ii});
17  end
18
19  for ii=1:4
20      idx1{ii}=find(ll{ii}==1);
21      idx2{ii}=find(ll{ii}==-1);
22  end
23
24  for ii=1:4
25   figure;plot(xx{ii}(idx1{ii}),yy{ii}(idx1{ii}),'.');axis([0 4 0
           12]);grid on;
26   hold on;text(xx{ii}(idx1{ii})+0.05,yy{ii}(idx1{ii})+0.2,'+1');
27   plot(xx{ii}(idx2{ii}),yy{ii}(idx2{ii}),'.');axis([0 4 0 12]);
           grid on;
28   hold on;text(xx{ii}(idx2{ii})+0.05,yy{ii}(idx2{ii})+0.2,'-1');
29  end
```

In this program, the block of code in lines 4–6 initializes the points and their labels. Four sets of random indexes are created from lines 8 to 11, and it provides indexes with repetition. The bootstrap samples are created from lines 13 to 17 using the above indexes. Class labels are extracted from lines 19 to 22. The figures in Fig. 7.13 are generated in the block of code in lines 25–28.

7.5 Layered Models

Layered models may be conceptualized as a transformation of a data domain through multiple layers of executions so that each point in the data domain can be characterized by some sort of probabilistic measure. Layered models may be divided into two groups: shallow learning models and deep learning models. In simple terms, the number of layers adopted in shallow learning models is significantly smaller than in the deep learning models. These two models are explained below using a simple example, and Chap. 12 is dedicated to a detailed discussion on deep learning models.

7.5.1 Shallow Learning

The standard machine-learning approaches typically adopt the shallow learning models, including support vector machine and logistic regression. A paper by Li Deng [19] provides excellent information. These standard approaches may be considered as single layer learning models. As mentioned by Yoshua Bengi [20], even if a machine-learning approach uses two to three layers, they should be considered as shallow learning models [20] because the adaptivity of the nonlinear transformation is almost nonexistence in these models. As Li Deng mentioned in his paper [19], the adaptivity of the nonlinear transformation of the features is the important factor that differentiates the shallow and deep learning models. Therefore, in essence, the rate of nonlinearity is the backbone of the shallow and deep learning models. The shallow learning model considered in this section is based on the models suggested by Hinton et al. [12] and Wan et al. [21] that provide building blocks for the understanding and the development of the modern deep learning architecture. To make the transition to deep learning easier, consider some examples that use two-to-three layers to transform the data domain to a probabilistic representation.

7.5.1.1 A Coding Example

The shallow and deep learning models provide methods that are suitable for online learning, and thus support big data classification. These models can also be used for batch learning. The model adopted for this explanation is illustrated in Fig. 7.14. This is a very simple example that shows how a data point (in this case (2.0,2.1)) on a two-dimensional data domain may be transformed into a probabilistic measure, which can be used to match the class label to reduce entropy in the training phase.

Listing 7.6 A Matlab example—it partially follows the model in [21]

```
1   clear all;
2   close all;
3
4   randn('seed',131);
5   W=randn(8,3);
6
7   randn('seed',181);
8   B=randn(2,8);
9
10  nn=400;
11
12  for ii=1:nn
```

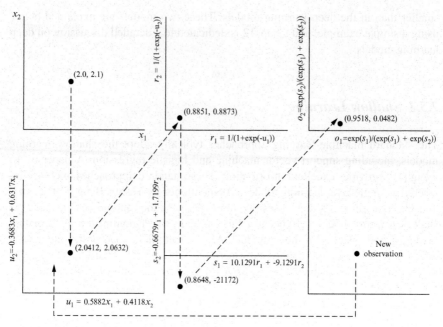

Fig. 7.14 The transformation of a data point by a layered model

```
13
14        if ii<(nn/2)
15            X=[6 6 6]';
16            %X=[6 6 6]'+randn(3,1);
17            y=1;
18        else
19            X=[-6 -6 -6]';
20            %X=[-6 -6 -6]'+randn(3,1);
21            y=1;
22        end
23
24        U=W*X;
25
26        R=1./(1+exp(-U));
27
28        P=B*R;
29        p1=P(1);
30        p2=P(2);
31
32        p=exp(p1)/(exp(p1)+exp(p2));
33        q=exp(p2)/(exp(p1)+exp(p2));
34
35        o(ii)=p;
36
37        dd1=repmat(p*(1-p),1,3);
38        K1=diag(dd1);
```

```
39
40        dd2=repmat(p*(1-p),1,8);
41        K2=diag(dd2);
42
43        neta1=(1/(X'*K1*X))*(y-p)*X;
44        neta2=(1/(R'*K2*R))*(y-p)*R;
45
46        daba1=repmat(neta1',8,1);
47        daba2=repmat(neta2',2,1);
48
49        ee(ii)=-y*log(p)-(1-y)*log(1-p);
50
51        W=W+0.1*daba1;
52        B=B+0.1*daba2;
53
54   end
55
56   figure;plot(o);grid on;
57   xlabel('Number_of_observations');ylabel('Probabilities');
58   figure;plot(ee);grid on;
59   xlabel('Number_of_observations');ylabel('Entropy');
```

We can see five domains, which include the given data domain and four other transformed domains. The point (2.0, 2.1) is shown in the given data domain and then it is transformed into a new domain defined by the linear combination of the features using randomly selected weights (0.5882, 0.4118). The transformed point (2.0412, 2.0632) is shown in this domain, and then the point is transformed into a nonlinear domain defined by an exponential function. The new point is (0.8851, 0.8873). It is the sigmoid function [22]. This data point is then transformed into an another domain defined by a linear combination using randomly selected weights (10.1291, −9.1291). In the next transformation, the values are converted to probabilities using a probabilistic measure. As a result, we have the probabilities (0.9518, 0.0482), and they can be assigned to the class label of the point (2.0, 2.1). When the new point arrives, the weights (0.5882, 0.4118) and (10.1291, −9.1291) will be updated using a method. The method used in the paper by Wan et al. [21] is the stochastic gradient descent [23].

This layered architecture is presented in the Matlab code in Listing 7.6. The code in this listing partially adopts the model in [21]. It uses two classes of data (three dimensional) to train a layered model, assuming the observations arrive one after the other in two batches. The block of code in lines 4–8 generates the parameters W and B (β) randomly. In line 10, the total number of observations is set to 400. From line 12 to line 54, the layered model's processes are iterated 400 times. The block of code from lines 14 to 22 generates observations $X = [6, 6, 6]$ and $X = [-6, -6, -6]$ from two classes, such that the first 200 observations come from the first class and the next 200 observations from the second class, respectively.

This scenario can help illustrate the nonlinearity of the model. In lines 24 and 26, the intermediate values U and R are calculated. The code in line 28 fits a model, and the code in lines 29 and 30 prints the values. These values are used to generate probabilities in lines 32 and 33. The code in line 35 stores the probability in an array

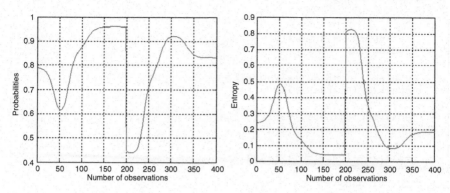

Fig. 7.15 Probabilities and entropy of two classes as separate batches

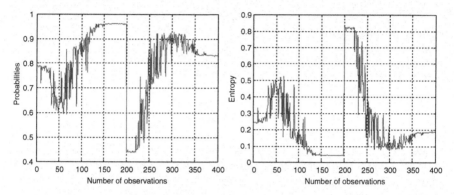

Fig. 7.16 Probabilities and entropy of two classes mixed

named o for plotting them later. The block of code in lines 37 to 47 implements the logistic regression model explained in Sect. 7.3.2 so that the parameters W and B updated in lines 51 and 52 according to Eq. (7.50) can be executed. The block of code in lines 56 to 59 plot the graphs presented in Fig. 7.15. They illustrate the probabilities and the entropy at each iteration.

The first figure shows that the probability for the classification of class 1 starts with 0.8, decreases up to the 5th iteration, and then starts to increase. It reaches its maximum at the 150th iteration and maintains until the 200th iteration, when the observations from the next class start to arrive. Hence, the probability suddenly drops and it makes sense. Then the classification of the second class increases to its maximum at about the 300th iteration, then becomes steady after iteration 350.

In the second figure of Fig. 7.15, we see similar results on the entropy measure, where we get the low entropy when we have high probability for the classification of the appropriate classes. Let us now consider dispersion (or error) in the data. That is, if we uncomment the code in lines 16 and 20, and comment the lines 15 and 19), then we will add random dispersion to the data. We will then get the results presented in Fig. 7.16 for this new data. We get similar results as the ones in Fig. 7.15, but with some local variations. Listing 7.6 provides us with a training algorithm.

Listing 7.7 A Matlab example—it also partially follows the model in [21]

```
1   clear all;
2   close all;
3
4   randn('seed',131);
5   W=randn(8,3);
6
7   randn('seed',181);
8   B=randn(2,8);
9
10  nn=400;
11  aa=round(rand(nn,1));
12
13  for ii=1:nn
14      if aa==1
15          X=[6 6 6]';
16          %X=[6 6 6]'+randn(3,1);
17          y=1;
18      else
19          X=[-6 -6 -6]';
20          %X=[-6 -6 -6]'+randn(3,1);
21          y=1;
22      end
23
24      U=W*X;
25
26      R=1./(1+exp(-U));
27
28      P=B*R;
29      p1=P(1);
30      p2=P(2);
31
32      p=exp(p1)/(exp(p1)+exp(p2));
33      q=exp(p2)/(exp(p1)+exp(p2));
34
35      oo(ii)=p;
36
37      dd1=repmat(p*(1-p),1,3);
38      K1=diag(dd1);
39
40      dd2=repmat(p*(1-p),1,8);
41      K2=diag(dd2);
42
43      neta1=(1/(X'*K1*X))*(y-p)*X;
44      neta2=(1/(R'*K2*R))*(y-p)*R;
45
46      daba1=repmat(neta1',8,1);
47      daba2=repmat(neta2',2,1);
48
```

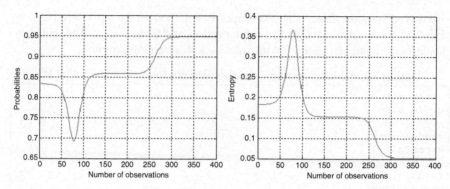

Fig. 7.17 The layered model applied on a stream of data with two classes that arrive separately

```
49        ee(ii)=-y*log(p)-(1-y)*log(1-p);
50
51        W=W+0.1*daba1;
52        B=B+0.1*daba2;
53
54  end
55
56  figure;plot(oo);grid on;
57  xlabel('Number_of_observations');ylabel('Probabilities');
58  figure;plot(ee);grid on;
59  xlabel('Number_of_observations');ylabel('Entropy');
```

What class does the observation $X = [-6.1 - 5.9 - 6.02]$ belong to? By looking at the code, you may say it belongs to class 1, not class 0. But it is dependent on the label array *aa* which is $0,0,0,0,0,0,0,1,1,\ldots$. The negative sign and the *else* condition in line 18 suggest this observation belongs to class 0. Now the next question is whether the trained algorithm gives the same results. To answer this question, we can use the trained parameters W and B together with the algorithm.

Listings 7.6 and 7.7 are similar except for a few lines, hence only the differences are explained. The first difference is in line 11, and the code creates an array *aa*, which has a sequence of 400 0s and 1s. Then the if statement in lines from 13 to 22 uses this array and creates an observation of two classes. These are the only differences between Listings 7.6 and 7.7. The block of code in lines 56 to 59 plots the graphs shown in Figs. 7.17 and 7.18.

In this case, the observations from the classes arrive randomly, and the first figure in Fig. 7.17 shows the changes in the accurate class labeling of the observation. As we can see, the probability is decreasing initially, and after about the 75th observation it starts to increase until about the 125th observation. Then it is steady until about the 225th observation and starts to increase after that until about the 300th observation. At the end, it is steady on the probability of 0.95. This property is also reflected in the entropy results presented in the second figure of 7.17. At the end it shows the entropy (error) is about 0.05. In this example, the dispersion is integrated

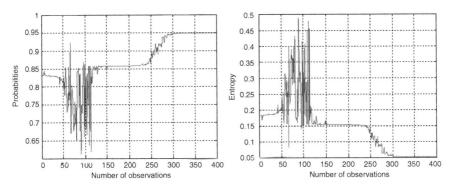

Fig. 7.18 The layered model applied on a stream of data with two classes that arrive mixed

in the data set. The results in the figures of Fig. 7.18 show the similar effect with local variations. The highest probability is 0.95 in this case as well. These results help praise the capability of the layered models.

7.5.2 Deep Learning

The extension of the layers discussed above with the multiple occurrences can lead to a strong adaptivity, and hence they can be referred to as deep learning. As illustrated in Fig. 7.8, it is easier to conceptualize the layered models with respect to feature space division, therefore deep learning can be viewed as the technique that belongs to the divisions of a feature space. Another important point to note about the deep learning is that it processes one observation at a time (i.e., called neuron), thus it facilitates the online learning. When we have information of one observation for processing, it is impossible to apply domain division approaches for developing learning models. We need to use the feature space information and its divisions, called the subspaces. Let us understand this problem using a simple example.

Thinking with Example 7.5:

Suppose we have a single observation x in a three-dimensional feature space: $x = (x_1, x_2, x_3)$. If you look at it *deeper*, you can find four observations hidden in four different subspaces (ignoring one-dimensional subspaces), and they are: $x_a = (x_1, x_2)$, $x_b = (x_1, x_3)$, $x_c = (x_2, x_3)$, and the original observation $x_d = (x_1, x_2, x_3)$. Let us represent the subspaces by s_1, s_2, s_3, and s_4, the original feature space. We can interpret this in a matrix form as follows:

$$S = \begin{bmatrix} s_1 \\ s_2 \\ s_3 \\ s_4 \end{bmatrix} = \begin{bmatrix} 1 & 1 & 0 \\ 0 & 1 & 1 \\ 1 & 0 & 1 \\ 1 & 1 & 1 \end{bmatrix} ⧓ \begin{bmatrix} x_1 \\ x_2 \\ x_3 \end{bmatrix} \tag{7.63}$$

The operator ⧓ is defined to interpret subspaces: the first row of the matrix on the right-hand side represents the subspace s_1 with each point represented by (x_1, x_2), the second row represents s_2 with each point represented by (x_2, x_3) and so on. If you analyze the transformed information *even deeper*, we can generate more observations by drawing several straight lines through each point (observation) in each subspace, and selecting the ratio between intercepts and the corresponding slopes as its related points. It can also be written as the following matrix:

$$U = \begin{bmatrix} u_1 \\ u_2 \\ u_3 \\ u_4 \\ u_5 \\ u_6 \\ u_7 \\ u_8 \end{bmatrix} = \begin{bmatrix} 0.5 & 1.8 & 0.0 \\ 2.2 & 0.8 & 0.0 \\ 0.0 & 1.3 & 0.4 \\ 0.0 & 0.3 & 3.5 \\ 2.7 & 0.0 & 1.3 \\ 3.0 & 0.0 & 0.7 \\ 0.1 & 1.4 & 0.6 \\ 0.7 & 1.2 & 0.1 \end{bmatrix} * \begin{bmatrix} x_1 \\ x_2 \\ x_3 \end{bmatrix} \tag{7.64}$$

The number of rows of the parametrized matrix on the right can be increased to go *deeper* into each subspace, analyze the data, and tune the parameters. Additionally, we can create similar matrices and transform the resulted (U) higher dimensional data to another dimensional and analyze the data. This provides a deep learning architecture. The matrix values are randomly selected. While increasing the information for each observation, it is important to induce randomness, nonlinearity, and adaptivity in the generated observation and in the subspaces so that probability theory can be applied successfully. The random selections of the straight lines (slopes and intercepts) can induce randomness in the generated observation $u_1, u_2, \ldots, u_8$. Assuming $x = (1, -2, 2)$, we can calculate U:

$$U = [-3.1, 0.6, -1.8, 6.4, 5.3, 4.4, -1.5, -1.5] \tag{7.65}$$

As a result of this layered process, we have transformed a single observation $x = (x_1, x_2, x_3)$ to multiple observations $u = (u_1, u_2, \ldots, u_8)$ using randomness. If we analyze these observations *more deeply*, we may find nonlinearity in them; however, it is advisable that we induce nonlinearity separately and generate new observations that are definitely nonlinear. The deep learning models, in general, use sigmoid functions for this purpose, and we can apply them to the U values and obtain the following:

$$R = [0.04, 0.64, 0.14, 0.99, 0.99, 0.98, 0.18, 0.18] \tag{7.66}$$

We can interpret this result in two ways: (1) a three-dimensional point is transformed into an eight-dimensional space where the new eight features are nonlinear; or (2) two straight lines are in each subspace s_1, s_2, s_3, and s_4. Considering this as a single observation, we can transform it into a set of real numbers and calculate probabilities. Each probability can be assigned to a class. Suppose we have two classes, then we need to create two probabilities, and this is done as follows:

$$P = \begin{bmatrix} p_1 \\ p_2 \end{bmatrix} = \begin{bmatrix} 1.1 \ 0.6 \ 0.5 \ 0.9 \ 1.0 \ 0.7 \ 0.2 \ 0.3 \\ 0.8 \ 1.1 \ 1.6 \ 1.2 \ 0.3 \ 0.1 \ 0.0 \ 1.5; \end{bmatrix} * \begin{bmatrix} 1 \\ -2 \\ 2 \end{bmatrix} \qquad (7.67)$$

where $p_1 = 3.1820$ and $p_2 = 2.8406$. Using these values and the softmax function described in Chap. 6, we can calculate the probabilities for the two classes as $p = 0.5845$ and $q = 0.4155$. In summary, we have transformed a three-dimensional observation $(1, -2, 2)$ through a series of steps that formed layers to probabilities $(0.5845, 0.4155)$. We can use these estimated class probabilities and the actual class probabilities $(1, 0)$ to minimize the entropy error through iterative steps. In deep learning algorithms, the stochastic gradient descent is used for this purpose, and it leads to the adaptivity of nonlinear transformation which is one of the requirements of the deep learning techniques [19, 20].

7.5.2.1 Some Modern Deep Learning Models

The modern deep learning approaches derived from the concept of artificial neural network are: no-drop, drop-out, and drop-connect, and these algorithms will be discussed in detail in Chap. 12. The papers by Hinton et al. [12] and Wan et al. [21] are the best papers to better understand these deep learning models.

Problems

7.1. By selecting the appropriate block of codes presented in the listing and different input data, produce three-dimensional figures to show the differences in ridge regression and elastic-net regression.

7.2. Deep Learning

(a) The equation in Eq. (7.63) provides a three-dimensional subspace architecture. Write a similar equation for a four-dimensional subspace architecture.
(b) Using a randomly generated matrix like the one in Eq. (7.64) for the four-dimensional scenario, derive the values for U, R, and P as done in Sect. 7.5.2.

Acknowledgements I would like to thank the authors/owners of the Latex materials that they have posted at https://jcnts.wordpress.com/ (for formatting the optimization problems, last accessed on April 20th, 2015) and http://www.tex.ac.uk/CTAN/info/symbols/comprehensive/symbols-a4.pdf (for the latex symbols, last accessed on April 20th, 2015). It helped the formatting of several mathematical equations in this book.

References

1. S. B. Kotsiantis. "Supervised machine learning: A review of classification techniques," Informatica 31, pp. 249–268, 2007.
2. T. G. Dietterich, "Machine-learning research: Four current directions," AI Magazine, vol. 18, no. 4, pp. 97–136,1997.
3. T. Hastie, R. Tibshirani, and J. Friedman. The Elements of Statistical Learning. New York: Springer, 2009.
4. G. Huang, H. Chen, Z. Zhou, F. Yin and K. Guo. "Two-class support vector data description." Pattern Recognition, 44, pp. 320–329, 2011.
5. D. Meyer, F. Leisch, and K. Hornik. "The support vector machine under test. Neurocomputing," 55, pp. 169–186, 2003.
6. G. M. Weiss, and F. Provost, F. "Learning when training data are costly: the effect of class distribution on tree induction," Journal of Artificial Intelligence Research, vol. 19, pp. 315–354, 2003.
7. Van der Kooij, A.J. and Meulman, J.J.(2006). "Regularization with Ridge penalties, the Lasso, and the Elastic Net for Regression with Optimal Scaling Transformations," https://openaccess.leidenuniv.nl/bitstream/handle/1887/12096/04.pdf (last accessed April 16th 2015).
8. H. Zou, and T. Hastie. "Regularization and variable selection via the elastic net," Journal of the Royal Society series, vol. 67, no. 2, pp. 301–320, 2005.
9. M. A. Hearst, S. T. Dumais, E. Osman, J. Platt, and B. Scholkopf. "Support vector machines." Intelligent Systems and their Applications, IEEE, 13(4), pp. 18–28, 1998.
10. L. Rokach, and O. Maimon. "Top-down induction of decision trees classifiers-a survey." IEEE Transactions on Systems, Man, and Cybernetics, Part C: Applications and Reviews, vol. 35, no. 4, pp. 476–487, 2005.
11. L. Breiman, "Random forests." Machine learning 45, pp. 5–32, 2001.
12. G. E. Hinton, N. Srivastava, A. Krizhevsky, I. Sutskever, and R. R. Salakhutdinov. "Improving neural networks by preventing co-adaptation of feature detectors," arXiv preprint arXiv:1207.0580, 2012.
13. M. Dunbar, J. M. Murray, L. A. Cysique, B. J. Brew, and V. Jeyakumar. "Simultaneous classification and feature selection via convex quadratic programming with application to HIV-associated neurocognitive disorder assessment." European Journal of Operational Research 206(2): pp. 470–478, 2010.
14. http://en.wikipedia.org/wiki/Distance_from_a_point_to_a_line
15. O. L. Mangasarian and D. R. Musicant. 2000. "LSVM Software: Active set support vector machine classification software," Available online at http://research.cs.wisc.edu/dmi/lsvm/.
16. V. Franc, and V. Hlavac. "Multi-class support vector machine." In Proceedings of the IEEE 16th International Conference on Pattern Recognition, vol. 2, pp. 236–239, 2002.
17. R. J. Lewis. "An introduction to classification and regression tree (CART) analysis" In Annual Meeting of the Society for Academic Emergency Medicine in San Francisco, California, pp. 1–14, 2000.
18. http://www.simafore.com/blog/bid/62482/2-main-differences- between- classification-and-regression-trees. (last accessed April 19, 2015).

19. Li Deng. "A tutorial survey of architectures, algorithms, and applications for deep learning," APSIPA Transactions on Signal and Information Processing, 3, e2 doi:10.1017/atsip.2013.9, 2014.

20. Y. Bengio. "Learning deep architectures for AI." Foundations and trends in Machine Learning, vol. 2, no. 1, pp. 1–127, 2009.

21. L. Wan, M. Zeiler, S. Zhang, Y. L. Cunn, and R. Fergus. "Regularization of neural networks using dropconnect." In Proceedings of the International Conference on Machine Learning, pp. 1058–1066, 2013.

22. B. L. Kalman and S. C. Kwasny. "Why tanh: choosing a sigmoidal function." International Joint Conference on Neural Networks, vol. 4, pp. 578–581, 1992.

23. T. Zhang. "Solving large scale linear prediction problems using stochastic gradient descent algorithms." In Proceedings of the International Conference on Machine Learning, pp. 919–926, 2004.

Chapter 8
Supervised Learning Algorithms

Abstract Supervised learning algorithms help the learning models to be trained efficiently, so that they can provide high classification accuracy. In general, the supervised learning algorithms support the search for optimal values for the model parameters by using large data sets without overfitting the model. Therefore, a careful design of the learning algorithms with systematic approaches is essential. The machine learning field suggests three phases for the design of a supervised learning algorithm: training phase, validation phase, and testing phase. Hence, it recommends three divisions (or subsets) of the data sets to carry out these tasks. It also suggests defining or selecting suitable performance evaluation metrics to train, validate, and test the supervised learning models. Therefore, the objectives of this chapter are to discuss these three phases of a supervised learning algorithm and the three performance evaluation metrics called domain division, classification accuracy, and oscillation characteristics. The chapter objectives include the introduction of five new performance evaluation metrics called delayed learning, sporadic learning, deteriorate learning, heedless learning, and stabilized learning, which can help to measure classification accuracy under oscillation characteristics.

8.1 Supervised Learning

In simple terms, supervised learning [1] means the tuning of model parameters using labeled data sets so that the tuned model parameters can work for larger and unseen data [2]. We may interpret this in a different way: say for example, we have n models $y = f_{\mathbf{w}_1}(\mathbf{x})$, $y = f_{\mathbf{w}_2}(\mathbf{x}),\ldots,$ $y = f_{\mathbf{w}_n}(\mathbf{x})$, and we select the best model $y = f_{\mathbf{w}_i}(\mathbf{x})$ through training and validation processes by using a labeled data set. The performance of the selected model is evaluated by testing it on another data set. Therefore, the objectives of the supervised learning can be divided into the following steps: (1) tuning model parameters, (2) generating algorithms for tuning, (3) improving the models to work with unseen data, and (4) applying efficient

© Springer Science+Business Media New York 2016

S. Suthaharan, *Machine Learning Models and Algorithms for Big Data Classification*, Integrated Series in Information Systems 36, DOI 10.1007/978-1-4899-7641-3_8

quantitative and qualitative measures for tuning. Supervised learning is similar to the sampling techniques used in statistics to estimate population parameters from the random samples. However, the distinction is the adoption of supervised learning in the development of the machine learning algorithms. These objectives may be divided systematically into three algorithms, namely training, testing, and validation algorithms [3]:

- Training Algorithm: The training algorithm must provide a systematic approach to generate model parameters and select the best parameters using a labeled data set. In this case, the labeled data set is called the training data set. The selection of the best parameters means the error between the predicted class labels and the actual class labels in the training data set is minimized. To achieve this, we need a good quantitative measure.
- Testing Algorithm: The testing algorithm must also provide a systematic approach to confirm if the model with tuned (best) parameters works efficiently with an another labeled data set. In this case, the data set is called the test data set. Confirming that the tuning parameters work efficiently means that the trained model gives high classification accuracy with the test (labeled) data set. To achieve this, we need a good qualitative measure.
- Validation Algorithm: The validation algorithm must provide a systematic approach to train and test the models under different conditions to improve the model to perform efficiently on unseen data. To achieve this, a training is done on both training and validation sets. Several combinations of training and validation sets from a given labeled data set are created first, and then the above training and testing (i.e., validation) algorithms are applied. One may interpret the validation task, in an informal way, as *testing the model before actually testing it.*

One of the other important factors that influences the successful implementation of these algorithms is the measure (quantitative or qualitative). In general, the quantitative measure contributes to the training algorithms, and the qualitative measure contributes to the testing and validation algorithms. The definitions and the differences between the quantitative measure and the qualitative measure are presented in a simple form at [4, 5]. In supervised learning algorithms, the quantitative measure provides an absolute measure (distance or a probabilistic) between the predicted and the actual class labels to minimize the error between them and select the best model parameters at training. Similarly, the qualitative measure provides a relative measure between the predicted and the actual labels and assesses the performance of the best model at testing.

The connections between these three algorithms, the possible ways the models are selected, and the ways the measures are used are illustrated in Fig. 8.1. In this figure, the top training and testing algorithms explain the *holdout* approach. The holdout approach is the standard supervised learning algorithm used in machine learning [6] as a combination of just training and testing algorithm. A very good discussion on the holdout algorithm can be found in [7], and readers should review this paper to acquire additional knowledge about some of the validation approaches. The training and validation algorithm on the left side of Fig. 8.1 and the testing algorithm

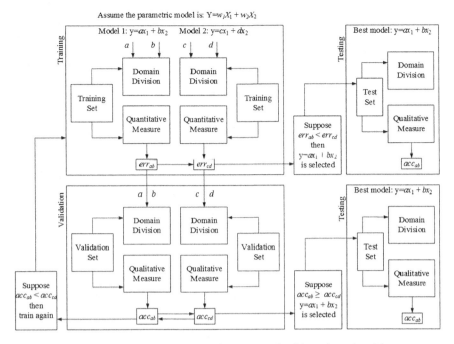

Fig. 8.1 The design structure of the supervised learning algorithms

at the bottom right side of the figure together form the *validation* approach (which includes cross-validation, bootstrap, and random subsampling) [7]. This figure explains the differences between the holdout and the validation approaches using two simple linear models $y = ax_1 + bx_2$ and $y = cx_1 + dx_2$ that divide the data domain for classification and select one as the best model. In the holdout approach, the errors (quantitative measure) are calculated (err$_{ab}$ and err$_{cd}$) in the training, and the model that gives the minimum error (e.g., err$_{ab} <$ err$_{cd}$) is selected as the best model, and then tested to obtain its accuracy (e.g., acc$_{ab}$). In the validation algorithm, the training is continued with the validation set, and the accuracies are calculated. If acc$_{ab} \geq$ acc$_{cd}$, then we can confirm the model $y = ax_1 + bx_2$ is the best, and the testing will be carried out; otherwise, new models ($y = ex_1 + fx_2$) will be used in the training to find the best model. Note that the notation acc$_{ab}$ is used here to match the notation used in [7] to represent classification accuracy.

8.1.1 Learning

The supervised learning algorithms may involve batch processing or online processing techniques; in that case they are called batch learning or online learning, respectively. In batch learning, the assumption is that a set of observations with all the class details are available in batches for processing, as we have seen in Chap. 3. Hence, we can estimate the statistical and mathematical characteristics of the data domain. We also have the estimates of the global parameters, and thus we can understand the data characteristics to determine suitable parameters for the model. The estimates of the global parameters also help the selection of a suitable quantitative measure for optimization of the model parameters. The distance measures like the mean squared error (MSE), or the root mean squared error (RMSE) can help accomplish the objective. Absolute measures like the true and false positive ratios also can help.

In online learning, we don't have global information of the data, and hence we don't see the data domain for defining the model and divide it for classification. Instead, the observations are arriving one at a time, and the model is trained using one observation at a time, as we have seen in Chap. 7. In this particular case, the probabilistic measure like the entropy can help optimize the classification error. One of the recent findings by Bottou and Lecun supports online learning over batch learning. They discussed batch learning and online learning briefly in their paper [8] and argue that if the online learning algorithms are designed correctly, they can outperform the batch learning algorithms on large data sets. Therefore, a careful design of the supervised learning algorithms is essential. The modern algorithms (e.g., deep learning) provide online learning, and hence they are suitable for big data, which is also supported by the research conducted by Bottou and Lecun [8].

8.1.2 Training

Training algorithms mainly help tune the model parameters and optimize them with labeled data sets. Training algorithms require quantitative measures to successfully train learning models using labeled data sets. Some examples of the quantitative measures are the false positive and true positive ratios. These measures will be discussed in detail later in the chapter. Training is a process of optimizing the model parameters using a set of labeled data sets. In general, it involves seven steps or subprocesses, which are illustrated in Fig. 8.2 using a simple two-dimensional data representation. The steps are numbered from 1 to 7 and are described below:

1. Extraction of data domain: In this step, the data domain, which is formed by the feature variables, extracted from the data set given. The purpose of doing this is to calculate the statistical mean and the variance of the independent variables.
2. Extraction of response set: The input data provides class labels, and thus we can extract the labels of each observation and create a response set so that the data domain is mapped to the response set. This set is useful for calculating the prediction error using the predicted responses by the model and the model parameters.
3. Standardization: The third step is to calculate the statistical mean (μ) and the standard deviation (σ) of each feature (X) and standardize them using the standard score transformation $(X - \mu)/\sigma$.

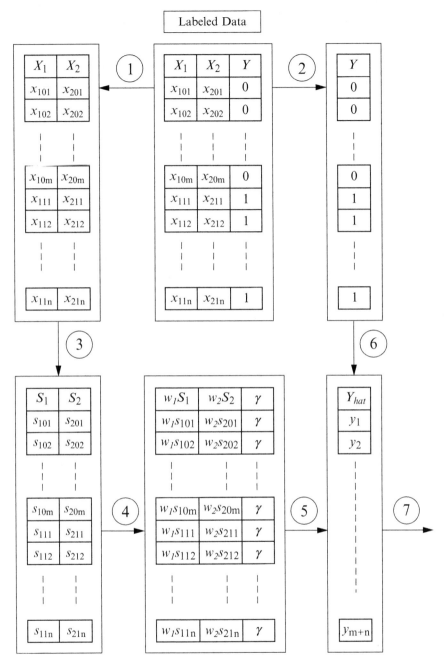

Fig. 8.2 The design structure of a training algorithm

4. Parametrization: Parametrization means the integration of parameters into the model (linear or nonlinear), such that the model divides the data domain with respect to the parameters. It means making the model and its capability to divide the model dependent on the parameters. As an example, $w_1 \times x_1$, $w_2 \times x_2$ and $+\gamma$.
5. Modeling: Modeling means making a connection between the parametrized variables. For example, we can make a linear relationship like $w_2 x_2 = w_1 x_1 + \gamma$.
6. The use of class labels: The training of a model is a supervised learning algorithm, hence the assumption is that the training data have classes that are correctly labeled. If the classes are not labeled correctly, then the training is not valid. The correct labels are used in the comparison with the predicted class labels.
7. Optimization: The final step is to update the parameters w_1, w_2, and γ to make the majority of the calculated responses match the actual class labels. To do this, we need a quantitative measure, and it may include distance measures, such as hamming distance, MSE, RMSE, and probabilistic measures (entropy).

Although the seven steps are presented above, they will have some differences when the batch learning and online learning are compared. The processes illustrated in Fig. 8.2 describe batch learning. The entire data of the data set is available; therefore, it is easier to find suitable values for the parameters w_1, w_2, and γ that can help to divide the data domain to classify the classes based on the class labels. If the data arrive one observation at a time for processing, then what do we do to tune the parameters? In this case, we may have to adopt online learning approaches.

8.1.3 Testing

The testing of models is a process of evaluating the performance of the model trained by the training algorithm. In simple terms, we can say that the testing will confirm that the trained model works on a different data set (test data set), which is also labeled. The processes (or steps) for testing models are presented in Fig. 8.3, and they are similar to the training processes presented in Fig. 8.2.

1. Extraction of data domain: This is the same step as the training, in which the data domain is identified and extracted from the test data set. The test data set is generally smaller than the training data set, hence the extraction process is much faster. The purpose is the same for calculating the mean and the variance of the features.
2. Extraction of response set: In the training phase, the response set information has been used to optimize the model parameters, but in the test case it is used in the final step of the testing process to obtain the classification accuracy. Therefore, the assumption is that the labels are not attached to the test data, and the extraction is not required. However, keep in mind that the labels are available for the performance evaluation as the qualitative measure.
3. Standardization: The standardization process must be done in the testing as well; therefore, the mean (μ) and the standard deviation (σ) are calculated for each feature (X). The same standard score transformation $(X - \mu)/\sigma$ is used in this step for standardization.

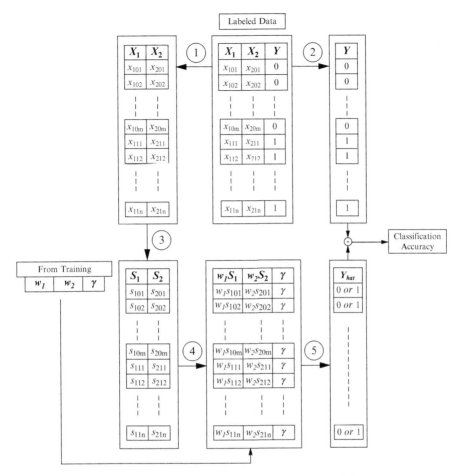

Fig. 8.3 The design structure of a testing algorithm

4. Parametrization: The parametrization process has already been done in the training phase, and the optimal parameters have been selected for the model. That is, the optimal model has been built to divide the data domain. In the testing process, we use this parametrized model to evaluate it to determine if the model divides the data domain optimally.
5. Modeling: Modeling is performed only in the training phase; therefore, this step is not part of the testing phase. The testing phase uses the model that has been built during the modeling objective of the training phase.
6. The use of class labels: The distinct nature of the use of class labels in training and testing phase is such that the training algorithms use the labels in the intermediate steps of the training process, and the testing algorithms use them at the final step of the testing process, which is the performance analysis.

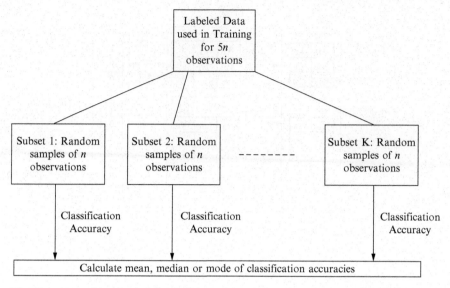

Fig. 8.4 A combination of the training and test data for testing of models on seen data

7. Optimization: In the testing phase, there is no question about optimization objectives. The result—the classification accuracy—that we get in the testing phase is considered to be final. The optimality obtained at the training phase must give the best domain division in the test data set.

In simple terms, most of the steps involved in the training algorithms are used in the testing phase, and the only difference is that these steps are repeated in the training until the optimal parameters are obtained; but in the testing, they are done only once.

8.1.4 Validation

In general, the classification problem may be interpreted as the classification of seen data and the classification of unseen data. The best model should perform efficiently in both situations, and the validation of models can help achieve this. The validation of a model may be defined as the testing of the model on multiple combinations of training and test data sets and aggregating the results. Now the challenge is how to generate or obtain multiple combinations of training and test data sets that can guarantee that the selected model will perform well with future data. The processes of generating such combinations of data sets and the statistical characteristics of the data determine the effectiveness of the validation algorithm. The qualitative measures also contribute to its effectiveness. The validation of supervised learning models may be categorized into three objectives based on the availability of data (seen or unseen data): (1) testing of models on seen data; (2) testing of models on unseen data; and (3) testing of models on partially seen and unseen data.

8.1.4.1 Testing of Models on Seen Data

In this approach, multiple validation sets may be generated from the data set used for training. One may choose to select 20 % of the data randomly and create a validation data set. This random sampling may be repeated, and multiple validation data sets may be created as shown in Fig. 8.4. In this particular case, the ratio between the training and the validation sets is 100:20. The training algorithm is applied to the 100 % training data set once errors are calculated, and then the best model parameters are selected. This model is applied to multiple validation sets (20 %) with the testing algorithm. The classification accuracies are recorded for each combination of training and validation data set, and the average accuracy is calculated as illustrated in Fig. 8.4. Based on this calculation, the model is selected as the best one if the trained and the validated models are the same. Otherwise, the training process will be repeated using another model. The mean, median, or mode can be used for this final classification accuracy.

8.1.4.2 Testing of Models on Unseen Data

This validation objective may be divided into two approaches. The first approach is the standard testing of the models with the 80:20 or 70:30 ratios for the training and test data sets. Because the training is done on 80 % (or 70 %) of the data set and the testing is done on the other 20 % (or 30 %) of the data set, the model has not seen the test data during training. This process will help us understand how efficiently the trained model will work with the unseen data. However, this holdout approach will not help detect the overfitting problem and the hidden statistical structures.

The second approach is to divide the data set into 60:20:20 and allocate them for training, validation, and testing. In this particular case, the validation process helps us envision the issues that will happen with the unseen data and revise the model and then test. That is, sensing the future is always good because it can help us prepare better and face the future challenges. For example, we can envision an overfitting problem and stop the training early. Similarly, sense the invariable statistical structures and integrate them in training. In this approach, we can imaging the validation process helps us bridge the training process and testing process, and revise the model.

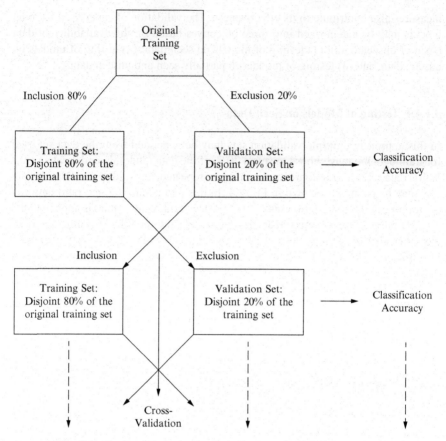

Fig. 8.5 The working mechanism of a cross-validation approach

8.1.4.3 Testing of Models on Partially Seen and Unseen Data

The cross-validation approaches are the best examples of the "testing of models on partially seen and unseen data." There are several cross-validation approaches to discuss, therefore separate subsections are allocated and presented in Sect. 8.2.

8.2 Cross-Validation

This validation algorithms designed with the above objectives are called cross-validation. I recommend the paper [7] by Kohavi to acquire additional knowledge on cross-validation and the related techniques. The book [3] by Hastie et al. is another resource for advanced readers to get in-depth knowledge on cross-validation. Three cross-validation approaches are selected from the machine learning literature [9] and discussed in this section. The first approach is called the n-fold cross-validation and, in practice, tenfold cross-validation is used in supervised learning. This may be called a deterministic approach. Another deterministic approach is called Leave-p-out cross-validation [9], but in practice Leave-1-out cross-validation (i.e., $p = 1$) has been widely used [10]. The third approach may be called a randomized approach, and in this case the n-folds are created using random subsampling techniques [7]. Now a simple question is that why these approaches are called cross-validation? Figure 8.5 explains the processes that illustrate cross-validation.

8.2.1 Tenfold Cross-Validation

We may call the n-fold cross-validation [11] a block-based, circular-shift algorithm where a block is a fold, and it carries a subset of data, and they are of equal sizes. The n-fold cross-validation is explained here using the tenfold cross-validation, and it is illustrated in Fig. 8.6. In the first step of this approach, the entire data set is divided into 10 disjointed subsets of equal sizes, and we may call them fold 1, fold 2,..., fold 10 as illustrated in the figure. In case we cannot divide the data set into equal sizes, a padding may be done with the observations that are selected randomly from the set. In the first step, we train the model using the first ninefolds and test it using the unseen 10th fold data. In the second step, the 9th fold is selected for testing, and the other folds are used for training. As you see, the 9th fold was seen from the first step, but the trained model in the second step didn't see the fold 9. Hence, the test set is both seen and unseen data. The process is applied to other combinations of training set and test set as illustrated in Fig. 8.6. As a result, we will have ten classification accuracies (or qualitative measure) $cv_1, cv_2, \ldots, cv_{10}$. The average will be considered as the final test error.

8.2.2 Leave-One-Out

The leave-one-out cross-validation technique [10] can be easily explained by an example. Suppose we have five observations $\{o_1, o_2, o_3, o_4, o_5\}$ in the original training set. We can then generate the following pairs of training and validation sets for the validation algorithm:

$T_{01} = \{o_1, o_2, o_3, o_4\}; V_{01} = \{o_5\}$
$T_{02} = \{o_1, o_2, o_3, o_5\}; V_{02} = \{o_4\}$
$T_{03} = \{o_1, o_2, o_4, o_5\}; V_{03} = \{o_3\}$
$T_{04} = \{o_1, o_3, o_4, o_5\}; V_{04} = \{o_2\}$
$T_{05} = \{o_2, o_3, o_4, o_5\}; V_{05} = \{o_1\}$

Now suppose we have two models, $M1$ and $M2$, to train and validate these sets, then we will have five errors (err_i; $i, \ldots, 5$) and five accuracies (acc_i; $i, \ldots, 5$) for each

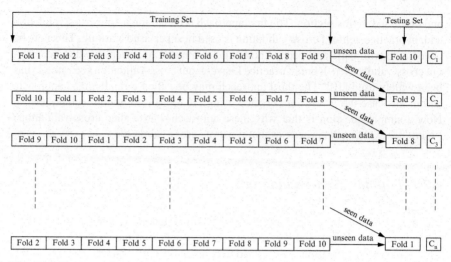

Fig. 8.6 The commonly used tenfold cross-validation is illustrated in this figure using the seen and unseen data concept

model. We can then use the average of all errors and the average of all accuracies to train and validate each model. Then the best model will be selected, or a retraining decision will be determined as explained in Fig. 8.1.

8.2.3 Leave-p-Out

The leave-p-out cross-validation [9] is computationally very expensive. Therefore it has been difficult to make use of this validation technique with standard technology platforms. Now we have a big data computing platform like the Hadoop distributed file systems [12]. This platform can help us to revisit and use this cross-validation technique. We can explain this technique with a simple example as follows: Suppose we have five observations $\{o_1, o_2, o_3, o_4, o_5\}$ in the original training set, and $p = 2$ is selected randomly. It means we can have three observations in the training set and two observations in the validation set. As such, we can generate the following pairs of training and validation sets for the validation algorithm:

$$T_{01} = \{o_3, o_4, o_5\}; V_{01} = \{o_1, o_2\}$$
$$T_{02} = \{o_2, o_4, o_5\}; V_{02} = \{o_1, o_3\}$$
$$T_{03} = \{o_2, o_3, o_5\}; V_{03} = \{o_1, o_4\}$$
$$T_{04} = \{o_2, o_3, o_4\}; V_{04} = \{o_1, o_5\}$$
$$T_{05} = \{o_1, o_4, o_5\}; V_{05} = \{o_2, o_3\}$$
$$T_{06} = \{o_1, o_3, o_5\}; V_{06} = \{o_2, o_4\}$$
$$T_{07} = \{o_1, o_3, o_4\}; V_{07} = \{o_2, o_5\}$$

$T_{08} = \{o_1, o_2, o_5\}; V_{08} = \{o_3, o_4\}$
$T_{09} = \{o_1, o_2, o_4\}; V_{09} = \{o_3, o_5\}$
$T_{10} = \{o_1, o_2, o_3\}; V_{10} = \{o_4, o_5\}$

As before, if we are training two models and validating them, we will have ten errors (err$_i$; $i, \ldots, 10$) and ten accuracies (acc$_i$; $i, \ldots, 10$) for each model. We can then use the average of all ten errors and the average of all ten accuracies to train and validate each model. Then the best model will be selected, or retraining will be determined as explained in Fig. 8.1.

8.2.4 Random Subsampling

The random subsampling approach [7] may be explained with three simple steps. Say $T = \{o_1, o_2, \ldots, o_n\}$ is a given training set. As we know, we need to create several pairs of training and validation sets for cross-validation. In order to do this, in the first step, we generate k integers $\{p_1, p_2, \ldots, p_k\}$ randomly, where $p_i < n; i = 1, \ldots, k$. In the second step, we shuffle the original training set k times randomly and create k new sets $\{S_1, S_2, \ldots, S_k\}$. In the third step, we create a pair (T_i, V_i) of training and validation sets by partitioning the set S_i such that the number of observations in T_i is p_i, and the number of observations in V_i is p_{n-i}, where $i = 1, \ldots, k$. Now the cross-validation processes can be executed, as explained before, on these sets.

8.2.5 Dividing Data Sets

Why is the dividing of the data sets for training, validation, and testing with particular ratios so important in supervised learning? The answer is that it will help the model to be fully trained, validated, and tested so that the classification error can be minimized, and the accuracy can be maximized for the unseen data. The book by Hastie et al. [3] discusses the ratio (in their Chap. 7, p. 222). In a simple form, the Pareto Principle, which is based on the Pareto distribution, suggests 80:20 ratio for training and test data sets [13, 14]. However, the question still remains if it is an optimal ratio or not.

In 1997, Guyon suggested [15] an approach to determine the ratio between the training and testing data sets. This ratio is nonlinearly proportional to the complexity in the minimization of the validation error and the minimization of the error resulted from the training set. To date there is no perfect approach that gives an optimal ratio. Therefore, dividing data sets for training, validation, and testing efficiently is still a challenging task. The ratio between the data sets plays an important role in controlling the classification accuracy and the computational complexity.

8.2.5.1 Possible Ratios

A careful selection of these ratios is mandatory for supervised learning. Let us discuss some of the commonly used ratios in supervised learning. Although extensive research has not been done in the selection of optimal ratio between these data sets, there are some common practices in selecting the size for these data sets. The commonly used ratio is 80:20 for training and testing data sets, based on the Pareto Principle [13]. Similarly, if training, validation, and testing phases are chosen, then the commonly used ratio is 50:25:25 as suggested in Hastie et al. [3]. However, several other ratios such as 100:20, 90:10, 70:30, 60:20:20, and random ratios have been used in different supervised learning applications. These ratios are now very subjective, and it is useful to develop an objective ratio. Therefore, the question still remains: What is the best split-ratio between the training, validation, and test data sets? However, the paper by Guyon [15] gives an objective measure, based on some intuitive assumptions, to derive a ratio for the training and test data sets.

8.2.5.2 Significance

The validation of "testing with seen data" requires the training on 100 % of the data and testing on 20 % that is selected randomly from the 100 %. This leads to many 20 % data sets and several results of classification accuracies. Hence, the final classification accuracy may be calculated as an average of these classification results. The random sampling of the 20 % from the data set increases the probability that the future data follow the same distribution (or characteristics) of the trained and test data. Hence, the classification accuracy on the future data is expected to be higher. Similarly, the validation of "testing with unseen data" requires either an 80:20 ratio or a 60:20:20 ratio depending on whether the cross-validation is not included or included [11]. How about a 70:30? Compared to an 80:20 ratio a 70:30 provides lesser number of observations for the training set, which provides a disadvantage to the training algorithm. In the meantime, the 30 % test set ratio may not bring a big advantage to the classification accuracy. Therefore, in practice, 80:20 and 60:20:20 ratios have been used widely. However, we need further research to develop a mechanism to select a very good ratio.

8.3 Measures

We have seen two measures, the quantitative measure and the qualitative measure, for tuning the model parameters toward obtaining optimal values through training, validation, and testing processes. Note that the measures and metrics are two important pillars that support the supervised learning algorithms. When a comparative value is calculated in the training, we call it a quantitative measure and if that is calculated in the testing or validation; then it is called a qualitative measure.

The quantitative measures used in the training algorithms are simply called measures, and the qualitative measures used in the testing and validation processes are called metrics. In this section, these two groups of measures are discussed in detail.

8.3.1 Quantitative Measure

Several quantitative measures have been used in supervised learning for training the models, and again they are associated with the types of modeling and algorithms. Some of the quantitative measures are the MSE, the false positive ratio, false negative ratio, and the entropy. For example, the supervised learning techniques support vector machine [16, 17] uses a distance-based measure and the decision tree [18], random forest [19, 20], and deep learning [21, 22] use probabilistic measures. These quantitative measures may be grouped into three: distance-based measure, irregularity-based measure, and probability-based measure.

8.3.1.1 Distance-Based

The distance-based measure is the measure that provides the differences in the magnitudes or in the labels. The measures like the mean absolute error (MAE), the MSE, and the RMSE are some examples of the distanced-based measures that have been used in the supervised learning algorithms [3]. The hamming distance is the best example for distance-based measure, which can better capture the differences in the labels [3].

8.3.1.2 Irregularity-Based

It is based on the differences in labels (e.g., signs) rather than differences in the magnitudes. Let us consider a set $P = \{+, +, +, +, +, -, +, +, +, +\}$ of plus signs. Well! the statement says it is a set of plus signs, but we don't see all of them as plus signs. We can see one "false positive" and nine "true positives." Therefore, we can see one irregularity and nine regularities in the set. Now suppose we have a set $P = \{-, -, -, -, -, +, -, -, -, -\}$ of minus signs. The statement now says, it is a set of minus signs, but we see one plus sign. That is we see one "false negative" and nine "true negatives." Therefore, we can use "false positives," "true positives," "false negatives," and "true negatives" as irregularity-based measures for defining quantitative measures.

8.3.1.3 Probability-Based

The entropy (even cross-entropy) is the best example for a probabilistic measure, and it plays an important role in the development of supervised learning algorithms. It is sometimes called an information value, and it is defined as [23]:

$$e(p_1, p_2, \ldots, p_n) = -\Sigma_i p_i \log(p_i) \tag{8.1}$$

Let us consider a simple example: suppose the class labels are [1 1 0 1], but the calculated responses are [0.9 0.8 0.1 1], then the entropy error is: $-1 \times \log(0.9) - 1 \times \log(0.8) - 0 \times \log(0.1) - 1 \times \log(1) = 0.105 + 0.223 - 0 - 0 = 0.328$. If the responses are the same as the actual labels, then there is no entropy error: $-1 \times \log(1) - 1 \times \log(1) - 0 \times \log(0) - 1 \times \log(1) = -1 \times 0 - 1 \times 0 - 0 \times \infty - 1 \times 0 = 0$.

8.3.2 Qualitative Measure

The confusion matrix and its associated performance metrics, accuracy (i.e., classification accuracy), precision, sensitivity, and specificity are some of the popular qualitative measures used in the validation and testing algorithms. The definition of the confusion matrix is presented in Fig. 8.7. These qualitative measures are built on the basic quantitative measures such as the false positive ratio, the false negative ratio, true positive ratio, and the true negative ratio [25]. The first figure in Fig. 8.7 shows two classes, A and B, as well as two regions, positive region and negative region. The positive region indicates that we are measuring the classification accuracy with respect to the classification measure of class A.

This figure also shows the transition state from an actual state to its classified state. If the class A is classified as A, then it is a true positive, and if it is classified as B then it is a false negative. Similarly, if the class B is classified as B then it is a true negative (because it is in the negative region), and if it is classified as A then it is a false positive. The second figure in Fig. 8.7 presents this scenario in a table form. The qualitative measures may be grouped into three categories: visualization-based measure, confusion-based measure, and oscillation-based measure. These categories of qualitative measures are discussed in the following subsections.

8.3.2.1 Visualization-Based

In the proposed performance evaluation, the domain division property and the classification accuracy are used as measures to evaluate the performance of the models visually and numerically, respectively. Inthe domain-division-based evaluation, the parameters are calculated at each iteration using the observations from the classes and applied to the entire input domain, and then the domain division properties of the parameters at each iteration are extracted. This will demonstrate the evolution of the final classification result of the model in action through domain divisions.

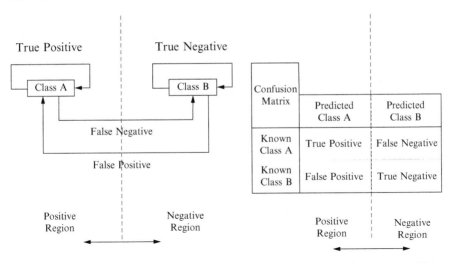

Fig. 8.7 The relationship between the false positive, false negative, true positive, true negative, and the confusion matrix [24]

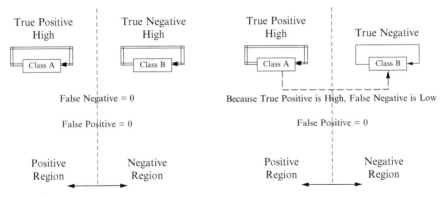

Fig. 8.8 Visual interpretation of accuracy and precision performance metrics, showing the effect of false positive, false negative, true positive, and true negative ratios

8.3.2.2 Confusion-Based

The confusion matrix is useful in generating four different qualitative measures: accuracy, precision, sensitivity, and specificity. The performance metric, accuracy, can be written in the following form and explained as follows [24]:

$$\text{accuracy} = \frac{1}{1 + \left(\frac{\text{FP+FN}}{\text{TP+TN}}\right)} \tag{8.2}$$

It describes the performance of the model based on the proportionality between the false positive and the true positive. As illustrated in the first figure of Fig. 8.8, if the accuracy is high, then it means that the classification of both classes are highly

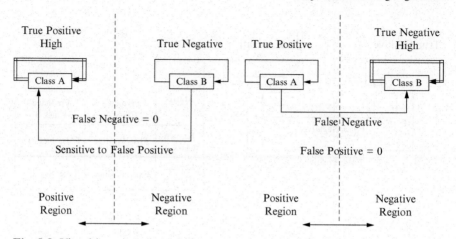

Fig. 8.9 Visual interpretation of sensitivity and specificity metrics showing the effect of false positive, false negative, true positive, and true negative ratios

accurate (it is indicated by the double lines), and the false negative and false positives are ignorable (i.e., zero). Similarly, the performance metric, precision, can be written as follows [24]:

$$\text{precision} = \frac{1}{1 + \left(\frac{\text{FP}}{\text{TP}}\right)} \qquad (8.3)$$

It describes the performance of the model based on the proportionality between the false positives and the true positives. As illustrated in the second figure of Fig. 8.8, if the precision is high, then it means that the classification of A is precisely high (double line) with low false negatives (dotted line from A to B). As presented in [24], the sensitivity measure can be defined as follows:

$$\text{sensitivity} = \frac{1}{1 + \left(\frac{\text{FN}}{\text{TP}}\right)} \qquad (8.4)$$

It describes the performance of the model based on the proportionality between the false negatives and the true positives, and it is illustrated in the first figure of Fig. 8.9. It shows that if the sensitivity is high, then the classification of true positives is highly sensitivity to false positives, which is indicted by the single line from class B to A. Finally, the specificity metric can be written as follows [24]:

$$\text{specificity} = \frac{1}{1 + \left(\frac{\text{FP}}{\text{TN}}\right)} \qquad (8.5)$$

This measure describes the performance of the model based on the proportionality between the true negatives and the false positives. As illustrated in the second figure of Fig. 8.9, if the specificity is high then the true negatives are high with significant false negatives (indicated by the single line from A to B).

8.3.2.3 Oscillation-Based

The oscillation characteristics can be highly found in online learning algorithms because of the stochastic gradient descent approach used to update the model parameters at each iteration with the new unseen observation. Hence, the classification accuracy also oscillates, and the high accuracies are sparse. It is therefore desirable to define a set of new learning metrics that may be used for performance evaluation of the online models. We can now define five new performance metrics (qualitative measures) to validate the online models: delayed learning measure, sporadic learning measure, deteriorate learning measure, heedless learning measure, and stabilized learning measure. These measures can help improve the performance of learning models on unseen data.

1. Delayed Learning: In online learning, it takes time (i.e., number of iterations) for the classification accuracy to jump to a high value during the training of a model. This is due to unseen data problems and the mixture of multiple classes during the training process. Therefore, taking delayed learning as a qualitative measure and describing the performance of the model is appropriate.
2. Sporadic Learning: The oscillation characteristics in the online learning influences the fluctuations in the maximum classification accuracy. Therefore, it is important to measure the sparsity of the occurrence of the maximum classification accuracies, and this will help avoid the overfitting problem by imposing early stopping. This qualitative measure will bring computational advantages to the learning algorithms as well.
3. Deteriorate Learning: Sometimes in online learning, the high classification accuracy can occur in very early stage of the training, but remain unnoticed due to the lack of learning with very few observations. This qualitative measure describes the severity of the model elimination with the declining accuracy of the model.
4. Heedless Learning: The algorithm sometimes believes that the high classification occurs after completing the training with all the observations, but the highest classification accuracy might have occurred earlier, and training must have been stopped early. This ignorance leads to heedless learning, and it also occurs due to the oscillation characteristics resulted from the processing of one observation at a time (i.e., online learning).
5. Stabilized Learning: In online learning, the classification accuracies oscillates with constant values over a single small period of time, or multiple small periods of time, forming a square wave-like representation. This can also form a qualitative measure and describe the stabilization of the model with the unseen data. It is thus called stabilized learning.

8.4 A Simple 2D Example

We have seen how the training, validation, and testing of the models work, and what measures must be used at training and testing/validation to optimize the performance of the model on seen and unseen data. Now, it is time for us to look at a simple example that can help conceptualize training and testing processes. The example taken here is the same one used previously with five point and two classes: $(2, 2, 1)$, $(3, 3, 1)$, $(1, 6, -1)$, $(2, 6.5, -1)$, and $(2.5, 9.5, -1)$. We select two of the four straight line models used in that example. The training and testing processes of these two models using the five labeled points are listed in Listings 8.1 and 8.2, respectively.

Listing 8.1 A Matlab example—training processes

```
1   clear all;
2   close all;
3
4   x1=[2 3 1 2 2.5];
5   x2=[2 3 6 6.5 9.5];
6   yy=[-1 -1 1 1 1];
7
8   s1=(x1-mean(x1))./std(x1);
9   s2=(x2-mean(x2))./std(x2);
10
11  figure;plot(s1,s2,'.');axis([-2 2 -2 2]);grid on;
12
13  % Not Good one in training
14  w1=3.5;
15  w2=1;
16  gm=3;
17
18  ws1=w1*s1;
19  ws2=w2*s2;
20
21  err1=ws2-(ws1+gm);
22
23  sign(err1)
24
25  % Good one in training
26  w1=1.5;
27  w2=1;
28  gm=0.5;
29
30  ws1=w1*s1;
31  ws2=w2*s2;
32
33  err2=ws2-(ws1+gm);
34
35  sign(err2)
```

The code listed in Listing 8.1 implements the processes described in Fig. 8.2 step by step. Lines 4–6 show the two-dimensional data (feature 1 is x_1 and feature 2 is x_2) and the corresponding labels (yy) used. Lines 8 and 9 standardize the input data initialized in lines 4 and 5. Line 11 is just a plot to see the scattering of the standardized data. In lines 14–16, the parameters are selected and in lines 18 and 19 they are used to parameterize the features. In lines 21 and 23, data domain and the response variable are modeled as a straight line. The output of line 23 is $[-1, -1, 1, -1, -1]$, and it does not match 100 % with the actual labels in line 6. We now take a different set of parameter values in lines 26–28, and the parametrization and modeling are carried out. Now the output of line 35 is $[-1, -1, 1, 1, 1]$ and it matches 100 % with the actual labels in line 6. Therefore, the trained model is $y = s_2 - (1.5s_1 + 0.5)$.

Listing 8.2 A Matlab example—testing processes

```
1   clear all;
2   close all;
3
4   # Testing data set
5   x1=[2 2.5];
6   x2=[2 9.5];
7
8   # Actual labels
9   yy=[-1 1];
10
11  # Standardized
12  s1=(x1-mean(x1))./std(x1);
13  s2=(x2-mean(x2))./std(x2);
14
15  figure;plot(s1,s2,'.');axis([-2 2 -2 2]);grid on;
16
17  # Use the good parameter values obtained in training
18  w1=1.5;
19  w2=1;
20  gm=0.5;
21
22  # Calculate the model
23  ws1=w1*s1;
24  ws2=w2*s2;
25
26  # Predict the labels
27  err=ws2-(ws1+gm);
28  sign(err)
29
30  #Predicted labels are [-1 -1], but actual labels are [1 -1]
31  # Therefore if we call 1 as true and -1 as false, and sub domain
32  # where the 1 is positive domain and the sub domain where the -1
33  # is negative domain then in the prediction the true (1) value is
34  # predicted in negative sub domain -1 true negative is detected
35
36  hold on;plot(-2:2,1.5*(-2:2)+0.5);
```

The quantitative measure that we have used here is a simple distance measure (like the hamming distance). Now we have to test the model using test data (smaller than the training data). Listing 8.2 shows the testing and describes the steps illustrated in Fig. 8.3. The data selected here is the seen data $(2, 2, -1)$ and $(2.5, 9.5, 1)$ (i.e., two points from the training data). Lines 5, 6, and 9 show these points and

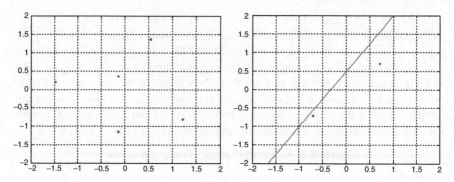

Fig. 8.10 The results of the Listings 8.1 and 8.2, respectively

labels, respectively. The standardization steps are in lines 12 and 13, and the use of model parameter values are in lines 18–20, and 23 and 24. The use of the model and the prediction of the responses (i.e., class labels) are in lines 27 and 28. The predicted labels are $[-1 - 1]$ and they are shown in the second figure of Fig. 8.10. It shows 50 % classification accuracy.

Problems

8.1. Effect of Standardization
The examples provided in Listings 8.1 and 8.2 show that the model has failed even in the seen data. It means we trained on 5 points, and two of the same points are used in the testing, but the model has failed to classify 100 %. Do you think it would have worked if the standardization was not applied? Implement it and justify.

8.2. A Simple 3D Example
(a) Generate a labeled data table with three features and 5–10 observations.
(b) Repeat the training and testing illustrated in Listings 8.1 and 8.2 with appropriate changes.

8.3. Nonlinear Modeling
(a) Use the same data sets.
(b) Model it with a quadratic equation (you need four parameters).

Acknowledgements The oscillation-based measures have been developed during my visit to University of California, Berkeley in Fall 2013. I take this opportunity to thank Professor Bin Yu for her financial support and valuable discussions.

References

1. S. B. Kotsiantis. "Supervised machine learning: A review of classification techniques," Informatica 31, pp. 249–268, 2007.
2. C.M. Bishop. "Pattern recognition and machine learning," Springer Science+Business Media, LLC, 2006.
3. T. Hastie, R. Tibshirani, and J. Friedman. The Elements of Statistical Learning. New York: Springer, 2009.
4. https://cio.gov/performance-metrics-and-measures/ (last accessed April 22nd, 2015).
5. http://samate.nist.gov/index.php/Metrics_and_Measures.html (last accessed April 22nd, 2015).
6. T. G. Dietterich, "Machine-learning research: Four current directions," AI Magazine, vol. 18, no. 4, pp. 97–136,1997.
7. R. Kohavi. "A study of cross-validation and bootstrap for accuracy estimation and model selection," International joint Conference on Artificial Intelligence (IJCAI), p. 7, 1995.
8. L. Bottou, and Y. Lecun. "Large scale online learning," Advances in Neural Information Processing Systems 16. Eds. S. Thurn, L. K. Saul, and B. Scholkopf. MIT Press, pp. 217–224, 2004.
9. S. Arlot, and A. Celisse. "A survey of cross-validation procedures for model selection," Statistics surveys, vol. 4, pp. 40–79, 2010.
10. A. Elisseeff and M. Pontil. "Leave-one-out error and stability of learning algorithms with applications," NATO science series sub series iii computer and systems sciences, 190, pp. 111–130, 2003.
11. H. Suominen, T. Pahikkala and T. Salakoski. "Critical points in assessing learning performance via cross-validation," In Proceedings of the 2nd International and Interdisciplinary Conference on Adaptive Knowledge Representation and Reasoning, pp. 9–22, 2008.
12. S. Suthaharan. "Big data classification: Problems and challenges in network intrusion prediction with machine learning," ACM SIGMETRICS Performance Evaluation Review, vol. 41, no. 4, pp. 70–73, 2014.
13. http://en.wikipedia.org/wiki/Pareto_principle
14. K. Macek. "Pareto principle in datamining: an above-average fencing algorithm," Acta Polytechnica, vol. 48, no. 6, pp. 55–59, 2008.
15. I. Guyon. "A scaling law for the validation-set training-set size ratio." AT&T Bell Laboratories, pp.1–11, 1997.
16. M. A. Hearst, S. T. Dumais, E. Osman, J. Platt, and B. Scholkopf. "Support vector machines." Intelligent Systems and their Applications, IEEE, 13(4), pp. 18–28, 1998.
17. O. L. Mangasarian and D. R. Musicant. 2000. "LSVM Software: Active set support vector machine classification software." Available online at http://research.cs.wisc.edu/dmi/lsvm/.
18. L. Rokach, and O. Maimon. "Top-down induction of decision trees classifiers-a survey." IEEE Transactions on Systems, Man, and Cybernetics, Part C: Applications and Reviews, vol. 35, no. 4, pp. 476–487, 2005.
19. L. Breiman, "Random forests. "Machine learning 45, pp. 5–32, 2001.
20. L. Breiman. "Bagging predictors." Machine learning 24, pp. 123–140, 1996.
21. G. E. Hinton, N. Srivastava, A. Krizhevsky, I. Sutskever, and R. R. Salakhutdinov. "Improving neural networks by preventing co-adaptation of feature detectors," arXiv preprint arXiv:1207.0580, 2012.
22. L. Wan, M. Zeiler, S. Zhang, Y. LeCun, and R. Fergus. "Regularization of neural networks using dropconnect." In Proceedings of the 30th International Conference on Machine Learning (ICML-13), pp. 1058–1066, 2013.
23. I.H. Witten, E. Frank, and M.A. Hall. Data Mining – Practical machine learning tools and techniques. Morgan Kaufmann, 3rd Edition, 2011.

24. Machine Learning Corner (Design models that learn from data), "Evaluation of Classifier's
     Performance," https://mlcorner.wordpress.com/tag/specificity/, Posted on April 30, 2013 (last
     accessed April 22nd, 2015).
25. G. M. Weiss, and F. Provost. "Learning when training data are costly: the effect of class dis-
     tribution on tree induction," Journal of Artificial Intelligence Research, vol. 19, pp. 315–354,
     2003.

Chapter 9
Support Vector Machine

Abstract Support Vector Machine is one of the classical machine learning techniques that can still help solve big data classification problems. Especially, it can help the multidomain applications in a big data environment. However, the support vector machine is mathematically complex and computationally expensive. The main objective of this chapter is to simplify this approach using process diagrams and data flow diagrams to help readers understand theory and implement it successfully. To achieve this objective, the chapter is divided into three parts: (1) modeling of a linear support vector machine; (2) modeling of a nonlinear support vector machine; and (3) Lagrangian support vector machine algorithm and its implementations. The Lagrangian support vector machine with simple examples is also implemented using the R programming platform on Hadoop and non-Hadoop systems.

9.1 Linear Support Vector Machine

Support vector machine [1], as mentioned in Chap. 6, provides a classification learning model and an algorithm rather than a regression model and an algorithm. It uses the simple mathematical model $\mathbf{y} = \mathbf{wx}' + \gamma$, and manipulates it to allow linear domain division. The support vector machine can be divided into linear and nonlinear models [2]. It is called linear support vector machine if the data domain can be divided linearly (e.g., straight line or hyperplane) to separate the classes in the original domain. If the data domain cannot be divided linearly, and if it can be transformed to a space called the feature space where the data domain can be divided linearly to separate the classes, then it is called nonlinear support vector machine.

Therefore, the steps in the linear support vector machine are: the mapping of the data domain into a response set and the dividing of the data domain. The steps in the nonlinear support vector machines are: the mapping of the data domain to a feature space using a kernel function [3], the mapping of the feature space domain into

© Springer Science+Business Media New York 2016

S. Suthaharan, *Machine Learning Models and Algorithms for Big Data Classification*, Integrated Series in Information Systems 36, DOI 10.1007/978-1-4899-7641-3_9

the response set, and then the dividing of the data domain. Hence, mathematically, we can say that the modeling of a linear support vector machine adopts the linear equation $\mathbf{y} = \mathbf{wx}' + \gamma$, and the modeling of a nonlinear support vector machine adopts the nonlinear equation $\mathbf{y} = \mathbf{w}\phi(\mathbf{x}') + \gamma$. The kernel function makes it nonlinear. The classification technique using a support vector machine includes the parametrization and the optimization objectives. These objectives mainly depend on the topological class structure on the data domain. That is, the classes may be linearly separable or linearly nonseparable. However, linearly separable classes may be nonlinearly separable. Therefore, the parametrization and optimization objectives that focus on the data domain must take these class properties into consideration.

9.1.1 Linear Classifier: Separable Linearly

This section mainly focuses on the two-class classification problem [4] using the support vector machine. However, a multiclass support vector machine can easily be derived from a combination of two-class support vector machines by integrating an ensemble approach [5]. This chapter focuses only on the two-class classification using the support vector machine learning models. Let us first consider the linear case. In Chap. 7, some preliminaries for the support vector machine were discussed, and a straight line equation was derived as:

$$\mathbf{wx}' + \gamma = 0 \tag{9.1}$$

Considering a data domain, this parameterized straight line divides the data domain into two subdomains, and we may call them left subdomain and right subdomain (as we state in decision tree-based models), denote them by D_1 and D_2, and define them as follows:

$$D_1 = \{\mathbf{x} : \mathbf{wx}' + \gamma \leq 0\}$$
$$D_2 = \{\mathbf{x} : \mathbf{wx}' + \gamma > 0\} \tag{9.2}$$

The points falling in these subdomains may be distinguished with labels 1 for the subdomain D_1 and -1 for the subdomain D_2. Therefore, the parametrization objective of the support vector machine can be defined as follows:

$$\mathbf{wx}' + \gamma = 1, \mathbf{x} \in D_1$$
$$\mathbf{wx}' + \gamma = -1, \mathbf{x} \in D_2 \tag{9.3}$$

In the parametrization objectives, we have modeled two straight lines (or hyperplanes) that can help to define boundaries between the classes. The optimization objective is to define an objective function (in this case, the distance between the straight lines) and search for the parameter values that maximize the distance. These lines are parallel to each other; therefore, we can simply use the standard distance formula between two parallel lines $y = mx + b_1$ and $y = mx + b_2$ as follows [6]:

$$d = \frac{(b_2 - b_1)}{\sqrt{m^2 + 1}} \tag{9.4}$$

where the slopes of the straight lines are $m = \mathbf{w}$, and their intercepts are $b_1 = \gamma + 1$ and $b_2 = \gamma - 1$. By substituting these variables, we can establish the following:

$$d = \frac{\pm 2}{\sqrt{\mathbf{w}\mathbf{w}' + 1}} \tag{9.5}$$

Ultimately, this distance formula will be the measure for the optimization problem that we build; therefore, without loss of generality, we can rewrite it as follows:

$$d = \frac{\pm 2}{\sqrt{\mathbf{w}\mathbf{w}'}} \tag{9.6}$$

In practice, the support vector machine optimization problem is written using the mathematical *norm* notation, therefore we rewrite the above equation as follows:

$$d = \frac{\pm 2}{||\mathbf{w}||^2} \tag{9.7}$$

By squaring both sides of the equation, and then dividing both sides of the equation by the value of 2, we can obtain the following simple mathematical relationship:

$$\frac{d^2}{2} = \frac{1}{\frac{||\mathbf{w}||^2}{2}} \tag{9.8}$$

It states that instead of maximizing the distance function $d^2/2$, we can minimize $||\mathbf{w}||^2/2$. In other words, we can minimize the prediction error with respect to the above classifier while maximizing the distance between them (this is the optimization objective). Therefore, the following mathematical expression can be defined for the prediction error between $\mathbf{x} \in D$ and its response variables y:

$$e = 1 - y(\mathbf{w}\mathbf{x}' + \gamma) \tag{9.9}$$

This error function plays a major role in the development of an optimization problem for the support vector machine. Let us now understand its role through the following thinking with examples.

Thinking with Example 9.1

Suppose the actual response y is -1, and the predicted response based on the classifier $\mathbf{w}\mathbf{x}' + \gamma = -1$ is -1, then we have $e = 1 - (-1)(-1) = 1 - 1 = 0$. Similarly, suppose the actual response y is 1, and the predicted response based on the classifier is $\mathbf{w}\mathbf{x}' + \gamma = 1$ is 1, then $e = 1 - (1)(1) = 1 - 1 = 0$. Therefore, it is clear the classification error is 0. However, if the actual response y is 1 and the predicted response based on the classifier $\mathbf{wx}' + \gamma = -1$ is -1, then $e = 1 - (1)(-1) = 1 + 1 = 2$. This indicates the error in the predicted response. Similarly, if the actual response y is -1, and the predicted response based on the classifier $\mathbf{wx}' + \gamma = 1$ is 1, then $e = 1 - (-1)(1) = 1 + 1 = 2$—this also gives the error indicator 2.

Suppose the actual response y is -1.1, and the predicted response of the classifier $\mathbf{wx}' + \gamma = -1$ is -1, then what is the value of e? Well! $e = 1 - (-1.1)(-1) = 1 - 1.1 = -0.1$. This means the variable x that corresponds to the response $y = -1.1$ is on the correct side of the classifier. Now suppose the actual response y is -0.9, and the response of the classifier $\mathbf{wx}' + \gamma = -1$, then what is the value of e? The answer is: $e = 1 - (-0.9)(-1) = 1 - 0.9 = 0.1$. It means the variable x that corresponds to $y = -1.1$ is on the wrong side of the classifier. Therefore, we can conclude that the negative error e is preferred when we optimize the classification.

9.1.1.1 The Learning Model

These examples show that the parameters $\mathbf{w}$ and γ must be selected such that the error $e \leq 0$. This leads to the following inequality:

$$1 - y(\mathbf{wx}' + \gamma) \leq 0. \tag{9.10}$$

$$y(\mathbf{wx}' + \gamma) \geq 1. \tag{9.11}$$

By combining the minimization goals, we can create the following optimization problem, and it is the basis for the two-class support vector machine [7]:

$$\begin{array}{ll} \underset{\mathbf{w},\gamma}{\text{Minimize:}} & \dfrac{||\mathbf{w}||^2}{2} \\ \text{subject to:} & y(\mathbf{wx}' + \gamma) \geq 1 \end{array} \tag{9.12}$$

We can now extend this optimization problem to a multidimensional data domain with a complete matrix representation as follows [8]:

$$\begin{array}{ll} \underset{\mathbf{w},\gamma}{\text{Minimize:}} & \dfrac{||\mathbf{w}||^2}{2} \\ \text{subject to:} & \mathbf{s}(\mathbf{wx}' + \gamma \mathbf{I}) \geq \mathbf{I} \end{array} \tag{9.13}$$

We can call the above "Minimize" term the *svm-measure* and the "subject to" term the *label error*. In this equation, $\mathbf{x}$ represents the matrix or the n points in the data domain D, and $\mathbf{s}$ is the set that represents the response variables of $\mathbf{x}$. The matrix I is the identity matrix, and γ is the intercept of the straight line (or the hyperplane). Three coding examples are designed to help you understand the svm-based optimization problem presented in Eq. (9.13). These examples are based on: (1) two points and single line svm-based domain division, (2) two points and three lines svm-based domain division, and (3) five points and three lines svm-based domain division, which will help you extend it to a generalized svm-based domain division.

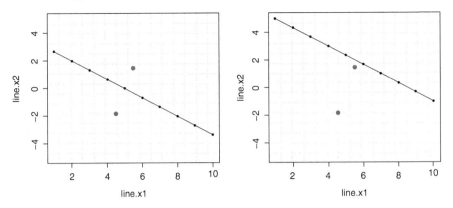

Fig. 9.1 The results of the "two point, straight line" coding example in Listing 9.1

9.1.1.2 A Coding Example: Two Points, Single Line

The main objective of this coding example is to illustrate the first iterative step of the svm-based optimization problem presented in Eq. (9.13). In Listing 9.1, a coding example is given to illustrate the problem of dividing the data domain linearly without applying any optimization mechanism. It is written in the R programming language, and it is expected that this example will help you build the concepts of the support vector machine. In this example, two-class points $x_1 = (5.5, 1.5)$ and $x_2 = (4.5, -1.8)$ are considered as illustrated in the first figure of Fig. 9.1 on a two-dimensional data domain. The goal is to find a straight line that separates the points.

Listing 9.1 An R programming example—a svm-based domain division

```
1   # Date: May 21st, 2015
2   # svm-prog1-new
3
4   # select weights for the straight line
5   weight.w = matrix(c(2,3),nrow=1,ncol=2,byrow=TRUE)
6   weight.w
7
8   # select intercept for the straight line
9   gamma.g = matrix(c(-10,-10),nrow=1,ncol=2,byrow=TRUE)
10  #gamma.g = matrix(c(-17,-17),nrow=1,ncol=2,byrow=TRUE)
11  gamma.g
12
13  # select points
14  point.x = matrix(c(5.5,1.5,4.5,-1.8),nrow=2,ncol=2,byrow=TRUE)
15  t(point.x)
16
17  # assign class labels
18  label.s = matrix(c(1,-1),nrow=1,ncol=2,byrow=TRUE)
19  label.s
20
21  # determine label error
```

```
22  hat.y = weight.w %*% t(point.x) + gamma.g
23  hat.y
24
25  # check for minimum error
26  label.s * hat.y
27
28  # calculate SVM measure
29  (weight.w %*% t(weight.w))/2
30
31  # display the straight line and points
32  line.x1 = rep(0,10)
33  line.x2 = rep(0,10)
34
35  slope = weight.w[1]/weight.w[2]
36  intercept = gamma.g[1]/weight.w[2]
37
38  for (i in 1:10) {
39      line.x1[i] = i
40      line.x2[i] = -intercept - slope * line.x1[i]
41  }
42
43  plot(line.x1, line.x2, type="o", pch=20, ylim=c(-5,5))
44  points(point.x[1,1], point.x[1,2], col="red", pch=19)
45  points(point.x[2,1], point.x[2,2], col="blue", pch=19)
46  grid(15, 15, lwd=2)
```

The block of code from line 4 to line 11 sets the parameters for a straight line, which could be the svm-based classifier. Two parameter values -10 and 17 are selected for the intercept parameter of the straight line. The codes in lines 14 and 18 select two points and assign labels, respectively. The code in line 26 helps us select the index of the minimum error and will be used for selecting the weights and intercept values as shown in the codes in lines 35 and 36. In line 22, the label error is determined based on the straight line defined earlier, and the svm-measure is calculated in line 29.

The slope and the intercept are calculated as shown in lines 35 and 36. The block of code in lines 38–46 produced the figures in Fig. 9.1. The first figure is related to the intercept value selected according to line 9, and the second figure is related to line 10 when uncommented. The program statements are written sequentially to help you understand the mathematical processes for the support vector machine presented at the beginning of this chapter. Comparing the two choices of the parameters, we can see the first set of parameters provides a better domain division than the second set for svm-based classification. It also illustrates the effect of the intercept parameter.

9.1.1.3 A Coding Example: Two Points, Three Lines

The main objective of the coding example in Listing 9.2 is to illustrate the iterative steps that lead to an optimization in the svm-based classification problem which is

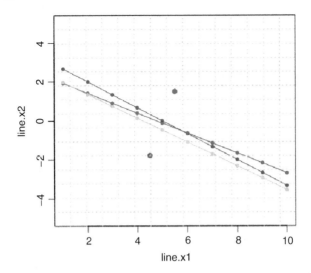

Fig. 9.2 A possible classifier for two points

presented in Eq. (9.13). However, the iterative steps are shown sequentially in the program, so that you can understand the algorithm better. As an exercise, once you understand the algorithm, make the program efficient using loops and functions.

Listing 9.2 An R programming example—the svm-based optimization problem

```
1   # Date: May 21st, 2015
2   # svm-prog1-new
3
4   # ITERATION 1 ################
5
6   # select weights for parametrization
7   weight.w = matrix(c(2,3),nrow=1,ncol=2,byrow=TRUE)
8   weight.w
9
10  # select intercept for parametrization
11  gamma.g = matrix(c(-10,-10),nrow=1,ncol=2,byrow=TRUE)
12  gamma.g
13
14  # select points
15  point.x = matrix(c(5.5,1.5,4.5,-1.8),nrow=2,ncol=2,byrow=TRUE)
16  t(point.x)
17
18  # assign class labels
19  label.s = matrix(c(1,-1),nrow=1,ncol=2,byrow=TRUE)
20  label.s
21
22  # determine label error
23  hat.y = weight.w %*% t(point.x) + gamma.g
24  hat.y
25
```

```
26  # check for minimum error
27  label.s * hat.y
28
29  # calculate SVM measure for optimization
30  measure.one = (weight.w %*% t(weight.w))/2
31
32  # display the straight line and points
33  line.x1 = rep(0,10)
34  line.x2 = rep(0,10)
35
36  slope = weight.w[,1]/weight.w[,2]
37  intercept=gamma.g/weight.w[,2]
38
39  for (i in 1:10) {
40    line.x1[i] = i
41    line.x2[i] = -intercept - slope*line.x1[i]
42  }
43
44  plot(line.x1, line.x2, type="o", col="blue", pch=20, ylim=c(-5,5)
        )
45  points(point.x[1,1], point.x[1,2], col="red", pch=19)
46  points(point.x[2,1], point.x[2,2], col="blue", pch=19)
47  grid(15, 15, lwd=2)
48
49  # ITERATION 2 #################
50
51  # select weights for parametrization
52  weight.w = matrix(c(2.1,4.1),nrow=1,ncol=2,byrow=TRUE)
53  weight.w
54
55  # select intercept for parametrization
56  gamma.g = matrix(c(-10,-10),nrow=1,ncol=2,byrow=TRUE)
57  #gamma.g = matrix(c(-17,-17),nrow=1,ncol=2,byrow=TRUE)
58  gamma.g
59
60  # select points
61  point.x = matrix(c(5.5,1.5,4.5,-1.8),nrow=2,ncol=2,byrow=TRUE)
62  t(point.x)
63
64  # assign class labels
65  label.s = matrix(c(1,-1),nrow=1,ncol=2,byrow=TRUE)
66  label.s
67
68  # determine label error
69  hat.y = weight.w %*% t(point.x) + gamma.g
70  hat.y
71
72  # check for minimum error
73  label.s * hat.y
74
75  # calculate SVM measure for optimization
76  measure.two = (weight.w %*% t(weight.w))/2
77
78  # display the straight line and points
```

```
79  line.x1 = rep(0,10)
80  line.x2 = rep(0,10)
81
82  slope = weight.w[,1]/weight.w[,2]
83  intercept=gamma.g/weight.w[,2]
84
85  for (i in 1:10) {
86    line.x1[i] = i
87    line.x2[i] = -intercept - slope*line.x1[i]
88  }
89
90  lines(line.x1, line.x2, type="o", col="red", pch=20, ylim=c(-5,5)
        )
91
92  # ITERATION 3 #################
93
94  # select weights for parametrization
95  weight.w = matrix(c(1.9,3.1),nrow=1,ncol=2,byrow=TRUE)
96  weight.w
97
98  # select intercept for parametrization
99  gamma.g = matrix(c(-8,-8),nrow=1,ncol=2,byrow=TRUE)
100 #gamma.g = matrix(c(-17,-17),nrow=1,ncol=2,byrow=TRUE)
101 gamma.g
102
103 # select points
104 point.x = matrix(c(5.5,1.5,4.5,-1.8),nrow=2,ncol=2,byrow=TRUE)
105 t(point.x)
106
107 # assign class labels
108 label.s = matrix(c(1,-1),nrow=1,ncol=2,byrow=TRUE)
109 label.s
110
111 # determine label error
112 hat.y = weight.w %*% t(point.x) + gamma.g
113 hat.y
114
115 # check for minimum error
116 label.s * hat.y
117
118 # calculate SVM measure for optimization
119 measure.three = (weight.w %*% t(weight.w))/2
120
121 # display the straight line and points
122 line.x1 = rep(0,10)
123 line.x2 = rep(0,10)
124
125 slope = weight.w[,1]/weight.w[,2]
126 intercept=gamma.g/weight.w[,2]
127
128 for (i in 1:10) {
129   line.x1[i] = i
130   line.x2[i] = -intercept - slope*line.x1[i]
131 }
```

```
132
133   lines (line.x1, line.x2, type="o", col="green", pch=20, ylim=c
          (-5,5))
134
135   # optimization
136   measure.one
137   measure.two
138   measure.three
```

The first iteration with the first set of weights is presented in the block of code from line 6 to line 47, and it reflects the code presented in Listing 9.1. Similarly, with the other sets of weights, the iterations 2 and 3 are presented in the blocks of code from line 51 to line 90 and from line 94 to line 133, respectively. In the block of code from line 136 to line 138, the results of svm-measures are displayed, and we can then select the one with the smaller value for the best classifier. Thus this program calculates the label errors for the straight line equations $y = 2x_1 + 3x_2 - 10$, $y = 2.1x_1 + 4.1x_2 - 10$, and $y = 1.9x_1 + 3.1x_2 - 8$, and the svm-measures to determine the straight line that minimizes the svm-measure. It also produced the graph in Fig. 9.2, and we can see the three classifiers and the best among them.

9.1.1.4 A Coding Example: Five Points, Three Lines

The main objective of the coding example in Listing 9.3 is to generalize the iterative steps that lead to optimization in the svm-based optimization problem presented in Eq. (9.13) using matrix formulation. This example inputs a file "file3.txt," which contains the data points and class labels. The file contains three columns where the first two columns represent the two features, and the third column represents the class labels. It has two features f_1 and f_2 with values $f_1 = \{5.5, 5.7, 6.1, 4.5, 4.3\}$ and $f_2 = \{1.5, 0.5, 1.1, -1.8, -1.5\}$, and their corresponding label set $L = \{1, 1, 1, -1, -1\}$.

Listing 9.3 An R programming example—linear svm-based classifiers

```
1    # Date: May 21st, 2015
2    # svm-prog2-new
3
4    # read data from a file
5    data <- read.table("file3.txt", sep="")
6
7    # extract feature and separate the labels
8    point.x = matrix(c(data$V1, data$V2),nrow=2,ncol=5,byrow=TRUE)
9    point.x
10
11   # select weights for parametrization
12   weight.w=matrix(c(2,3,2.1,4.1,1.9,3.1),nrow=3,ncol=2,byrow=TRUE)
13   weight.w
14
15   # select intercepts for parametrization
16   gamma.g = matrix(c(-10,-10,-8),nrow=3,ncol=1,byrow=TRUE)
17   gamma.g
18
```

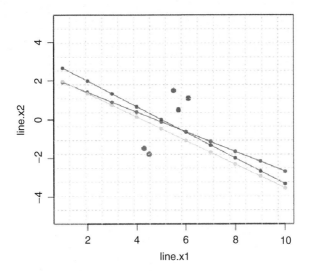

Fig. 9.3 A possible classifier for five points

```
19  mgamma.g = matrix(rep(gamma.g,5),nrow=3,ncol=5)
20  mgamma.g
21
22  # assign class labels
23  label.s = matrix(c(data$V3),nrow=5,ncol=1,byrow=TRUE)
24  label.s
25
26  label.ss=matrix(rep(label.s,3),ncol=3)
27  label.ss
28
29  # determine label error
30  hat.y = weight.w %*% point.x + mgamma.g
31  hat.y
32
33  # check for minimum error
34  t(label.ss) * hat.y
35
36  # calculate SVM measure for optimization
37  measure.m = (weight.w %*% t(weight.w))/2
38  measure.m
39
40  # display the straight line and points
41  line.x1 = rep(0,10)
42  line.x2 = rep(0,10)
43
44  slope = weight.w[,1]/weight.w[,2]
45  intercept=gamma.g/weight.w[,2]
46
47  line.x1 = 1:10
48  line.x2 = -intercept[1]-slope[1]*line.x1
49
```

```
50  plot(line.x1, line.x2, type="o", col="blue", pch=20, ylim=c(-5,5)
        )
51  points(point.x[1,], point.x[2,], col=ifelse(data$V3==1,"blue","
        red"), pch=19)
52  grid(15, 15, lwd=2)
53
54  line.x1 = 1:10
55  line.x2 = -intercept[2]-slope[2]*line.x1
56  lines(line.x1, line.x2, type="o", col="red", pch=20, ylim=c(-5,5)
        )
57
58  line.x1 = 1:10
59  line.x2 = -intercept[3]-slope[3]*line.x1
60  lines(line.x1, line.x2, type="o", col="green", pch=20, ylim=c
        (-5,5))
61
62  # optimization - select the weights that correspond
63  # to the smallest measure.
64  diag(measure.m)
```

This program has produced the figure presented in Fig. 9.3, and we can see the five points in the data domain with two classes separated by the same three straight lines considered previously. The program has also produced svm-measures that are calculated in line 37 and displayed in line 64. The difference between Listing 9.3, and Listings 9.2 and 9.1 is the calculations using the matrix form rather than the iterative steps; hence, the diagonal values of the matrix variable "measure.m" are the svm-measures for the three lines considered.

9.1.2 Linear Classifier: Nonseparable Linearly

In the above section we studied the classification problem of separable classes. If classes are nonseparable to an acceptable level, then a slack variable that describes the false positives must be introduced to the optimization problem described in Eq. (9.12). This will lead to the following equation [7]:

$$
\begin{aligned}
\text{Minimize:} &\quad \frac{\|\mathbf{w}\|^2}{2} + \varepsilon(\zeta) \\
\underset{\mathbf{w},\gamma,\zeta \geq 0}{} &
\end{aligned}
\tag{9.14}
$$
$$
\text{subject to:} \quad s(\mathbf{w}\mathbf{x}' + \gamma\mathbf{I}) + \zeta \geq \mathbf{I}
$$

where the new variable ζ is called the slack variable, and it describes the acceptance of false positive and true negative errors in the classification results. Incorporating this error variable in the optimization goal of the support vector machine, we can obtain a better and acceptable classifier.

9.2 Lagrangian Support Vector Machine

The Lagrangian Support Vector Machine may be conceptualized as matrix expansion and matrix multiplications. The paper [9] by Mangasarian and Musicant provides mathematical modeling of this approach with a detail explanation. It is mathematically intensive; therefore, this approach is simplified in this section with the usage of matrix expansions and multiplications with a conceptualized example.

9.2.1 Modeling of LSVM

The modeling of the Lagrangian support vector machine can be easily understood if you have a clear understanding of the support vector machine theory presented in Chap. 7 and in the earlier sections of this chapter. The Lagrangian support vector machine may be explained based on the details in [7, 9], however, adopting the following optimization problem proposed by Dunbar [10] as a new formulation (called $L_1 + L_2 - SVM$) can help with better implementation:

$$\text{Minimize:} \quad \frac{\mathbf{W}'\mathbf{L_1}\mathbf{W}}{2} + \frac{\gamma^2}{2} + \frac{\lambda_2}{2}\hat{\zeta}'\hat{\zeta}$$
$$\mathbf{W},\gamma,\hat{\zeta} \geq 0$$
$$\text{subject to:} \quad \mathbf{S}(\mathbf{XW} + \hat{I}\gamma) + \hat{\zeta} \geq \hat{I} \tag{9.15}$$

where

$$\mathbf{W} = \begin{bmatrix} \mathbf{w} \\ \mathbf{v} \end{bmatrix}; \mathbf{L_1} = \lambda_1 \begin{bmatrix} \mathbf{I} & \mathbf{0} \\ \mathbf{0} & \mathbf{0} \end{bmatrix}; \mathbf{S} = \begin{bmatrix} \mathbf{s} & \mathbf{0} \\ \mathbf{0} & \mathbf{I} \end{bmatrix}; \hat{I} = \begin{bmatrix} \mathbf{I} \\ \mathbf{0} \end{bmatrix}; \tag{9.16}$$

$$\mathbf{X} = \begin{bmatrix} \mathbf{x} & \mathbf{0} \\ \mathbf{I} & \mathbf{0} \\ -\mathbf{I} & \mathbf{0} \end{bmatrix}; \hat{\zeta} = \begin{bmatrix} \zeta \\ \mathbf{v} \\ \mathbf{0} \end{bmatrix}. \tag{9.17}$$

It can be considered as the generalized model of the support vector machine presented in Eq. (9.14). Say, for example, if you substitute value 1 for λ_1 and λ_2 with appropriate matrix dimensions, then we will be able to obtain the same optimization model as the one presented in Eq. (9.14).

9.2.2 Conceptualized Example

The optimization model $L_1 + L_2 - SVM$ proposed in [10] and presented above may be simplified for its implementation by the process diagram with data flow illustrated in Figs. 9.4 and 9.5. These figures illustrate the approach using a simple example with two classes (labeled 1 and -1), and 5 data points $\{(5.5, 1.5), (5.7, 0.5), (6.1, 1.1), (4.5, -1.8), (4.3, -1.5)\}$, $\lambda_1 = 0.95$, and $\lambda_2 = 1$. Let us begin our explanation with the "Start" from the top of the diagram. The data table is first divided into the data domain and the response set. The data domain is then processed via the left side of the diagram, and the response set is processed via the right side of the diagram, and the results are combined to generate the input to the Mangasarian and Musicant code, which provides the results in the bottom right-hand corner of the figure. The step to get the final weights for the slope and the intercept of the classifier is illustrated in Fig. 9.5. The process in Figs. 9.4 and 9.5 reflects the code in Listing 9.4. This conceptualized example provides a simple visual tool to understand the code of $L_1 + L_2 -$ SVM in Listing 9.4.

9.2.3 Algorithm and Coding of LSVM

The code in Listing 9.4 is written in R programming language, based on the process diagram with the data flow in Fig. 9.4, which was developed based on the $L_1 + L_2 -$ SVM formulation proposed by Dunbar [10] and the pseudo code presented by Mangasarian and Musicant in [9].

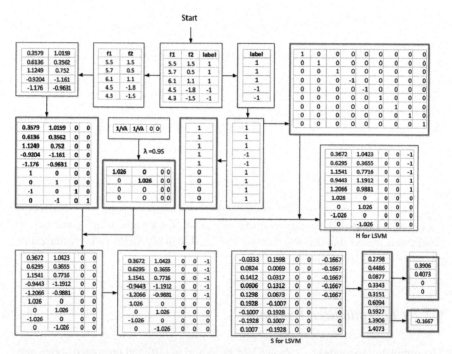

Fig. 9.4 The process diagram with data flow to develop the classifier based on $L_1 + L_2 -$ SVM and the Mangasarian and Musicant pseudo code in [9]

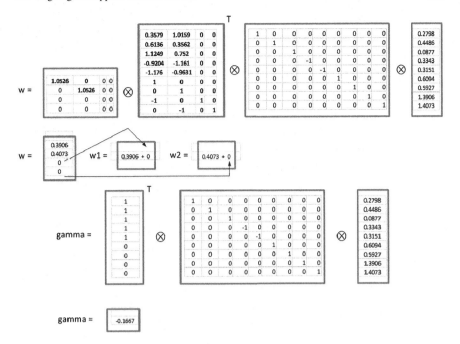

Fig. 9.5 Calculation of the final output of the process diagram presented in the previous figure in Fig. 9.4

Listing 9.4 An R programming example—implementation of LSVM

```
1   # Date: October 4th, 2014
2   # my-svm
3
4   data <- read.table("file3.txt", sep="")
5
6   A = data[1:2]
7   tmp1.A = scale(A)
8
9   scaled.A = tmp1.A[,]
10  class.label = data[3]
11  plot(scaled.A[,1], scaled.A[,2], col=ifelse(data$V3==1,"blue","
        red"), pch=19)
12
13  dim1.A = dim(A)[1]
14  dim2.A = dim(A)[2]
15
16  tmp1.D = c(t(class.label),rep(1,2*dim2.A))
17  diag.D = diag(tmp1.D)
18
19  tmp2.A = cbind(scaled.A, matrix(0,dim1.A,dim2.A))
20  tmp3.A = cbind(diag(dim2.A),0.0*diag(dim2.A))
21  tmp4.A = cbind(-diag(dim2.A),diag(dim2.A))
22
```

```
23
24   tmp.expanded.A = rbind(tmp2.A, tmp3.A, tmp4.A)
25   dim1.expanded.A = dim(tmp.expanded.A)[1]
26   dim2.expanded.A = dim(tmp.expanded.A)[2]
27   expanded.A = matrix(tmp.expanded.A, dim1.expanded.A, dim2.
         expanded.A)
28
29   lamda = 0.95
30   tmp1.lamda = sqrt(1/lamda)*diag(dim2.A)
31   tmp2.lamda = 0*diag(dim2.A)
32   tmp3.lamda = cbind(tmp1.lamda, tmp2.lamda)
33   tmp4.lamda = cbind(tmp2.lamda, tmp2.lamda)
34
35   expanded.lamda = rbind(tmp3.lamda, tmp4.lamda)
36
37   one.zero = c(rep(1,dim1.A), rep(0,2*dim2.A))
38
39   inter1.A = expanded.A \%*\% expanded.lamda
40   inter2.A = cbind(inter1.A, -one.zero)
41
42   lsvm.H = diag.D \%*\% inter2.A
43
44
45   ##### Mangasarian code starts #####
46   nu =1
47   lsvm.S = lsvm.H \%*\% solve((1/nu)*diag(2*dim2.A + 1) + t(lsvm.H)
         \%*\% lsvm.H)
48
49   lsvm.u = nu*(1-lsvm.S \%*\% (t(lsvm.H) \%*\% one.zero))
50
51   prev.lsvm.u = lsvm.u + 1
52
53   ii=0
54   alpha = 1.9/nu
55   while(ii < 1000 & norm(prev.lsvm.u-lsvm.u) > 0.0001) {
56     z = ((1/nu) + lsvm.H \%*\% t(lsvm.H) - alpha) \%*\% lsvm.u - 1
57     z = 1 + (abs(z) + z)/2
58     prev.lsvm.u = lsvm.u
59     lsvm.u = nu*(z-lsvm.S \%*\% (t(lsvm.H) \%*\% z))
60     ii = ii+1
61   }
62   ##### Mangasarian code ends #####
63
64   lsvm.y = expanded.lamda \%*\% t(expanded.A) \%*\% diag.D \%*\%
         lsvm.u
65   lsvm.y
66
67   lsvm.gamma = -t(one.zero) \%*\% diag.D \%*\% lsvm.u
68   lsvm.gamma
69
70   lsvm.w = lsvm.y[1:dim2.A] - lsvm.y[(dim2.A+1):(2*dim2.A)]
71   lsvm.w
72
73   intercept = lsvm.gamma/lsvm.w[2]
```

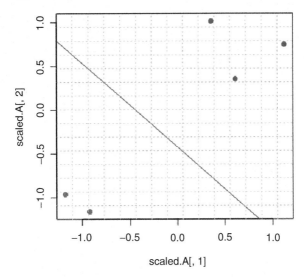

Fig. 9.6 The implementation of SVM and the classifier

```
74   slope = -lsvm.w[1]/lsvm.w[2]
75
76   abline(a=intercept, b=slope, col=2)
77   grid(15, 15, lwd=2)
```

The output of this program is presented in Fig. 9.6. It shows the scatter plot of the input data in file "file3.txt" and the support vector machine classifier calculated by this program. We can easily agree with this linear classification result.

9.3 Nonlinear Support Vector Machine

We have seen that the scatter plots play a major role in classification by facilitating the domain divisions. In the scatter plots, the dimension (i.e., each axis) is defined by a feature, and the space defined by the feature is called the vector space. The scatter plot describes the relationship between the features, and thus the correlated and uncorrelated data points can be identified in the vector space. The classification (in other words, the domain division) may be carried out either in a vector space or in a feature space, where the vector space is defined as the space that contains the scatter plot of the original features, and the feature space is defined as the space that contains the scatter plot of the transformed features using kernel functions [3].

9.3.1 Feature Space

Suppose there are p features $X_1, X_2, \ldots, X_p$ and the ith observation is denoted by $x_{i1}, x_{i2}, \ldots, x_{ip}$, where $i = 1, \ldots, n$. Then we can plot these n data points in a p-dimensional space to form a multidimensional scatter plot. This space is the vector space, and it displays both the magnitude and the directional information of the data. This set of p features may be transformed to a new set of d features using a polynomial kernel [3]. This space is called the feature space and, in general, each data point in the feature space carries information about a single data point in the vector space. The advantage of a feature space is that the nonseparable classes in the vector space may be turned into separable classes using a right choice of a kernel. However, finding a kernel and generating such a transformation are not simple.

$$\phi : R^p \to R^d \tag{9.18}$$

where R^p is the vector space (original domain) and R^d is the feature space, which is high dimensional (generally $d >> p$). It is possible to find ϕ that helps transform the vector space to a feature space where the classes are linearly separable. Hence, the support vector machine classifier in the feature space can be written as follows:

$$\begin{aligned} \text{Minimize:} \quad & \frac{||\mathbf{w}||^2}{2} \\ \text{subject to:} \quad & \mathbf{s}(\mathbf{w}\phi(\mathbf{x}') + \gamma \mathbf{I}) \geq \mathbf{I} \end{aligned} \tag{9.19}$$

However, $\phi(\mathbf{x})$ is high dimensional, thus the computation becomes very expensive. This can be tackled using an approach called a *kernel trick*. Very useful lecture notes on kernel trick can be found at http://www.cs.berkeley.edu/~jordan/courses/281B-spring04/lectures/lec3.pdf.

9.3.2 Kernel Trick

The usefulness of the kernel trick technique is explained in this section using the data points shown in Fig. 9.7. This figure shows classes that are not linearly separable. However, if we transform them to a three-dimensional feature space (higher dimensional) using the following transformation, then we can obtain linear separability as shown in Fig. 9.8:

$$\phi(u_1, u_2) = (au_1{}^2, bu_2{}^2, cu_1u_2) \tag{9.20}$$

Therefore, the support vector machine technique can be applied to this higher dimensional space, and a hyperplane can be derived as a classifier. In many real applications, such linear separability may be achieved in a very high-dimensional space, which makes it infeasible to apply the support vector machine techniques.

This is where the kernel tricks help. What exactly is the kernel trick? It is explained with the following simple example: Let us take two points (u_1, u_2) and (v_1, v_2) from the two-dimensional space presented in Fig. 9.7. Then we can have their transformed points as follows:

$$\phi(u_1, u_2) = (au_1{}^2, bu_2{}^2, cu_1u_2)$$
$$\phi(v_1, v_2) = (av_1{}^2, bv_2{}^2, cv_1v_2) \tag{9.21}$$

Let us now define a new function, which is called the kernel function, as follows:

$$k(u, v) = \phi(u_1, u_2).\phi(v_1, v_2) \tag{9.22}$$

It gives us

$$k(u, v) = a^2u_1{}^2v_1{}^2 + b^2u_2{}^2v_2{}^2 + c^2u_1v_1u_2v_2 \tag{9.23}$$

If we select $c^2 = 2ab$, then we can have

$$k(u, v) = (au_1v_1 + bu_2v_2)^2 \tag{9.24}$$

This can be written in the following matrix form:

$$k(u, v) = \left(\begin{bmatrix} u_1 & u_2 \end{bmatrix} * \begin{bmatrix} a & 0 \\ 0 & b \end{bmatrix} * \begin{bmatrix} v_1 \\ v_2 \end{bmatrix} \right)^2 \tag{9.25}$$

It shows that even if the function ϕ transforms the original data domain to a higher dimensional domain, the product $\phi.\phi$ can be easily defined based on the data in the original domain. Therefore, we can conclude that the kernel functionpresented

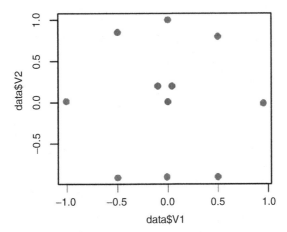

Fig. 9.7 It shows nonlinear classifiers are required to classify these two classes—a circle or an ellipse is needed to separate these two classes

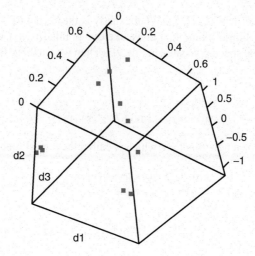

Fig. 9.8 This example shows that the classification of nonlinear separable classes is possible in a higher dimensional space called feature space

in Eq. (9.22) can be obtained by the matrix operations inside the original vector space rather than in the higher dimensional feature space. With the dual form [10] and the kernel function, the support vector machine can be applied in the original space (which is the lower dimension) with the same effect as its application inside the higher dimensional feature space.

Listing 9.5 An R programming example—Kernel trick example

```
1   # Date: May 23rd, 2015
2   # kernel-trick
3
4   library("rgl")
5
6   data <- read.table("file4.txt", sep="")
7
8   png("nonlinear2d.png", width=4, height=4, units="in",res=300)
9   plot(data$V1, data$V2, col=ifelse(data$V3==1,"blue","red"), pch
        =19)
10  grid(15, 15, lwd=2)
11  dev.off()
12
13  a = 1
14  b = 1
15  c = sqrt(2*a*b)
16
17  d1 = a*data$V1*data$V1
18  d2 = b*data$V2*data$V2
19  d3 = c*data$V1*data$V2
20
21  plot3d(d1,d2,d3,col=ifelse(data$V3==1,"blue","red"))
22  rgl.snapshot("somefile.png")
```

This R program reads the contents of "file4.txt" and first generates the scatter plot in Fig. 9.7. We can see the need for a nonlinear classifier. A kernel trick code in the rest of the program transforms the data to a higher dimension (in this case, 3D) and generates the plot as shown in Fig. 9.8. We can clearly see a linear separation in the transformed data.

> The kernel trick generally increases the dimensionality and, in turn, it can increase the computational time.

9.3.3 SVM Algorithms on Hadoop

Big data classification requires the support vector machine to be implemented on the system like the RHadoop, which provides a distributed file system and the R programming framework. As we recall, this framework provides mapper(), reducer(), and mapreduce() functions. Therefore, the MapReduce programming on Hadoop distributed files systems allows the implementation of svm-based algorithms either inside the mapper() function or inside the reducer() function. Two examples are considered in this section: the first example adopts the five points, three lines svm-based example discussed earlier and implements it inside the reducer() function, and the second example implements the lsvm algorithm inside the mapper() function and illustrates the conceptual example presented previously.

9.3.3.1 SVM: Reducer Implementation

Once again, the $L_1 + L_2 - $ SVM formulation proposed by Dunbar [10] and the pseudo code presented by Mangasarian and Musicant in [9] have been used in this implementation. The RHadoop system requires a number of environment variables [11]; therefore, they are included in the program from lines 4 to 6 in Listing 9.6. They provide path to the home of MapReduce (to access necessary libraries), to the Hadoop command (for program execution), and streaming jar file in the Linux system. In line 8, the data is uploaded into the R environment. The implementations on RHadoop requires two libraries [12, 13], rmr2, and rhdfs, and they are included in lines 10 and 11.

Listing 9.6 An RHadoop example—LSVM as a reducer() function

```
1  # Date: May 21st, 2015
2  # svm-on-hadoop
3
4  Sys.setenv(HADOOP_HOME='/usr/lib/hadoop-0.20-mapreduce')
5  Sys.setenv(HADOOP_CMD='/usr/bin/hadoop')
```

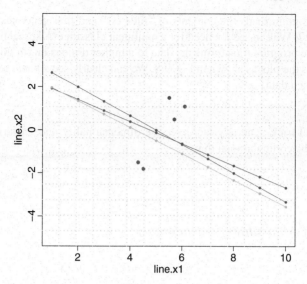

Fig. 9.9 It shows the implementation of SVM and the classifier

```
6   Sys.setenv(HADOOP_STREAMING='/usr/lib/hadoop-0.20-mapreduce/
        contrib/streaming/hadoop-streaming-2.0.0-mr1-cdh4.7.0.jar')
7
8   data <- read.table("file3.txt", sep="")
9
10  library(rmr2)
11  library(rhdfs)
12
13  hdfs.init()
14  data.content <- to.dfs(data)
15
16  data.map.fn <- function(k,v) {
17    key <- 1
18    val <- c(v[,1],v[,2],v[,3])
19    #val <- c(scale(v[,1]),scale(v[,2]),v[,3])
20    keyval(key,val)
21  }
22
23  data.reduce.fn <- function(k,v) {
24
25    # extract feature and separate the labels
26    rmr.str(v)
27    point.x = matrix(v[1:10],nrow=2,ncol=5,byrow=TRUE)
28
29    # select weights for parametrization
30    weight.w = matrix(c(2,3,2.1,4.1,1.9,3.1),nrow=3,ncol=2,byrow=
          TRUE)
31    weight.w
32
33    # select intercepts for parametrization
```

```
34   gamma.g = matrix(c(-10,-10,-8),nrow=3,ncol=1,byrow=TRUE)
35   gamma.g
36
37   mgamma.g = matrix(rep(gamma.g,5),nrow=3,ncol=5)
38   mgamma.g
39
40   # assign class labels
41   label.s = matrix(c(v[11:15]),nrow=5,ncol=1,byrow=TRUE)
42   label.s
43
44   label.ss=matrix(rep(label.s,3),ncol=3)
45   label.ss
46
47   # determine label error
48   hat.y = weight.w %*% point.x + mgamma.g
49   hat.y
50
51   # check for minimum error
52   t(label.ss) * hat.y
53
54   # calculate SVM measure for optimization
55   measure.m = (weight.w %*% t(weight.w))/2
56   measure.m
57
58   # display the straight line and points
59   line.x1 = rep(0,10)
60   line.x2 = rep(0,10)
61
62   slope = -weight.w[,1]/weight.w[,2]
63   intercept = -gamma.g/weight.w[,2]
64
65   line.x1 = 1:10
66   line.x2 = intercept[1]+slope[1]*line.x1
67
68   plot(line.x1, line.x2, type="o", col="blue", pch=20, ylim=c
         (-5,5))
69   points(point.x[1,], point.x[2,], col=ifelse(data$V3==1,"blue","
         red"), pch=19)
70   grid(15, 15, lwd=2)
71
72   line.x1 = 1:10
73   line.x2 = intercept[2]+slope[2]*line.x1
74   lines(line.x1, line.x2, type="o", col="red", pch=20, ylim=c
         (-5,5))
75
76   line.x1 = 1:10
77   line.x2 = intercept[3]+slope[3]*line.x1
78   lines(line.x1, line.x2, type="o", col="green", pch=20, ylim=c
         (-5,5))
79
80   # optimization - select the weights that correspond
81   # to the smallest measure.
82   kk = diag(measure.m)
83   ii = which(kk == min(kk))
```

```
84      ss=c(slope[ii],intercept[ii])
85      keyval(k, ss)
86  }
87
88  classify <- mapreduce(input=data.content,
89                           map = data.map.fn,
90                           reduce = data.reduce.fn)
91
92  results = from.dfs(classify)
93  results
```

We should initialize the Hadoop environment and feed the data to it, and these tasks are presented in lines 13 and 14. Once these tasks are performed, we can define mapper() and reducer() functions, and then input them to the MapReduce model. The mapper() function is defined from line 16 to 21, and it creates a (key, value) pair from the input data. The integer value of 1 is used as key (see line 17) because of the single file processing, and the features in the first and the second column $(v[,1], v[,2])$ of the file are used as values (see line 18) in the key value pair presented in line 20. The reducer() function accepts the (key, value) pair, and uses the values to find the classifier (i.e., the slope and the intercept), which gives the minimum measure adopted in the svm's optimization approach [see Eq. (9.13)]. These steps are in the code from lines 23 to 86. Then these optimal parameters are tagged with the key (see line 85). Each block of code in this program is commented such that they are self explanatory. The block of code from line 58 to line 78 produces the scatter plot and the straight lines (possible svm-based classifiers) presented in Fig. 9.9. Because this program is executed inside the RHadoop it saves this result as Rplots.pdf file. The MapReduce model in lines 88–90 then assigns them to the variable called "classify." These data processing tasks occur inside the Hadoop environment, and they must be transferred to outside the Hadoop environment as performed with the command in line 92.

9.3.3.2 LSVM: Mapper Implementation

The mapper implementation of the $L_1 + L_2 - $ SVM formulation proposed by Dunbar [10] is presented, and it uses the pseudo code presented by Mangasarian and Musicant in [9]. In the reducer() implementation, the sorted data was obtained from the mapper(), and then the reducer() implemented the LSVM-based approach to derive the weights for the slope and intercept parameters of the svm classifier. But in the mapper implementation, the LSM-based approach is implemented in the mapper() function, and the slope and intercept parameters are calculated. These parameters are passed to the reducer() function. In both cases, a single key is used. However, multiple keys can be used to take advantage of the parallelization and sorting features of the MapReduce framework.

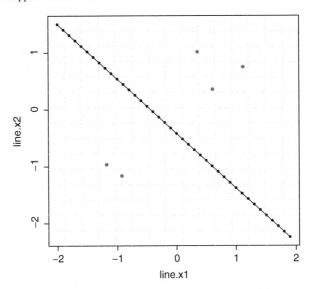

Fig. 9.10 The implementation of SVM on RHadoop and the classifier

Listing 9.7 An RHadoop example—LSVM as a mapper() function

```
1   # Date: May 21st, 2015
2   # lsvm-on-hadoop
3
4   Sys.setenv(HADOOP_HOME='/usr/lib/hadoop-0.20-mapreduce')
5   Sys.setenv(HADOOP_CMD='/usr/bin/hadoop')
6   Sys.setenv(HADOOP_STREAMING='/usr/lib/hadoop-0.20-mapreduce/
        contrib/streaming/hadoop-streaming-2.0.0-mr1-cdh4.7.0.jar')
7
8   data <- read.table("file3.txt", sep="")
9
10  library(rmr2)
11  library(rhdfs)
12
13  hdfs.init()
14  data.content <- to.dfs(data)
15
16  data.map.fn <- function(k,v) {
17    key <- 1
18    vw <- cbind(scale(v[,1]),scale(v[,2]))
19
20    scaled.A <- matrix(vw, ncol=2, byrow=FALSE)
21    class.label <- v[,3]
22    rmr.str(class.label)
23
24    dim1.A = dim(scaled.A)[1]
25    dim2.A = dim(scaled.A)[2]
26
```

```
27    tmp1.D = c(t(class.label),rep(1,2*dim2.A))
28    diag.D = diag(tmp1.D)
29
30    tmp2.A = cbind(scaled.A, matrix(0,dim1.A,dim2.A))
31    tmp3.A = cbind(diag(dim2.A),0.0*diag(dim2.A))
32    tmp4.A = cbind(-diag(dim2.A),diag(dim2.A))
33
34    tmp.expanded.A = rbind(tmp2.A, tmp3.A, tmp4.A)
35    dim1.expanded.A = dim(tmp.expanded.A)[1]
36    dim2.expanded.A = dim(tmp.expanded.A)[2]
37    expanded.A = matrix(tmp.expanded.A, dim1.expanded.A, dim2.
          expanded.A)
38
39    lamda = 0.95
40    tmp1.lamda = sqrt(1/lamda)*diag(dim2.A)
41    tmp2.lamda = 0*diag(dim2.A)
42    tmp3.lamda = cbind(tmp1.lamda, tmp2.lamda)
43    tmp4.lamda = cbind(tmp2.lamda, tmp2.lamda)
44
45    expanded.lamda = rbind(tmp3.lamda, tmp4.lamda)
46    one.zero = c(rep(1,dim1.A), rep(0,2*dim2.A))
47
48    inter1.A = expanded.A %*% expanded.lamda
49    inter2.A = cbind(inter1.A, -one.zero)
50
51    #rmr.str(scaled.A)
52    lsvm.H = diag.D %*% inter2.A
53
54    ##### Mangasarian code starts ###############
55    nu =1
56    lsvm.S = lsvm.H %*% solve((1/nu)*diag(2*dim2.A + 1) + t(lsvm.H)
          %*% lsvm.H)
57
58    lsvm.u = nu*(1-lsvm.S %*% (t(lsvm.H) %*% one.zero))
59
60    prev.lsvm.u = lsvm.u + 1
61
62    ii=0
63    alpha = 1.9/nu
64    while(ii < 1000 & norm(prev.lsvm.u-lsvm.u) > 0.0001) {
65      z = ((1/nu) + lsvm.H %*% t(lsvm.H) - alpha) %*% lsvm.u - 1
66      z = 1 + (abs(z) + z)/2
67      prev.lsvm.u = lsvm.u
68      lsvm.u = nu*(z-lsvm.S %*% (t(lsvm.H) %*% z))
69      ii = ii+1
70    }
71    ###### end of Mangasarian
72
73    lsvm.y = expanded.lamda %*% t(expanded.A) %*% diag.D %*% lsvm.u
74
75    lsvm.gamma = -t(one.zero) %*% diag.D %*% lsvm.u
76    lsvm.gamma
77
78    lsvm.w = lsvm.y[1:dim2.A] - lsvm.y[(dim2.A+1):(2*dim2.A)]
```

```
79    lsvm.w
80
81    intercept = lsvm.gamma/lsvm.w[2]
82    slope = -lsvm.w[1]/lsvm.w[2]
83
84    line.x1 = rep(0,10)
85    line.x2 = rep(0,10)
86
87    xx = -2.0
88    for (i in 1:40) {
89      line.x1[i] = xx
90      line.x2[i] = slope*line.x1[i] + intercept
91      xx=xx+0.1
92    }
93
94    plot(line.x1, line.x2, type="o", pch=20)
95    points(vw[,1], vw[,2], col=ifelse(v[,3]==1,"blue","red"), pch
           =19)
96    grid(15, 15, lwd=2)
97
98    val <- c(intercept,slope)
99    keyval(key,val)
100  }
101
102  data.reduce.fn <- function(k,v) {
103    keyval(k, v)
104  }
105
106  classify <- mapreduce(input=data.content,
107                        map = data.map.fn,
108                        reduce = data.reduce.fn)
109
110  aa = from.dfs(classify)
111  aa
```

The output of this program is presented in Fig. 9.10. This is similar to the one in Fig. 9.6, except this classifier is obtain using the RHadoop and MapReduce computing tools. However, the results show a significant similarity. The slopes and the intercepts may be numerically compared to determine their similarities.

9.3.4 Real Application

In this real application, the hardwood floor and carpet floor data sets are used. As you recall, these data sets have 1024 observations in each with 64 features that correspond to the intensity values of the pixels. To show the performance of the support vector machine implemented in Listing 9.7 in a two-dimensional data domain, the features 48 and 49 are selected. The scatter plots of the data sets corresponding

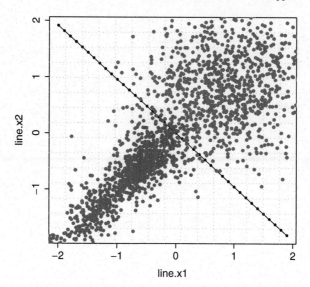

Fig. 9.11 The implementation of SVM on RHadoop, and the classifier with hardwood floor and carpet floor data sets

to these two features and the support vector machine classifier obtained using the algorithm are presented in Fig. 9.11. We can clearly see the linear classification performance of the Lagrangian support vector machine.

Problems

9.1. Code Revision
Revise the MapReduce programs presented in this chapter using the coding principles taught in Chap. 5.

9.2. Coding Efficiency

(a) Study the programs presented in the listings and draw the structure diagrams, data flow diagrams, and process diagrams based on the software engineering principles.
(b) Study the R programs in the Listings and improve their efficiencies using coding principles and modularization. Make this program more efficient using arrays and input files as well.

9.3. Comparison
Discuss the advantages and disadvantages of the mapper() and the reducer() implementations of the svm-based approaches. You may also run these implementations and obtain the system times to support the discussion.

9.4. Split-Merge-Split

(a) Assuming that you have completed the problem presented in "Problem 3.1," perform the same steps using the RHadoop system with the R programming framework.

(b) Compare the results that you obtained in (a) with the results that you obtained in Problem 3.1.

Acknowledgements I would like to thank Professor Vaithilingam (Jeya) Jeyakumar of the University of New South Wales, Australia, for giving me an opportunity to work with him and his research team on support vector machine problems and associated implementations to different applications. I also participated in the research focusing on enhancing the support vector machine technique and published our theory, results, and findings. This research contributed to this chapter.

References

1. M. A. Hearst, S. T. Dumais, E. Osman, J. Platt, and B. Scholkopf. "Support vector machines." Intelligent Systems and their Applications, IEEE, 13(4), pp. 18–28, 1998.
2. T. Hastie, R. Tibshirani, and J. Friedman. The Elements of Statistical Learning. New York: Springer, 2009.
3. B. Scholkopf, S. Mika, C. J. C. Burges, P. Knirsch, K. R. Muller, G. Ratsch and A. J. Smola. "Input space versus feature space in kernel-based methods," IEEE Trans. On Neural Networks, vol. 10, no. 5, pp. 1000–1017, 1999.
4. G. Huang, H. Chen, Z. Zhou, F. Yin and K. Guo. "Two-class support vector data description." Pattern Recognition, 44, pp. 320–329, 2011.
5. V. Franc, and V. Hlavac. "Multi-class support vector machine." In Proceedings of the IEEE 16th International Conference on Pattern Recognition, vol. 2, pp. 236–239, 2002.
6. http://en.wikipedia.org/wiki/Distance_between_two_straight_lines, accessed June 5th, 2015.
7. M. Dunbar, J. M. Murray, L. A. Cysique, B. J. Brew, and V. Jeyakumar. "Simultaneous classification and feature selection via convex quadratic programming with application to HIV-associated neurocognitive disorder assessment." European Journal of Operational Research 206(2): pp. 470–478, 2010.
8. V. Jeyakumar, G. Li, and S. Suthaharan. "Support vector machine classifiers with uncertain knowledge sets via robust optimization." Optimization, pp. 1–18, 2012.
9. O. L. Mangasarian and D. R. Musicant. 2000. "LSVM Software: Active set support vector machine classification software." Available online at http://research.cs.wisc.edu/dmi/lsvm/.
10. M. Dunbar. "Optimization approaches to simultaneous classification and feature selections," Technical Report (supervised by V. Jeyakumar) School of Mathematics and Statistics, The University of New South Wales, Australia, pp. 1–118, 2007.
11. http://www.meetup.com/Learning-Machine-Learning-by-Example/pages/Installing_R_and_R Hadoop/
12. http://projects.revolutionanalytics.com/rhadoop/
13. http://bighadoop.wordpress.com/2013/02/25/r-and-hadoop-data-analysis-rhadoop/

Chapter 10
Decision Tree Learning

Abstract The main objective of this chapter is to introduce you to hierarchical supervised learning models. One of the main hierarchical models is the decision tree. It has two categories: classification tree and regression tree. The theory and applications of these decision trees are explained in this chapter. These techniques require tree split algorithms to build the decision trees and require quantitative measures to build an efficient tree via training. Hence, the chapter dedicates some discussion to the measures like entropy, cross-entropy, Gini impurity, and information gain. It also discusses the training algorithms suitable for classification tree and regression tree models. Simple examples and visual aids explain the difficult concepts so that readers can easily grasp the theory and applications of decision tree.

10.1 The Decision Tree

In practice, the decision tree-based supervised learning is defined as a rule-based, binary-tree building technique (see [1–3]), but it is easier to understand if it is interpreted as a hierarchical domain division technique. Therefore, in this book, the decision tree is defined as a supervised learning model that hierarchically maps a data domain onto a response set. It divides a data domain (node) recursively into two subdomains such that the subdomains have a higher information gain than the node that was split. We know the goal of supervised learning is the classification of the data, and therefore, the information gain means the ease of classification in the subdomains created by a split. Finding the best split that gives the maximum information gain (i.e., the ease of classification) is the goal of the optimization algorithm in the decision tree-based supervised learning.

Suppose we have a system that produces events (observations) that can be one of the classes 0 or 1 (e.g., rain or no rain, head or tail), and these events depend on only one feature. Hence, let us define the data domain as $D = \{e_1, e_2, \ldots, e_n\}$ (assume

© Springer Science+Business Media New York 2016
S. Suthaharan, *Machine Learning Models and Algorithms for Big Data Classification*, Integrated Series in Information Systems 36,
DOI 10.1007/978-1-4899-7641-3_10

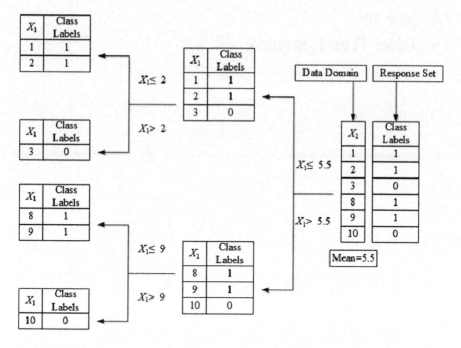

Fig. 10.1 Classification example. A decision tree building with a one-dimensional data domain—output is a discrete value

this is a sorted list), and their corresponding class labels are $L = \{r_1, r_2, \ldots, r_n\}$, where $r_i \in \{0, 1\}$, and $i = 1 \ldots n$. The spread (or the distribution pattern) of the class labels over the data domain determines the ease of classification. Let us represent the information gain of D with respect to L by I_i and split the sorted set at the location m to form two subdomains $D_1 = \{e_1, e_2, \ldots, e_m\}$ and $D_2 = \{e_{m+1}, e_2, \ldots, e_n\}$ with the corresponding response sets $L_1 = \{r_1, r_2, \ldots, r_m\}$ and $L_2 = \{r_{m+1}, r_2, \ldots, r_n\}$. If their information gains are I_{i1} and I_{i2}, then m will be considered as the best split if $average(I_{i1}, I_{i2}) > I_i$. Of course, we need a good quantitative measure to measure the information gain, or the ease of classification, with respect to the domain split.

Suppose p_0 and p_1 represent the probabilities that class 0 and class 1 can be drawn from the domain D, respectively. Take an example that $|p_0 - p_1| \to 1$; then we can see one particular class dominates highly in that domain, hence further domain division is not required. Similarly if $|p_0 - p_1| \to 0$, then the classes have equal domination in that domain; therefore, further split is needed. In that case, we generate two subdomains D_1 and D_2. Say, q_0 and q_1 are the probabilities that class 0 and class 1 can be drawn from the subdomain D_1, respectively. If the split is efficient, $q_0 > p_0$ or $q_1 > p_1$. Assume $q_0 > p_0$, then $q_0 = p_0 + \varepsilon$, where $\varepsilon > 0$.

$$|q_0 - q_1| = |2q_0 - 1| = |2(p_0 + \varepsilon) - 1| = |2p_0 + 2\varepsilon - 1| \tag{10.1}$$

$$|q_0 - q_1| = |p_0 + 1 - p_1 + 2\varepsilon - 1| = |p_0 - p_1 + 2\varepsilon|. \tag{10.2}$$

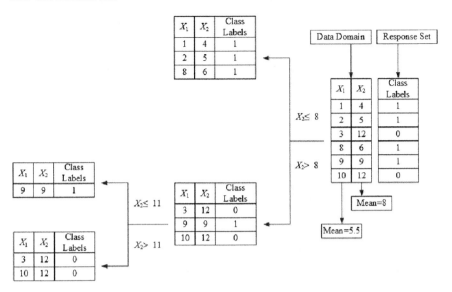

Fig. 10.2 Classification example. A decision tree building with a two-dimensional data domain—output is a discrete value

This mathematical equation emphasizes the following inequality (when $q_0 > p_0$):

$$|q_0 - q_1| > |p_0 - p_1|. \tag{10.3}$$

The absolute differences in the above inequality are the quantitative measures that measures the proportionality between the classes in the respective subdomains. This probabilistic measure is a good measure to address the optimization objectives of the decision tree. Let us look at some "Thinking with Examples" and understand the decision tree better in terms of domain division focusing on information gain.

Thinking with Example 10.1:

The purpose of this example is to show you how a data domain formed by a single feature may be divided and mapped to a two-class (discrete) response set. Suppose the data domain is a single feature set $X_1 = \{1, 2, 3, 8, 9, 10\}$ with a set of assigned class labels $L = \{1, 1, 0, 1, 1, 0\}$, respectively. Then the root node of the decision tree is the feature X_1, and its value is used to divide the data domain as shown in Fig. 10.1. We now need a parameter and an approach to divide this root node to build a decision tree. For simplicity, we can choose the mean value ($m = 5.5$) as the parameter value, and the approach as the values $\leq m$ form the left subdomain and the values $> m$ form the right subdomain. We can see these subdomains at the second level of the tree (assuming the root is the first level). The mean values of

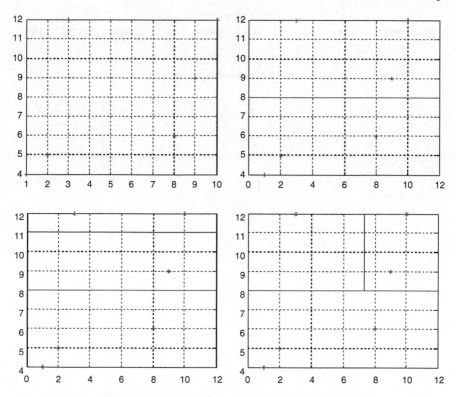

Fig. 10.3 Results from the code in Listing 10.1

the subdomains ($m = 2$ and $m = 9$) can be used to expand the tree as shown in Fig. 10.1. Finally, the leaves that show the class labels are determined by the mean as the split criterion and feature X_1 as the domain and subdomains variables. Let us now consider a two-dimensional data domain example.

Thinking with Example 10.2:

Suppose the system adds another feature set $\{4, 5, 12, 6, 9, 12\}$ to the same data with the same labeling order. Hence, it creates the two-dimensional data domain formed by the features X_1 and X_2. We now have two features, thus we must adopt an approach to select one feature for the root node first. For simplicity, assume that the feature X_2 is selected randomly. Then the data domain considered at the root of the tree is $\{4, 5, 12, 6, 9, 12\}$, as shown in Fig. 10.2. Once again, if we use the mean as the split criterion with the same splitting approach, then we get the subdomains as shown in the figure. The left node at this level has the same class (i.e., class 1), so no further split is required. The right node needs a split, and now we have a choice

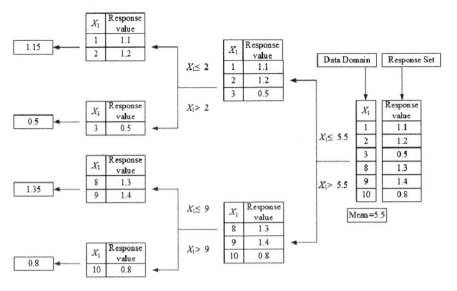

Fig. 10.4 Regression example. A decision tree building with a one-dimensional data domain—output is a real number

to have either X_1 or X_2. The tree shows the selection of the same feature. The mean is calculated, and the node is split. Now the leaves have the class labels from the same classes. The code in Listing 10.1 provides the results of the domain division example in Fig. 10.2.

10.1.1 A Coding Example—Classification Tree

The block of code in line 4 to line 14, a two-dimensional data set with two classes is created, a data domain and a response set are established, and these data points are plotted as shown in the first figure in Fig. 10.3. In lines 18–20, the data domain is divided into two subdomains using the mean value of feature 2 as the split location. This statistical mean value is a part of the classifier. Note that this is the place where the decision tree calculates the information gain using Gini index to find the optimal split location. The block of code in lines 22–23 creates the subdomains (or the children of the tree node). The classifier mean at this node is plotted in the second figure of Fig. 10.3.

Listing 10.1 A Matlab example—classification tree

```
1  clear all;
2  close all;
3
4  x1=[1 2 3 8 9 10];
```

```
 5   x2=[4  5  12  6  9  12];
 6   yy=[1  1  0  1  1  0];
 7
 8   xx=[x1'  x2'  yy'];
 9
10   ind1=find(xx(:,3)==1);
11   ind2=find(xx(:,3)==0);
12
13   figure;plot(xx(ind1,1),xx(ind1,2),'b*');grid on;
14   hold on;plot(xx(ind2,1),xx(ind2,2),'r*');grid on;
15
16   %%%%%%%%%%%%%%%%%%%%%%%%%%%%%%%%%%%%%%%%%%%%%%%%%
17
18   m1=mean(xx(:,2));
19   indL=find(xx(:,2)<m1);
20   indR=find(xx(:,2)>=m1);
21
22   xxL=xx(indL,:)
23   xxR=xx(indR,:)
24
25   hold on;line([0,  max(xx(:,2))],[m1,m1]);
26
27   %%%%%%%%%%%%%%%%%%%%%%%%%%%%%%%%%%%%%%%%%%%%%%%%%
28
29   ind=2;
30   m2=mean(xxR(:,ind));
31   indRL=find(xxR(:,ind)<m2);
32   indRR=find(xxR(:,ind)>=m2);
33
34   xxRL=xxR(indRL,:)
35   xxRR=xxR(indRR,:)
36
37   if (ind==2)
38       hold on;line([0,  max(xxR(:,ind))],[m2,m2],'color','k');
39   else
40       hold on;line([m2,m2],[8,  12],'color','k');
41   end
```

This is a toy example; therefore, we can see the intermediate output and observe that the left domain does not need the split. Only the right subdomain is further divided using the same feature (i.e., feature 2) in lines 29–32. By changing the value of the variable ind in line 29 to 1, we can perform the split based on feature 1. The third and fourth figures show the second split using the statistical means of features 1 and 2, respectively. The block of code in lines 37–41 performs this task. The numerical output of this program is (if ind = 2):

xxL =				xxR =		
1	4	1		3	12	0
2	5	1		9	9	1
8	6	1		10	12	0

xxRL =			xxRR =		
9	9	1	3	12	0
			10	12	0

These results are presented in a two-column format only for the purpose of improving the presentation of the results. Similarly, the output of this program is (if ind = 1):

xxL =			xxR =		
1	4	1	3	12	0
2	5	1	9	9	1
8	6	1	10	12	0

xxRL =			xxRR =		
3	12	0	9	9	1
			10	12	0

These outputs are also presented in a two-column format for the purpose of improving the presentation. This example leads us to ask the following questions: (1) Which features must be selected for the nodes? (2) How do we parametrize the node split? (3) What parameter values must be chosen? (4) How do we parametrize the depth of the tree? and (5) How do we optimize the tree structure?

We can simply state: in decision tree supervised learning, there is a data domain which must be split into two subdomains at a location on a feature set with the focus of obtaining an information gain at each split. This process must be recursively carried out until the data domain is divided into several subdomains, where each domain presents an optimal classification.

Thinking with Example 10.3:

The purpose of this example is to show you how a data domain formed by a single feature may be divided and mapped to a continuous response set. Suppose the data domain is a single feature set $X_1 = \{1, 2, 3, 8, 9, 10\}$ with a set of assigned continuous responses $R = \{1.1, 1.2, 0.5, 1.3, 1.4, 0.8\}$. We use the same decision tree building as shown in Fig. 10.1, and it is presented in Fig. 10.4 with minor differences. The responses are averaged over the values of the subdomains resulting in at the leaves of the tree. This is called the regression tree, and we will study this in detail later in this chapter. The code in Listing 10.2 provides the results of the domain division for a regression tree.

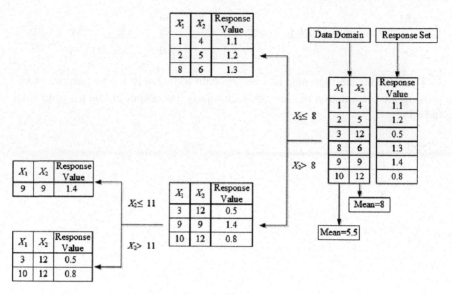

Fig. 10.5 Regression example. A decision tree building with a two-dimensional data domain—output is a real number—result of Listing 10.2

10.1.2 A Coding Example—Regression Tree

The program in this section can be explained by the diagram in Fig. 10.5. The block of code in lines 4–6 defines the two-dimensional data domain and the response set with real numbers for regression. Line 8 defines a single matrix which contains both data domain and response set.

Listing 10.2 A Matlab example—regression tree

```
1   clear all;
2   close all;
3
4   x1=[1 2 3 8 9 10];
5   x2=[4 5 12 6 9 12];
6   yy=[1.1 1.2 0.5 1.3 1.4 0.8];
7
8   xx=[x1' x2' yy'];
9
10  ind1=find(xx(:,3)==1);
11  ind2=find(xx(:,3)==0);
12
13  figure;plot3(xx(:,1),xx(:,2),xx(:,3),'*');grid on;
14
15  %%%%%%%%%%%%%%%%%%%%%%%%%%%%%%%%%%%%%%%%%%%%%%%%%%%%
16
17  m1=mean(xx(:,2));
18  indL=find(xx(:,2)<m1);
```

```
19  indR=find(xx(:,2)>=m1);
20
21  xxL=xx(indL,:);
22  xxR=xx(indR,:);
23
24  mean(xxL(:,3))
25
26  %%%%%%%%%%%%%%%%%%%%%%%%%%%%%%%%%%%%%%%%%%%%%%%%%%%%
27
28  ind=2;
29  m2=mean(xxR(:,ind));
30  indRL=find(xxR(:,ind)<m2);
31  indRR=find(xxR(:,ind)>=m2);
32
33  xxRL=xxR(indRL,:);
34  xxRR=xxR(indRR,:);
35
36  mean(xxRL(:,3))
37  mean(xxRR(:,3))
```

The block of code from line 17 to 24 performs the first split using feature 2 and prints the average of the responses of the subdomain in the left side of the tree. The block of code in lines 28–34 splits the subdomain in the right side of the tree further using feature 2. The averages of the responses in the new branches of the tree are printed in lines 36–37. Hence, the final output of this program is:

```
ans =
     1.2000

ans =
     1.4000

ans =
     0.6500
```

This program is hardcoded; therefore, you can modify the program in appropriate places to investigate the effect of the features at different tree nodes. For example, modify the code in line 28 to ind = 1, and study the effect.

10.2 Types of Decision Trees

In supervised learning, the decision tree has been divided into classification trees and regression trees by Breiman et al. [4]. In simple terms, we can say the classification tree helps predict a class label (i.e., discrete) for a response variable whereas the regression tree helps predict a value (i.e., continuous) for the response variable. In Figs. 10.6 and 10.7, the processes of a classification tree and regression tree are illustrated using a hierarchical structure to show the evolution of domain division properties.

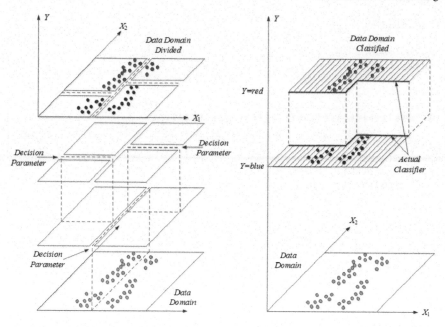

Fig. 10.6 The classification tree is illustrated in 3D using two classes with domain division properties. Response variable *Y* has two discrete values, *red* or *blue*

10.2.1 Classification Tree

The classification tree helps assign a label to a new data set. For example, it can help us decide if a new observation belongs to a class 1 or a class 0. The concept of the classification tree is explained using the illustration in Fig. 10.6, where two classes (red and blue) are used. Note that the explanation is the construction of a classification tree at the training phase, and it gives a visual example of a decision tree building. It also uses the data domain and its changes during the construction of a decision tree. The left diagram shows the propagation of tree split that divides the data domain and creates subdomains for appropriate classification based on the given class labels. It can be seen as the generation of simple multiple thin layers of data domains with split-regions. The first thin layer shows the given data domain and a split condition which is applied to the first feature. The domain is divided into two subdomains, and it is shown in the second thin layer. These subdomains are further divided into four subdomains based on the second feature, and they are shown in the third thin layer. Finally, the class labels are highlighted and we can see they are classified into different disjointed subdomains.

The diagram on the right side shows the given data domain and the final classified data domain. It illustrates the effect on the response variable (discrete) with two classes, where the related subdomains are combined to show the class separation. The main parameters of the classification tree models are the values of the features

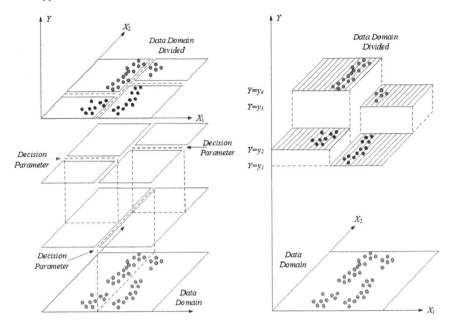

Fig. 10.7 The regression tree is illustrated in 3D using two classes with domain division properties. Response variable Y has two continuous *red* and *blue* values

used to split the tree at a particular node, and these parameters are trained using information gain as a quantitative measure. The combination of parameters selected by the classification tree at training is considered the classifier. The decision parameters and the actual classification with the tree-based classifier are explained later in the chapter.

In classification trees, the split criterion must give an information gain so that the subdomains (i.e., the leaves of the current tree) have class information that help separate the classes. The split criterion needs decision parameters that form the classification model. The decision parameters (a feature and its split location) are calculated based on the maximization of the information gain. That is, the decision parameters shown in Fig. 10.6 can be calculated according to this principle.

10.2.2 Regression Tree

The regression tree helps assign a value for new data. The objective of the regression tree model is to divide the data domain into disjoint, rectangular subdomains by splitting features, and then map the subdomains to nonoverlapping groups of responses that are estimated with the minimum error criterion (e.g., least square method). See Fig. 10.7. This statement shows four tasks: (1) feature selection for a node, (2) parametrization of the split location, (3) parametrization of the depth of the tree, and (4) estimation of the response variables.

The PhD thesis by Torgo [5] provides a very good explanation, and I encourage readers refer to it for additional information. The full version of the thesis can be found at the following website: http://www.dcc.fc.up.pt/~ltorgo/PhD/. The popular book by Breiman et al. [4] is another best resource for exploring regression trees in depth. The decision parameters are chosen based on the least square criterion (see Leo Breiman's classification and regression trees book [4] and Torgo's thesis [5]). The example in the figure shows the decision parameters that are calculated based on the mean value of the respond variable for each subdomain and the domain.

10.3 Decision Tree Learning Model

We have seen in a previous chapter that modeling means the definition of a function or a mapping between a data domain and a response set followed by the parametrization of the model and the optimization of the parameters. It is clear that the decision tree satisfies this definition and forms a supervised learning model because it can be trained, validated, and tested using the supervised learning algorithms. Let us now study the processes of parametrization and optimization of the decision tree supervised learning model.

10.3.1 Parametrization

As discussed before, a supervised model must be parametrized so that it can be trained, validated, and tested. This is true for a decision tree as well. The question now is how to parametrize a tree-like structure and find the parameters. In building a tree-like structure, the nodes are split and leaves are generated, and this process is recursively done. Therefore, we can parametrize (1) the choice of features for a node, (2) the threshold that splits the node and divides the feature set into two subsets, and (3) the number of levels that the entire tree should have. It is illustrated in Figs. 10.8 and 10.9.

- Parametrization: select the features for the root node and intermediate nodes of the decision tree. Hence, I would say the feature must be considered as one of the parameters for the decision tree. We have two options: (1) We may select a feature for a node randomly, or (2) We may select a feature that can give some information gain (or error reduction) when it is used and subdomains are constructed.

- Parametrization: select a parameter to split criterion (e.g., split location in the feature set). Hence, a threshold for the feature values can form a parameter for the decision tree. We have two options: (1) We may select the statistical tech-

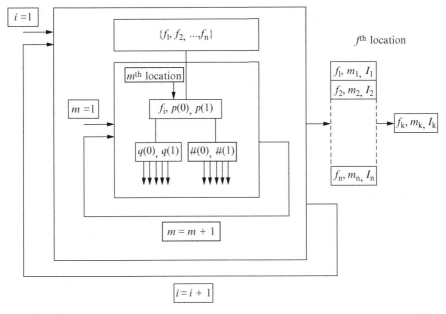

Fig. 10.8 The process of selecting the best features (with its split location) that give the maximum information gain ($i = 1, \ldots, n$)

niques like mean or median to find the split location, or (2) We can find the split location which will give two subdomains that lead to an acceptable information gain (or error reduction) by splitting.

- Parametrization: select a parameter to stop the tree building. It means that the number of levels in the decision tree must be a parameter.

- Optimization: select an algorithm that helps optimize the parameters such that the final decision tree is optimal so that the tree can perform a very good prediction of class labels. This may lead to a computationally expensive process, because all of the possible combinations of features and the split locations must be processed toward obtaining information gain values and selecting the feature and split location combination that gives maximum gain or minimum error.

10.3.2 Optimization

The example in Fig. 10.1 shows the dividing of a tree node (i.e., building a model) and building a decision tree, but it doesn't show how to divide a tree node *efficiently* (i.e., the training). To find an answer to this question, we may need to ask several other questions: Which feature must be selected first to start building the tree? Which features must be selected at the intermediate steps of the tree building? It

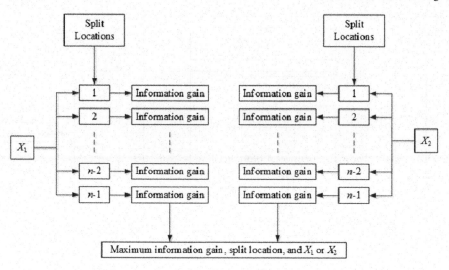

Fig. 10.9 The process of finding the best split location using the maximum information gain—a sub process for Fig. 10.8

means that we need a good quantitative measure which is applicable to tree building structure. Tree building means the generation of leaves (or branches) from a node, and carrying out this process iteratively. Let me explain the standard quantitative measures like entropy [6], Gini impurity [3, 7], information gain [3], and cross-entropy [8].

10.4 Quantitative Measures

In decision tree modeling, the quantitative measures are required in two places: (1) to measure the information gain resulted by a feature split over data domains (or subdomains), and (2) to measure the significance in the class difference at each node to decide further split. Useful measures for the first requirement are the entropy, Gini impurity, and information gain. Useful measures for the second requirement are the class proportions, count differences, and a probability measure (e.g., ratios and percentages).

10.4.1 Entropy and Cross-Entropy

Entropy provides a measure based on the proportionality of the events. For example, if one event occurs more than another event in a place or with an object, then we have good knowledge about that place or the object relative to the majority event. If both events occur the same number of times in that place or with the object, then it is hard to characterize the place or the object. Say, for example, if a football team

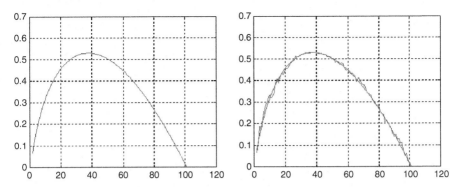

Fig. 10.10 The entropy characteristics with and without an error factor, respectively—horizontal axis represents the probability index and the vertical axis represents the entropy

has 9 wins and 1 loss, then we should be able to characterize the team as a "hard to beat team." Similarly, the rainfall recorded over 365 days in a place shows 360 days of rain, then we may characterize the place possibly as a "rainforest." This is the characteristic of the entropy measure. The entropy is defined as follows [6]:

$$en = -\sum_i p_i \log_2(p_i), \tag{10.4}$$

where p_i is the probability of the ith event. To understand better, take four different examples. In all examples, the assumption is that two events are occurring in an environment.

Thinking with Example 10.4:

Say, for example, "rain" or "no rain." In this first example, we take the probability for the first event is 1 (i.e., $p_1 = 1$) and the second event is 0 (i.e., $p_1 = 0$), and let us denote the probabilities of the first and the second events by $[1,0]$ matrix. Then the entropy is: en $= -1 \times \log(1) - 0 \times \log(0) = -1 \times 0 - 0 \times \infty = 0 - 0 = 0$. This result indicates that there is no-error, and it means we can characterize the environment by the first event at 100 %. The characteristics of entropy are illustrated in Fig. 10.10 and the results are generated using the Matlab code in Listing 10.3.

Listing 10.3 A Matlab example—shows entropy noise

```
1  clear all;
2  close all;
3
4  p=0:0.01:1;
5  s=length(p);
6
```

```
 7   randn('seed',13);
 8   r=0.01*randn(1,s);
 9   q=p+r;
10   q=(q-min(q))/(max(q)-min(q));
11
12   x=-p.*log2(p);
13   y=-q.*log2(q);
14
15   figure;plot(x);grid on;
16   figure;plot(x);grid on;
17   hold on;plot(y,'color','red');
```

Thinking with Example 10.5:

Now suppose we take the probability for the first and second events as 0.5 (i.e., $p_1 = p_2 = 0.5$). Then we can denote the probabilities of the first and second events by $[0.5, 0.5]$ matrix. In this case, the entropy is: $en = -0.5 \times \log(0.5) - 0.5 \times \log(0.5) = 1$. This is the maximum error as shown in Fig. 10.10, and it means that we cannot characterize the environment by either of these two events.

Thinking with Example 10.6:

In the next example, suppose the probability for the first and second events are $p_1 = 0.9$ and $p_2 = 0.1$, then we can denote the probabilities of the events by $[0.9, 0.1]$ matrix. If we calculate the entropy for these events, then we have $en = -0.9 \times \log(0.9) - 0.1 \times \log(0.1) = 0.4690$.

Thinking with Example 10.7:

Similarly, if we take the probabilities as $p_1 = 0.7$ and $p_2 = 0.3$, then the entropy is 0.8813. We can see the probabilities reach $[0.5, 0.5]$ and the entropy (i.e., error) is getting higher.

10.4.2 Gini Impurity

The Gini impurity is another type of measure which can be used to measure incorrect labelling [3, 7] with matching the patterns. The abbreviation Gini stands for generalized inequality index. The Gini impurity may be used in decision tree building, instead of entropy, and it is defined as follows [3]:

$$\text{Gini} = -\sum_i p_i(1 - p_i), \tag{10.5}$$

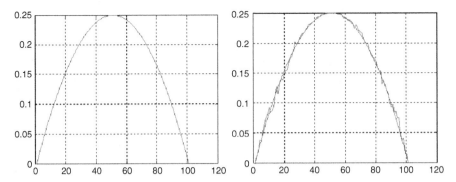

Fig. 10.11 The Gini indexes characteristics with and without an error factor, respectively—horizontal axis represents the probability index and the vertical axis represents the Gini impurity

where p_i is the probability of the ith event. The characteristics of Gini impurity are illustrated in Fig. 10.11. We can see the differences in entropy (in Fig. 10.10) and Gini impurity (in Fig. 10.11) clearly. One difference is the spread and the other is skewness (symmetry).

Listing 10.4 A Matlab example—shows Gini impurity

```
1   clear all;
2   close all;
3
4   p=0:0.01:1;
5   s=length(p);
6
7   randn('seed',13);
8   r=0.01*randn(1,s);
9   q=p+r;
10  q=(q-min(q))/(max(q)-min(q));
11
12  x=p.*(1-p);
13  y=q.*(1-q);
14
15  figure;plot(x);grid on;
16  figure;plot(x);grid on;
17  hold on;plot(y,'color','red');
```

We have seen that the entropy measure is useful when multiple events occur at a particular instance or a location. In contrast, the cross-entropy is used to measure the error when multiple events (but the same events) occur at two different instances or locations. We can distinguish these two cases as follows: in the first case, the events come from the same statistical distribution, but in the second case, the events are from two distributions. Therefore, we can say the entropy measures within as the intra-error (i.e., within a distribution) and cross-entropy as the inter-error between two distributions. Suppose two events a and b occur at two different instances with probabilities $[p_1, p_2]$, and $[q_1, q_2]$, where $p_1 + p_2 = 1$ and $q_1 + q_2 = 1$, then the cross-entropy is defined as follows [6]:

$$x\_en = -p_1 \log_2(q_1) - p_2 \log_2(q_2). \tag{10.6}$$

In the actual entropy definition, the probabilities p_1 and p_2 occupy the places of q_1 and q_2. Therefore, the difference in the probability q from p is reflected on the cross-entropy. We can generalize this as follows [8]:

$$x\_en = -\sum_i p_i \log_2(q_i), \tag{10.7}$$

where $\sum p_i = 1$ and $\sum q_i = 1$. Let us now understand the meaning of the cross-entropy through some examples.

Thinking with Example 10.11:

In this example, suppose a container has 10 balls, and the only additional information given to you is that either all of them are red balls or all of them are blue balls. However, I know that the container has only 10 red balls. The game is that I draw a ball without showing it to you, but you must predict its color by guessing it 10 times. Because I know that all the balls are red, the actual probability matrix is $[1, 0]$. Now suppose your predicted probability is $[1, 0]$ (i.e., all 10 guesses you said red), then the cross-entropy is $x\_en = -1 \times \log(1) - (0) \times \log(0) = 0 - 0 \times \infty = 0$. This indicates that there is no error in actual and predicted values. Suppose your predicted probability is $[0, 1]$. It means all 10 guesses you said blue, then the cross-entropy is: $x\_en = -1 \times \log(0) - (0) \times \log(1) = -1 \times \infty - 0 \times 0 = -\infty$. It indicates a very large error in your prediction. Suppose your probability matrix is $[0.9, 0.1]$. It means you guessed 9 times as red and 1 time as blue. Then the cross-entropy is: $x\_en = -1 \times \log(9/10) - (0) \times \log(1/9)$. The program Listing 10.5 may be used for this purpose and it produces the results in Fig. 10.12.

Listing 10.5 A Matlab example—shows cross-entropy

```
1   clear all;
2   close all;
3
4   p=0.01:0.01:0.5;
5   x_en=-p.*log2(p) - (1-p).*log2(1-p);
6   figure;plot(p,x_en);grid on;
7
8   q1=0.01:0.01:0.99;
9   p1=ones(1,length(q1));
10
11  x_en1=-p1.*log2(q1) - (1-p1).*log2(1-q1);
12  figure;plot(q1,x_en1);
13  hold on;plot(0.5,1,'o');grid on;
```

Thinking with Example 10.12:

Now suppose the container has 9 red balls and 1 blue ball, then the actual probability matrix is $[0.9, 0.1]$, and your predicted probability is $[0.9, 0.1]$, then the cross-entropy is: $x\_en = -0.9 \times \log(0.9) - (0.1) \times \log(0.1) = 0.4690$. Suppose your predicted probability is $[0.1, 0.9]$, then the cross-entropy is $x\_en = -0.9 \times \log(0.1) - (0.1) \times \log(0.9) = 3.0049$. In another example, if the container has 5 red balls and 5 blue balls, and if you predict 5 times red and 5 times blue, then the actual probability matrix is $[0.5, 0.5]$, and the predicted probability measure is also $[0.5, 0.5]$. Therefore, the cross-entropy is: $x\_en = -0.5 \times \log(0.5) - (0.5) \times \log(0.5) = 1$. It is highlighted in the second figure of Fig. 10.12.

10.4.3 Information Gain

Suppose we have set of binary events, such as success or failure, rain or no rain, head or tail, etc. A set of binary events carries information that characterize the system that generated these events. This is true for any number of events, not just binary events. As we have seen, the entropy measure or the Gini impurity may be used to describe these characteristics. However, if we divide the set into two subsets, these subsets may lead to gain in the information. For example, the original set of events may have an entropy (error), and when the set is divided into subsets then the average of the entropies of these subsets may have a reduced error (entropy) leading to an information gain.

Thinking with Example 10.8:

An example is selected and the steps involved in analyzing the information gain is presented. Consider two events a and b, and a set of these binary events is $S = \{a, b, a, a, b, a, b, b, b, a, a, a\}$. There are seven observations in event a and five observations in event b. Let us write this in a matrix form: $[7a, 5b]$. They can be written as the following probability matrix: $[7/12, 5/12]$, where the first element corresponds to event a and the other event b. Therefore, the entropy of this set of binary events is: $en = -(7/12) \times \log(7/12) - (5/12) \times \log(5/12) = 0.9799$.

Thinking with Example 10.9:

Let us now split the set into two subsets. The question is, where to split? The different split locations will give different subsets and, in turn, will give a different information gain. The best information gain will help select the best split. Let us first split the set at the middle, and it gives us two subsets S_1 and S_2, where $S_1 = \{a, b, a, a, b, a\}$ and $S_2 = \{b, b, b, a, a, a\}$. We can write their event matrices

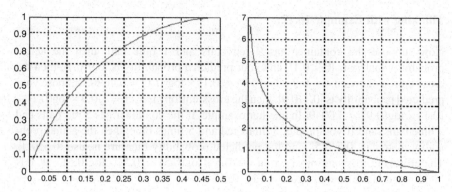

Fig. 10.12 The cross-entropy results of Listing 10.5

as $[4a, 2b]$ and $[3a, 3b]$. Therefore, their probability matrices are: $[4/6, 2/6]$ and $[3/6, 3/6]$. If we calculate their entropies as before, we get en $= 0.9183$ and en $= 1$ for these subsets of events. As we can see, the second subset has an equal number of events, and the entropy is high as illustrated earlier. The fractions of these subsets with respect to the original set are: 6/12 and 6/12. Therefore, the average entropy is: $(6/12) \times 0.9183 + (6/12) \times 1 = 0.9591$, which is smaller than the entropy 0.9799 of the original set. Therefore, there is a gain in the information or the reduction in the error (entropy) from 0.9799 to 0.9591 through the split at the middle of the set.

Thinking with Example 10.10:

What will happen if we split the data set at the 9th location and create the subsets $S_1 = \{a, b, a, a, b, a, b, b, b\}$ and $S = \{a, a, a\}$? The entropies of these subsets can be calculated, and they are 0.9911 and 0, respectively. The fractions of the subsets from the original set are 9/12 and 3/12; therefore, the average entropy of the subsets is: $(9/12) \times 0.9911 + (3/12) \times 0 = 0.7433$. This is a significant reduction in the entropy, and thus it gives a very good information gain. Among these two splits, the split at the 9th location is preferred.

10.5 Decision Tree Learning Algorithm

The goal of the decision tree learning algorithm is to focus on each one-dimensional subspace (i.e., single feature at a time), select the best feature (the best one-dimensional subspace) and best split location, extract the feature value at the best split location, and divide the domain into two subdomains. Then repeat the same process with the subdomains until no domain divisions are required (until a subdomain has a particular class significantly higher than others).

10.5.1 Training Algorithm

The best feature and the best split location of that feature are the first and the most important requirement in the training of a decision tree. As we have discussed earlier, the parametrization and the optimization are performed simultaneously at each node while a decision tree is built (i.e., the data domain and subdomains are divided). The parameters of a decision tree (at each node) are: the best features and the best features' value at the best split location—the value at the split location that gives the maximum information gain. The leafs of a node are the subdomains. Hence, the training algorithm is as follows:

1. Assuming the data is p-dimensional, analyze all the p, one-dimensional subspaces (i.e., a feature at a time) to search for the best features and split locations. If p is high, then the search will be exhaustive, and the process will be computationally expensive.

2. In each one-dimensional subspace, its data domain will be split at each location (i.e., $n-2$ locations, if there are n observations) and the information gain resulted from the split to two subdomains will be calculated.

3. For each feature, the best split location is selected based on the split that gives the highest information gain, and the feature values at that location will be recorded.

4. The best feature and the feature value at the split location will be assigned to the node that is being processed.

5. The data domain is then divided into two subdomains ($SD1$ and $SD2$) at the split locations.

6. Steps 1–5 will be repeated for the subdomains $SD1$ and $SD2$ to get the best feature, best split location, and the best split feature value for the new nodes.

7. The decision tree will be built following these processes until the subdomain that does not need a split because of the subdomain that has a significantly large number of observations from a single class.

The Matlab code, created as a function named *calc_ig_fn* and presented in Listing 10.6, illustrates these tasks. It uses the hardwood floor and carpet floor data sets presented previously and generates a decision tree. It generates only a two-level decision tree as illustrated in Fig. 10.13.

Listing 10.6 A Matlab example—a function to create information gain

```
1   function [sl,mx,ig]=calc_ig_fn(xx,yy)
2
3       ll=length(yy);
4       for ii=2:ll-1
5           %sp is the split location
```

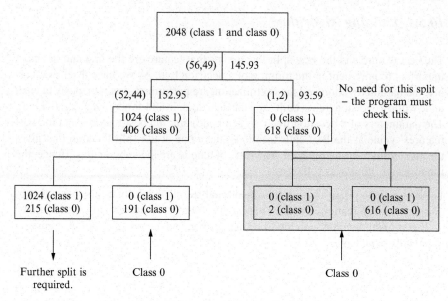

Fig. 10.13 This is the two-level decision tree of the data. The visual effects of these results are presented in Fig. 10.14

```
 6          sp=xx(ii);
 7
 8          %build left and right tree
 9          xl=yy(xx<sp);
10          xr=yy(xx>=sp);
11
12          %length of the left tree
13          l1=length(xl);
14          %sum of class 1s
15          n1=sum(xl);
16          %sum of class 0s
17          n2=l1-n1;
18
19          %probabilities
20          p1=n1/(n1+n2)+0.0001; %1.0e-14; %0.000001;
21          p2=n2/(n1+n2)+0.0001; %1.0e-14; %0.000001;
22
23          %entropy of the left tree
24          en1 = -p1*log(p1)-p2*log(p2);
25
26          %length of the right tree
27          l2=length(xr);
28          %sum of class 1s
29          n1=sum(xr);
30          %sum of class 0s
31          n2=l2-n1;
32
```

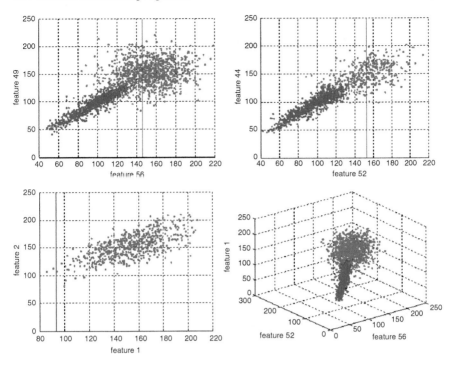

Fig. 10.14 The visual effects of the results obtained in the two-level decision tree presented in the previous figure

```
33          %probabilities
34          p1=n1/(n1+n2)+0.0001; %1.0e-14; %0.000001;
35          p2=n2/(n1+n2)+0.0001; %1.0e-14; %0.000001;
36
37          %entropy of the right tree
38          en2 = -p1*log(p1)-p2*log(p2);
39
40          %Calculates information gain
41          ig(ii-1)=1-((l1/ll)*en1 + (l2/ll)*en2);
42       end
43       %find the split location with the maximum information gain
44       tmp=find(ig==max(ig));
45       sl=tmp(1);
46       mx=max(ig);
47    end
```

This function accepts the data domain stored in a variable *xx* together with their corresponding class labels (only two classes), and then gives the best feature *mx* and best feature split *sl*. It also gives information gain values *ig* for each feature at each split. The second task is to customize the data, pass it through the function, obtain the best feature and best split location, find the feature value at that location, split the data domain (i.e., the data table) at that location, and analyze if the subdomains (left and right) require further split. The Matlab code in Listing 10.7 perform these tasks only at two nodes sequentially. The program has been written to simplify the explanation, and thus it requires programming enhancement. One way to do it is to write this program with recursive, iterative statements or functions.

Listing 10.7 A Matlab example—decision tree building algorithm

```
1   function best_subspaces=dt_build_fn(hw,cp)
2
3   %%%%%%%%%%%%%%%%%%%%%%%%%%%%%%%%%%%%%%%%%%%%%%%%%%%%%
4   % Building the root node
5   %%%%%%%%%%%%%%%%%%%%%%%%%%%%%%%%%%%%%%%%%%%%%%%%%%%%%
6
7   yy=[ones(1,size(hw,1)) zeros(1,size(cp,1))];
8   xx=[hw;cp]';
9
10  for ii=1:size(xx,1)
11      [slx(ii),fmx(ii),igx{ii}]=calc_ig_fn(xx(ii,:),yy);
12  end
13
14  fmxsort=sort(fmx,'descend');
15  tmp1=find(fmx==fmxsort(1));
16  f1=tmp1(1);
17  fmx(f1)=0;
18  tmp2=find(fmx==fmxsort(2));
19  f2=tmp2(1);
20  fval=xx(f1,slx(f1));
21
22  %%%%%%%%%%%%%%%%%%%%%%%%%%%%%%%%%%%%%%%%%%%%%%%%%%%%%
23  % Splitting the root node
24  %%%%%%%%%%%%%%%%%%%%%%%%%%%%%%%%%%%%%%%%%%%%%%%%%%%%%
25
26  idxL=find(xx(f1,:)<fval);
27  idxR=find(xx(f1,:)>=fval);
28
29  xxL=xx(:,idxL);
30  xxR=xx(:,idxR);
31
32  yyL=yy(idxL);
33  yyR=yy(idxR);
34
35  fprintf('\n');
36  fprintf('Left_side_class_1_=_%d\n',sum(yyL));
37  fprintf('Left_side_class_0_=_%d\n\n',length(yyL)-sum(yyL));
38
39  fprintf('Right_side_class_1_=_%d\n',sum(yyR));
40  fprintf('Right_side_class_0_=_%d\n',length(yyR)-sum(yyR));
41
42  %%%%%%%%%%%%%%%%%%%%%%%%%%%%%%%%%%%%%%%%%%%%%%%%%%%%%
43  % Building the left node
44  %%%%%%%%%%%%%%%%%%%%%%%%%%%%%%%%%%%%%%%%%%%%%%%%%%%%%
45
46  for ii=1:size(xxL,1)
```

```
47          [slxL(ii),fmxL(ii),igxL{ii}]=calc_ig(xxL(ii,:),yyL);
48   end
49
50   fmxsortL=sort(fmxL,'descend');
51   tmp3=find(fmxL==fmxsortL(1));
52   f1L=tmp3(1);
53   fmxL(f1L)=0;
54   tmp4=find(fmxL==fmxsortL(2));
55   f2L=tmp4(1);
56   fvalL=xx(f1L,slxL(f1L));
57
58   %%%%%%%%%%%%%%%%%%%%%%%%%%%%%%%%%%%%%%%%%%%%%%%%%%%
59   % Splitting the left node
60   %%%%%%%%%%%%%%%%%%%%%%%%%%%%%%%%%%%%%%%%%%%%%%%%%%%
61
62   idxLL=find(xxL(f1L,:)<fvalL);
63   idxRL=find(xxL(f1L,:)>=fvalL);
64
65   xxLL=xxL(:,idxLL);
66   xxRL=xxL(:,idxRL);
67
68   yyLL=yyL(idxLL);
69   yyRL=yyL(idxRL);
70
71   fprintf('\n');
72   fprintf('Left side class 1 = %d\n',sum(yyLL));
73   fprintf('Left side class 0 = %d\n\n',length(yyLL)-sum(yyLL));
74
75   fprintf('Right side class 1 = %d\n',sum(yyRL));
76   fprintf('Right side class 0 = %d\n',length(yyRL)-sum(yyRL));
77
78   %%%%%%%%%%%%%%%%%%%%%%%%%%%%%%%%%%%%%%%%%%%%%%%%%%%
79   % Building the right node
80   %%%%%%%%%%%%%%%%%%%%%%%%%%%%%%%%%%%%%%%%%%%%%%%%%%%
81
82   for ii=1:size(hw,2)
83          [slxR(ii),fmxR(ii),igxR{ii}]=calc_ig(xxR(ii,:),yyR);
84   end
85
86   fmxsortR=sort(fmxR,'descend');
87   tmp5=find(fmxR==fmxsortR(1));
88   f1R=tmp5(1);
89   fmxR(f1R)=0;
90   tmp6=find(fmxR==fmxsortR(2));
91   f2R=tmp6(1);
92   fvalR=xx(f1R,slxR(f1R));%%%%%%%%%%%%%%%%%%%%%%%%
93
94   %%%%%%%%%%%%%%%%%%%%%%%%%%%%%%%%%%%%%%%%%%%%%%%%%%%
95   % Splitting the right node
96   %%%%%%%%%%%%%%%%%%%%%%%%%%%%%%%%%%%%%%%%%%%%%%%%%%%
97
98   idxLR=find(xxR(f1R,:)<fvalR);
99   idxRR=find(xxR(f1R,:)>=fvalR);
100
```

```
101   xxLR=xxR(:,idxLR);
102   xxRR=xxR(:,idxRR);
103
104   yyLR=yyR(idxLR);
105   yyRR=yyR(idxRR);
106
107   fprintf('\n');
108   fprintf('Left side class 1 = %d\n',sum(yyLR));
109   fprintf('Left side class 0 = %d\n\n',length(yyLR)-sum(yyLR));
110
111   fprintf('Right side class 1 = %d\n',sum(yyRR));
112   fprintf('Right side class 0 = %d\n',length(yyRR)-sum(yyRR));
113   fprintf('==============================================\n');
114
115   %%%%%%%%%%%%%%%%%%%%%%%%%%%%%%%%%%%%%%%%%%%%%%%%%%%%%%
116   % Printing root node and split
117   %%%%%%%%%%%%%%%%%%%%%%%%%%%%%%%%%%%%%%%%%%%%%%%%%%%%%%
118
119   figure; grid on;
120   for ii=1:size(xx,2)
121      if(yy(ii)==1)
122         hold on;plot(xx(f1,ii),xx(f2,ii),'.');
123      else
124         hold on;plot(xx(f1,ii),xx(f2,ii),'r.');
125      end
126   end
127   hold on;line([fval fval],[0 250]);
128
129   %%%%%%%%%%%%%%%%%%%%%%%%%%%%%%%%%%%%%%%%%%%%%%%%%%%%%%
130   % Printing left node and split
131   %%%%%%%%%%%%%%%%%%%%%%%%%%%%%%%%%%%%%%%%%%%%%%%%%%%%%%
132   figure; grid on;
133   for ii=1:size(xxL,2)
134      if(yyL(ii)==1)
135         hold on;plot(xxL(f1L,ii),xxL(f2L,ii),'.');
136      else
137         hold on;plot(xxL(f1L,ii),xxL(f2L,ii),'r.');
138      end
139   end
140   hold on;line([fvalL fvalL],[0 250]);
141
142   %%%%%%%%%%%%%%%%%%%%%%%%%%%%%%%%%%%%%%%%%%%%%%%%%%%%%%
143   % Printing right node and split
144   %%%%%%%%%%%%%%%%%%%%%%%%%%%%%%%%%%%%%%%%%%%%%%%%%%%%%%
145   figure; grid on;
146   for ii=1:size(xxR,2)
147      if(yyR(ii)==1)
148         hold on;plot(xxR(f1R,ii),xxR(f2R,ii),'.');
149      else
150         hold on;plot(xxR(f1R,ii),xxR(f2R,ii),'r.');
151      end
152   end
153   hold on;line([fvalR fvalR],[0 250]);
154
```

```
155 | best_subspaces=[f1 f2; f1L f2L; f1R f2R];
156 |
157 | end
```

In this program the first two blocks of codes from line 3 to line 20 and from line 22 to 40 perform the building and splitting the root node, respectively. After splitting, it builds the left node which is provided in the lines 42–56 and then split the left node. The block of code from line 58 to 76 performs this left node split and then the code from line 78 to 113 perform the right node split. The rest of the code prints the results as commented in the program.

Listing 10.8 A Matlab example—initiates decision tree training

```
1 | clear all;
2 | close all;
3 |
4 | hw=csvread('hardwood.csv');
5 | cp=csvread('carpet.csv');
6 |
7 | best_subspaces=dt_build_fn(hw,cp);
```

This program simply calls the function presented in the Listing 10.7 and performs the two-level decision tree construction for the input data the hardwood floor (Fig. 10.15) and the carpet floor (previously used). The results will be the best sub spaces.

10.5.2 Validation Algorithm

The cross-validation may be conducted to determine the depth of the tree, and it can allow a tree pruning mechanism to speed up the testing when the new data arrives to be classified. Hence, it can bring computational advantages.

10.5.3 Testing Algorithm

The testing algorithm is simple in decision tree learning. It takes one observation at a time from the test data (Fig. 10.16) and puts it through the decision tree constructed using the training algorithm. The feature and the feature value at the root node of the decision tree classifier are observed, and they are used to assign the observation to the left or the right tree. It is pushed into the tree until it reaches one of the leaves. Then the corresponding class label is assigned to the observation if it is a classification tree, and if it is a regression tree then the actual predicted value is assigned.

Fig. 10.15 Training Image Hardwood Floor

Listing 10.9 A Matlab example—a simple decision tree testing

```
1   clear all;
2   close all;
3
4   hw=csvread('hardwood.csv');
5   cp=csvread('carpet.csv');
6
7   oo=size(hw,1);
8   ff=size(hw,2);
9   rand('seed',131);
10  rr=1:2048; %randperm(2048);
11
12  %1 represents hardwood floor and 0 represents carpet floor
13  ty=[ones(1,oo) zeros(1,oo)];
14  tx=[hw;cp]';
15  yy=ty(rr);
16  xx=tx(:,rr);
17
18  %For each feature xx{ii}, it provides information gains igx{ii}
19  %For each feature xxii}, it also provides split locations slx{ii}
20  for ii=1:ff
21      [slx(ii),fmx(ii),igx{ii}]=calc_ig(xx(ii,:),yy);
22  end
23
24  fnum=find(fmx==max(fmx))
25  w1=slx(fnum)+1;
26  fmx(fnum);
```

Fig. 10.16 Test Image Hardwood Floor

```
27
28  in=xx(fnum,w1)
29
30  tt1=csvread('test_hw3.csv');
31  hw=tt1';
32
33  f1=find(hw(fnum,:)<in);
34  f2=find(hw(fnum,:)>=in);
35
36  %total on the left side is 1430
37  length(yy(f1))
38
39  %left hand side all 1024 hardwood and 1430-1024=406 carpet
40  sum(yy(f1))
41
42  %right hand side ALL carpets 618
43  sum(yy(f2))
44
45  figure; grid on;
46  for ii=1:1024
47      if(yy(ii)==1)
48          hold on;plot(hw(56,ii),hw(52,ii),'.');
49      else
50          hold on;plot(hw(56,ii),hw(52,ii),'r.');
51      end
52  end
53  hold on; line([in in],[0 250]);
```

10.6 Decision Tree and Big Data

In this section, a toy example to help implement decision tree modeling and algorithm is presented. It uses the sorting and parallelization features of the big data processing platform, a single node RHadoop with R programming environment, and the MapReduce framework presented in Chaps. 4 and 5. The structure of the toy example may be used to write the full implementation of the decision tree and process real data sets to illustrate the performance of the decision tree classification on a Hadoop platform.

10.6.1 Toy Example

This example does not provide a program for building a decision tree; instead, it brings the features of MapReduce framework that can help you write a program to implement decision tree supervised learning. The content of the data file used for this purpose is presented below:

```
1  4   1
2  5   1
3  12  0
8  6   1
9  9   1
1  12  0
```

It shows a three-column table with six observations. The first two columns show the data points (or the data domain), and the last column shows the class labels (or the response set). The goal of this program is to divide the data domain based on the mean value of feature 2 (second column) first, then map them to the labels. This will be the split at the root node of the tree. Then repeat the process on the left side (left subdomain) of the tree and the right side (right subdomain) of the tree until the split is no longer necessary.

Listing 10.10 An RHadoop example—it can help you write a decision tree technique for big data applications

```
1   Sys.setenv(HADOOP_HOME='/usr/lib/hadoop-0.20-mapreduce')
2   Sys.setenv(HADOOP_CMD='/usr/bin/hadoop')
3   Sys.setenv(HADOOP_STREAMING='/usr/lib/hadoop-0.20-mapreduce/
        contrib/streaming/hadoop-streaming-2.0.0-mr1-cdh4.7.0.jar')
4
5   data <- read.table("tree1.txt", sep="")
6
7   library(rmr2)
8   library(rhdfs)
9
10  hdfs.init()
11
```

```
12  gauss.data = to.dfs(data)
13
14  gauss.map.fn = function(k, v) {
15
16    #Split at the root
17    m1=mean(v[,2])
18    k=ifelse(v[,2]<m1,1,0)
19    v[,2]=k
20    keyval(k,v)
21
22    #divide the tree
23    l=which(v[,2]==0)
24    r=which(v[,2]==1)
25
26    vl=v[l,]
27    vr=v[r,]
28
29    #Split needed on the left side
30    m2=mean(vl[,1])
31    kl=ifelse(vl[,1]<m2,0,1)
32    vl[,1]=kl
33    keyval(kl,vl)
34
35    #Split not needed on the right side
36    kr=vr[,3]
37    vr[,1]=kr
38    keyval(kr,vr)
39
40    #Concatenate (key, value) pair
41    c.keyval(keyval(kl,vl),keyval(kr,vr))
42  }
43
44  gauss.reduce.fn = function(k, v) {
45
46      keyval(k, v)
47  }
48
49  mr.gauss = mapreduce(input = gauss.data, map = gauss.map.fn,
            reduce = gauss.reduce.fn)
50
51  mr.results = from.dfs(mr.gauss)
52  mr.results
```

We have already seen some of the statements required for performing MapReduce using rmr2 package [9]. The codes needed for this specific example are described below. The block of code in lines 16–20 splits the data domain based on the mean of feature 2 (line 17) and labels them with 1 and 0 (line 18). Then it generates (key, value) at lines 19 and 20—this will help the mapreduce() function to sort them with respect to the key value, which is the label. In the block of code in lines 23–27, the subdomains (or the left and right children) are created. The block of code from lines 29–33 performs the split using feature 1 as in lines 16–20. This should be done either iteratively or recursively as, this being a toy example, these tasks are performed sequentially. The right split is not required, as we can see the output after labeling the data based on the split condition of feature 2. However, a (key, value) pair is generated for the right child of the tree. The (key, value) pairs are then concatenated in line 41. The output of the program is given below, which gives the sorted (key, value) pair:

```
$key
[1] 0 0 1 1 1 1

$val
  V1 V2 V3
3  0  0  0
6  0  0  0
5  1  0  1
1  1  1  1
2  1  1  1
4  1  1  1
```

As we can see, the data is sorted with respect to the key, which is the label of the classes in column three of the data set. Based on the mean value of feature 2, the data domain is split at the third row, and class 0 is assigned to the top half of feature 2, and class 1 is assigned to the bottom half of feature 2. If we compare the feature 2 column (V2) and the labels column (V3), then we can see the majority of the actual labels matches, except the third row. If we now extend this to feature 1, then its label correctly matches with the actual label. This output is similar to the results presented in Fig. 10.2.

Problems

10.1. Code Revision
Revise the MapReduce programs presented in this chapter using the coding principles taught in Chap. 5.

10.2. Building a Decision Tree
The decision tree illustrated in Fig. 10.1 used the tree split using X_3, X_2, and X_1 order. Reproduce the decision tree with the order X_2, X_1, and X_3. Then compare the classifiers and the results.

10.3. Real Example
(a) Complete the toy example using iteration (or recursion) together with the actual method of calculating split location and selection of features using the Gini index and the information gain approaches.
(b) Use this implementation to the real data sets like the hardwood floor and carpet floor data sets. Make sure the programs follow the coding principles presented in a previous chapter.

References

1. S. B. Kotsiantis. "Supervised machine learning: A review of classification techniques," Informatica 31, pp. 249–268, 2007.
2. S.K. Murthy. "Automatic construction of decision trees from data: A multi-disciplinary survey," Data Mining and Knowledge Discovery, Kluwer Academic Publishers, vol. 2, no. 4, pp. 345–389, 1998.
3. http://en.wikipedia.org/wiki/Decision_tree_learning
4. L. Breiman, J. Friedman, C.J. Stone, and R.A. Olshen. "Classification and Regression Trees," CRC Press, 1984.
5. L. Torgo. "Inductive learning of tree-based regression models," PhD Thesis, Department of Computer Science, Faculty of Science, University of Porto, Porto, Portugal, pp. 57–104, 1999.
6. T. Hastie, R. Tibshirani, and J. Friedman. The Elements of Statistical Learning. New York: Springer, 2009.
7. https://www.stat.berkeley.edu/~breiman/RandomForests/cc_home.htm
8. L. Wan, M. Zeiler, S. Zhang, Y. LeCun, and R. Fergus. "Regularization of neural networks using dropconnect." In Proceedings of the 30th International Conference on Machine Learning (ICML-13), pp. 1058–1066, 2013.
9. http://www.rdocumentation.org/packages/rmr2.

Part IV
Understanding Scaling-Up Machine Learning

Chapter 11
Random Forest Learning

Abstract The main objective of this chapter is to introduce you to the random forest supervised learning model. The random forest technique uses the decision tree model for parametrization, but it integrates a sampling technique, a subspace method, and an ensemble approach to optimize the model building. The sampling approach is called the bootstrap, which adopts a random sampling approach with replacement. The subspace method also adopts a random sampling approach, but it helps extract smaller subsets (i.e., subspaces) of features. It also helps build decision trees based on them and select decision trees for the random forest construction. The ensemble approach helps build classifiers based on the so-called bagging approach. The objectives of this chapter include detailed discussions on these approaches. The chapter also discusses the training and testing algorithms that are suitable for the random forest supervised learning. The chapter also presents simple examples and visual aids to better understand the random forest supervised learning technique.

11.1 The Random Forest

The random forest is a supervised learning technique and, as the name suggests, it forms forest-like structures with decision trees that are generated using the random sampling with replacement [1, 2]. These decision trees may either be the classification trees or the regression trees; therefore, the random forest can be applied to both classification problems and regression problems. In Chap. 10, we have discussed and learned that the decision tree supervised learning technique provides a single trained decision tree classifier for the testing phase. The advantage of the random forest is that it provides multiple trained decision tree classifiers for the testing phase. This property of the random forest supervised learning technique makes the random forest a preferred technique over regular decision tree learning.

© Springer Science+Business Media New York 2016

S. Suthaharan, *Machine Learning Models and Algorithms for Big Data Classification*, Integrated Series in Information Systems 36, DOI 10.1007/978-1-4899-7641-3_11

273

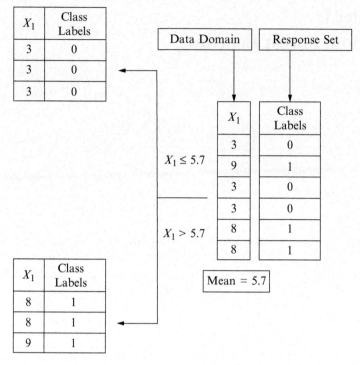

Fig. 11.1 The construction of a decision tree using one-dimensional data domain and bootstrap sampling

Thinking with Example 11.1

The purpose of this example is to show that sampling with replacement may help the decision trees improve their classification performances and reduce the depth of the tree. Look at the same example used in "Thinking with Example 10.1," where a single feature set $f_1 = \{1, 2, 3, 8, 9, 10\}$ with a set of class labels $L = \{1, 1, 0, 1, 1, 0\}$ was considered. Suppose we applied the sampling technique with replacement and created a new data domain as shown in Fig. 11.1. If we compare the classification results at each node of the tree with the depth of the tree in Figs. 10.1 and 11.1, we can say the sampling with replacement (i.e., the bootstrap sampling, or simply the bootstrapping approach) has helped the decision tree building.

11.1.1 Parallel Structure

Parallelization is one of the contributing properties of the random forest supervised learning toward the enhanced classification performances. The parallel structure of the random forest technique may be described as illustrated in the diagram in

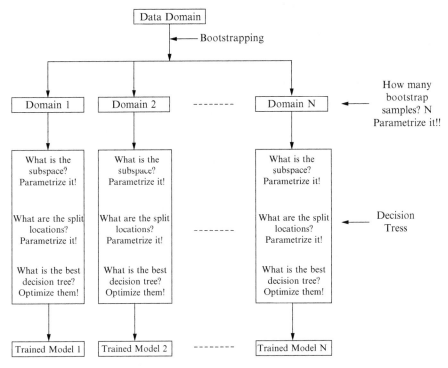

Fig. 11.2 The parallelization feature of the random forest technique

Fig. 11.2. We can interpret random forest modeling as the parallelization of the decision trees because multiple decision trees are built at the same time for classification. To carry out this task, it creates multiple domains using bootstrapping [2, 3] from the data domain and applies the decision tree technique to each domain using a procedure to generate classifiers. This parallel structure of random forest can help big data classification, which is required by the modern big data technologies like the Hadoop distributed file system [4] and the MapReduce [5] framework.

11.1.2 Model Parameters

The parametrization of random forest includes the parametrization of a decision tree model because it adopts the decision tree model. Therefore, all the parameters of the decision tree model are also the parameters of the random forest model. However, it adds a new parameter that represents the number of feature subsets (i.e., the subspaces) selected for the number of decision trees for the construction of a random forest. This is stated in the questions for parametrization in Fig. 11.2.

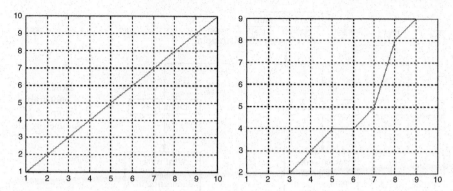

Fig. 11.3 A simple example is provided to illustrate the effect of bootstrapping

11.1.3 Gain/Loss Function

The parameters are optimized based on bootstrap sampling and the subspace integration in model building. The tree building, as in the decision tree, uses the quantitative approaches like entropy [2], the Gini impurity [3, 6], and the information gain [6] to select the best features for building the optimal decision trees. These measures are used to answer the optimization question in Fig. 11.2.

11.1.4 Bootstrapping and Bagging

In random forest supervised learning, the statistical measures, the bootstrapping, and the bagging, play important roles for optimizing the classification objectives. These two measures are discussed in the following subsections. Their definitions and their data domain division properties are also discussed with simple examples.

11.1.4.1 Bootstrapping

Bootstrapping is a simple randomization technique, but its effect on the supervised learning algorithms, especially on the random forest, is magnificent. It helps generate several subsets from a set of data by randomly selecting the same number of observations as the original data set, but with the replacement. This allows some observations from the original data to be repeated in a subset of the data set. The notion of bootstrap sampling in random forest models is to maximize the "class-distance" at each intermediate node and the leaves of the decision trees.

Bootstrapping is applied at the training phase of the random forest algorithm.

Thinking with Example 11.4

The purpose of this example is to show how bootstrap samples may be generated from a given data domain. In this example, ten consecutive integers form the data domain and show how the bootstrapping makes changes to these consecutive integers. The data domain (sorted) is: $D = \{1, 2, 3, 4, 5, 6, 7, 8, 9, 10\}$. A domain (sorted) generated by bootstrapping in Listing 1: $D_1 = \{2, 2, 2, 3, 4, 4, 5, 8, 9, 9\}$. This set is generated using the Matlab program listed in Listing 11.1. The sorted data domain and the sorted bootstrap sample are plotted in Fig. 11.3. It clearly shows the repetition of some integers and the dropping of other integers.

Listing 11.1 A Matlab example—a simple bootstrapping example

```
1   clear all;
2   close all;
3
4   mm=10;
5   sig=1:mm;
6   figure;plot(sig);grid on;
7
8   rand('seed',131);
9   rnd=round(mm*rand(1,mm));
10
11  figure;plot(sort(rnd));grid on;
```

The code in lines 4 and 5 generates ten consecutive integers from 1, and then the code in line 6 plots the points (see Fig. 11.3). The code in line 8 sets a seed value to generate pseudorandom numbers as shown in line 9. It generates ten random numbers between 0 and 1, multiply them by 10, and rounds the results. Hence, the duplicated indexes may appear, which provides sampling with replacement. Note that a minor modification is needed for the code in line 9 to get the values from 1 to 10 inclusive.

11.1.4.2 Overlap Thinning

Let us study some of the effects that bootstrapping brings to a data domain. In simple terms, we can say that bootstrapping generates several domains where the classes may be isolated more than the original data domain. Suppose we have a data domain $D = \{1, 2, 3, 4\}$ with the corresponding class labels $L = \{1, 0, 1, 0\}$ indicating odd and even classes, then some of the possible bootstrap samples are: $S_1 = \{1, 1, 3, 4\}$,

$S_2 = \{1,1,2,2\}$, and $S_2 = \{1,1,3,3\}$. They provide the following domains: $D_1 = \{1,-,3,4\} = \{1,3,4\}$, $D_2 = \{1,2,-,-\} = \{1,2\}$, and $D_3 = \{1,-,3,-\} = \{1,3\}$ with the class labels $L_1 = \{1,1,0\}$, $L_2 = \{1,0\}$, and $L_3 = \{1,1\}$. The classes in these domains can be easily separated by single splits. According to L_1, we can split D_1 at the second location; according to L_2, we can split D_2 at the first location; and according to L_3, no split is needed—it forms the odd class. However, to separate the classes in actual domain D, three splits are required.

11.1.4.3 Bagging

Bagging means the averaging of the prediction (or classification) responses the bootstrap samples gave to obtain the final prediction (or classification) result. The term Bagging comes from Bootstrap aggregating [7]. Bootstrapping is applied as a part of the training algorithm in random forest technique. It helps generate multiple domains with simple class overlap thinning, and these domains help create multiple classification models. The multiple classification models allow the testing algorithm to evaluate the performance of the classifiers efficiently.

Bagging is applied at the testing phase of the random forest algorithm.

How does bagging work? Suppose N decision trees $T = \{T_1, T_2, \ldots, T_N\}$ were generated from N bootstrap samples of a data domain D as the random forest classifier through training. Now we have a new data X that must be classified or predicted based on if the tree was a classification tree or a regression tree. This is a test case. Then the bagging suggests to insert the new data X through each decision tree and get its class label or the predicted value. Hence, we will have N classification results $C = c_i, c_i \in 0, 1, i = 1 \ldots N$ (assuming it is a two-class problem) or N predicted values $Y = y_i, i = 1 \ldots N$. Then the bagging suggests the final class label for the new data as the label, which is majority in the set C if it is a classification problem, and mean(Y) if it is a regression problem.

11.2 Random Forest Learning Model

The random forest learning model, like the other machine learning models discussed previously, accomplishes the parametrization objectives and optimization objectives. These two objectives are discussed in the following two subsections. Note that the random forest learning model adopts the decision tree learning model, and thus includes the parametrization and optimization objectives of the decision tree learning model. We have already studied these objectives in the previous chapter so they are not included in these subsections.

11.2.1 Parametrization

We have already selected the parameters for the random forest learning model, and they are the number of domains generated using bootstrapping, the size of the subspace for each node (domain), and the threshold for a domain split. For the purpose of parametrization, we need to find or suggest possible values for the parameters. The typical number of bootstrap samples used to build the random forest are 10; however, it is appropriate to conduct cross-validation and determine a suitable range of values for the number of bootstrap samples (or domains). For the subspace size selection, there are two possible constraints that may be used, [3] and [6]. The first constraint is from Leo Breiman and it can be found at [3]. The recommendation is that $n << p$, and it must be kept constant throughout the construction of the decision tree. The second constraint, from [6], and it suggests $n \leq \sqrt{p}$. We should be able to show this intuitively. Suppose there are p features in the data domain, and n of them are good ones, but we don't know what they are. Therefore, the fraction of good ones is n/p. Among the good ones let us assume 1 of them is the best one, then its fraction among the good ones is $1/n$. Therefore we can write it as follows:

$$\frac{1}{n} \geq \frac{n}{p} \tag{11.1}$$

It give us $n^2 \leq p$. Therefore, we have $n \leq \sqrt{p}$. Several papers have used the random selection of $\sqrt{p}$ number of features for the nodes of a tree, where p is the number of features which determines the dimensionality of the data and contributes to the scalability problem in the big data applications.

11.2.2 Optimization

In general, after the parameters are selected for the model, and the model is parametrized, then the parameters must be optimized. However, in random forest, the parametrization and the optimization are nested, and they are performed at the same time. The optimization has been done at each node of the tree. The major players for the optimization of the random forest learning model are the Gini index (entropy) and the information gain. Hence, random forest modeling provides a mechanism to parametrize and optimize the model during the application of the training algorithm.

11.3 Random Forest Learning Algorithm

The random forest learning algorithms, like other machine learning algorithms, have three parts: training, validation, and testing algorithms. However, the cross-validation is already integrated in the training algorithm; therefore, no separate validation algorithm is required for the random forest technique [3].

In simple terms, we can say that random forest learning gives us several subspaces (i.e., best feature combinations), where the best domain divisions can be performed and high classification accuracies can be obtained.

Hence, in practice, the classification objectives of the random forest techniques are divided into only training algorithms and testing algorithms.

11.3.1 Training Algorithm

The training algorithm of random forest supervised learning provides a systematic approach to developing multiple classifiers (decision trees) so that the testing algorithm uses multiple classifiers to select the best way to classify the new data. Let us understand this process step by step:

- Step 1: Multiple subspaces are created from the given data set. For example, if the dimension of the space (number of features) of a given data set is p, then we can generate multiple subspaces with dimension r, where $r \le \sqrt{p}$. We may call this a subspace division.

- Step 2: Now we have an r-dimensional subspace, where r is significantly smaller, and we can find the best feature and the best split location (domain division) for the root node of a decision tree using the decision tree-building process explained in the previous chapter. However, we do not perform this process to this subspace; instead, we do the next step first.

- Step 3: We alter the subspace randomly using bootstrap samples and create multiple bootstrap-subspaces where the overlap thinning occurred in their respective data domains.

- Step 4: Apply the decision tree learning algorithm to find the best feature and the best split location (together with the feature value at that split location) for each bootstrap-subspace to construct the nodes for the decision trees.

- Step 5: As a result of step 4, we have a decision tree (classifier) for each bootstrap sample. Therefore, if we create m bootstrap samples, then we will have m decision trees for the random forest classifier. These trees can be used by the testing algorithm to classify the new data.

Therefore, the advantages of the random forest algorithm over the decision tree algorithm are: (1) multiple decision trees are available for classification at the testing phase, which will increase the classification accuracy; (2) bootstrap samples are used for multiple decision trees, which will help increase the sharpening of the classification boundary (i.e., domain divisions) through overlap thinning; and (3) the exhaustive search done for finding the best feature and best split location in the entire space is eliminated by the subspace search with a small additional computation cost in the bootstrap sampling. This process still brings the computational advantages to the random forest algorithm over the decision tree algorithm.

11.3.1.1 Coding Example

Using two-level trees, this example shows how the random forest learning algorithm splits the bootstrap samples and creates forests of decision trees. This example will help you understand the algorithm, and then take overthe incremental development of the code to build iterative or recursive functions to construct the complete decision trees and then the entire forest. This coding example is presented in Listing 11.2, followed by the explanation. This program uses the Matlab modules (or functions) developed in the previous chapter to build a decision tree with two

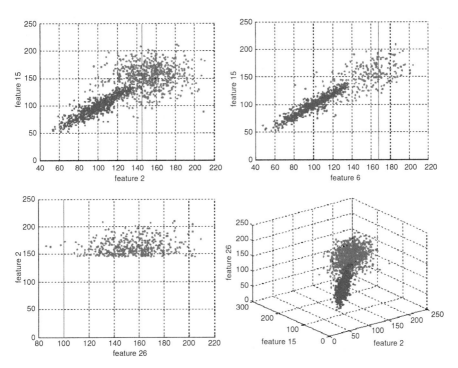

Fig. 11.4 A partial result of the random forest application to classify hardwood floor and carpet floor data sets

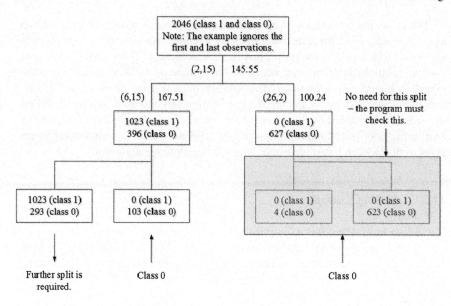

Fig. 11.5 This is the two-level decision tree built for the first bootstrap sample. The visual effects of these results are presented in the next figure

levels. The results of the program are presented in Fig. 11.4, and its tree structure is given in Fig. 11.5.

Listing 11.2 A Matlab example—random forest training

```
1   clear all;
2   close all;
3
4   hw1=csvread('hardwood.csv');
5   cp1=csvread('carpet.csv');
6
7   %%%%%%%%%%%%%%%%%%%%%%%%%%%%%%%%%%%%%%%%%%%%%%%%%%%%%%%%
8   % Subspace selection
9   %%%%%%%%%%%%%%%%%%%%%%%%%%%%%%%%%%%%%%%%%%%%%%%%%%%%%%%%
10  rand('seed',189);
11  rp1=randperm(64);
12  rp2=rp1(1:8)
13
14  hw2=hw1(:,rp2);
15  cp2=cp1(:,rp2);
16
17  % Loops over 10 bootstrap samples
18  for tt=1:10
19      %%%%%%%%%%%%%%%%%%%%%%%%%%%%%%%%%%%%%%%%%%%%%%%%%%%%
20      % Bootstrapping
21      %%%%%%%%%%%%%%%%%%%%%%%%%%%%%%%%%%%%%%%%%%%%%%%%%%%%
22      rand('seed',131*tt); %111, 131,
23      rn=round(1023*rand(1,1023))+1;
```

```
24      hw=hw2(rn',:);
25      cp=cp2(rn',:);
26
27      % Decision tree building
28      best_subspaces=dt_build_fn(hw,cp)
29
30 end
```

The random forest implementation selects feature 2 as the best feature with the split location 15 and the data value of 145.55, as shown in the first level of the tree presented in Fig. 11.5. This selection divides the data domain, as shown in the first figure of Fig. 11.4. This domain division gives 1023 points of class 1 and 396 points of class 0 on the left leaf of the tree, and 0 points from class 1 and 627 points of class 0 on the right side leaf. The random forest implementation then selects feature 6 as the best feature on the left side of the tree, with the split location 15 and the data value 167.51. This is described in the tree in Fig. 11.5. The corresponding domain division is presented in the second figure of Fig. 11.4. You can now follow the tree in Fig. 11.5 and interpret the third figure in Fig. 11.4. The fourth figure is the original plot of both hardwood floor and carpet floor data sets.

11.3.2 Testing Algorithm

The testing algorithm requires the entire random forest be constructed using several bootstrap samples, typically ten samples. It provides a systematic approach to label newly arriving data using the random forest classifier generated in the training phase. We can describe this process by the following steps:

- Feature selection: In this step, the correct sequence of features from the incoming data for the nodes of the trees must be observed.

- Tree selection: Suppose we have generated N random forest classifiers (decision trees of the bootstrap samples), then we push the new data according to the features through all of these decision trees and obtain its class labels.

- Bagging: In this step, the trees selected in the previous steps are used to find the aggregate of the results obtained—this is the bagging technique as explained earlier.

Suppose you have ten decision trees in your random forest, and you push the new data through the trees and determine that nine trees labeled it as class 1. You can then use a voting mechanism and conclude that the new observation belongs to class 1, because of the majority votes. This is applicable if the problem is the classification problem. If it is a regression problem, then you can use the average of the results obtained from the trees for prediction.

11.4 Random Forest and Big Data

Random forest supervised learning is an excellent technique to deal with the big data classification problems because of its flexible parallelized structure, which co-operates with the requirements of the modern big data technologies like the Hadoop distributed files systems and the MapReduce framework. The usage of subspaces and bootstrapping to build trees can deal with the scalability problems associated with big data applications. The recent technique proposed by Li et al. [8] is briefly discussed in the following subsections. For additional information, I encourage you to consult the original paper by Li et al. [8].

11.4.1 Random Forest Scalability

In a typical data science application, the number of features is fixed and the random forest technique selects a subspace from them and builds the depth-first decision trees based on bootstrapping to construct the random forest. But in a big data application, the feature set can dynamically grow (e.g., text processing application like the email-spam filtering) causing a scalability problem. The approach proposed by Li et al. [8] can handle this problem by constructing the breadth-first decision trees for the random forest. In a typical random forest implementation, the root node for a tree is built first (i.e., the data domain is divided) and then it is split into two sub-trees (i.e., subdomains). This process is repeated until the entire tree is built. Then the next tree is constructed, and this is the process of the standard random forest technique. But in the approach they proposed, the trees were built in parallel. As an example, they first selected K nodes, then generated $2K$ children (two children per node), and then repeated the process to build the next level of the trees which will have $4K$ altogether, and so on.

11.4.2 Big Data Classification

The dynamic parallelization can be achieved by using the big data processing platform that uses the MapReduce engine with the mapper() and reducer() functions. The paper by Li et al. [8] presents pseudo codes for implementing these functions and illustrates that their breadth-first random forest can be successfully implemented to handle scalability problems. The coding example in Listing 11.3 will help you develop a scalable random forest algorithm. The data set used for this illustration is:

```
1  4  1
2  5  1
3  12  0
```

```
8  6  1
9  9  1
1 12  0
```

This data set has three columns where the first two columns define the data domain and the last column defines the class labels. The goal is to generate bootstrap samples and show the parallelism and sorting feature of the MapReduce framework.

Listing 11.3 An RHadoop example—toward the depth-first random forest

```
1  Sys.setenv(HADOOP_HOME='/usr/lib/hadoop-0.20-mapreduce')
2  Sys.setenv(HADOOP_CMD='/usr/bin/hadoop')
3  Sys.setenv(HADOOP_STREAMING='/usr/lib/hadoop-0.20-mapreduce/
      contrib/streaming/hadoop-streaming-2.0.0-mr1-cdh4.7.0.jar')

5  data <- read.table("tree1.txt", sep="")
6  data

8  library(rmr2)
9  library(rhdfs)

11 hdfs.init()

13 gauss.data = to.dfs(data)

15 gauss.map.fn = function(k, v) {
16   # Extract the number of observations
17   nn=dim(v)[1]

19   # Create the first bootstrap sample
20   set.seed(129)
21   ind1=round(runif(nn,min=1,max=nn))
22   oo=matrix(1,nn,1)
23   v1=cbind(v[ind1,],oo) # add the bootstrap index too

25   # Create the second bootstrap sample
26   set.seed(131)
27   ind2=round(runif(nn,min=1,max=nn))
28   oo=matrix(2,nn,1)
29   v2=cbind(v[ind2,],oo) # add the bootstrap index too

31   # Combine the bootstrap samples
32   vv=rbind(v1,v2)

34   # Assign key value pairs
35   # key is the bootstrap sample index
36   k=vv[,4]
37   keyval(k,vv)
38 }

40 gauss.reduce.fn = function(k, v) {

42   # Find split location for the feature 2
43   # Use a loop and the information gain to find
```

```
44    # the feature and its best split location
45    #v[,2]=ifelse(v[,2]<mean(v[,2]),1,0)
46    keyval(k, v)
47  }
48
49  mr.gauss = mapreduce(input = gauss.data, map = gauss.map.fn,
          reduce = gauss.reduce.fn)
50
51  mr.results = from.dfs(mr.gauss)
52  mr.results
```

Some of the blocks of code in this program are already familiar to you; therefore, the explanation in this section only focuses on the blocks of code that are directly related to the example. The block of code in lines 17–23 extracts the number of obs-ervations in the data set, generates integers uniformly between 1 and the number of observations (inclusive), uses them to draw observations with repetition, and labels them with the bootstrap sample number 1. Similarly, the block of code in lines 26–29 creates the second bootstrap sample. You can use a loop control structure to generate as many bootstrap samples as needed. Line 32 then combines them using the rbind() function, and lines 36 and 37 create (key, value) pairs assuming the bootstrap sample number as the key. Therefore, each key (in this example 1 and 2) holds a set of related bootstrap samples. Thus the job instructed in the reducer() function executes on them parallel with respect to the sorted key. If uncommented, the job in line 45 is to change the feature 2 with the class labels determined by the mean value of the feature. The output of this program, with line 45 commented, is given below:

```
$key
  [1]  1 1 1 1 1 1 2 2 2 2 2 2

$val
        V1 V2 V3  oo
2        2  5  1   1
3        3 12  0   1
2.1      2  5  1   1
3.1      3 12  0   1
1        1  4  1   1
4        8  6  1   1
21       2  5  1   2
2.11     2  5  1   2
2.2      2  5  1   2
31       3 12  0   2
5        9  9  1   2
41       8  6  1   2
```

We can see a column is added to the table, and this column carries the bootstrap sample number. The data table is sorted with respect to these "key" numbers as expected. By uncommenting line 45, we can obtain the following output:

```
$key
 [1] 1 1 1 1 1 1 2 2 2 2 2 2

$val
      V1 V2 V3 oo
2      2  1  1  1
3      3  0  0  1
2.1    2  1  1  1
3.1    3  0  0  1
1      1  1  1  1
4      8  1  1  1
21     2  1  1  2
2.11   2  1  1  2
2.2    2  1  1  2
31     3  0  0  2
5      9  0  1  2
41     8  1  1  2
```

In this output, the values of feature 2 are substituted with the class labels determined by the mean value of each set of bootstrap samples separately based on the
key assignment. This indicates the use of the parallelization feature of the MapReduce framework, and it forms the depth-first scenario.

Problems

11.1. Code Revision

Revise the MapReduce programs presented in this chapter using the coding principles taught in Chap. 5.

11.2. Revising the Programs

Revise the programs presented in this chapter by applying the coding principles
taught in Chap. 5. While revising, understand the program and complete all required
tasks to satisfy the goal of each program.

11.3. Random Forest for Big Data

(a) Write a mapper() function based on random forest implementation. Use the
    hardwood floor and carpet floor data sets, or your own data set to show the
    working mechanism of your program.
(b) Write a reducer() function based on random forest implementation. Once again,
    use the hardwood floor and carpet floor data sets, or your own data set to show
    the working mechanism of your program.

References

1. L. Breiman, "Random forests." Machine learning 45, pp. 5–32, 2001.
2. T. Hastie, R. Tibshirani, and J. Friedman. The Elements of Statistical Learning. New York: Springer, 2009.
3. https://www.stat.berkeley.edu/~breiman/RandomForests/cc_home.htm
4. T. White. Hadoop: the definitive guide. OReilly, 2012.
5. J. Dean, and S. Ghemawat, "MapReduce: simplified data processing on large clusters." Communications of the ACM, vol. 51, no. 1, pp. 107–113, 2008.
6. http://en.wikipedia.org/wiki/Decision_tree_learning
7. L. Breiman. "Bagging predictors." Machine learning 24, pp. 123–140, 1996.
8. B. Li, X. Chen, M.J. Li, J.Z. Huang, and S. Feng. "Scalable random forests for massive data," P.N. Tan et al. (Eds): PAKDD 2012, Part I, LNAI 7301, pp. 135–146, 2012.

Chapter 12
Deep Learning Models

Abstract The main objective of this chapter is to discuss the modern deep learning techniques, called the no-drop, the dropout, and the dropconnect in detail and provide programming examples that help you clearly understand these approaches. These techniques heavily depend on the stochastic gradient descent approach; and this approach is also discussed in detail with simple iterative examples. These parametrized deep learning techniques are also dependent on two parameters (weights), and the initial values of these parameters can significantly affect the deep learning models; therefore, a simple approach is presented to enhance the classification accuracy and improve computing performance using perceptual weights. The approach is called the perceptually inspired deep learning framework, and it incorporates edge-sharpening filters and their frequency responses for the classifier and the connector parameters of the deep learning models. They preserve class characteristics and regularize the deep learning model parameters.

12.1 Introduction

One of the requirements in a big data environment is scalability of learning algorithms, especially the scaling-up of machine learning [1]. The scaling-up problem may occur due to the rapid growth in the number of observations that define the size of the data, the number of features that define the dimensionality of the data, and the number of classes that define the variety of data types. This scaling-up problem can be handled by the modern machine learning technique called deep learning [2], which is an alternative version of the artificial neural network models [3] used in the Artificial Intelligence arena for decades. The main goal of deep learning algorithms is to develop computational models that can find an optimal mapping between the input variables (also called input neurons or predictors) and their corresponding class labels. There are several contributors to the successful

© Springer Science+Business Media New York 2016   289
S. Suthaharan, *Machine Learning Models and Algorithms for Big
Data Classification*, Integrated Series in Information Systems 36,
DOI 10.1007/978-1-4899-7641-3_12

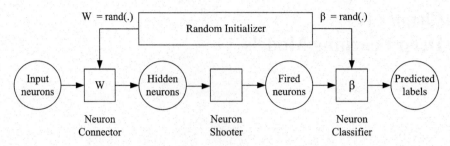

Fig. 12.1 Insight of a deep learning model, known as the no-drop deep learning

development of deep learning models. Among them, the neuron connector, the neuron shooter, and the neuron classifier are the major and minimum number of contributors required. The methodological processes between these modules are presented in Fig. 12.1. The first module, the neuron connector, establishes a connection between the input neurons, using a neural network approach and the tuning parameter w, called weights [4]. Subsequently, the neuron shooter fires the neurons suitable for classification using activation functions like sigmoid [5] and tanh [6]. Finally, the neuron classifier assigns a map between the fired neurons and the class labels using a parametrized transformation and the tuning parameter β. Hence, w and β parametrize the map between the input neurons and the class labels, and they help optimize the map by iteratively tuning them using training data sets. In the deep learning models, the Stochastic Gradient Descent (SGD) with backward propagation approach [5, 7, 8] has been used for learning the parameters and scaling-up machine learning.

The performance of a deep learning model is heavily dependent on the starting values of the parameters w and β. The overfitting problem caused by the incorrect value choices of w and β has been reported in the book by Hastie et al. [4]. In general, these starting values are selected randomly, and this randomization is the cause for the unpredictable overfitting problem manifested from the integration of the SGD-based backward propagation technique. The randomization also causes inconsistent and unpredictable arrival of an optimal solution between applications. Another cause for the overfitting and the time delay problems is the independent selection of the starting values. Currently, there is no standard mechanism to determine a suitable connection between these parameters. Therefore, one of the objectives of this chapter is to present a technique to control the independent updates of the parameters. This technique employs the edge-sharpening filters [9] for the classification parameter and their frequency responses [10] for the neuron connector parameters to connect them so that the class characteristics can be preserved and the deep learning parameters can be regularized.

12.2 Deep Learning Techniques

The classification problem for a deep learning technique can be defined as follows: Suppose we denote a given training example by the following equation:

$$X = \{(X_i, Y_i) | X_i \in R^p; Y_i \in \{1, \ldots, k\}; i = 1, \ldots, n\}, \tag{12.1}$$

where X_i is the ith training example (or input neuron) with dimension p, and Y_i is its corresponding class label. Then the goal of classification is to find an optimal function

$$f : R^p \to \{1, 2, \ldots, k\} \text{ such that } f(X_i) = Y_i, i = 1, \ldots, n. \tag{12.2}$$

Finding such an optimal function mathematically is a difficult task; hence, deep learning models have been proposed in which a set of parameters may be estimated using training and cross-validation techniques. This definition can be used to define the deep learning models [2, 3]: no-drop, dropout, and dropconnect, and they are discussed in detail in the following subsections.

12.2.1 No-Drop Deep Learning

The no-drop deep learning model is defined based on the paper [3] by Hinton et al. For no-drop, the classification function f (i.e., the classifier) is defined by a composition of two parametric functions, h and s, and a sigmoid function a [3]:

$$f(X_i) = s_{\beta_i}(a(h_{w_i}(X_i))), \tag{12.3}$$

where w_i and β_i are the parameters of the functions h and s at iteration i, and $i = 1, \ldots, n$, and they are iteratively updated using the SGD approach with back propagation [8]. The no-drop model is described in Fig. 12.1, and it shows the processes and the modeling parameters.

12.2.2 Dropout Deep Learning

The dropout deep learning model is presented here based on the papers by Hinton et al. [3] and Wan et al. [2]. Similarly, the classifier f for the dropout is defined by Wan et al. [2]:

$$f(X_i) = s_{\beta_i}(m_i \odot a(h_{w_i}(X_i))), \tag{12.4}$$

where the operator $\odot$ denotes the element-by-element matrix multiplication. It introduces the parameter m_i, which is generated using a Bernoulli distribution with probability 0.5 to drop output neurons. The dropout model is illustrated in Fig. 12.2.

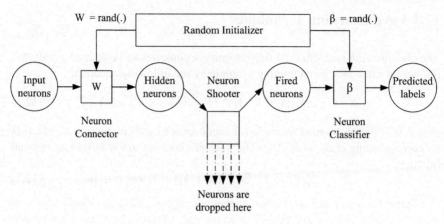

Fig. 12.2 Insight of the dropout deep learning model

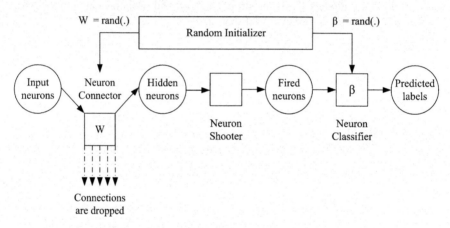

Fig. 12.3 Insight of the dropconnect deep learning model

12.2.3 Dropconnect Deep Learning

The dropconnect is discussed based on the information available in the paper [2] by Wan et al. Similarly, the dropconnect defines [2]:

$$f(X_i) = s_{\beta_i}(a(M_i \odot h_{w_i}(X_i))). \tag{12.5}$$

This model introduces the parameter M_i, which is generated using a Bernoulli distribution with probability 0.5 to drop input neurons (i.e., the connections as defined in neural networks). The dropconnect model is illustrated in Fig. 12.3. The dropout and dropconnect can remove some important information randomly, and it may adversely affect the model's classification accuracy and the computing

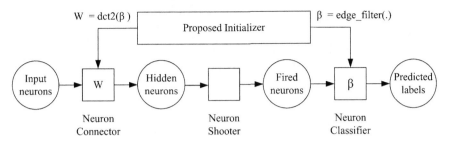

Fig. 12.4 Insight of the proposed perceptually inspired deep learning model

time. Additionally, the initial values for w_0 and β_0 are selected randomly. The proposed approach will focus on the preservation of feature variability in dropout and dropconnect models as illustrated in Fig. 12.4 which will be discussed in Sect. 12.3. These modern deep learning approaches require an iterative technique for optimization through the updates of the parameters, and they use the gradient descent-based approach. It is discussed in the following subsection.

12.2.4 Gradient Descent

In this section, two examples, a conceptualized example and a numerical example, are formulated to help you understand the gradient descent and the SGD techniques. These examples will also help you distinguish these two techniques and apply them correctly to various applications.

In the gradient descent approach, multiple models are assumed, and the best model is selected based on the minimization of the global misclassification error using all the misclassified observations *together*.

In the SGD approach, one model is assumed, and it is updated using the minimization of the misclassification error using a single misclassified observation at a time.

While the gradient descent can use the global characteristics of the observations to derive a model, the SGD uses the local characteristics of the observation to iteratively revise the model to drive a final model. The following two subsections provide a conceptualized example and a numerical example that can help you understand and describe the meaning of these statements in detail.

12.2.4.1 Conceptualized Example

Suppose we have the data domain D with the response set C, where $x \in D$ and its response $y \in C$, and we want to find the optimal model $y = \beta x + \gamma$. For simplicity, let us assume we want to find the best model among the following two models:

$$y = \beta_1 x + \gamma_1, \tag{12.6}$$

$$y = \beta_2 x + \gamma_2. \tag{12.7}$$

Then the gradient descent suggests the minimization of the misclassified responses as follows [4]:

$$e_{\beta,\gamma} = \sum y_i \hat{y}_i, \tag{12.8}$$

where $\hat{y}_i$ are the predicted, but misclassified responses, and y_i are their actual responses. It means that the values of y_i and $\hat{y}_i$ are opposite to each other. For example, their values may be either 1 and -1 or -1 and 1. Then the gradient descent is [4]:

$$\frac{\partial e}{\partial \beta} = -\sum y_i x_i, \tag{12.9}$$

$$\frac{\partial e}{\partial \gamma} = -\sum y_i. \tag{12.10}$$

Obviously, the parameters β and γ that make these partial derivatives 0 give their respective optimal values through the minimization of the error factor in Eq. (12.8). However, to select the best among the two models, we can select the parameters β and γ that make the partial derivatives minimum rather than 0.

Therefore, conceptually we can say that the models are assumed, and the best model that minimizes the misclassification (i.e., minimizes the incorrect labels) is selected as the optimal model in the gradient descent method, which uses the global characteristics of the data domain. The "global characteristics" means that all the data points are used *together* in the selection of the model as noted in Eqs. (12.9) and (12.10). In SGD, as stated before, one model is assumed:

$$y = \beta_{\text{curr}} x + \gamma_{\text{curr}} \tag{12.11}$$

and then they are updated using the following iterative sequences:

$$\frac{\beta_{\text{next}} - \beta_{\text{curr}}}{h} = y_i x_i, \tag{12.12}$$

$$\frac{\gamma_{\text{next}} - \gamma_{\text{curr}}}{h} = y_i, \tag{12.13}$$

where h is called the learning rate, but it is the small displacement used in the calculation of the derivatives. If you compare Eqs. (12.12) and (12.13) with Eqs. (12.9) and (12.10), then we can see the localization and globalization properties in the SGD and the standard gradient descent approaches.

12.2.4.2 Numerical Example

Let us consider the classification example used in Chap. 7, Sect. 7.1.2 (see the second figure of Fig. 7.4). Let us also select the worst classifier $x_2 = 3.5x_1 + 3.0$. The following table shows the actual and predicted label with this worst classifier.

x1	x2	yi	ei
1.00	6.00	-1	1
2.00	2.00	1	1
2.00	6.50	-1	1
2.50	9.50	-1	1
3.00	3.00	1	1

We can now demonstrate the steps to show how the SGD improves this worst model. As you can see, the predicted label of the first observation suggests the observation is misclassified, and we can start the parameter correction from there. The parameters $\beta = (3.5, -1)$ and $\gamma = 3.0$ used here will be corrected (or updated) using Eqs. (12.12) and (12.13) as follows:

$$\beta = (3.5, -1) - 1(1,6) = (2.5, -7), \tag{12.14}$$

$$\gamma = 3.0 - 1 = 2.0. \tag{12.15}$$

Therefore, the new classifier is $7x_2 = 2.5x_1 + 2.0$. We must now check to see if the next observation will be misclassified with this new classifier. We can observe that it is misclassified, too. Therefore, we must update the parameters again. This time we have the following corrections:

$$\beta = (2.5, -7) + 1(2,2) = (4.5, -5), \tag{12.16}$$

$$\gamma = 2.0 + 1 = 3.0. \tag{12.17}$$

Therefore, the new classifier is $5x_2 = 4.5x_1 + 3.0$, and it predicts the actual labels for the rest of the points, and it is illustrated in the Matlab code given in Listing 12.1.

Listing 12.1 A Matlab example—SGD dynamic parameter correction

```
1   clear all;
2   close all;
3
4   x=[1 2 2 2.5 3;
5       6 2 6.5 9.5 3];
6
7   l=[-1 1 -1 -1 1];
8
9   b=[3.5 -1];
10  g=3.0;
11  %%%%%% classifier is x2 = 3.5 x1 + 3.0
12
13  % Misclassified- actual is -1 predicted is 1
14  den=sqrt(b*b');
```

```
15  d=sign((b*x + g)/den);
16
17  fprintf('\n\n\n%4s_%8s_%8s_%8s\n','x1', 'x2', 'yi', 'ei');
18
19  for i=1:5
20      fprintf('%4.2f_%8.2f_%8d_%8d\n',x(1,i), x(2,i), l(1,i), d(1,i
            ));
21  end
22
23  % 1. dynamic correction to the parameters beta (b) and gamma (g)
24
25  b = b + l(1)*x(:,1)'
26  g = g + l(1)
27  %%%%%% we have updated classifier is 7.0 x2 = 2.5 x1 + 2.0
28
29  % Misclassified- actual is 1 predicted is -1
30  den=sqrt(b*b');
31  d=sign((b*x(:,2) + g)/den)
32
33  % 2. dynamic correction to the parameters beta (b) and gamma (g)
34  b = b + l(2)*x(:,2)'
35  g = g + l(2)
36  %%%%%% we have updated classifier is 5.0 x2 = 4.5 x1 + 3.0
37
38  % No misclassification, no update - actual is -1 predicted is -1
39  den=sqrt(b*b');
40  d=sign((b*x(:,3) + g)/den)
41
42  % 3. no correction required
43
44  % No misclassification- original is -1 predicted is -1
45  den=sqrt(b*b');
46  d=sign((b*x(:,4) + g)/den)
47
48  % 4. no correction required
49
50  % No misclassification- original is 1 predicted is 1
51  den=sqrt(b*b');
52  d=sign((b*x(:,5) + g)/den)
53
54  % 5. no correction required
55
56  %%%%%% final classifier is 5.0 x2 = 4.5 x1 + 3.0
```

As you can see, the block of code in lines 4–7 declare the data domain and the response set. The data domain has five points, as listed above, together with the labels. The initial model selected for this illustration is $x_2 = 3.5x_1 + 3.0$, and its parameters are listed in lines 9 and 10. The rest of the code follows the steps described above, and the relevant blocks of code are also presented with comments. Each iterative step and the parameter updates are numbered 1 through 4 from lines 23 to 56.

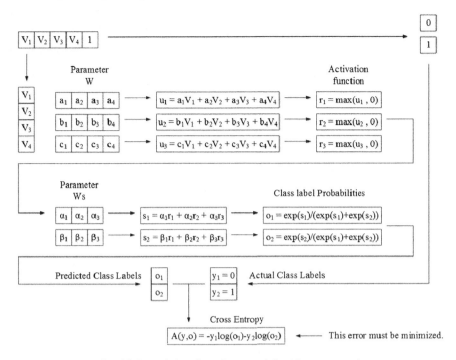

Fig. 12.5 Insight of no-drop model with an example

12.2.5 A Simple Example

These techniques may be easily understood using the simple example, which is extended from the explanation provided in Chap. 7 in the "Thinking with Example 7.5." This example provides the explanation of the no-drop model based on the steps explained in the paper [2] by Wan et al. , but it can easily be modified to explain the other two techniques. The example uses a four-dimensional single point (or neurons) (V_1, V_2, V_3, V_4) to explain this approach and two classes $(0,1)$, and it is illustrated in Fig. 12.5. The two parameters W and Ws, as denoted in [2]; are presented in the illustration. The activation function $max(.)$ is used in the illustration; however, the implementation uses the sigmoid function. The first parameter W connects the neurons, the activation function transmits impulses (or fires neurons), and the second parameter Ws generates a predictive model. Then the softmax function is used to predict the labels with probabilities. Finally, the cross-entropy is calculated using the predicted and the actual labels. This model is implemented in the next section.

12.2.6 MapReduce Implementation

The example presented in the Listing 12.1 showed the usefulness of the stochastic descent in updating the model parameters toward optimality. In this section, a MapReduce implementation of the no-drop model, based on the modeling procedures presented in the paper [2] by Wan et al., is partially adopted. However, it will help you understand its MapReduce implementation and develop your own complete implementation for the big data classification.

Listing 12.2 An RHadoop example—implementation of no-drop model

```
1   Sys.setenv(HADOOP_HOME='/usr/lib/hadoop-0.20-mapreduce')
2   Sys.setenv(HADOOP_CMD='/usr/bin/hadoop')
3   Sys.setenv(HADOOP_STREAMING='/usr/lib/hadoop-0.20-mapreduce/
        contrib/streaming/hadoop-streaming-2.0.0-mr1-cdh4.7.0.jar')
4
5   deep.data.fi <- read.table("deep1.txt", sep="")
6
7   library(rmr2)
8   library(rhdfs)
9
10  hdfs.init()
11
12  deep.data.df = to.dfs(deep.data.fi)
13
14  deep.map.fn = function(k, v) {
15    # get the number of observations
16    nn=dim(v)[1]
17
18    # initialize the weight parameter W
19    set.seed(129)
20    m1=rnorm(12,0.5,2.1)
21    m1=m1/max(m1)
22    W=matrix(m1,nrow=3,ncol=4)
23
24    # initialize the beta parameter B
25    set.seed(131)
26    m2=rnorm(6,0.5,2.1)
27    m2=m2/max(m2)
28    B=matrix(m2,nrow=2,ncol=3)
29
30    # initialize arrays of weight matrices
31    WW<-list()
32    BB<-list()
33
34    # initialize entropy matrices
35    ee<-NULL
36
37    # update the W and B using the observations
38    for(ii in 1:nn){
39
40      # get the data domain
41      X=v[ii,1:4]
```

```
42        # get the response set
43        y=v[ii,5]
44
45        # store the W and B to get them later
46        WW[[ii]]=W
47        BB[[ii]]=B
48
49        # calculate U
50        U=W %*% t(X)
51
52        # calculate R
53        R=1/(1+exp(-U))
54
55        # calculate the P matrix
56        P=B %*% R
57
58        # calculate probabilities
59        p1=P[1]
60        p2=P[2]
61
62        p=exp(p1)/(exp(p1)+exp(p2))
63        q=exp(p2)/(exp(p1)+exp(p2))
64
65        # calculate entropy
66        ee[ii]=-y*log(p)-(1-y)*log(1-p)
67
68        # calculate parameters for logistic regression
69        pq=p*(1-p)
70
71        dd1=rep(pq,1,4)
72        K1=diag(dd1)
73
74        dd2=rep(pq,1,3)
75        K2=diag(dd2)
76
77        # calculate parameters to update W and B
78        Y=t(X)
79        neta1=as.numeric((1/(t(Y) %*% K1 %*% Y)) * (y-p)) * Y
80        neta2=as.numeric((1/(t(R) %*% K2 %*% R)) * (y-p)) * R
81
82        # convert to the matrix forms
83        daba1=matrix(rep(t(neta1),3),nrow=3,byrow=TRUE)
84        daba2=matrix(rep(t(neta2),2),nrow=2,byrow=TRUE)
85
86        # update W and B
87        W=W+0.1*daba1
88        B=B+0.1*daba2
89     }
90
91     # entropy as the key
92     k=ee
93
94     keyval(k,c(WW,BB))
95  }
```

```
96   deep.reduce.fn = function(k, v) {
97
98     keyval(k, v)
99   }
100
101  deep.output.mr = mapreduce(input = deep.data.df, map = deep.map.
        fn, reduce = deep.reduce.fn)
102
103  deep.output.df = from.dfs(deep.output.mr)
104  deep.output.df
```

It reads the following deep1.txt file, which consists of a four-dimensional data domain with six observations and their corresponding class labels, and generates parameter updates together with their corresponding entropy at each observation.

```
2.0  8  1  4  1
2    5  5  1  1
3    4  2  12 0
8    8  5  6  1
9    2  7  9  1
1   11  1  12 0
```

The entropy values are nominated as the key of the (key, value) pair as shown in line 93. In line 95, the (key, value) pairs are generated where the value is tuple, which transmits the model parameters W and β (i.e., B).

```
$key
 [1]  0.4182887 0.4182887 0.4368713 0.4368713 0.4397458
 0.4397458 0.4602714 0.4602714
 [9]  1.0281549 1.0281549 1.0489053 1.0489053

$val
$val[[1]]
            [,1]          [,2]        [,3]          [,4]
[1,]  -0.3840013 -0.4710894 0.4689858 -0.341270869
[2,]  -0.3253059  1.0289663 0.1222893  0.608256671
[3,]  -0.4975646  0.4468758 0.5748454 -0.007758183

$val[[2]]
            [,1]          [,2]        [,3]
[1,]  -0.4439768 1.0751781 -0.0762585
[2,]  -0.2255478 0.3013913  0.1132608

$val[[3]]
            [,1]          [,2]        [,3]          [,4]
[1,]  -0.3905531 -0.4776412 0.4648909 -0.34618470
[2,]  -0.3318576  1.0224145 0.1181945  0.60334284
[3,]  -0.5041164  0.4403240 0.5707506 -0.01267201
```

```
$val[[4]]
              [,1]          [,2]             [,3]
[1,] -0.4440815  0.9901814  -0.15328188
[2,] -0.2256525  0.2163946   0.03623744
 :
 :
```

You can observe, each entropy value appears twice in the key-list that indicating the sequence $W, \beta, W, \beta, \ldots$. In each iteration presented in the val-list, the first 3×4 matrix is the parameter W, and the next 2×3 matrix is the parameter β. This list shows only a partial output of the program in Listing 12.2.

12.3 Proposed Framework

The proposed framework provides an approach, which is a combination of a deep learning model and a mapper, which connects the modeling parameters of the deep learning models (see Fig. 12.4). It allows the deep learning models, such as no-drop, dropout, and dropconnect, to be integrated in the framework. The mapper provides an initialization mechanism to the initial w_0 and β_0 parameters.

12.3.1 Motivation

The motivation behind the proposed approach is to incorporate perceptual parameters in the mapper between the deep learning parameters w and β. The output of the neuron shooter (see Fig. 12.1) displays edge-like structures because of the application of a sigmoid function. This structure is strengthened using edge-sharpening filters and is assigned to the initial parameter β_0 to rectify class characteristics. The original class characteristics of an observation are propagated using the discrete cosine transform (DCT) coefficients [11] of the edge-sharpening filters by assigning the DCT coefficients to the initial parameter w_0 of the neuron connector.

12.3.2 Parameters Mapper

In the proposed deep learning framework, the parameters mapper is a simple mathematical function that uses the edge-sharpening filters, and it is defined as follows:

$$\beta_0 = \text{edge\_sharp}(w_0), \tag{12.18}$$

where the function edge_sharp helps manipulate important information from the drop mechanism adopted in modern deep learning models and algorithms like the

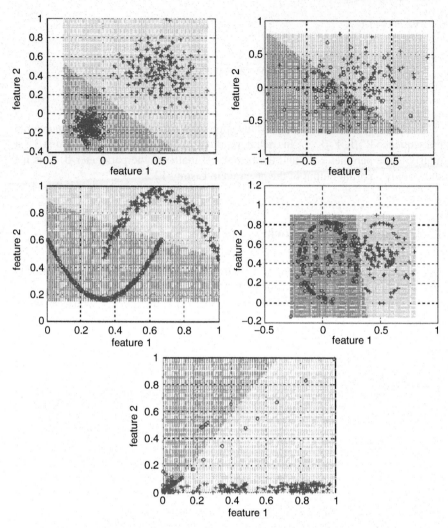

Fig. 12.6 Domain division (standard approach)

dropout and the dropconnect, and it must be defined selectively by the user. In this paper, the two-dimensional discrete cosine transformation has been selected because its coefficients carry useful edge (vertical, horizontal, and diagonal) information, and it can help preserve edge effect [11]. The parameters β_0 and w_0 represent an edge-sharpening filter and its discrete transform coefficients, respectively.

12.4 Implementation of Deep Learning

The simulation compares the classification and domain division performances of no-drop, dropout, dropconnect, and the proposed mapper model. For this simulation, five data sets are considered: (E1) a Gaussian data set with two separable classes; (E2) a Gaussian data set with nonseparable classes (from the historical example presented by Leo Breiman [12]); (E3) a data set with concave-shaped classes (a good example for evaluating nonlinear classification properties of the models)—the concave-shaped classes have been previously used [13, 14]; (E4) the publicly available intrusion data set NSL-KDD [15] (only the regular network traffic and the "neptune" attack traffic are considered in this simulation); and (E5) a data set in which the neptune attack traffic data and regular traffic data are transformed into circular patterns, and the intersection of these circles are computed. Figures 12.6 and 12.7 show the results of these data, respectively.

12.4.1 Analysis of Domain Divisions

Domain division results of the dropconnect model for the five data sets are presented in Fig. 12.6. Similar domain division results are obtained for the no-drop and dropout model. As we can see, the dropconnect model provides linear classification boundaries for these examples with two features. Domain division results of the no-drop with mapper model (i.e., the proposed model) for the same five data sets are presented in Fig. 12.7. In these examples, nonlinear boundaries can be seen. Several noticeable observations make the proposed approach more unique than the no-drop, dropout, and dropconnect models. For example, the first result shows that the proposed approach gives an importance to a single data point in the classification results. We can observe that the classification boundary bends at a location (0, 0.2) classifies the data point at that location correctly. Another interesting result is in the third example. The classification boundaries bend at both tips of the concave classes, making the proposed approach far more superior with two features. Similar nonlinear and desired results are obtained in the other three examples as well.

12.4.2 Analysis of Classification Accuracies

The classification accuracies are first calculated at the end of all iterations (i.e., no early stopping). The results for all data sets and the models no-drop, dropout, and dropconnect are presented in Table 12.1. The results show that the dropconnect model performs poorly on the concave-shaped data set. Overall, no-drop performs better than the other two models. The maximum classification accuracies with early-stopping strategy are presented in Table 12.2. It has five columns (data sets), and the values show equal performance in the models.

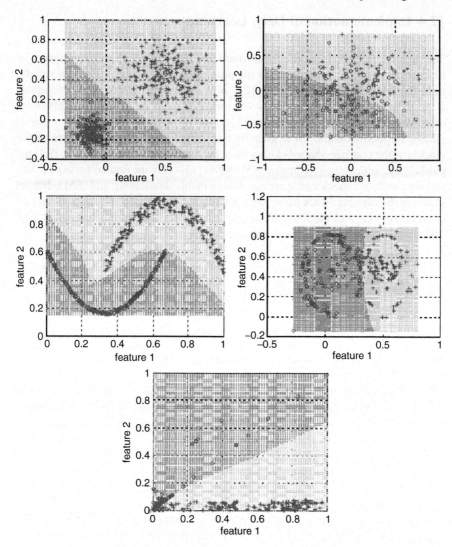

Fig. 12.7 Domain division (proposed approach)

The classification accuracies calculated for no-drop with the mapper model are presented in the first row of Table 12.3 (i.e., without an ensemble approach). These results show improvements overall; however, it shows excellent performance on concave-shaped data sets. The empirical observation indicated that combining several domain division results could improve the performance; hence, an ensemble approach is proposed and discussed in the next section.

Table 12.1 Final step classification accuracies

Models	E1	E2	E3	E4	E5
No-drop	100.00	70.59	92.53	94.83	96.00
Dropout	100.00	65.88	89.07	95.00	82.13
Dropconnect	100.00	71.76	50.13	88.50	92.27

Table 12.2 Maximum classification accuracies

Models	E1	E2	E3	E4	E5
No-drop	100.00	75.88	93.07	98.33	97.60
Dropout	100.00	75.88	92.80	98.17	94.93
Dropconnect	100.00	74.71	91.47	98.33	94.93

Table 12.3 Classification accuracy of the proposed approach

Models	E1	E2	E3	E4	E5
W/o ensemble	100.00	76.60	99.73	95.47	94.50
With ensemble	100.00	78.82	99.73	97.60	99.27

12.5 Ensemble Approach

The proposed approach provides many parameter-pairs, w and β, that can give high classification accuracies. Therefore, several robust domain divisions can be obtained. These domain divisions may give better classification accuracies when combined selectively. An ensemble approach is proposed for this purpose in this section. The goal of the ensemble approach is to select a number of parameter-pairs, (say L) that can help improve the classification accuracy. Suppose the training provides n pairs, then we can denote this set by: $w_s = \{(w_1, \beta_1), (w_2, \beta_2), \ldots, (w_n, \beta_n)\}$. If this set is sorted in descending order using their classification accuracies, then our new set is: $w'_s = \{(w'_1, \beta'_1), (w'_2, \beta'_2), \ldots, (w'_n, \beta'_n)\}$. We can notice that the first 7, 6, 16, 5, and 2 % parameter-pairs give the maximum classification accuracies for the examples E1–E5, respectively. Hence, these percentages can be used to derive L for these examples. The classification results produced by these L parameters for their corresponding examples can be combined in the ensemble classification. However, this process must be automated.

Suppose we select the first L parameter-pairs (i.e., the L parameter-pairs with highest classification accuracies) from the sorted set w'_s and apply them to the entire domain for classification. Now, to ensemble the data points (i.e., input neurons), each data point in an example is analyzed against the L domain division results produced by the L high classification accuracy parameters selected. If a data point belongs to a class domain more than $L/2$ times, then the data point is marked with that class label. Otherwise, it is marked with the other class label. The entire domain will undergo this threshold-based labeling process. The ensemble classification results for the examples E1–E5 are presented in the second row of Table 12.3. We can see the improvements in the classification accuracies for no-drop with mapper and the ensemble approach.

Problems

12.1. Code Revision
Revise the MapReduce programs presented in this chapter using the coding principles taught in Chap. 5.

12.2. Real Example with No-Drop Model

(a) Modify the program in Listing 12.2 to read all the features from the hardwood floor and carpet floor data sets with appropriate labels.
(b) Run the program with these data sets and produce the results. Observe the characteristics of this deep learning model and interpret the results.

12.3. Implementation of DropConnect

(a) Understand the SGD explained in this chapter and derive similar iterative sequences for the deep learning parameters W and Ws (or β) stated in the paper [2] by Wan et al.
(b) Incorporate this SGD in the code in Listing 12.2 by modifying the block of code in lines 69–89 based on the Algorithm 1 in [2]. Run and observe the results. Then interpret the results and discuss the differences (if any) with the results obtained from the code in Listing 12.2.

Acknowledgements I would like to thank Professor Bin Yu from the University of California, Berkeley for giving me an opportunity to visit the Statistics Department and work on the Deep Learning research. This work was carried out with Professor Bin Yu. I also would like to thank Dr. Jinzhu Jia from Peaking University, who was a visiting scholar at the University of California, Berkeley during this research, for his help in validating the SGD implementation.

References

1. B. Dalessandro. "Bring the noise: Embracing randomness is the key to scaling up machine learning algorithms." Big Data vol. 1, no. 2, pp. 110–112, 2013.
2. L. Wan, M. Zeiler, S. Zhang, Y. L. Cun, and R. Fergus. "Regularization of neural networks using dropconnect." In Proceedings of the International Conference on Machine Learning, pp. 1058–1066, 2013.
3. G. E. Hinton, N. Srivastava, A. Krizhevsky, I. Sutskever, and R. R. Salakhutdinov. "Improving neural networks by preventing co-adaptation of feature detectors." Technical Report, arXiv:1207.0580, pp. 1–18, 2012.

4. T. Hastie, R. Tibshirani, and J. Friedman. The Elements of Statistical Learning. New York: Springer, 2009.

5. J. Han and C. Moraga. "The influence of the sigmoid function parameters on the speed of backpropagation learning." In From Natural to Artificial Neural Computation, pp. 195–201, Springer, 1995.

6. B. L. Kalman and S. C. Kwasny. "Why tanh: choosing a sigmoidal function." International Joint Conference on Neural Networks, vol. 4, pp. 578–581, 1992.

7. Y. LeCun, L. Bottou, Y. Bengio, and P. Haffner. "Gradient-based learning applied to document recognition." Proceedings of the IEEE, vol. 86, no. 11, pp. 2278–2324, 1998.

8. T. Zhang. "Solving large scale linear prediction problems using stochastic gradient descent algorithms." In Proceedings of the International Conference on Machine learning, pp. 919–926, 2004.

9. Subtle Sharpen Filter, http://lodev.org/cgtutor/filtering.html.

10. S. Suthaharan. "No-reference visually significant blocking artifact metric for natural scene images." Signal Processing, vol. 89, no. 8, pp. 1647–1652, 2009.

11. N. Ahmed, T. Natarajan, and K. R. Rao. Discrete cosine transform. IEEE Transactions on Computers, vol. 100, no. 1, pp. 90–93, 1974.

12. Twonorm, http://www.cs.toronto.edu/$\sim$delve/data/datasets.html, (dataset used by Leo Breiman).

13. G. Montavon, M. L. Braun, and K. R. Muller. "Kernel analysis of deep networks," The Journal of Machine Learning Research, vol. 12, pp. 2563–2581, 2011.

14. C. Jose, P. Goyal, P. Aggrwal, and M. Varma. "Local deep kernel learning for efficient non-linear svm prediction," In Proceedings of the 30th International Conference on Machine Learning, pp. 486–494, 2013.

15. NSL-KDD, https://archive.ics.uci.edu/ml/datasets/KDD+Cup+1999+Data.

Chapter 13
Chandelier Decision Tree

Abstract This chapter proposes two new techniques called the *chandelier decision tree* and the *random chandelier*. This pair of techniques is similar to the well-known pair of techniques, the decision tree and the random forest. The chapter also presents a previously proposed algorithm called the unit circle algorithm (UCA) and proposes a family of UCA-based algorithms called the unit circle machine (UCM), unit ring algorithm (URA), and unit ring machine (URM). The unit circle algorithm integrates a normalization process to define a unit circle domain, and thus the other proposed algorithms adopt the phrase "unit circle." The chandelier decision tree and the random chandelier use the unit ring machine to build the chandelier trees.

13.1 Unit Circle Algorithm

The unit circle algorithm (UCA) proposed in a recent paper [1] is one of the important contributors to the chandelier decision tree and random chandelier techniques presented in this chapter. The main concept of the UCA is the transformation of a given data domain to a circular data domain (or hypersphere) and the execution of domain division on that circular domain for classification. To achieve these objectives, the data have been represented in unit circles with two regions called the inner circle and the outer circle and then used to classify two classes. One of the advantages of this algorithm is that it can provide a classifier with a fewer number of parameters compared to the current algorithms.

Another advantage is that it can classify the similar unseen data that maps to the classified data; as a result, it is very useful for big data classification. However, its application is limited because, as you will see, it is heavily dependent on the topographical structure (especially the orientation) of the data and the degree of separability of the classes. The step-by-step enhancement of this algorithm can lead

© Springer Science+Business Media New York 2016
S. Suthaharan, *Machine Learning Models and Algorithms for Big Data Classification*, Integrated Series in Information Systems 36, DOI 10.1007/978-1-4899-7641-3_13

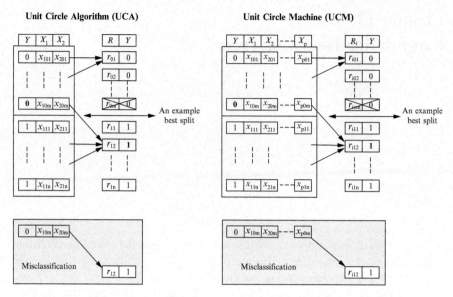

Fig. 13.1 UCA and UCM algorithms are illustrated in this figure

to a good classification algorithm, and it is discussed in this chapter. In simple terms, the goal of this algorithm is to represent the data domain using circles, and then parametrize the learning model with the radius of the circles.

13.1.1 UCA Classification

The UCA classification is demonstrated on the left side of Fig. 13.1 using two feature sets, X_1 and X_2 with a response set Y, and two class labels, 0 and 1. In this example, the two-dimensional data domain D_1, which is defined by the features X_1 and X_2, is transformed into a one-dimensional data domain defined by R as follows:

$$r = \sqrt{(x_1{}^2 + x_2{}^2)}, \qquad (13.1)$$

where $r \in R$, $x_1 \in X_1$, and $x_2 \in X_2$. This mathematical transformation is also shown in the left figure of Fig. 13.1. The transformation provides the radius of a circle on which an observation resides. Hence, all the unseen observations which reside on the circle can be classified when the given observation is classified.

Also note that multiple observations in the data domain D_1 may be mapped to a single observation in the newly created circular data domain D_2. This brings the advantage of data reduction as well. Also note that the misclassification can occur as illustrated in this example (i.e., an observation with class label 0 can map to a class

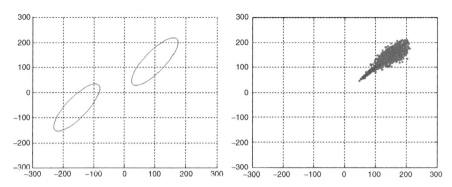

Fig. 13.2 UCA's class location requirements

label 1 and vice versa). This figure also shows a possible domain division (split) which encounters a misclassification problem. The misclassification causes a fuzzy boundary in the domain division at classification. As reported in [1], the classifier $r = 0.7071$ was obtained for classifying two intrusion attacks with a fuzzy boundary of 0.005. We can simply say that in this approach a circular learning model has been proposed, and it has been parametrized using the radius of the unit circles.

We can also say that the regions formed by the circles have been used for classification. It is a good technique to classify separable classes, and its performance is poor when the classes are nonseparable. The first figure in Fig. 13.2 shows the preferred location and orientation of the classes on a data domain. The second figure shows the overlapping classes obtained from the hardwood floor and carpet floor images—it illustrates a fuzzy boundary. The fuzzy boundary can be captured by defining a ring boundary, and it becomes the new technique called, unit ring algorithm, which will be explained later. Let us now look at a coding example, which implements an improved version of unit circle machine (UCM) in which the data domain is divided using the entropy-based information gain approach.

13.1.2 Improved UCA Classification

The original UCA does not incorporate any algorithms to find an optimal split location for the domain division. In this section, the original UCA has been improved by integrating the entropy-based information gain technique to find the best split location on the circular domain R. The best split algorithm will help to minimize the misclassification and reduce the fuzzy boundary. This improved approach is implemented in Matlab and presented in the following subsection.

13.1.3 A Coding Example

This section provides two Matlab programs, the first one is a function that implements the information gain calculator as before in Chap. 10, and the second one is the main program that implements the UCA classification using the information gain calculator. The main objective of the function is to read a feature variable with its label information and find the best split location for domain division.

Listing 13.1 A Matlab example—information gain calculator

```
1   function [sl,mx,ig]=uca_calc_ig_fn(xx,yy)
2
3       ll=length(xx);
4       for ii=2:ll-1
5           %sp is the split location
6           sp=xx(ii);
7
8           %build left and right tree
9           xl=yy(xx<sp);
10          xr=yy(xx>=sp);
11
12          %length of the left tree
13          l1=length(xl);
14          %sum of class 1s
15          n1=sum(xl);
16          %sum of class 0s
17          n2=l1-n1;
18
19          %probabilities
20          p1=n1/(n1+n2)+0.00001;
21          p2=n2/(n1+n2)+0.00001;
22
23          %entropy of the left tree
24          en1 = -p1*log(p1)-p2*log(p2);
25
26          %length of the right tree
27          l2=length(xr);
28          %sum of class 1s
29          n1=sum(xr);
30          %sum of class 0s
31          n2=l2-n1;
32
33          %probabilities
34          p1=n1/(n1+n2)+0.00001;
35          p2=n2/(n1+n2)+0.00001;
36
37          %entropy of the right tree
38          en2 = -p1*log(p1)-p2*log(p2);
39
40          %Calculates information gain
41          ig(ii-1)=1-((l1/ll)*en1 + (l2/ll)*en2);
42      end
43      %find the split location with the maximum information gain
```

```
44        tmp=find(ig==max(ig));
45        sl=tmp(1);
46        mx=max(ig);
47  end
```

In line 1, the function *uca_calc_ig_fn* is defined, and it accepts a single feature set (*xx*) and its class labels (*yy*) (only two classes) and outputs the best split location (*sl*), the maximum information gain (*mx*), and the list of information gains at each location (*ig*). Line 3 provides the number of observations in the data domain (*ll*). The for-loop in lines 4–42 carries out the task of calculating the information gain when split occurs, starting from the observation 2 to the observation *ll*-1. The program has comments for each block of code, and it explains the purpose of the code. The goal of each step is to complete a set of tasks that will lead to the information gain for each split. Finally, the split location that gives the maximum information gain is selected as the best split location.

Listing 13.2 A Matlab example—improved UCA-based classification

```
1   clear all;
2   close all;
3
4   % Two-classes input data sets
5   hw1=csvread('hardwood.csv');
6   cp1=csvread('carpet.csv');
7
8   % The first two features are used
9   tw1=hw1(:,1); tw2=hw1(:,2);
10  tw3=sqrt(tw1.*tw1+tw2.*tw2);
11  figure;plot(tw1,tw2,'.');grid on
12  axis([-300 300 -300 300]);
13
14  tp1=cp1(:,1); tp2=cp1(:,2);
15  tp3=sqrt(tp1.*tp1+tp2.*tp2);
16  hold on;plot(tp1,tp2,'r.');grid on;
17  axis([-300 300 -300 300]);
18
19  % Labels are added
20  yy=[ones(1,size(tw3,1)) zeros(1,size(tp3,1))];
21  xx=[tw3;tp3]';
22
23  % Finding the best split using information gain
24  [slx,fmx,igx]=uca_calc_ig_fn(xx,yy);
25
26  fmxsort=sort(fmx,'descend');
27  tmp1=find(fmx==fmxsort(1));
28  f1=tmp1(1);
29  fval=xx(f1,slx(f1));
30
31  % Splitting the circular domain
32  idxL=find(xx(f1,:)<fval);
33  idxR=find(xx(f1,:)>=fval);
34
35  xxL=xx(:,idxL);
36  xxR=xx(:,idxR);
```

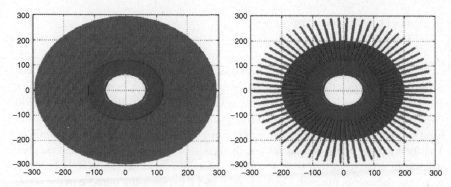

Fig. 13.3 UCA's circular domain division and overlap revelation

```
37  yyL=yy(idxL);
38  yyR=yy(idxR);
39
40  % Showing the classification counts
41  fprintf('\n');
42  fprintf('Left side class 1 = %d\n',sum(yyL));
43  fprintf('Left side class 0 = %d\n\n',length(yyL)-sum(yyL));
44
45  fprintf('Right side class 1 = %d\n',sum(yyR));
46  fprintf('Right side class 0 = %d\n',length(yyR)-sum(yyR));
47
48  % Showing the classes using circles
49  figure;
50  for ii=1:size(xx,2)
51      if yy(ii)==1
52          circle(0,0,xx(f1,ii),'.',0.01);
53      else
54          circle(0,0,xx(f1,ii),'r.',0.01);
55      end
56      hold on;grid on;
57  end
58
59  %Showing the overlapping region
60  figure;
61  for ii=1:size(xx,2)
62      if yy(ii)==1
63          circle(0,0,xx(f1,ii),'.',0.01);
64      else
65          circle(0,0,xx(f1,ii),'r.',0.09);
66      end
67      hold on;grid on;
68  end
```

The block of code in lines 50–58 has produced the result presented in the first figure of Fig. 13.3, where we can see circular subdomains for two classes represented by blue (label 1) and red (label 0). This figure gives the impression of perfect separation (classification) between the classes, but there is a hidden circular subdomain, where we can see a large quantity of misclassified data. The block of code in line 61 to line 69 makes the red class thinner, thus the hidden subdomain can be seen. Observe it in the second figure of Fig. 13.3. This is the fuzzy boundary problem in UCA-based approaches.

13.1.4 Drawbacks of UCA

One of the problems is that the circular domains from different classes may overlap. The overlapping region may also be significantly high as illustrated in Fig. 13.3. We cannot see the overlap in the first figure, but the overlapping region is disclosed in the second figure by thinning the circular domain of the class 0 (in red). Despite this fuzzy boundary problem, it can work nicely with the classification of separable classes. There are several features in the problem space, and therefore nonoverlapping regions may be found in other subspaces. We must deploy an optimization process to find the best feature pair and the best split. This is the goal of UCM which is discussed in the next section.

13.2 Unit Circle Machine

The UCA provides a machine learning model and algorithms. However, it does not provide a good optimization because of the absence of a simultaneous feature selection algorithm. The UCM fulfills this requirement through an iterative approach. The main difference is that the UCM technique scans through all the features and selects the best feature that gives the best split on the circular domain using the information gain approach as performed in decision tree [2] and random forest [3] approaches. The UCM classification is also good for the separable classes, but it tries to find the separability in subspaces and gives the subspace that has the best separability or split. It brings the same advantages as UCA, but it also helps to optimize the classification to a certain extent.

13.2.1 UCM Classification

The UCM classification is illustrated on the right side of Fig. 13.1 using p feature sets $X_1, X_2, \ldots, X_p$ with a response set Y and two class labels 0 and 1. The same as UCA, the misclassification is also illustrated in this figure. In this example, the

p dimensional data domain D_1, which is defined by the features $X_1, X_2, \ldots, X_p$, is transformed into $p-1$ one-dimensional data domains defined by R_i as follows:

$$r = \sqrt{(x_i^2 + x_j^2)}, \tag{13.2}$$

where $r \in R_i, x_i \in X_i, x_j \in X_{i+1}$, and $i = 1, \ldots, p-1$. It means that the circular domain is defined iteratively pairing the features and calculating the radius of the circle for each observation. The second figure in Fig. 13.1 shows the construction of circular domain for the ith feature pair and the domain split with a misclassification example. This process is done repeatedly for $i = 1, \ldots, p-1$, and the feature that gives the best split (maximum information gain) is selected as the best feature. Hence, we have the best feature and the best split location on the data domain.

13.2.2 A Coding Example

The Matlab code for UCM classification is presented in this section. It uses the UCA function presented in Listing 13.1. The overall goal of the code is to find the best feature that gives the best split location for domain division. It uses the hardwood floor and carpet floor data sets introduced earlier in this book.

Listing 13.3 A Matlab example—UCM classification

```
1   clear all;
2   close all;
3
4   hw1=csvread('hardwood.csv');
5   cp1=csvread('carpet.csv');
6
7   % Iteration over the features
8   tw1=hw1(:,1:1:end-1); tw2=hw1(:,2:1:end);
9   hw=sqrt(tw1.*tw1+tw2.*tw2);
10
11  tp1=cp1(:,1:1:end-1); tp2=cp1(:,2:1:end);
12  cp=sqrt(tp1.*tp1+tp2.*tp2);
13
14  % Labels are added
15  yy=[ones(1,size(hw,1)) zeros(1,size(cp,1))];
16  xx=[hw;cp]';
17
18  % Finding the best split and the best feature
19  % using information gain
20  for ii=1:size(xx,1)
21      sig=std(xx(ii,:));
22      [slx(ii),fmx(ii),igx{ii}]=uca_calc_ig_fn(xx(ii,:),yy);
23  end
24
25  fmxsort=sort(fmx,'descend');
26  tmp1=find(fmx==fmxsort(1));
27  f1=tmp1(1);
```

```
28   fval=xx(f1,slx(f1));
29
30   % Splitting the circular domain
31   idxL=find(xx(f1,:)<fval);
32   idxR=find(xx(f1,:)>=fval);
33
34   xxL=xx(:,idxL);
35   xxR=xx(:,idxR);
36
37   yyL=yy(idxL);
38   yyR=yy(idxR);
39
40   % Showing the classification counts
41   fprintf('\n');
42   fprintf('Left_side_class_1_=_%d\n',sum(yyL));
43   fprintf('Left_side_class_0_=_%d\n\n',length(yyL)-sum(yyL));
44
45   fprintf('Right_side_class_1_=_%d\n',sum(yyR));
46   fprintf('Right_side_class_0_=_%d\n',length(yyR)-sum(yyR));
47
48   % Showing the classes using circles
49   figure;
50   for ii=1:size(xx,2)
51       if yy(ii)==1
52           circle(0,0,xx(f1,ii),'.',0.01);
53       else
54           circle(0,0,xx(f1,ii),'r.',0.09);
55       end
56       hold on;grid on;
57   end
58
59   % Showing the features 1 and 2
60   figure;plot(hw1(:,1),hw1(:,2),'.');
61   hold on;plot(cp1(:,1),cp1(:,2),'r.');
62   axis([40 240 40 240]);grid on;
63
64   % Showing the best features 48 and 49
65   figure;plot(hw1(:,48),hw1(:,49),'.');
66   hold on;plot(cp1(:,48),cp1(:,49),'r.');
67   axis([40 240 40 240]);grid on;
```

The block of code in line 60 to line 62 has produced the scatter plot in the first figure of Fig. 13.4, which shows the two classes (hardwood floor and carpet floor) in the data domain defined by features 1 and 2. But UCM selects the features 48 and 49 as the best features to construct the circular domain and to obtain the best split (domain division), and the results are presented in the second figure of Fig. 13.4. In this figure, we can clearly see a better separation between the classes.

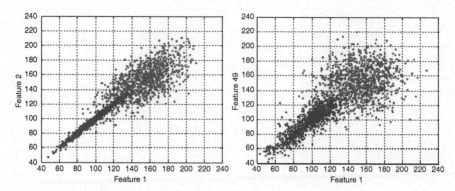

Fig. 13.4 We can see the UCM technique selects the best features to construct circular classifiers and gives good classification—compared to the first plot, we can see less class overlap. The same scales are used to show the effect

13.2.3 Drawbacks of UCM

As illustrated in Fig. 13.2, the topological structure is the major restriction in both UCA and UCM approaches. Although the UCM approach helps find the best feature pair, still the overlapping subdomain can be high, and the misclassification can be increased. There is an alternative way of handling this problem, which is called the unit ring algorithm [4]. The main goal of URA is to find the ring split that minimizes the misclassification by absorbing the observations that increase the misclassification.

13.3 Unit Ring Algorithm

The UCA and UCM techniques suffer from the fuzzy boundary problem, which leads to high misclassification. Therefore, it is desirable to search for the best feature that gives the best split in order to minimize the misclassification, meaning the reduction of fuzzy boundary. For this purpose, the unit ring algorithm is proposed. In the URA approach, the circular domain is split by a ring, such that the ring-split minimizes the misclassification by finding the subdomains that give the maximum information gain on the ring-split. Thus, it helps alleviate the problem of misclassification by identifying the fuzzy boundary which falls within the ring and gives the best domain split. It is also called best-split, worst-ring technique because it gives the subdomains that have the maximum information gain while the ring does not have the maximum information gain. The first diagram in Fig. 13.5 illustrates this technique. It shows that the ring absorbs the misclassification and thus reduces misclassification in the separated circular sub domains.

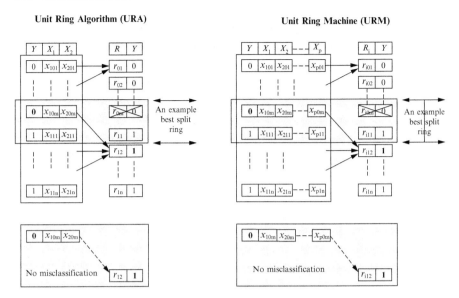

Fig. 13.5 URA and URM algorithms are illustrated in this figure—the iteration over feature space to find the best feature is integrated in URM

To accomplish this task, URA deploys an iterative mechanism with a ring concept, which is similar to the sliding window technique used in many computer science applications. It also adopts the entropy-based information gain approach (as the same as UCA and UCM) to find the best split. The width of the ring (i.e., the window size) is selected as a proportion of the standard deviation (σ) of the observations. The examples presented in this section use 0.5σ. However, URA suggests finding a suitable value for the window size using cross-validation approach.

By sliding the window (i.e., by expanding the ring over the circular data domain, but keeping the window size fixed), the information gains of domain split are calculated, and the ring that gives the maximum information gain is selected as the best split ring. This is called the URA approach, and the algorithm is provided in Matlab code in the following subsection.

13.3.1 A Coding Example

This section presents a Matlab function. The objective of this function is to accept a feature variable with its labels and standard deviation, and then outputs the best split ring with two circular subdomains. It also returns other variables (or information) for readers to explore.

Listing 13.4 A Matlab example—unit ring algorithm

```matlab
function [s1,mx,ig,md1,md0,n1,n2,o1,o2]=ura_calc_ig_fn(xx,yy,sig)

    l1=length(yy);
    for ii=2:ll-1
        %sp is the split location
        sp=xx(ii);

        %build left and right tree
        wd=0.5*sig;
        xl=yy(xx<sp);
        xr=yy(xx>=(sp+wd));
        xm=yy(xx>=sp & xx<(sp+wd));

        %length of the node
        m1=length(xm);
        %sum of class 1s
        md1=sum(xm);
        %sum of class 0s
        md0=m1-md1;

        %length of the left tree
        l1=length(xl);
        %sum of class 1s
        n1=sum(xl);
        %sum of class 0s
        n2=l1-n1;

        %probabilities
        p1=n1/(n1+n2)+0.00001;
        p2=n2/(n1+n2)+0.00001;

        %entropy of the left tree
        en1 = -p1*log(p1)-p2*log(p2);

        %length of the right tree
        l2=length(xr);
        %sum of class 1s
        o1=sum(xr);
        %sum of class 0s
        o2=l2-o1;

        %probabilities
        p1=o1/(o1+o2)+0.00001;
        p2=o2/(o1+o2)+0.00001;

        %entropy of the right tree
        en2 = -p1*log(p1)-p2*log(p2);

        %Calculates information gain
        ig(ii-1)=1-((l1/ll)*en1 + (l2/ll)*en2);
    end
    %find the split location with the maximum information gain
```

```
53      tmp=find(ig==max(ig));
54      sl=tmp(1);
55      mx=max(ig);
56  end
```

The URA technique is applied to features 1 and 2 and the result is presented in the first figure of Fig. 13.6. It shows that URA requires a feature selection algorithm to find the best feature with the best split location.

13.3.2 Unit Ring Machine

The unit ring machine is an extension of the URA approach like the way the UCM approach was developed from UCA. In URM, the URA approach is applied to all pairs of features iteratively as performed previously, and the best feature pair that gives the best URA split over the circular domain is selected as the classifier. It uses all the feature pairs iteratively with the sliding window technique and finds the best feature pair that forms a ring, which provides the maximum information gain at ring split. The URM approach is illustrated in the second figure of Fig. 13.5.

13.3.3 A Coding Example

Listing 13.5 A Matlab example—URM classification

```
1   clear all;
2   close all;
3
4   hw1=csvread('hardwood.csv');
5   cp1=csvread('carpet.csv');
6
7   % Iteration over the features
8   tw1=hw1(:,1:1:end-1); tw2=hw1(:,2:1:end);
9   hw=sqrt(tw1.*tw1+tw2.*tw2);
10
11  tp1=cp1(:,1:1:end-1); tp2=cp1(:,2:1:end);
12  cp=sqrt(tp1.*tp1+tp2.*tp2);
13
14  % Labels are added
15  yy=[ones(1,size(hw,1)) zeros(1,size(cp,1))];
16  xx=[hw;cp]';
17
18  % Finding the best split and the best feature
19  % using information gain
20  for ii=1:size(xx,1)
```

```
21        sig=std(xx(ii,:));
22        [slx(ii),fmx(ii),igx{ii},md1(ii),md0(ii),n1(ii),n2(ii), \
             ldots
23           o1(ii),o2(ii)]=ura_calc_ig_fn(xx(ii,:),yy,sig);
24   end
25
26   fmxsort=sort(fmx,'descend');
27   tmp1=find(fmx==fmxsort(1));
28   f1=tmp1(1);
29   fval=xx(f1,slx(f1));
30
31   % Splitting the circular domain
32   idxL=find(xx(f1,:)<fval);
33   idxR=find(xx(f1,:)>=fval);
34
35   xxL=xx(:,idxL);
36   xxR=xx(:,idxR);
37
38   yyL=yy(idxL);
39   yyR=yy(idxR);
40
41   % Showing the classification counts
42   fprintf('\n');
43   fprintf('Left side class 1 = %d\n',sum(yyL));
44   fprintf('Left side class 0 = %d\n\n',length(yyL)-sum(yyL));
45
46   fprintf('Right side class 1 = %d\n',sum(yyR));
47   fprintf('Right side class 0 = %d\n',length(yyR)-sum(yyR));
48
49   % Showing the classes using circles
50   figure;
51   for ii=1:size(xx,2)
52       if yy(ii)==1
53           circle(0,0,xx(f1,ii),'.',0.01);
54       else
55           circle(0,0,xx(f1,ii),'r.',0.09);
56       end
57       hold on;grid on;
58   end
59
60   % Showing the features 1 and 2
61   figure;plot(hw1(:,1),hw1(:,2),'.');
62   hold on;plot(cp1(:,1),cp1(:,2),'r.');
63   axis([40 240 40 240]);grid on;
64   xlabel('Feature 1');ylabel('Feature 2');
65
66   % Showing the best features 48 and 49
67   figure;plot(hw1(:,48),hw1(:,49),'.');
68   hold on;plot(cp1(:,48),cp1(:,49),'r.');
69   axis([40 240 40 240]);grid on;
70   xlabel('Feature 48');ylabel('Feature 49');
71
72   figure;plot(md1);hold on;plot(md1,'.');grid on;
73   hold on;plot(md0,'color','r');hold on;plot(md0,'r.');
```

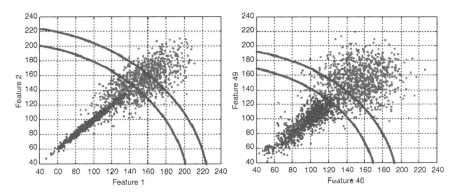

Fig. 13.6 Comparison between URA and URM

```
74
75  figure;plot(fmx);grid on;
76  xlabel('Feature_number');ylabel('Information_gain');
```

The final result of this program is presented in the second figure of Fig. 13.6. It shows that URM selects feature 48 and feature 49 as best features and divided it with a unit ring at the best split location. Comparing the results in the first and second figure, we can appreciate the capability of URM over URA.

13.3.4 Drawbacks of URM

The overlapping region may be very high. As presented earlier, the second figure in Fig. 13.3 discloses the overlapping region. However, nonoverlapping regions may be found in other subspaces. Therefore, an optimization process must be integrated to find the best feature pair and the best split. The chandelier decision tree addresses this process and it is discussed in the next section.

13.4 Chandelier Decision Tree

The chandelier decision tree is the machine learning technique that integrates the URM approach and the concepts used in the decision tree. It divides the circular data domain into a tree of circular subdomains, where a node has the ring with data that gives two branches (subdomains) that have maximum information gain.

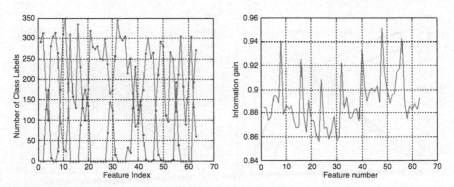

Fig. 13.7 Number of class labels and information gain for each feature split with chandelier decision tree

---

The main difference between the decision tree and the chandelier decision tree
The decision tree builds the best node that gives the best split, but the chandelier decision tree builds the worst node that gives the best split. However, each node in the tree has a ring of subdomains, which is split as arcs to give a good classification.

13.4.1 CDT-Based Classification

As mentioned before, the CDT approach adopts URM, divides the data domain iteratively, and builds a decision tree. The use of URM provides a best split ring at each node and circular subdomains for two leaves. The URM approach is repeatedly applied on the subdomains and a tree like structure is built. It looks like a chandelier; therefore, it is called the chandelier decision tree. The nodes of the tree are the best split rings, and these rings must also be divided to get additional classifiers.

This process also makes this approach unique and differentiates it from the standard decision tree approach. The subdomains of these best split rings form arc shapes, and thus the entire tree looks like the chandelier. Hence, the name chandelier decision tree fits very well for this approach. The examples presented for the CDT approach in this chapter build the first level of the chandelier tree, which has a node with a unit ring, and the leaves have circular subdomains. It can be easily extended (iteratively or recursively) to a complete CDT as we do with the regular decision tree. The program in Listing 13.6 demonstrates the concept of CDT and some of its results are presented in Figs. 13.7 and 13.8. The calculation of information gain for each feature is one of the information tasks of CDT and it is carried out in the block of code in lines 20–24, and the results are presented in Fig. 13.7. The first figure shows the number of class labels in the best split ring associated with each feature, and the second figure shows information gain of each feature—we can see the maximum information gain is achieved with the split of feature 48.

Listing 13.6 A Matlab example—CDT classification

```matlab
1   clear all;
2   close all;
3
4   hw1=csvread('hardwood.csv');
5   cp1=csvread('carpet.csv');
6
7   % Iteration over the features
8   tw1=hw1(:,1:1:end-1); tw2=hw1(:,2:1:end);
9   hw=sqrt(tw1.*tw1+tw2.*tw2);
10
11  tp1=cp1(:,1:1:end-1); tp2=cp1(:,2:1:end);
12  cp=sqrt(tp1.*tp1+tp2.*tp2);
13
14  % Labels are added
15  yy=[ones(1,size(hw,1)) zeros(1,size(cp,1))];
16  xx=[hw;cp]';
17
18  % Finding the best split and the best feature
19  % using information gain
20  for ii=1:size(xx,1)
21      sig(ii)=std(xx(ii,:));
22      [slx(ii),fmx(ii),igx{ii},md1(ii),md0(ii),n1(ii),n2(ii), \
           ldots
23          o1(ii),o2(ii)]=ura_calc_ig_fn(xx(ii,:),yy,sig(ii));
24  end
25
26  fmxsort=sort(fmx,'descend');
27  tmp1=find(fmx==fmxsort(1));
28  f1=tmp1(1);
29  fval=xx(f1,slx(f1));
30
31  % Splitting the circular domain
32  idxL=find(xx(f1,:)<fval);
33  idxR=find(xx(f1,:)>=fval+0.5*sig(f1));
34  idxM=find(xx(f1,:)>=fval & xx(f1,:)<fval+0.5*sig(f1));
35
36  xxL=xx(:,idxL);
37  xxR=xx(:,idxR);
38  xxM=xx(:,idxM);
39
40  yyL=yy(idxL);
41  yyR=yy(idxR);
42  yyM=yy(idxM);
43
44  % Showing the classification counts
45  fprintf('\n');
46  fprintf('Left_side_class_1_=_%d\n',sum(yyL));
```

```
47   fprintf('Left_side_class_0_=_%d\n\n',length(yyL)-sum(yyL));
48
49   fprintf('Middle_class_1_=_%d\n',sum(yyM));
50   fprintf('Middle_class_0_=_%d\n\n',length(yyM)-sum(yyM));
51
52   fprintf('Right_side_class_1_=_%d\n',sum(yyR));
53   fprintf('Right_side_class_0_=_%d\n',length(yyR)-sum(yyR));
54
55   % Showing the classes using circles
56   figure;
57   for ii=1:size(xx,2)
58       if yy(ii)==1
59           circle(0,0,xx(f1,ii),'.',0.01);
60       else
61           circle(0,0,xx(f1,ii),'r.',0.09);
62       end
63       hold on;grid on;
64   end
65
66   % Showing the maximum IG for each feature
67   figure;plot(md1);hold on;plot(md1,'.');grid on;
68   hold on;plot(md0,'color','r');hold on;plot(md0,'r.');
69
70   figure;plot(fmx);grid on;
71   xlabel('Feature_number');ylabel('Information_gain');
72
73   % Showing the features 1 and 2
74   figure;plot(hw1(:,1),hw1(:,2),'.');
75   hold on;plot(cp1(:,1),cp1(:,2),'r.');
76   axis([40 240 40 240]);grid on;
77   xlabel('Feature_1');ylabel('Feature_2');
78
79   jj=48;
80   % Showing the best features 48 and 49
81   figure;plot(hw1(:,jj),hw1(:,jj+1),'.');
82   hold on;plot(cp1(:,jj),cp1(:,jj+1),'r.');
83   axis([40 240 40 240]);grid on;
84   xlabel('Feature_48');ylabel('Feature_49');
85
86   quartcircle(0,0,fval,'m.',0.001);
87   quartcircle(0,0,fval+0.5*sig(jj),'m.',0.001);
88
89   %%%%%%%%%%%%%%%%
90   idxx=find(xx(f1,:)>=fval & xx(f1,:)<fval+0.5*sig(jj));
91   hww1=hw1(idxx(idxx<=1024),:);
92   cpp1=cp1(idxx(idxx>1024)-1024,:);
93
94   % figure;plot(hww1(:,jj),hww1(:,jj+1),'.');
95   % hold on;plot(cpp1(:,jj),cpp1(:,jj+1),'r.');grid on;
96
97   % Unit Ring Domain Division
98   tww1=hww1(:,1:1:end-1); tww2=hww1(:,2:1:end);
99   hww=tww2./tww1;
100
```

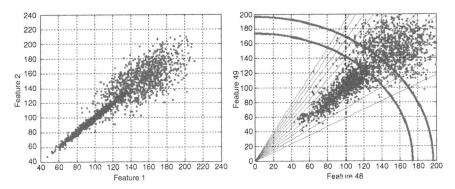

Fig. 13.8 Domain division by chandelier decision tree is illustrated

```
101  tpp1=cpp1(:,1:1:end-1); tpp2=cpp1(:,2:1:end);
102  cpp=tpp2./tpp1;
103
104  wyy=[ones(1,size(hww,1)) zeros(1,size(cpp,1))];
105  wxx=[hww;cpp];
106
107  uu=(max(wxx(:,jj))-min(wxx(:,jj)))/9;
108  for tt=min(wxx(:,jj))-0.05:uu:max(wxx(:,jj))+0.05
109      iddx=find((tt<wxx(:,jj) & wxx(:,jj)<tt+uu));
110      s1=sum(wyy(iddx));
111      l1=length(wyy(iddx));
112      fprintf('(%4.2f,%4.2f),(%4.2f,%4.2f),\n',s1,(l1-s1)\ldots
113          ,s1/l1,(l1-s1)/l1);
114  end
115
116  m1=0;
117  m2=max(cpp1(:,jj))+40;
118
119  for tt=min(wxx(:,jj))-0.05:uu:max(wxx(:,jj))+uu
120      tt
121      hold on;line([m1:m2],tt*[m1:m2]);
122      axis([0 200 0 200]);
123  end
```

The block of code in lines 73–77 plots feature 1 and feature 2 of hardwood floor and carpet floor data sets and it is presented in the first figure of Fig. 13.8. We can see a significant overlap between classes. The block of code in lines 80–84 plots feature 48 and feature 49 of hardwood floor and carpet floor data sets. These features are selected by CDT as the best features. This scatter plot is presented in the second figure of Fig. 13.8. The overlap between classes is significantly lower than the one presented in the first figure. The second figure also shows the best ring (based on URM) of the CDT technique and the ring splits (arcs) forming a chandelier like structure. Within each arc significant classification can clearly be seen.

13.4.2 Extension to Random Chandelier

The proposed *random chandelier* approach is similar to the random forest approach. The extension is similar to the extension of the decision tree to random forest in the sense that it is an extension from the chandelier decision tree. Bootstrapping [5] and bagging [6] are the two techniques that play important roles in the approach, just as they played a role in the extension of the decision tree to random forest. Hence these techniques are also adopted in the development of the random chandelier from the chandelier decision tree. However, this extension has a slight difference in the sense that it is applied on the circular subdomains. It brings the computational and classification accuracy advantages.

Problems

13.1. Chandelier Decision Tree
The examples presented in this chapter only illustrated the creation of the first level of the chandelier decision tree. Now write a Matlab program to perform the entire chandelier decision tree building. Use the knowledge that you gained on the standard decision tree learning.

13.2. Random Chandelier

(a) Generate bootstrap samples from the hardwood floor and carpet floor data sets. You may select your own data sets as well.
(b) Generate chandelier decision trees using these bootstrap samples and the knowledge that you gained from random forest and decision tree techniques. (c) Using the bagging techniques and the CDT classifiers that you created, perform a testing process using a test set. Identify the training and test data sets clearly.

References

1. S. Suthaharan. "unit-circle classification algorithm to characterize back attack and normal traffic for network intrusion detection systems," in Proceedings of the IEEE International Conference on Intelligence and Security Informatics, pp. 150–152, 2012.
2. L. Rokach, and O. Maimon. "Top-down induction of decision trees classifiers-a survey." IEEE Transactions on Systems, Man, and Cybernetics, Part C: Applications and Reviews, vol. 35, no. 4, pp. 476–487, 2005.
3. L. Breiman, "Random forests." Machine learning 45, pp. 5–32, 2001.
4. S. Suthaharan. "A single-domain, representation-learning model for big data classification of network intrusion," Machine Learning and Data Mining in Pattern Recognition, Lecture Notes in Computer Science Volume 7988, pp. 296–310, 2013.
5. T. Hastie, R. Tibshirani, and J. Friedman. The Elements of Statistical Learning. New York: Springer, 2009.
6. L. Breiman. "Bagging predictors." Machine learning 24, pp. 123–140, 1996.

Chapter 14
Dimensionality Reduction

Abstract The main objective of this chapter is to explain the two important dimensionality reduction techniques, feature hashing and principal component analysis, that can support scaling-up machine learning. The standard and flagged feature hashing approaches are explained in detail. The feature hashing approach suffers from the hash collision problem, and this problem is reported and discussed in detail in this chapter, too. Two collision controllers, feature binning and feature mitigation, are also proposed in this chapter to address this problem. The principal component analysis uses the concepts of eigenvalues and eigenvectors, and these terminologies are explained in detail with examples. The principal component analysis is also explained using a simple two-dimensional example, and several coding examples are also presented.

14.1 Introduction

Scaling-up machine learning is one of the important and recent research topics in machine learning, as stated in [1]. It can help solve many emerging big data problems, including scalability, reliability, and maintainability. In general, it deals with the scaling-up problems between finite and infinite data. In particular, it focuses on the scaling-up problems associated with a massive data set (big data controller: observations), dynamically changing objects (big data controller: features), and large numbers of classes (big data controller: labels). As stated in [1], stochastic gradient descent [2, 3] and feature hashing [4, 5] are the two most important mathematical techniques that have recently shown significant positive impact on scaling-up machine learning. Additionally, the modern technologies like Hadoop distributed file system [6] with the MapReduce framework [7] can also help to evaluate machine learning techniques in a big data environment [8]. The stochastic gradient descent technique mainly focuses on the size of the dynamically growing data set, whereas

© Springer Science+Business Media New York 2016
S. Suthaharan, *Machine Learning Models and Algorithms for Big Data Classification*, Integrated Series in Information Systems 36, DOI 10.1007/978-1-4899-7641-3_14

the feature hashing focuses on the size of the dynamically growing feature set. Similarly, the hierarchical classification techniques, like the decision tree [9] and the random forest [10], have been used to handle the size of the dynamically growing number of labels. The main focus of the stochastic gradient descent is to efficiently manage three different types of errors—called the estimation error, the approximation error, and the optimization error, as stated in [1] and [11]. The main focus of the feature hashing techniques is to reduce the dimension of the data through hashing an infinite feature space to a finite feature space.

We have reviewed deep learning in detail in a previous chapter, and it can address all of these scaling-up problems simultaneously. Many real-world applications, like document classification, speech recognition, and email spam filtering, can easily be affected by the drawbacks of feature hashing techniques. Therefore, it is important to understand the drawbacks of the feature hashing techniques so that efficient solutions can be found. The main drawback of the feature hashing techniques is the hash collision, and a solution for this problem is needed to improve scaling-up machine learning techniques. Many electronic (digital) applications can benefit from this solution. In the past decade, scaling-up machine learning has been studied in different directions. In [12], Domingos and Hulten proposed a method that minimizes the learner's loss function while controlling the error in the cases of finite and infinite input data. Then they demonstrated its effectiveness to large data sets using K-means clustering.

In recent years, the benefits of feature hashing to scaling-up machine learning have been emphasized through research. In 2009, Shi et al. [13] proposed a hash kernels approach that maps a large feature space to a finite feature space as a dimensionality reduction approach, and its effectiveness to multiclass classification problems has also been presented in their work. They also studied and presented the hash kernels to structured data in another paper [14]. Subsequently, Weinberger et al. [4] improved the feature hashing approach by combining two hash functions to flag the hash collisions. The difficulty of avoiding hash collisions led to a new approach called supervised semantic indexing [15], in which a multiple binning technique has been used. Similarly, Caragea et al. [16] combined hashing and abstraction (hierarchical binning) to enhance feature hashing. However, minimization of feature collision is not achieved satisfactorily.

14.2 Feature Hashing Techniques

In this section, the mathematics behind the standard feature hashing technique presented in [4] and the flagged feature hashing technique in [13] are briefly discussed. The subtle differences between these two approaches are highlighted, and the need for an improvement is also pointed out.

14.2.1 Standard Feature Hashing

Suppose F is a set of N features denoted by $F = \{f_1, f_2, \ldots, f_N\}$, and they are available for learning (or training), where N is very large. Then the goal is to explore a suitable feature hashing technique that hashes these features to a set I of indices denoted by $I = \{1, 2, \ldots, n\}$ and reduces the dimension to n as defined by the user specifications and requirements, where $n << N$. In the standards feature hashing approach, this process may be defined as follows [13]:

$$j = h(f); f \in F;\qquad(14.1)$$
$$i = j \bmod n; i \in I\qquad(14.2)$$

This two-step hashing technique, by ignoring the intermediate results j, may be written as follows:
$$i = \phi(f)\qquad(14.3)$$

The hashing process leads to several features $(f \in F)$ that map to a single index i, hence we can construct a set of features that map to the index i as follows [4]:

$$s(i) = \bigcup_{f:\phi(f)=i} f\qquad(14.4)$$
$$\phi_i = \#(s(i))\qquad(14.5)$$

Where the symbol # denotes the number of elements in the set $s(i)$.

14.2.2 Flagged Feature Hashing

In general, the standard feature hashing [5] creates bias in the hash kernel of $\phi(.)$ as stated in [4] and does not flag hash collisions. Hence, a new hash function ξ was suggested in the alternative hashing approach and added to the process as an additional step to remove this bias as follows [13]:

$$s(i) = \bigcup_{f:\phi(f)=i} \xi(f)f\qquad(14.6)$$

The binary hash function ξ helps decide if a feature should be added to or removed from the hashed set $s(i)$. This process helps remove the bias and flag 50% of the hash collisions. It has also been suggested to add more binary hash functions to flag more hash collisions. Therefore, in the following section, a new hashing technique, which suggests steps to address this issue, is proposed.

14.3 Proposed Feature Hashing

In the proposed feature hashing technique, as an object arrives, it is assigned to a bin with similar features (e.g., word length). This object is then processed with the feature mitigation unit before applying the hash function. The hash function is then applied, and an index is created to assign its feature. Hence, the object receives the index for its feature. This proposed approach is expected to reduce the hash collision as shown in the forthcoming examples. The combined processes, binning and mitigation are especially designed so that the MapReduce framework with the Hadoop distributed file system can be effectively used.

14.3.1 Binning and Mitigation

Suppose X is a set of N objects denoted by $X = \{x_1, x_2, \ldots, x_N\}$, and they have variable length (size). The maximum length is denoted by L, and it is treated as a scalable parameter. Hence, L number of bins, denoted by $B = \{b_1, b_2, \ldots, b_L\}$ can be defined, and the rth bin will be used to store the objects of length r. The bins are of equal size, and the maximum size for a bin is denoted by M. It means that the maximum number of objects that can be stored in a bin is M, and it is also treated as a scalable parameter.

The maximum length for an object is L; therefore, L number of weights $W = \{w_1, w_2, \ldots, w_L\}$ are generated to mitigate features pertinent to an object. The weights will be learned using machine learning techniques. In the proposed feature hashing technique, each object is hashed to an index which serves as a feature for the objects. Consider the ith object $x_i, (i = 1 \ldots N)$ and suppose the length of this object is l with the content $x_i = x_{i1}x_{i2}\ldots x_{il}$, where $l \leq L$; then, the first il weights $\{w_1, w_2, \ldots, w_{il}\}$ will be selected for the feature mitigation process. Also, this object will be indexed by bin l. The feature mitigation is then done as follows:

$$h_i = \sum_{k=1}^{l} w_{ik}x_{ik} \tag{14.7}$$

Then the hashed index j for the object x_i in bin l is defined by

$$(l, j) = (l - 1) * M + h_i \bmod M \tag{14.8}$$

$$f_{(l,j)} = f_{(l,j)} + 1 \tag{14.9}$$

The first term in Eq. (14.8) describes the *interbin indexing* and the second term describes the *intrabin indexing*. It means that the interbin indexing completely eliminates the collision that can occur between dissimilar features (i.e., different length objects). However, the intrabin indexing may cause hash collision. The careful training and selection of W, as well as the suitable selection of scaling parameters, can avoid hash collisions. In the other feature hashing algorithms, the collision between dissimilar objects exists, and this collision must be avoided.

14.3.2 Mitigation Justification

The objective of this section is to justify the effectiveness of the feature mitigation approach to feature hashing when applied together with feature binning. Suppose X and Y are words selected at two instances. It is obvious that X and Y collide when $X = Y$, but it is a good collision, hence we can write

$$H(X) = H(Y); X = Y \qquad (14.10)$$

In the feature mitigation, we make them not collide when the words detected at two instances are the same. In this case, we want to degrade X using parameters a and b, such that

$$H(aX) - H(bX) = t_1 \qquad (14.11)$$

Although we made them not collide, the feature binning based on the length of the words helps them assign in the same bin. Consider the case of collision, (i.e., $H(X) = H(Y)$ when $X \neq Y$) then we have:

$$H(aX) - H(bY) = H(aX) - H(bX) + H(bX) - H(bY) \qquad (14.12)$$
$$H(aX) - H(bY) = t_1 + H(bX) - H(bY) \qquad (14.13)$$

X and Y already collide; hence, according to the strong hash function definition, for every b, bX and bY do not collide. Therefore, we can write $H(bX) \neq H(bY)$, and

$$H(aX) - H(bY) = t_1 + t_2 \qquad (14.14)$$

where t_1 and t_2 are greater than 0; therefore, aX and bY do not collide. It shows that using the feature mitigation in Eq. (14.7), we can reduce collision, and the randomness can play a major role in this objective. In summary, when the two words are the same, we select weight to make them not collide; these weights can help the two distinct words not collide if a robust hash function is selected. The strong cryptographic hash functions must be used for this purpose.

14.3.3 Toy Example

In this section, a simple text classification example has been used to demonstrate the effectiveness of the proposed feature hashing technique. In this example, 21 words (objects), which include regular English dictionary words, the author's name, and a dictionary word with a typo, are considered. This information is presented in Table 14.1. The words "catch," "accommodation," and "machine" occur multiple times as shown in the third column of the table. The words are of varying lengths, from 2 to 14 characters, but the maximum length is defined as 16. Therefore, 16 bins are selected with the bin sizes of 8, 16, and 32 for three separate simulations.

Table 14.1 Some of the objects and their length and frequency

Object (X)	$L \leq 16$	Freq.	$M = 8$	$M = 16$	$M = 32$
"bat"	3	1	–	–	–
"ballu"	5	1	–	–	–
"tab"	3	1	–	–	–
"catch"	5	2	–	–	–
"suthaharan"	10	1	–	–	–
"patch"	5	1	–	–	–
"dad"	3	1	–	–	–
"god"	3	1	–	–	–
"dog"	3	1	–	–	–
"accommodation"	13	2	–	–	–
"performance"	11	1	–	–	–
"degradation"	11	1	–	–	–
"methods"	7	1	–	–	–
"telephone"	9	1	–	–	–
"computer"	8	1	–	–	–
"science"	7	1	–	–	–
"machine"	7	3	–	–	–
"learning"	8	1	–	–	–
"am"	2	1	–	–	–
"to"	2	1	–	–	–
"shanmugathasan"	14	1	–	–	–

14.4 Simulation and Results

Two programs that implement the proposed binning and feature mitigation approach are presented in this section. The first program has been written in Matlab and is presented in the first subsection, and the second program has been written in R and is presented in the second subsection.

14.4.1 A Matlab Implementation

The set of words in Table 14.1 has been used as the input to this program, and it is presented in Listing 14.1. This input is hardcoded; however, you can read this data from an external file for efficiency.

Listing 14.1 A Matlab example—proposed feature hashing

```
1  clear all;
2  close all;
3
4  data={'bat', 'ballu', 'tab', 'catch', 'suthaharan', 'catch', '
       patch', \ldots
```

```
 5        'dad', 'god', 'dog', 'accommodation', 'accommodation', '
              performance', \ldots
 6        'degradation', 'methods', 'telephone', 'computer', 'science',
              'machine', \ldots
 7        'learning', 'am', 'to', 'shanmugathasan','machine','machine'
              }; %ballu and patch collide
 8
 9   NN=size(data,2); %number of features
10   LL=16; %predefined number of bins
11   MM=8; %predefined size for the bins (bin cells)
12   randn('seed',129);
13   tt-10+floor(131*randn(1,LL));
14
15   bin=zeros(1,LL*MM); %size for 2D vector
16
17   for ii=1:NN
18       xx{ii}=(data{ii}+data{ii})/2;
19       sz{ii}=length(data{ii}); %length of the word in process
20       ww{ii}=tt(1:size(xx{ii},2));
21       hh{ii}=sum(ww{ii}.*xx{ii});
22
23       ind{ii}=(sz{ii}-1)*MM + mod(hh{ii},MM); %indexing of vector
24       bin(1+ind{ii})=bin(1+ind{ii}) + 1; %updating at each index
25   end
26
27   LL=find(bin>0);
28
29   figure;plot(bin,'.');grid on;axis([min(LL)-100 max(LL)+100 0 3]);
30   xlabel('Feature_Index');ylabel('Number_of_Features');
31
32   figure
33   au=find(bin>0);
34   ax=au;
35   ay=bin(au);
36   plot(ax,ay,'.');grid on;
37   for ii=1:size(au,2)
38       line([ax(ii) ax(ii)],[0 ay(ii)]);
39   end
40   set(gca,'YLim',[0 max(ay)]);
41
42   gg=[data; sz; ind];
43   jj=0;ii=1;
44   while(jj<size(data,2))
45       fprintf('%17s_\t_%4d_\t_%4d_\n',gg{ii},gg{ii+1},gg{ii+2})
46       jj=jj+1;
47       ii=3*jj+1;
48   end
49
50   sortrows(gg',2)
```

The block of code in lines 4–7 declares the input data presented in the first column of Table 14.1. These are considered features in scalable machine learning, and the number of features in this example is calculated in line 9. The number of bins

Table 14.2 Output of the program presented in Listing 14.1

Object (X)	8(i)	8(j)	16(i)	16(j)	32(i)	32(j)
"am"	[2]	[10]	[2]	[18]	[2]	[50]
"to"	[2]	[8]	[2]	[24]	[2]	[40]
"bat"	[3]	[20]	[3]	[36]	[3]	[84]
"tab"	[3]	[16]	[3]	[32]	[3]	[80]
"dad' '	[3]	[16]	[3]	[40]	[3]	[88]
"god"	[3]	[22]	[3]	[46]	[3]	[78]
"dog"	[3]	[20]	[3]	[36]	[3]	[68]
"ballu"	[5]	[33]	[5]	[73]	[5]	[137]
"catch"	[5]	[37]	[5]	[77]	[5]	[157]
"catch"	[5]	[37]	[5]	[77]	[5]	[157]
"patch"	[5]	[39]	[5]	[71]	[5]	[135]
"methods"	[7]	[50]	[7]	[106]	[7]	[218]
"science"	[7]	[55]	[7]	[111]	[7]	[207]
"machine"	[7]	[48]	[7]	[96]	[7]	[208]
"machine"	[7]	[48]	[7]	[96]	[7]	[208]
"machine"	[7]	[48]	[7]	[96]	[7]	[208]
"computer"	[8]	[58]	[8]	[122]	[8]	[234]
"learning"	[8]	[57]	[8]	[113]	[8]	[241]
"telephone"	[9]	[71]	[9]	[143]	[9]	[271]
"suthaharan"	[10]	[79]	[10]	[151]	[10]	[295]
"performance"	[11]	[80]	[11]	[160]	[11]	[320]
"degradation"	[11]	[81]	[11]	[161]	[11]	[321]
"accommodation"	[13]	[96]	[13]	[200]	[13]	[392]
"accommodation"	[13]	[96]	[13]	[200]	[13]	[392]
"shanmugathasan"	[14]	[106]	[14]	[210]	[14]	[418]

and the size of these bins are predefined in lines 10 and 11, respectively. As you recall, the proposed feature hashing technique requires weights for feature mitigation and they are generated pseudorandomly in lines 12 and 13. The total memory of the bins is initialized to zero in line 15. For each feature, the hashed index is generated according to Eqs. (14.7)–(14.9), and this process is presented in lines 17–25. The block of code in lines 27–40 prints the figure in Fig. 14.1. However, by changing the bin size (MM) to 16 and 32, other two figures in Figs. 14.2 and 14.3 can be generated, respectively. The block of code in lines 42–50 prints the results in Table 14.2. The results in Figs. 14.1, 14.2, and 14.3, and Table 14.2 show the hashed values and the collisions when the proposed feature hashing is applied to the examples with bin sizes of 8, 16, and 32.

As we can see, there is no collision between dissimilar words as they are indexed into different bins. However, there are collisions within a bin under restricted conditions. For example, when $M = 8$, we can see two collisions in bin 3: bat collides with dog, and tab collides with dad. Similarly, when $M = 16$ is considered, we can see one collision: bat collides with dog. In the case of $M = 32$, we don't see any collision. This simple example demonstrates that the proposed concepts of feature binning and feature mitigation helped feature hashing controls feature

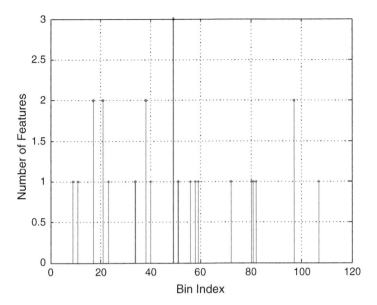

Fig. 14.1 The collision results with bin size of 8

collision. These algorithms provide flexibility and scalability; therefore, the combined approach is capable of supporting scaling-up machine learning. The structure of the algorithms shows that the capabilities of the modern MapReduce framework with Hadoop distributed file systems can be adopted to enhance its scaling-up machine learning objectives.

14.4.2 A MapReduce Implementation

In this section, the proposed feature hashing approach is implemented using the mapper(), the reducer(), and the mapreduce() functions using the R programming framework on the RHadoop system. The same input table is used, and same as before, it is hardcoded.

Listing 14.2 An RHadoop example—proposed feature hashing

```
1  Sys.setenv(HADOOP_HOME='/usr/lib/hadoop-0.20-mapreduce')
2  Sys.setenv(HADOOP_CMD='/usr/bin/hadoop')
3  Sys.setenv(HADOOP_STREAMING='/usr/lib/hadoop-0.20-mapreduce/
      contrib/streaming/hadoop-streaming-2.0.0-mr1-cdh4.7.0.jar')
4
5  data=c('bat', 'ballu', 'tab', 'catch', 'suthaharan', 'catch', '
      patch',
6
```

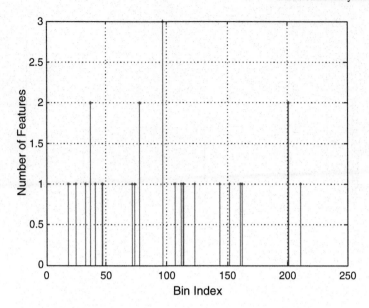

Fig. 14.2 The collision results with bin size of 16

```
 7              'dad', 'god', 'dog', 'accommodation', 'accommodation', '
                   performance',
 8
 9              'degradation', 'methods', 'telephone', 'computer', '
                   science', 'machine',
10
11              'learning', 'am', 'to', 'shanmugathasan','machine','
                   machine')
12
13   library(rmr2)
14   library(rhdfs)
15
16   hdfs.init()
17
18   gauss.data = to.dfs(data)
19
20   gauss.map.fn = function(k, v) {
21
22     NN=length(v)
23     k=nchar(v)
24
25     # generate weights for mitigation
26     LL=16
27     MM=16
28     set.seed(5)
29     ww = rnorm(LL,10,131)
30
```

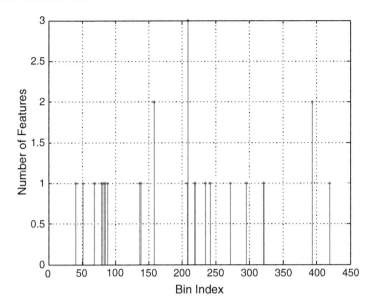

Fig. 14.3 The collision results with bin size of 32

```
31   vv=matrix(0,nrow=1, ncol=NN)
32   for(ii in 1:NN) {
33     # crop the weights w.r.t feature length
34     tt=strtoi(charToRaw(v[ii]),16L)
35     ss=length(tt)
36     pp=floor(ww[1:ss])
37
38     # apply binning and mitigation
39     uu=sum(tt * pp)
40     vv[ii]=(ss-1)*MM + uu %% MM
41   }
42
43   # generate key value pairs
44   keyval(k, c(v,vv))
45 }
46
47 gauss.reduce.fn = function(k, v) {
48
49   keyval(k,v)
50 }
51
52 mr.gauss = mapreduce(input = gauss.data, map = gauss.map.fn,
       reduce = gauss.reduce.fn)
53
54 mr.results = from.dfs(mr.gauss)
55 mr.results
```

The output of this program is presented below as sorted (key, value) pairs:

```
$key
 [1]  2  2  2  2  3  3  3  3  3  3  3  3  3  3  5  5
  5  5  5  5  5  5  7  7  7  7  7  7

[29]  7  7  7  7  8  8  8  8  9  9 10 10 11 11 11 11
 13 13 13 13 14 14
```

```
$val
 [1] "am"                "to"              "30"
 "29"                "bat"

 [6] "tab"               "dad"             "god"
 "dog"               "41"

[11] "37"                "47"              "34"
"32"                "ballu"

[16] "catch"             "catch"           "patch"
"71"                "77"

[21] "77"                "76"              "methods"
"science"           "machine"

[26] "machine"           "machine"         "108"
"99"                "101"

[31] "101"               "101"             "computer"
"learning"          "121"

[36] "123"               "telephone"       "134"
"suthaharan"        "158"

[41] "performance"       "degradation"     "163"
"174"               "accommodation"

[46] "accommodation"  "199"                "199"
"shanmugathasan"  "215"
```

14.5 Principal Component Analysis

In general, the feature variables of a system that produces observations (or responses) are assumed to be independent variables, and the responses are dependent variables. But some of the independent variables may be correlated. Therefore, if we detect the correlated variables, then we should be able to reduce the dimensionality of the data by selecting the uncorrelated variable. As we know, the dimensionality of data is determined by the independent variables (or features). The goal of principal component analysis is to find such a set of linearly uncorrelated features called principal components [17]. It is always preferable to understand complicated theory by using simple examples and the PCA is simplified and explained in the following subsections.

14.5.1 Eigenvector

The Eigenvector plays a major role in PCA. What does eigenvector mean? What does eigenvalue mean? What does eigenspace mean? A discussion on eigenvectors can be found in the book "Advanced Engineering Mathematics" by Erwin Kreyszig (6th edition, John Wiley and Sons, Inc., 1988). The major player of the eigenvector theory is the following simple equation:

$$A\mathbf{x} = \mathbf{x}\lambda \tag{14.15}$$

where A is a matrix, x is a vector (data), and λ is a scalar. The left-hand side of this equation simply transforms the input data $\mathbf{x}$, and the right-hand side of the equation scales the data by λ. Hence, it simply says the new point that we get after transforming it by A and the new point that we get after moving it by a scalar λ are the same. The questions are: (1) How to find such an A and λ pair for a specific data $\mathbf{x}$? and (2) most importantly, Does this pair exist for the data $\mathbf{x}$? If the above equation is satisfied, then we can define the following three important terms in the eigenvector theory:

1. If there is a scalar λ and a matrix A such that they can satisfy the above equation, then we call the scalar λ the eigenvalue of A.

2. If there is a scalar λ and a matrix A such that they can satisfy the above equation, then we call the data $\mathbf{x}$ the eigenvector of A.

3. If there is a scalar λ and a matrix A such that they can satisfy the above equation, then we call the vector space formed by $\mathbf{x}$ the vector space with the parameters A and λ the eigenspace.

It is easier to understand the properties of this simple equation in the eigenvector theory. Therefore, the following "thinking with example" has been developed and presented here.

Thinking with Example 14.1

Suppose we take a set of points and transform them using a matrix. What will happen to the original points? The points and the matrix selected for the example can be found in the code provided in Listing 14.3. Similarly, the points are scaled using a scalar λ, and the scalar selected for the example is $3 + \mathrm{sqrt}(7)$ to move the points. Note that the example is a toy example, and thus the points are artificially generated to help explain the eigenvector and the eigenvalue in a meaningful way using visual tools. The block of code in lines 5 to 6 selects the parameters A and λ, creates eight points pseudorandomly, and modifies a sub set of three points to satisfy the eigenvector equation.

Listing 14.3 A Matlab example—eigenvector theory is explained

```
1   clear all;
2   close all;
3
4   %%%%%%%%%%%%%%%%%%%%%%%%%%%%%%%%%%%%%%%%%%%%%%%%%%
5   A=[5 -3; -1 1];
6   lamda=(3+sqrt(7));
7
8   %%%%%%%%%%%%%%%%%%%%%%%%%%%%%%%%%%%%%%%%%%%%%%%%%%
9   randn('seed',129);
10  x1=0.1+0.1*randn(1,8);
11  randn('seed',131);
12  x2=0.2+0.2*randn(1,8);
13
14  rand('seed',3);
15  ind=1+floor(8*rand(1,3));
16  yy=(1/(1-lamda))*x1;
17
18  x2(1,ind)=yy(1,ind);
19
20  figure;plot(x1,x2,'.','MarkerSize',14);
21  %hold on;plot(x1(1,ind),x2(1,ind),'r.','MarkerSize',14);
22  grid on;axis([-1.5 1.6 -1 3.5]);
23
24  %%%%%%%%%%%%%%%%%%%%%%%%%%%%%%%%%%%%%%%%%%%%%%%%%%
25  lhs=A*[x1;x2];
26  figure;plot(x1,x2,'.','MarkerSize',14);
27  hold on;plot(lhs(1,:),lhs(2,:),'m.','MarkerSize',14);
28  grid on;axis([-1.5 1.6 -1 3.5]);
29
30  %%%%%%%%%%%%%%%%%%%%%%%%%%%%%%%%%%%%%%%%%%%%%%%%%%
31  rhs=lamda*[x1;x2];
32  figure;plot(x1,x2,'.','MarkerSize',14);
33  hold on;plot(rhs(1,:),rhs(2,:),'m.','MarkerSize',14);
34  grid on;axis([-1.5 1.6 -1 3.5]);
35
36  %%%%%%%%%%%%%%%%%%%%%%%%%%%%%%%%%%%%%%%%%%%%%%%%%%
37  figure;plot(lhs(1,:),lhs(2,:),'.','MarkerSize',14);
38  hold on;plot(rhs(1,:),rhs(2,:),'r.','MarkerSize',14);
39  grid on;axis([-1.5 1.6 -1 3.5]);
```

```
40
41  ind1=find(abs(lhs(1,:)-rhs(1,:))<0.000001);
42  hold on;plot(rhs(1,ind1),rhs(2,ind1),'o','MarkerSize',10);
43  grid on;axis([-1.5 1.6 -1 3.5]);
44
45  %%%%%%%%%%%%%%%%%%%%%%%%%%%%%%%%%%%%%%%%%%%%%%%%%%%
46  figure;plot(x1,x2,'.','MarkerSize',14);grid on;
47  hold on;plot(x1(ind1),x2(ind1),'o','MarkerSize',10);
48  axis([-1.5 1.6 -1 3.5]);
49
50  figure;plot(x1,x2,'.','MarkerSize',14);
51  hold on;plot(x1(1,ind),x2(1,ind),'r.','MarkerSize',14);
52  grid on;axis([-1.5 1.6 -1 3.5]);
```

The block of code in lines 20–22 plots the eight points artificially created, and this scatter plot is given in Fig. 14.4a. Line 25 executes the left side of eigenvector equation, and then the block of code in lines 26–28 plots the transformed data as shown in Fig. 14.4b. Similarly, line 31 executes the right side of eigenvector equation and then the block of code in lines 32–34 plots the scaled data as shown in Fig. 14.4c. The block of code in lines 37–43 plots both scatter plots in Fig. 14.4b, c, and circles the overlapping points as shown in Fig. 14.4d—the points that satisfy eigenvector equation. The block of code in lines 46–52 provides the results in Fig. 14.5 and validates the eigenvectors calculated by the program.

14.5.2 Principal Components

The principal component analysis and its effect of dimensionality reduction can be easily understood if we comprehend the eigenvector equation and a suitable linear transformation. The following two simple equations play important roles in the principal component analysis and the dimensionality reduction [17, 18]:

$$\mathbf{Aw} = \mathbf{w}\lambda \tag{14.16}$$

$$\mathbf{y} = \mathbf{w}'\mathbf{x} \tag{14.17}$$

In the first equation, $\mathbf{A}$ represents a matrix, $\mathbf{w}$ represents its eigenvector, and λ represents its eigenvalues. In the second equation, $\mathbf{x}$ represents the input data centered with respect to their statistical means, and $\mathbf{y}$ represents the transformed variable using the eigenvectors. For a better description of these equations, they are rewritten to show their dimensions below:

$$\mathbf{A}_{p \times p} \mathbf{W}_{p \times k} = \mathbf{w}_{p \times k} \lambda_{k \times k} \tag{14.18}$$

$$\mathbf{y}_{k \times n} = \mathbf{w}'_{k \times p} \mathbf{x}_{p \times n} \tag{14.19}$$

Therefore, the first equation defines the eigenvalues/eigenvectors equation, whereas the second equation transforms the original data set X from p dimensions

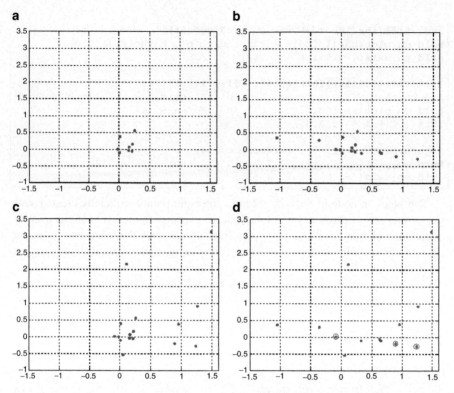

Fig. 14.4 Intermediate steps of eigenvector explanation—the horizontal axis represents x1 and vertical axis represents x2

to k (where $k \leq p$) dimensions data set Y. In other words, we can say the number of features are reduced from p to k. Also note that the number of observations in each feature is represented by n.

In principal component analysis, the matrix **A** is defined by the covariance matrix **C** of **x** and, in this case, the eigenvector **w** is called the principal component. Thus the second equation describes the linear transformation from **x** to **y** using the principal components as the weights. Also note the matrix multiplications transform the p dimensional data **x** to k dimension data **y**. The challenge is the selection of k such that $k \leq p$, so that the dimensionality reduction can be achieved. Therefore, using the covariance matrix **C**, we can write these equations as follows:

$$\mathbf{C_{p \times p} w_{p \times k}} = \mathbf{w_{p \times k} \lambda_{k \times k}} \tag{14.20}$$

$$\mathbf{y_{k \times n}} = \mathbf{w'_{k \times p} x_{p \times n}} \tag{14.21}$$

The covariance matrix **C** is a symmetric square matrix, and its dimension is $p \times p$, which reflects the dimension of the data **x**. It can be calculated as follows (note that **x** is centered around its mean):

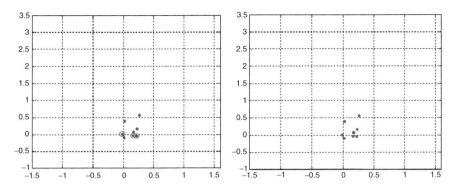

Fig. 14.5 Final step of eigenvector explanation—the horizontal axis represents x1 and vertical axis represents x2

$$\mathbf{C_{p \times p}} = \frac{1}{n-1}\mathbf{x_{p \times n}x'_{n \times p}} \tag{14.22}$$

If the dimensionality reduction is not required, then the dimension p of the original data set and the dimension k of the transformed data set are the same, hence the above equations can be written as follows:

$$\mathbf{C_{p \times p}w_{p \times p}} = \mathbf{w_{p \times p}\lambda_{p \times p}} \tag{14.23}$$

$$\mathbf{y_{p \times n}} = \mathbf{w'_{p \times p}x_{p \times n}} \tag{14.24}$$

Now the challenge is to solve the eigenvector equations to calculate the eigenvalues, λ, and eigenvectors, $\mathbf{w}$, for a covariance matrix $\mathbf{C}$. Once eigenvalues are available, if the dimensionality reduction is not required, then all the eigenvectors are used in the transformation of the input data $\mathbf{x}$. If the dimensionality reduction is required, then the eigenvalues are sorted, and the eigenvectors corresponding to the k largest eigenvalues are selected to transform the data to k dimensional data.

In Matlab, the *eig* function can be used to calculate the eigenvalue (*eval*) and eigenvector (*evec*) for the covariance matrix *C* as follows:

$[evec, eval] = eig(C);$

According to Matlab instructions, *eval* is a diagonal matrix which contains eigenvalues of *C*, and *evec* is a matrix that contains column wise eigenvectors, and it satisfies the eigenvector equation $C * evec = evec * eval$.

The principal components give the principal directions of a data set. This is demonstrated in the coding example presented in Listing 14.4, which uses the

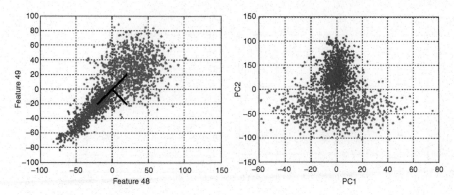

Fig. 14.6 PCA is explained in 2D, similar to the one at [17]

hardwood floor and carpet floor data sets. We have seen previously that the features 48 and 49 are highly suitable for getting a very good classification between the hardwood floor and carpet floor data. Therefore, these features are considered in this example.

14.5.3 The Principal Directions

The principal direction of a set of data can be obtained from the principal components of the data as demonstrated in the first figure of Fig. 14.6. This figure has been produced by the Matlab code in Listing 14.4. The second figure is also produced by this code, and it illustrates the classes in a new space defined by the principal components of these data sets.

Listing 14.4 A Matlab example—PCA characteristics

```
1   clear all;
2   close all;
3
4   % read class data files
5   hw1=csvread('hardwood.csv');
6   cp1=csvread('carpet.csv');
7
8   % select feature 48 and 49
9   x1=[hw1(:,48);cp1(:,48)];
10  x2=[hw1(:,49);cp1(:,49)];
11
12  % center them w.r.t their mean
13  x1=x1-mean(x1);
14  x2=x2-mean(x2);
15
16  % concatenate them
17  xx=[x1';x2'];
18
```

```
19  % plot the classes
20  figure;plot(xx(1,1:1024),xx(2,1:1024),'.');grid on;
21  hold on;plot(xx(1,1025:end),xx(2,1025:end),'r.');grid on;
22
23  % calculate covariance matrix
24  C=(xx*xx')/(length(xx)-1);
25
26  % calculate eignvectors and eigenvalue of C
27  [ww,ee]=eig(C);
28
29  % get eigenvalues
30  ss=sum(ee);
31
32  %validate eigenvector equation
33  C*ww(:,1)
34  ss(1)*ww(:,1)
35
36  C*ww(:,2)
37  ss(2)*ww(:,2)
38  %validation ends
39
40  % plot and show the principal directions
41  hold on;line([0 30*ww(1,2)],[0 30*ww(2,2)],'color','black','
        LineWidth',3);
42  hold on;line([0 -30*ww(1,2)],[0 -30*ww(2,2)],'color','black','
        LineWidth',3);
43  hold on;line([0 30*ww(1,1)],[0 30*ww(2,1)],'color','black','
        LineWidth',3);
44
45  % transform to a new space using principal components
46  yy=ww'*xx;
47
48  % plot the classes in the new space
49  figure;plot(yy(1,1:1024),yy(2,1:1024),'.');grid on;
50  hold on;plot(yy(1,1025:end),yy(2,1025:end),'r.');grid on;
```

The block of code in lines 5 and 6, 9 and 10, and 13 and 14 reads the data sets, selects the features 48 and 49, and centralizes the data, respectively. The code in line 17 concatenates them to form a single matrix. The block of code in lines 20 and 21 plots the two classes (in red and blue) and gives the first figure in Fig. 14.6. The code in line 24 gives the covariance matrix of the concatenated data. The eigenvector and eigenvalue are calculated using the Matlab's *eig* function in the block of code in lines 26–30. The block of code in lines 32–38 validates the eigenvector equation by comparing the left and right sides of the equation. The directional indicators displayed on the first figure of Fig. 14.6 have been produced by the code in lines 41–43. The data sets are transformed to a new space using the principal components using the code in line 46. Finally, the transformed data sets are presented in the second figure of Fig. 14.6.

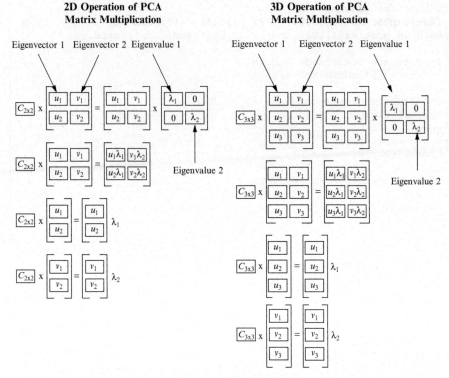

Fig. 14.7 PCA operations explained in 2D and 3D

14.5.4 A 2D Implementation

Understanding the operations of the principal component analysis using a simple two-dimensional example can help apply this technique in scalable machine learning. Hence, these operations are implemented, demonstrated, and explained in Listing 14.5. Its 2D implementation (i.e. $p = 2$), in a matrix form, is explained in the left figure of Fig. 14.7. Let us select four observations from each of the hardwood floor and carpet floor data sets used previously.

Listing 14.5 A Matlab example—PCA operations in 2D

```
1   clear all;
2   close all;
3
4   % read the class data files
5   [num1,txt1,raw1]=xlsread('hardwood.csv');
6   [num2,txt2,raw2]=xlsread('carpet.csv');
7
8   % [num1,txt1,raw1]=xlsread('biltmore31.csv');
9   % [num2,txt2,raw2]=xlsread('MyPrismacolors1.csv');
10
```

```
11  % shuffle the observations of a class randomly
12  rand('seed',129);
13  nd1=randperm(1024);
14
15  % select the observation corresponding to
16  % the first 4 indexes
17  t1=num1(nd1(1:4),:);
18
19  % shuffle the observations of a class randomly
20  rand('seed',131);
21
22  % select the observation corresponding to
23  % the first 4 indexes
24  nd2=randperm(1024);
25  t2=num2(nd2(1:4),:);
26
27  % collect the values of the 48th feature
28  x1=[t1(:,48);t2(:,48)];
29
30  % collect the values of the 49th feature
31  x2=[t1(:,49);t2(:,49)];
32
33  % center them w.r.t their means
34  xx1=x1-mean(x1);
35  xx2=x2-mean(x2);
36
37  % concatenate them
38  xx=[xx1';xx2'];
39
40  % plot the observations
41  figure;plot(xx1,xx2,'.','MarkerSize',14);
42  grid on;xlabel('Feature 48');ylabel('Feature 49');
43
44  % calculate covariance matrix
45  C=(xx*xx')/(length(xx)-1);
46
47  % calculate eigenvector (principal component)
48  % and eigenvalue
49  [ww,ee]=eig(C);
50
51  % transform using principal compoments
52  yy=ww'*xx;
53
54  % plot the original and pc-transformed values
55  figure;plot(xx1,xx2,'.','MarkerSize',14);
56  hold on;plot(yy(1,:),yy(2,:),'r.','MarkerSize',14);
57  grid on;xlabel('PC 1');ylabel('PC 2');
```

This program is self-explanatory as it gives comments for each block of code. These comments explain the steps illustrated in the first diagram (i.e., the 2D implementation of PCA) in Fig. 14.7. The results are presented in Fig. 14.8. Orthogonality effect of principal components can clearly be seen in the second figure.

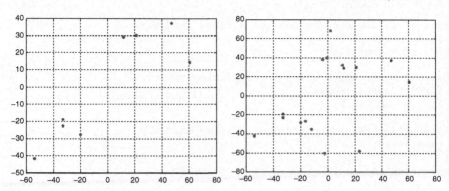

Fig. 14.8 PCA is explained in 2D scatter plot—the axes represent the PCs

14.5.5 A 3D Implementation

Let us now study the three-dimensional implementation of operations of the PCA to understand the differences between them so that the generalization of the PCA operations in higher dimensions can be easily understood. The 3D implementation example in Listing 14.6 and the right figure in Fig. 14.7 present the principal component analysis as the dimensionality reduction from $p = 3$ to $k = 2$.

Listing 14.6 A Matlab example—PCA operations in 3D

```
1   clear all;
2   close all;
3
4   % read the class data files
5   [num1,txt1,raw1]=xlsread('hardwood.csv');
6   [num2,txt2,raw2]=xlsread('carpet.csv');
7
8   % [num1,txt1,raw1]=xlsread('biltmore31.csv');
9   % [num2,txt2,raw2]=xlsread('MyPrismacolors1.csv');
10
11  % shuffle the observations of a class randomly
12  rand('seed',129);
13  nd1=randperm(1024);
14
15  % select the observation corresponding to
16  % the first 4 indexes
17  t1=num1(nd1(1:4),:);
18
19  % shuffle the observations of a class randomly
20  rand('seed',131);
21  nd2=randperm(1024);
22
23  % select the observation corresponding to
24  % the first 4 indexes
25  t2=num2(nd2(1:4),:);
26
```

```
27   % collect the values of the 47th feature
28   x1=[t1(:,47);t2(:,47)];
29
30   % collect the values of the 48th feature
31   x2=[t1(:,48);t2(:,48)];
32
33   % collect the values of the 49th feature
34   x3=[t1(:,49);t2(:,49)];
35
36   % center them w.r.t their means
37   xx1=x1-mean(x1);
38   xx2=x2-mean(x2);
39   xx3=x3-mean(x3);
40
41   % concatenate them
42   xx=[xx1';xx2';xx3'];
43
44   % plot the observations
45   figure;plot3(xx1,xx2,xx3,'.','MarkerSize',14);
46   grid on;
47
48   % calculate covariance matrix
49   C=(xx*xx')/(length(xx)-1);
50
51   % calculate eigenvector (principal component)
52   % and eigenvalue
53   [ww,ee]=eig(C);
54
55   % transform using principal components
56   yy=ww'*xx;
57
58   ss=sum(ee);
59   [r1,r2]=sort(ss,'descend');
60
61   kk=2;
62   wwt=ww(:,r2(1:kk));
63
64   yyt=wwt'*xx;
65
66   figure;plot3(xx1,xx2,xx3,'.','MarkerSize',14);
67   hold on;plot3(yy(1,:),yy(2,:),yy(3,:),'r.','MarkerSize',14);
68   grid on;
69
70   figure;plot(yyt(1,:),yyt(2,:),'.','MarkerSize',14);
71   grid on;
```

The results of this program are presented in Figs. 14.9 and 14.10. The first figure in Fig. 14.9 shows the three-dimensional scatter plot of the eight points based on their features 47–49. The second figure shows these points and their principal components. The dimensionality reduction using the best two principal components is presented in Fig. 14.10. We can see a clear classification between the classes.

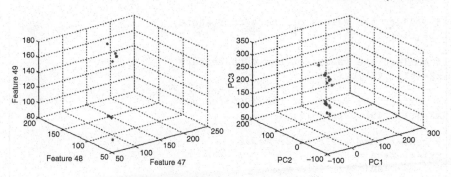

Fig. 14.9 PCA is explained in 3D

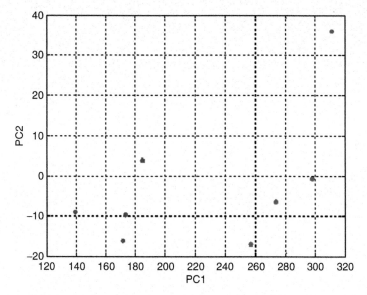

Fig. 14.10 PCA is explained with dimensionality reduction

14.5.6 A Generalized Implementation

This generalized implementation example in Listing 14.7 shows the principal component analysis as well as the dimensionality reduction from $p = 64$ to $k = 2$. It shows better separation than $p = 3$ to $k = 2$. It uses hardwood floor and carpet floor data sets as a one set, and Biltmore estate and MyPrismaColors data sets as another. The program reads the data sets, calculates the principal components (PCs), selects the first two PCs, and transforms the data using them.

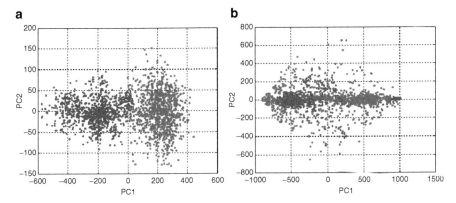

Fig. 14.11 PCA is explained with dimensionality reduction. (**a**) PC1 and PC2 of hardwood floor and carpet floor data sets. (**b**) PC1 and PC2 of Biltmore estate and MyPrismaColors data sets

Listing 14.7 A Matlab example—PCA's generalized operations

```matlab
1   clear all;
2
3   close all;
4
5   % read class data files
6   hw1=csvread('hardwood.csv');
7   cp1=csvread('carpet.csv');
8
9   % hw1=csvread('biltmore31.csv');
10  % cp1=csvread('MyPrismacolors1.csv');
11
12  % concatenate them
13  tt=[hw1;cp1];
14
15  for jj=1:64
16      qq(:,jj)=tt(:,jj)-mean(tt(:,jj));
17  end
18
19  xx=qq';
20
21  % calculate covariance matrix
22  C=(xx*xx')/(length(xx)-1);
23
24  % calculate eigenvector (principal component)
25  % and eigenvalue
26  [ww,ee]=eig(C);
27
28  % transform using principal components
29  yy=ww'*xx;
30
31  % sort the eigenvectors in descending order
```

```
32  ss=sum(ee);
33  [r1,r2]=sort(ss,'descend');
34
35  % dimensionality reduction
36  kk=2;
37  wwt=ww(:,r2(1:kk));
38
39  % transform using reduced principal components
40  yyt=wwt'*xx;
41
42  % plot the pc-transformed values
43  figure;plot(yyt(1,1:1024),yyt(2,1:1024),'.');
44  hold on;plot(yyt(1,1025:end),yyt(2,1025:end),'r.');
45  grid on;xlabel('PC_1');ylabel('PC_2');
```

The results are presented in Fig. 14.11 where the first image is the results of the pairs of data sets, hardwood floor and carpet floor; and the second image is the results of Biltmore estate and MyPrismaColors data sets. These are the best separations (or classification) we can obtain between classes using their principal components. Note that the dimensions are also reduced.

Problems

14.1. Code Revision

Revise the MapReduce programs presented in this chapter using the coding principles taught in Chap. 5.

14.2. Scaling-up Machine Learning

The MapReduce program provided for the feature hashing problem implemented the technique inside the mapper() function. Using your own data sets, implement a complete classification algorithm in the reducer() function that receives the feature indexes from the mapper() function.

14.3. 3D PCA

(a) Derive the principal components for three variables following the steps used in Sect. 14.5.2.
(b) Create a simple numerical example, similar to the one used in 14.5.2, and derive the principal component values.

References

1. B. Dalessandro. "Bring the noise: Embracing randomness is the key to scaling up machine learning algorithms." Big Data vol. 1, no. 2, pp. 110–112, 2013.
2. L. Bottou. "Large-scale machine learning with stochastic gradient descent." in Proceedings of COMPSTAT'2010. Physica-Verlag HD, pp. 177–186, 2010.

3. J. Han and C. Moraga. "The influence of the sigmoid function parameters on the speed of backpropagation learning." In From Natural to Artificial Neural Computation, pages 195–201. Springer, 1995.

4. K. Weinberger, A. Dasgupta, J. Langford, A. Smola, and J. Attenberg. "Feature hashing for large scale multitask learning." In Proceedings of the 26th Annual International Conference on Machine Learning, pp. 1113–1120. ACM, 2009.

5. http://en.wikipedia.org/wiki/Feature_hashing

6. K. Shvachko, H. Kuang, S. Radia, and R. Chansler. "The hadoop distributed file system." In Proceedings of the IEEE Symposium on Mass Storage Systems and Technologies, pp. 1–10, 2010.

7. J. Dean, and S. Ghemawat. "MapReduce: a flexible data processing tool." Communications of the ACM, vol. 53, no. 1, pp. 72–77, 2010.

8. B. Li, X. Chen, M.J. Li, J.Z. Huang, and S. Feng. "Scalable random forests for massive data," P.N. Tan et al. (Eds): PAKDD 2012, Part I, LNAI 7301, pp. 135–146, 2012.

9. L. Rokach, and O. Maimon. "Top-down induction of decision trees classifiers-a survey." Systems, Man, and Cybernetics, Part C: Applications and Reviews, IEEE Transactions on 35, no. 4, pp. 476–487, 2005.

10. L. Breiman, "Random forests." Machine learning 45, pp. 5–32, 2001.

11. L. Bottou, and O. Bousquet. "The tradeoffs of large scale learning." In Proceedings of NIPS, vol 4., p. 8, 2007.

12. P. Domingos, and G. Hulten. "A general method for scaling up machine learning algorithms and its application to clustering." In ICML, pp. 106–113. 2001.

13. Q. Shi, J. Petterson, G. Dror, J. Langford, A. Smola, A. Strehl, and V. Vishwanathan. "Hash kernels." In Proceedings of the International Conference on Artificial Intelligence and Statistics, pp. 496–503. 2009.

14. Q. Shi, J. Petterson, G. Dror, J. Langford, A. Smola, and V. Vishwanathan. "Hash kernels for structured data." The Journal of Machine Learning Research 10, pp. 2615–2637, 2009.

15. B. Bai, J. Weston, D. Grangier, R. Collobert, O. Chapelle, and K. Weinberger, "Supervised semantic indexing." In Proceedings of the 18th ACM conference on Information and knowledge management, pp. 187–196, 2009.

16. C. Caragea, A. Silvescu, and P. Mitra. "Combining hashing and abstraction in sparse high dimensional feature spaces." AAAI, p. 7, 2012.

17. http://en.wikipedia.org/wiki/Principal_component_analysis

18. http://www.math.northwestern.edu/~mlerma/papers/princcomp2d.pdf, Last accessed: May 14, 2015.

Index

© Springer Science+Business Media New York 2016
S. Suthaharan, *Machine Learning Models and Algorithms for Big Data Classification*, Integrated Series in Information Systems 36,
DOI 10.1007/978-1-4899-7641-3

CPSIA information can be obtained
at www.ICGtesting.com
Printed in the USA
LVOW01*1613051115
461256LV00001B/20/P